Gregory W. Rome

Civil Law Property
Outline & Case Briefs

Keyed to
YIANNOPOULOS' CIVIL LAW
PROPERTY COURSEBOOK
10TH EDITION

STRAYLIGHT
PUBLISHING

v1.0

Civil Law Property Outline & Case Briefs

Published in 2025 by Straylight Publishing, L.L.C. • New Orleans, Louisiana

ISBN-13: 978-0-9910433-2-3 (Paperback)
ISBN-13: 978-0-9910433-3-0 (Ebook)
Library of Congress Control Number: 2025942129

In loving memory of my friend Yippy.

Introduction

"The civil law is beautiful."

If you haven't already, you will hear and read this sentence time and time again during your legal education. It was a favorite of Professor Yiannopoulos's and marked a new phase of my life the first time I heard him exclaim it in the fall of 2007.

But the civil law is more than beautiful. It's durable. Its study forges you into the most recent link in an unbroken chain stretching back thousands of years and spanning the globe. On a more human scale, the way we study the law connects us to countless students, scholars, philosophers, and practitioners who have gone this way before and distinguishes us from the students of other legal traditions.

This may seem much too grandiose an introduction for the simple book of case briefs and topic outlines you hold in your hand. But make no mistake: we walk the same paths blazed over centuries by Romans, Byzantines, glossators, commentators, and all who followed — all the way down to Professor Yiannopoulos, the present authors of *Yiannopoulos' Civil Law Property Coursebook*, and now you.

But remember that the civil law is beautiful but is neither perfect nor complete. You should strive not merely to learn the law but to feel it and to understand it in its worldly context. It's tempting to sit apart and admire the law as a slick, unblemished ivory edifice. And while its veneer *is* impressive, it is even more so considering what lies beneath. It has been built up and torn down and built up again over millennia from mud and bricks and sweat by legions of people — some noble, others base, and most somewhere in the middle — with conflicting aims, viewpoints, cultures, and philosophies.

As you progress in your studies and your career, you may become part of the next cadre of builders and maintainers of our heritage. You get to decide what part you play and how. I hope the beauty of the civil law guides you, your intellectual journey, and your passions. And I hope this volume will aid you in that pursuit.

Gregory W. Rome
New Orleans, Louisiana
May 31, 2025

A Note on Usage

The outlines in this book follow the contours of the chapters in *Yiannopoulos' Civil Law Property Coursebook* as closely as possible to maximize their applicability when studying the material. Headers in the outlines may contain short phrases taken directly from the source material and used without quotation marks.

For example in chapter 10, the phrases "Proof of Ownership" and "Ownership Good Against the World" appear in the text and the outline as headers but are not set off by quotations marks in the outline because quotation marks would not add any additional information or value. It is already clear that the entire outline refers to the casebook. Nevertheless, where significant amounts text are copied from a source, the text is quoted and a citation is provided.

Generally, I have provided full reporter citations for cases referred to in the text of this book but not reproduced in the casebook or briefed herein. For cases that are briefed in this book, I have omitted the reporter citation and simply italicized the case name. In the electronic version of this book, the case name links to the appropriate brief and is likely formatted to show that it is a link (depending on your reader's settings).

Where the materials in this book refer to Louisiana code articles or statutes, I use the abbreviations in the table below in citations. If no date is given for a statutory citation, it is made to the version of the code or statute current as of this writing. Where a specific version of the statute is relevant, a year is typically given in parentheses.

Abbreviation	Citation
C.L.P.	Yiannopoulos's Civil Law Property Coursebook 10th Ed.
La. C.C. art.	Louisiana Civil Code Annotated article
La. C.C.P. art.	Louisiana Code of Civil Procedure article
La. M.C. art.	Louisiana Mineral Code article
La. R.S.	Louisiana Revised Statutes Annotated

If you notice a typo or other error, please write us at errata@straylightpublishing.com.

Contents

Part I

Things, Possession, and Ownership

Chapter 1

Common, Public, and Private Things

1. Things are classified as common, public, or private; corporeal or incorporeal; and movable or immovable. La. C.C. art. 448.

2. **Common Things.** Things that cannot be owned by anyone, e.g., the air and the high seas. La. C.C. art. 449.

   a) **Air.** Atmospheric air, as opposed to the airspace over the ground, is a common thing and insusceptible of ownership. But a finite quantity of air may be captured and reduced to possession and ownership, as when automobile tires are filled with compressed air.

   b) **High Seas.** The term "high seas" refers to the column of water, the surface, and airspace beyond the territorial sea. While Louisiana law treats the high seas as common things, the United States claims certain fishery management and other rights over the "exclusive economic zone," which stretches 200 miles out from the edge of the territorial seas surrounding the United States.

3. **Public Things.** Things dedicated to public use and owned by public bodies, e.g., state highways and municipal roads. La. C.C. art. 450.

   a) **Public things.** Certain public things are owned by the state or its political subdivisions in their capacities as public persons. Such things — like running water, the bottoms of natural navigable bodies of water, or public streets — are insusceptible of private ownership; only public bodies may own them. La. C.C. 450.

   b) **Public Trust Doctrine.** Public things are controlled by the state for the benefit of its citizens.

   c) "Public things and common things are subject to public use in accordance with applicable laws and regulations. Everyone has the right to fish in the rivers, ports, roadsteads, and harbors, and the right to land on the seashore, to fish, to shelter himself, to moor ships, to dry nets, and the like, provided that he does not cause injury to the property of adjoining owners." La. C.C. art. 452.

   d) **Private things owned by the state.** On the other hand, public entities may also own things in their capacities as private persons, for example, police cruisers. These are private things that happen to be owned by a public entity and remain susceptible of private ownership.

4. **Private Things.** Things that may be owned either by private persons or by public bodies in their capacities as private persons. La. C.C. art. 453.

    a) **Alienation.** Private persons may normally dispose of the private things they own freely, except as provided by law. But private things that belong to public entities may only be disposed of as allowed by law and regulation.

    b) **Prescription and seizure.**

        i. *Private things owned by private persons* are generally subject to acquisitive prescription and seizure, except as provided by law.

        ii. *Private things owned by political subdivisions* of the state in their capacities as private persons, however, are normally exempt from seizure but remain subject to acquisitive prescription.

        iii. *Private things owned by the state* in its capacity as a private person are exempt from seizure and acquisitive prescription.

    c) A road may be either public or private. A **public road** is one that is subject to public use. The public may own the land on which the road is built or merely have the right to use it. A **private road** is one that is not subject to public use. La. C.C. art. 457.

Chapter 2

Water Bodies and Related Lands

1. **State ownership of water bodies**.

   a) **Running water** is a public thing that belongs to the state in its capacity as a public person. La. C.C. art. 450.

      i. The water itself is distinct from the bed of the channel through which it runs. The bed of the waterway is either a public or a private thing, depending on the nature of the waterway. In either case, the water itself is a public thing subject to public use.

   b) **Natural navigable water bodies.** The state owns the waters and the bottoms of natural navigable bodies of water. La. C.C. art. 450.

      i. **Constitutional issues.** The United States purchased most of the area comprising modern Louisiana from France in 1803. Consequently, Louisiana had no claim to ownership of or sovereignty over the waters or bottoms inside its borders until it was admitted as a state in 1812. Two constitutional doctrines then operated to grant Louisiana this sovereignty:

         A. **Equal footing doctrine.** Under *Coyle v. Smith*, 221 U.S. 559 (1911), every state admitted to the union enters with the same powers and authority as all the existing states.

         B. **Sovereignty over waters.** In *Pollard v. Hagan*, 44 U.S. 212 (1845), the Court had already decided that control and ownership of the shores and beds of navigable waterways belonged to the states and not to the United States.

   c) **The territorial sea and the seashore**.

      i. "The State of Louisiana owns in full and complete ownership the waters of the Gulf of Mexico and of the arms of the Gulf and the beds and shores of the Gulf and the arms of the Gulf, including all lands that are covered by the waters of the Gulf and its arms either at low tide or high tide, within the boundaries of Louisiana." La. R.S. 49:3.

      ii. The bed of a natural navigable body of water or of an arm of the sea is a public thing and may not be owned by a private person. *Milne v. Girodeau*.

      iii. Land that is located far from the sea but is nevertheless subject to tidal overflow from bayous is not part of the seashore. *Buras v. Salinovich*.

   d) **The "Oyster Statutes."**

   i. **State ownership of bottoms.** By Act 258 of 1910, the state claimed ownership of the waters and bottoms of all bayous, streams, rivers, lagoons, lakes, and bays that were not already "directly owned" by someone else on the Act's effective date.

   A. **Application.** The Act has been ignored by Louisiana courts.

   B. **Constitutional issues.** The statute asserts state ownership of waters and bottoms. It exempts waters and bottoms "under the direct ownership" of any person, but the notions of direct and indirect ownership are meaningless under Louisiana law. Thus, the statute may be unconstitutional insofar as it deprives owners of their property, since the exception is meaningless.

   ii. **Private ownership of bottoms.** Inland non-navigable waters and bottoms are private things and may be owned by private persons or by public bodies in their capacities as private persons.

e) **Freeze Statute.** Changing ownership of land or water bottoms as a result of erosion, alluvion, dereliction, or other water action does not affect any oil, gas, or mineral lease encumbering those lands or bottoms. The new owner takes the land subject to the lease. La. R.S. 9:1151.

2. **Navigability.**

   a) **Question of fact.** The navigability of a body of water is a question of fact.

   b) **Test.** A "body of water is navigable if it is susceptible of being used, in its ordinary condition, as a highway of commerce 'over which trade and travel are or may be conducted in the customary modes of trade and travel on water." C.L.P. at 26.

3. **Navigable Rivers.**

   a) **Ownership of the beds and banks of rivers and streams.**

      i. The waters and bottoms of navigable water bodies, including rivers, belong to the state. La. C.C. art. 450.

      ii. Absent a title transfer, the beds of formerly navigable waterways continue to belong to the state if the waterway becomes non-navigable. *Wemple v. Eastham.*

      iii. "The bank of a navigable river or stream is the land lying between the ordinary low and the ordinary high stage of water." La. C.C. art. 456. Where there is a legally established levee near the waterway, the levee forms its bank. *Id.*

      iv. "The banks of navigable rivers or streams are private things that are subject to public use." La. C.C. art. 456.

      A. The banks of rivers navigable in 1812 which have become non-navigable are probably not under a public servitude. On the other hand, the banks of rivers that have become navigable since 1812 may be subject to public servitude.

      v. The "beds of non-navigable rivers or streams belong to the riparian owners along a line drawn in the middle of the bed." La. C.C. art. 506. This line is called the **thread**.

   b) **Alluvion and dereliction.**

      i. **Alluvion** is an accretion of land "formed successively and imperceptibly on the bank of a river or stream, whether navigable or not." La. C.C. art. 499.

     ii. Alluvion belongs to the owner of the bank on which it forms. La. C.C. art. 499. Alluvion that forms adjacent to properties owned by different people is divided equitably. La. C.C. art. 501. This division takes into account the frontage enjoyed by each owner before the alluvion and the relative value of frontage and acreage. *Id.*; *See Jones v. Hogue*, 241 La. 407, 129 So. 2d 194 (La. 1960).

     iii. **Dereliction** is dry land revealed by "water receding imperceptibly from a bank of a river or stream[, and belongs to the] owner of the land situated at the edge of the bank left dry." La. C.C. art. 501.

c) **Avulsion**.

     i. **Avulsion** is the sudden tearing away of an identifiable piece of ground from one bank of a river or stream and the subsequent attachment of that piece of ground to the other bank or to the same bank downstream. La. C.C. art. 502. *Cf.* this sudden action with the successive and imperceptible action characterizing alluvion and dereliction.

     ii. The owner of the land moved by avulsion does not lose ownership of it. He may "claim it within a year, or even later, if the owner of the bank with which it is united has not taken possession." La. C.C. art. 502.

d) **Opening a new channel**.

     i. The ownership of riparian land is not affected if the river or stream opens a new channel, surrounds the riparian land, and makes it an island. La. C.C. art. 503.

     ii. "When a navigable river or stream abandons its bed and opens a new one, the owners of the land on which the new bed is located shall take by way of indemnification the abandoned bed, each in proportion to the quantity of land that he lost. If the river returns to the old bed, each shall take his former land." La. C.C. art. 504.

     iii. Contrast this indemnification with the case where land erodes into a navigable river that does not change course. There, the state gains ownership of the eroded land because it becomes the river's bed, and the owner is not entitled to any indemnification. *See* La. C.C. art. 450.

     iv. The new owner of the former riverbed need not have been a riparian owner along the old bed. *See State v. Bourdon*, 535 So. 2d 1091 (La. App. 2d Cir. 1988).

     v. "Islands, and sandbars that are not attached to a bank, formed in the beds of navigable rivers or streams, belong to the state." La. C.C. art. 505.

e) **Public use of riverbanks**.

     i. "The banks of navigable rivers or streams are private things that are subject to public use." La. C.C. art. 456. Contrast this with lake and sea shores, which are public things, and the banks and shores of non-navigable inland waters, which are private things without any public servitude.

     ii. **Limitations on public use**.

       A. Members of the public may not cross private lands without permission to access the banks of navigable waterways. *Pizanie v. Gauthreaux*, 173 La. 737, 138 So. 650 (La. 1931).

       B. The public at large only has a right to use the banks of a river in a manner incidental to the navigable character of the river and its enjoyment as an avenue of commerce, e.g., for drying nets, temporary mooring, and unloading cargo.

C. Riparian servitudes of public use do not allow for hunting and fishing on the privately owned banks and batture of a navigable waterway, because those activities are not incidental to the nature and navigable character of the waterway. *Warner v. Clarke, Parm v. Shumate.*

iii. **Restrictions on private owners of banks**.

A. A riparian landowner may build structures on his land, including batture, provided that the structures do not obstruct the navigational use of that land. *Lake Providence Port Commission v. Bunge Corporation. See also* La. C.C. art. 459.

B. "Works built without lawful permit on public things, including the sea, the seashore, and the bottom of natural navigable waters, or on the banks of navigable rivers, that obstruct the public use may be removed at the expense of the persons who built or own them." La. C.C. art. 458.

C. The private owner's use of the bank can be limited by ordinances and other regulations, including zoning laws.

D. If a structure encroaches on the use of the bank and its removal would substantially harm the owner, it may be left in place until naturally destroyed, at which time the land is returned to the public use. La. C.C. art. 459.

E. "Port commissions of the state, or in the absence of port commissions having jurisdiction, municipalities may, within the limits of their respective jurisdictions, construct and maintain on public places, in beds of natural navigable water bodies, and on their banks or shores, works necessary for public utility, including buildings, wharves, and other facilities for the mooring of vessels and the loading or discharging of cargo and passengers." La. C.C. art. 460.

F. In general, the regulation of rural riparian land is looser than that of riparian land within urban areas or port facilities. For example, a rural riparian owner may collect fees for the permanent mooring of vessels or camping on the banks or engage in mineral exploration and exploitation on the banks.

4. **Lakes**.

a) The state owns the beds and bottoms of all navigable lakes. La. C.C. art. 450. This ownership extends to the lake's high water mark.

b) Classification as a lake, as opposed to a stream, is based on the physical and historical characteristics of the body of water, including but not limited to:

- its size, especially its width compared to the streams entering it;
- its depth;
- its banks;
- its channel;
- its current, especially compared to that of the streams entering it; and
- its historical designation on maps and other official documents. *State v. Placid Oil Company*.

c) "There is no right to alluvion or dereliction on the shore of the sea or of lakes." La. C.C. art. 500.

      i. Where the waters of the lake recede, the adjacent landowner still only owns property up to the former high water mark.

     ii. On the other hand, lakeshore that becomes part of the bed of a lake through erosion, subsidence, or other action ceases to be private property and becomes the property of the State. *Miami Corporation v. State*.

5. **Canals**.

   a) Canals built on private land with private funds are private things subject to the control of the owner, who may exclude the public from using the canals. *Vermilion Corporation v. Vaughn*.

   b) A navigable canal built with private funds on private property that destroys the navigability of surrounding waters may be subject to a navigational servitude under federal law. *See Vermilion Corp. v. Vaughn*, 387 So. 2d 698 (La. App. 3 Cir. 1980) (on remand from the United States Supreme Court, 444 U.S. 206 (1979)). Whether such a canal would be subject to a servitude under state law is undetermined. *See Ilhenny v. Broussard*, 172 La. 895, 135 So. 669 (La. 1931).

6. **Patents Conveying Navigable Water Bottoms**.

   a) As a general rule, the beds and bottoms of navigable waterbodies are public things and therefore inalienable by the state and insusceptible of private ownership.

   b) Alienation of navigable water bottoms by the state has been specifically prohibited by the Civil Code, by statute since 1886, and by the state constitution since 1921.

   c) In the 19th century, the state issued patents conveying tracts of swampland to various persons and entities without reserving the ownership of navigable water bottoms that happened to lie within those tracts.

   d) The Louisiana legislature passed the **Repose Statute of 1912**, which declared that all suits to annul the land patents issued by the state must be brought within six years of the Act. The statute was reenacted in 1950 to give a six year prescriptive period from the date of the patent for challenging its issuance.

   e) The repose statute was tested and found to apply to all patents, including those purporting to convey navigable water bottoms in contravention of the law. *California v. Price*, 74 So. 2d 1, 22 La. 706 (La. 1953).

   f) *Gulf Oil Corporation v. State Mineral Board*, 317 So. 2d 576 (La. 1974), overruled *Price* and established that state patents conveying navigable water bottoms to private persons are absolute nullities and could not be cured by the Repose Statute of 1912.

MILNE V. GIRODEAU
12 La. 324 (1838)

Facts & Procedure

Milne (P) filed a petitory action against Girodeau (D) to have the court recognize his ownership of a piece of ground along Lake Pontchartrain that stretched below its high water mark. Girodeau (D) maintained that the relevant lot formed part of the seashore and was, therefore, common property insusceptible of ownership. The trial court found for Girodeau (D) because the land was inside the high water mark of the lake and, therefore, part of its bed.

Milne (P) appealed.

Issue

Is the bed of a natural navigable body of water susceptible of private ownership?

Holding & Decision

No, in Louisiana, public things are not susceptible of private ownership. The bottoms of natural navigable bodies of water, the territorial sea, and seashore are all public things. Therefore the land in question in this case, part of the bed of the lake, is a public thing and not susceptible of private ownership.

The Court affirmed the trial court's judgment.

Rule of Law

The bed of a natural navigable body of water or of an arm of the sea is a public thing and may not be owned by a private person.

BURAS V. SALINOVICH
Landowner (P) v. Six hunters (D)
154 La. 594, 97 So. 748 (La. 1923)

Facts & Procedure

Buras (P) owned a large piece of marshland downriver from New Orleans. Nearly all of the land was subject to tidal overflow and unfit for cultivation or pasturage. Nevertheless, the Landowner (P) posted "no trespassing" signs along the perimeter of the land and along the bayous that criss-crossed it. He also employed a man to patrol the land and deliver written demands that hunters and trappers he encountered cease trespassing. Despite these efforts, Six Hunters (D) continued to hunt and trap on the land. The Hunters (D) possessed the appropriate state hunting and trapping licenses.

The Landowner (P) sought an injunction against the Hunters (D) forbidding them from going upon his land to hunt or trap. The Hunters (D) filed a reconventional demand for a declaratory judgment that they had the right to go upon the land to hunt and trap, for damages, and for attorney's fees.

The trial court refused to issue the Landowner (P) an injunction and found for the Hunters (D), recognizing their right to enter the land to hunt and trap. The trial court held that, while the Civil Code generally allows a landowner to deny hunters the right to enter his land to hunt or trap, that Code article was superseded with respect to marshes subject to tidal overflow by Section 20 of the Conservation law (Act 204 of 1912).

The Landowner (P) appealed.

Issue

Should land far from the sea but subject to tidal overflow from bayous be classified as seashore?

Holding & Decision

No, land that is located far from the sea but nonetheless subject to tidal overflow from bayous is not part of the seashore.

After disposing of the Hunters' (D) argument that the Conservation Law prevented Buras (P) from excluding them from his land, the Court turned to their alternative argument: since the marshland was regularly subject to tidal overflow, it is seashore within the meaning of the Civil Code and, therefore, not susceptible of private ownership. The Court held that land subject to tidal overflow is not necessarily seashore and found that, here, the Gulf of Mexico backed up into coves along the shoreline, which then caused the bayous in the land to rise and spread over most of the land. This mechanism does not make the land covered by rising bayous part of the seashore. The Court also noted that the nearest body of water that could properly be considered an arm of the sea was more than a mile from Buras's (P) land.

The Court annulled the lower court's judgment and issued the requested injunction.

Rule of Law

Land that is located far from the sea but nonetheless subject to tidal overflow from bayous is not part of the seashore.

STATE V. TWO O'CLOCK BAYOU LAND COMPANY
Government (P) v. Land Company & Lessee (D)
365 So. 2d 1175 (La. App. 3 Cir. 1978)

Facts & Procedure

Two O'Clock Bayou Land Company and its lessee, Creighton James Nail, (D) placed a cable across Two O'Clock Bayou that impeded the use of the canal for navigation.

The State and the St. Landry Parish Police Jury (P) sued the defendants, seeking an order enjoining the defendants from keeping the cable across the bayou and for a judicial declaration that the bayou was navigable and subject to public use.

One witness testified that the bayou appeared on an 1808 survey and that it could have been navigable at that time. On the other hand, he testified that, from time to time, the bed of the bayou had been dry enough to allow the germination of cypress trees but that there remained a ten or twelve foot open space between the remaining trees and stumps.

Other witnesses testified that the shallowest portions of the bayou were between three and seven feet deep and that, at its narrowest point, the bayou was eight to ten feet wide. The witnesses each recounted the activities they had seen on the bayou over the preceding forty-odd years, including logging, film production, recreational fishing, and commercial fishing. A dam prevented travel from the North end of the bayou into a nearby bay, but other parts of the bayou allowed access to other nearby bodies of water.

The trial court found that the bayou had an average depth of nine feet and an average width of eighteen to thirty feet. It also concluded that, despite occasional obstructions in its flow, the bayou was capable of sustaining commerce and, therefore, navigable. The trial court declared the bayou navigable and issued a permanent injunction against the Land Company and Lessee (D) impeding navigation.

The Land Company and Lessee (D) appealed.

Issue

Is Two O'Clock Bayou navigable?

Holding & Decision

Yes, a body of water is navigable in law when it is navigable in fact, which question turns on whether the evidence shows the body of water to be suitable by its depth, width, and location for commerce. The body of water need not actually be used for commerce in order to be navigable. The appeal court held that the evidence allowed for a reasonable inference that Two O'Clock Bayou is navigable in fact, with the exception of certain man-made obstructions, and affirmed the trial court's decision.

Rule of Law

A body of water is navigable in law when it is navigable in fact, which question turns on whether the evidence shows the body of water to be suitable by its depth, width, and location for commerce. The body of water need not actually be used for commerce in order to be navigable.

WEMPLE V. EASTHAM
Landowner (P) v. Mineral Lessee (D)
150 La. 247, 90 So. 637 (La. 1922)

Facts & Procedure

Mally Eastham (D) leased river and lake beds and bottoms from the state, including all the land owned by the state along Bayou Pierre and Bayou Dolet, for the production of oil, gas, and other minerals. Wemple (P) owned land along one side of Bayou Pierre and surrounding Bayou Dolet. After the Mineral Lessee (D) began drilling a well on the bank of Bayou Pierre, the Landowner (P) sued to cancel the Mineral Lessee's (D) lease and to enjoin him from drilling the well. The Mineral Lessee (D) made a reconventional for damages caused by the plaintiff's interference with his operations and for the right of passage over the plaintiff's land to the nearest public road.

The Landowner (P) argued that the two bayous had never been navigable and that he, therefore, owns all of Bayou Dolet and the bottom of Bayou Pierre out to it thread. He also argued that, even if the bayous were navigable, he owned their banks. The Mineral Lessee (D) admitted that Bayou Dolet was not navigable and that the state had no right to lease its bed but argued the Bayou Pierre was once navigable and that, accordingly, the state had a right to lease its bed and banks.

The trial court found in favor of the Landowner (P) and recognized his title to the bed and banks of Bayou Dolet and to one bank of Bayou Pierre between its ordinary high and low water marks. The court enjoined the Mineral Lessee (D) from going on the plaintiff's property but recognized the validity of the lease of Bayou Pierre's bed.

The Mineral Lessee (D) appealed the portions of the judgment concerning Bayou Pierre. The Landowner (P) answered and requested that the trial court's judgment be amended to declare him owner of Bayou Pierre to its thread.

Issue

Does the state own the bed of Bayou Pierre, a formerly navigable stream?

Holding & Decision

Yes, the bed of a navigable waterway belongs to the state and continues to belong to the state after the waterway becomes non-navigable. The banks of waterways between their ordinary high and low watermarks belong to the riparian landowners. The appeal court held that Bayou Pierre had been navigable and that, accordingly, the state owned it. Because the state continued to own the bed after Bayou Pierre ceased to be navigable, it had the right to lease it. The banks, on the other hand, belonged to the riparian owners and could not be used for mineral production without the owners' permission.

The appeal court affirmed the trial court's decision.

Rule of Law

The bed of a navigable waterway belongs to the state and continues to belong to the state after the waterway becomes non-navigable. The banks of waterways between their ordinary high and low watermarks belong to the riparian landowners.

WARNER V. CLARKE
Hunters (P) v. District Attorney & Sheriff (D)
232 So. 2d 99 (La. App. 2d Cir. 1970)

Facts & Procedure

Several Hunters (P) were arrested for trespassing while hunting and fishing on privately owned land near the Mississippi River, including the levee and the batture. These lands include navigable or formerly navigable water bodies. The Hunters (P) sued to enjoin the District Attorney and Sheriff of East Carroll Parish (D) from prosecuting them and sought a judgment declaring that the lands in question are subject to public use.

The trial court found for the public officials (D) and refused to issue an injunction. The court also declined to render a declaratory judgment because the plaintiffs failed to name the landowners as defendants. They were indispensable parties to such a judgment.

The Hunters (P) appealed.

Issue

Do riparian servitudes give members of the public the right to hunt and fish on privately owned riparian land?

Holding & Decision

No, the appeal court held the riparian servitudes do not give members of the public the right to hunt and fish on the lands and waters between the river and a levee because hunting and fishing are "unrelated to the nature and navigable character of the" river. Because the hunters had no property rights allowing them to hunt and fish, they were not entitled to an injunction.

The appeal court affirmed the trial court's decision.

Rule of Law

Riparian servitudes of public use do not allow for hunting and fishing on the privately owned banks and batture of a navigable waterway because those activities are not incidental to the nature and navigable character of the waterway.

PARM V. SHUMATE
Fishermen (P) v. Sheriff (D)
513 F.3d 135 (5th Cir. 2007)

Facts & Procedure

The Sheriff (D) arrested several Fisherman (P) for trespassing when they refused to stop fishing on waters covering normally dry private property. The Fishermen (P) sued the Sheriff for violating their civil rights through false arrest, arguing that the Sheriff (D) lacked probable cause to arrest them because they had a right under federal and state law to fish on the property when it was submerged under the waters of the Mississippi River during its regular spring flooding.

Gassoway Lake is located about three and a half miles from the ordinary low water mark of the Mississippi River and lies within privately owned land that is normally dry. During the spring, the Mississippi River floods the property, and it normally remains submerged for two months or more. The landowner objected to fishermen fishing on his property and complained to the Sheriff (D), who arrested the Fishermen (P) and other trespassers found on the property.

The landowner filed a separate lawsuit in state court seeking a declaration of its ownership and an injunction prohibiting the public from entering its property without permission. While that lawsuit was pending the Fishermen (P) filed this lawsuit in federal court, which was stayed until the state court rendered a decision.

The state court ruled that the landowner owned the property and could exclude the public from it. The court found that the land in question was farmland or forest when Louisiana entered the Union as a state. Several decades later, the Mississippi River changed course and submerged the land. It subsequently changed course again, leaving the property dry again save for a depression that became Gassoway Lake. The court also found that, but for a man-made drainage ditch connecting the lake to other waterways, Lake Gassoway would dry up during the summer. Accordingly, the state court held that the waters lying on the property were not navigable in fact and issued an injunction prohibiting the public from going on the property without permission.

The Louisiana Second Circuit Court of Appeal accepted the trial court's findings of fact and affirmed its holding that the lake and surrounding lands remained private things because they did not become part of the bed of the Mississippi during the temporary annual floods. But the appeal court lifted the injunction because the landowner could not have an injunction against the public in general, only against specific individuals. Neither state court addressed whether the lands between the river's ordinary low water mark and its flood stage water mark were subject to a public navigational servitude.

Once the state decisions became final, both sides moved for summary judgment in the United States District Court. The District Court denied the Fishermen's (P) motion for summary judgment and granted the Sheriff's (D) cross-motion. The District Court found that the property in question formed part of the bank of the Mississippi River and that it was therefore subject to a public servitude. But the court recognized that hunting and fishing are not part of that servitude. Accordingly, the District Court held that the Sheriff (D) had probable cause to arrest the Fishermen (P).

The Fishermen (P) appealed.

Issue

Does Louisiana law provide the public with a right to fish on privately owned land submerged during the Mississippi River's normal flood stage?

Holding & Decision

No, Louisiana law does not provide the public with a right to fish on flood-submerged private property, even where that property forms part of the bank of the Mississippi River. While the banks of navigable rivers are subject to public use under Civil Code article 456, that use is limited to navigational purposes. Fishing is not a navigational purpose and is, therefore, not protected by that servitude.

The appeal court affirmed the district court's judgment.

Rule of Law

Private lands submerged by the normal flooding of a navigable body of water may form part of the body of water's banks and, if so, are subject to public use under La. C.C. art. article 456. But the owner may deny individuals any use of that property unrelated to navigation.

LAKE PROVIDENCE PORT COMMISSION V. BUNGE CORPORATION

Commission (P) v. Grain Company (D)
193 So. 2d 363 (La. App. 2d Cir. 1966)

Facts & Procedure

The Lake Providence Port Commission (P), a state agency, developed port facilities on the Mississippi River in East Carroll Parish. A Grain Company (D) unsuccessfully bid on a portion of the port facility to build a grain elevator. The Grain Company (D) then purchased twenty-four acres of land along the banks of the Mississippi River several miles from the Commission's (P) port facility.

The Port Commission (P) sued for an injunction forbidding the Grain Company (D) from building the planned grain elevator on the banks of the river and for a declaratory judgment concerning its rights and status under the law. The Commission (P) maintained that the riparian servitude over riverbanks prohibited the Grain Company (D) and other members of the public from erecting any permanent structure on the bank of the Mississippi River in East Carroll Parish without the Commission (P)'s permission. The Grain Company (D), on the other hand, argued that while the Commission (P) certainly had some authority to regulate river commerce within the Parish, the Commission (P) could not prevent rural riparian owners from building structures on their property as long as the structures did not impinge on the navigational uses of the banks and other land burdened by public servitudes.

The trial court denied the Commission's (P) request for an injunction and declared that the Commission (P) is an executive department of the state with the exclusive authority to reasonably regulate navigable river commerce and traffic in East Carroll Parish.

The Commission (P) appealed.

Issue

May a landowner erect permanent structures on the batture of the Mississippi River if those structures do not obstruct the public use of the banks of the river for navigational purposes?

Holding & Decision

Yes, a landowner may erect permanent structures on the batture of a river if those structures do not impair the navigational use of its banks. The appeal court found that the Grain Company (D) wished to place its grain elevator in a rural area with free flowing river traffic and a large expanse of land between the ordinary high water mark of the River and the levee. Because of these factors, the court reasoned, restrictions on development of riparian land in these areas need not be as extensive as the restrictions present in more congested urban or industrial areas. Since there was no evidence to indicate that the Grain Company's (D) elevator would obstruct the public's use of the riverbank, there was no prohibition against its construction.

The appeal court affirmed the trial court's judgment.

Rule of Law

A riparian landowner may build structures on his land, including batture, provided that the structures do not obstruct the navigational use of that land.

STATE V. PLACID OIL COMPANY

Louisiana & its Mineral Lessee (P) v. Oil Company (D)
300 So. 2d 154 (La. 1973)

Facts & Procedure

Louisiana and Gulf Oil Corporation, one of its mineral lessees, (P) filed suit against Placid Oil Company (D) to recognize the state as owner of land lying below the high water mark of a body of water known as Grand Lake-Six Mile Lake. Several oil wells had been drilled on the disputed land.

The trial court found that the body of water was navigable when Louisiana joined the Union in 1812 and that the disputed land remained submerged until at least 1935. Sedimentary deposits, probably accelerated by channeling and dredging, built up on the edge of the lake and created the disputed land between the high and low water marks of the body of water.

The State (P) argued that it owned the beds of all waterways that were navigable in 1812 and all land below the high water mark of a lake. Placid Oil (D) argued that the land created by sedimentary buildup was alluvion, as the term is used in La. C.C. art. 499. Under that article alluvion formed on the shore of a river or other stream belongs to the owner of the adjoining ground. That code article does not apply to land formed on the shore of a lake.

The trial court found Grand Lake-Six Mile Lake to be a stream, despite its name, and held that the defendants owned the land created along its edge in accordance with the Civil Code. The appeal court affirmed that portion of the trial court's judgment, and the State and Gulf Oil (P) petitioned for certiorari. The Louisiana Supreme Court initially affirmed the appeal court's decision in large part because a substantial current flowed through the body of water but granted a rehearing.

Issue

Was Grand Lake-Six Mile Lake a lake, as opposed to a stream, at the time of Louisiana's admission to the United States in 1812?

Holding & Decision

Yes, Grand Lake-Six Mile Lake was a lake in 1812 and must now be classified as a lake. The Court reasoned that the existence of an accretion-forming current is not a sufficient basis on which to classify a body of water as a stream rather than a lake. Instead, the Court adopted and applied a multiple-factor test, finding that Grand Lake-Six Mile Lake is a wide, shallow, irregularly shaped body of water with a current substantially slower than that of the river feeding it. Thus, the Court held that Grand Lake-Six Mile Lake was a lake in 1812. The Court held that the State (P) owned the land created below the high water mark of Grand Lake-Six Mile Lake subject to Gulf Oil's (P) rights as mineral lessee.

Dissent

Justice Summers dissented, arguing that the majority ignored the principal characteristic of a water body for classification under Revised Civil Code article 499: "a moving or running body of water principally endowed with the capacity for change." He criticized the majority opinion for emphasizing irrelevant physical features over Grand Lake-Six Mile Lake's demonstrated ability to change itself through alluvion and dereliction.

Test

Classification of a body of water as a lake or stream is based on its physical and historical characteristics, including:

- its size, especially its width compared to the streams entering it;

- its depth;

- its banks;

- its channel;

- its current, especially compared to that of the streams entering it; and

- its historical designation on maps and other official documents.

Rule of Law

The classification of a body of water as a lake or a stream depends on its historical designation and its physical characteristics, including its size, depth, banks, channel, and current.

MIAMI CORPORATION V. STATE

Landowner (P) v. State (D)
186 La. 784, 173 So. 315 (La. 1936)

Facts & Procedure

The parties dispute the ownership of a piece of land that eroded into Grand Lake. Miami Corporation (P) owned land along Grand Lake's shore. A portion of that land eroded away and became part of the bed of the lake. The Landowner (P) claimed that it continued to own the eroded land, and the State (D) claimed that it became owner of the land when it became part of the bed of a navigable lake.

The trial court found that Grand Lake was a navigable lake and was navigable in 1812. The court also found that the Mermentau River is made up of wide, marshy areas locally called lakes connected by a relatively narrow channel. Grand Lake is the largest of the "lakes" in the river's chain. Finally, the trial court found that there is a substantial current running through Grand Lake which carries sediment into one end of the lake and out the other. Based on these factors, the trial court determined that Grand Lake was a lake and not a stream. Accordingly, the trial court found for the State (D), and Miami Corporation (P) appealed.

Issue

Does the State become owner of newly created lakebed when the shore subsides or erodes into the lake?

Holding & Decision

Yes, the state owns the bed of a navigable lake, even when it is created by subsidence or erosion of the lakeshore. The Court reasoned that, where the shore of a navigable body of water becomes a portion of the bed of that body of water, it becomes a public thing insusceptible of private ownership. Therefore, it is the property of the State (D) by virtue of its inherent sovereignty. The Court then held that the State (D) owned the disputed lands.

The Court also specifically overruled *State v. Erwin*, 173 La. 507, 138 So. 84 (La. 1931). That case held that the State only owned the bottoms of navigable lakes up to the shoreline of that lake as it existed in 1812. Any land that subsequently became submerged remained the property of the person who owned it before 1812. The *Miami Corporation* Court overruled *Erwin* in part because that precedent would create a ring of privately owned lakebed around the perimeter of navigable lakes, which would be "undesirable and destructive of progress."

Dissent

Chief Justice O'Niell denied that *Erwin* presented a dangerous precedent. The majority, he maintained, did not identify any particular danger, undesirable result, or public policy at issue. The real motive was to put money into the state's coffer's over a private entity's. After all, "oil derricks erected by the oil companies holding leases from the State are not any less objectionable to navigation on the lakes than the derricks erected by the oil companies holding leases from the owners of the submerged lands."

Rule of Law

Lakeshore that becomes part of the bed of a lake through erosion, subsidence, or other action ceases to be private property and becomes property of the State.

VERMILION CORPORATION V. VAUGHN
Lessee (P) v. Fishermen (D)
356 So. 2d 551 (La. App. 3d Cir. 1978)

Facts & Procedure

Vermilion Corporation (P) sued to enjoin Fishermen (D) from using its private canals. The corporation (P) leased a large tract of land containing a network of man-made canals. The canals were navigable, were dug with private funds, and had been continuously used and controlled by the present owner and its ancestors in title. The canal system connected to public waterways and was used by the Lessee (P) and its sub-lessees as part of their leasing arrangements.

The defendants are commercial Fishermen (D) who entered the Lessee's (P) property and used the man-made canals without permission. The Lessee (P) issued written warnings to the Fishermen (D) forbidding their use of the property, but they ignored them.

The Lessee (P) sued the Fishermen (D) seeking permanent injunctions enjoining them from trespassing on the property and using the canals. The Fishermen (D) argued that the artificial canals have rendered the surrounding waterways unnavigable and, as a result, the man-made waterways should be declared open to the public. The trial court found for the Lessee (P), and issued a permanent injunction prohibiting the Fishermen (D) from trespassing on the Lessee's (P) property and using the canals.

The Fishermen (D) appealed.

Issue

May the owner of a private, navigable canal built on private property using private funds exclude others from its use?

Holding & Decision

Yes, a canal built on private property with private funds is a private thing subject to private control. The appeal court distinguished this case from two earlier cases in which the canals were created in part with public funds or were dedicated to public use. The diversion of water from nearby public waterways to the private waterway does not give rise to a right for the public to use the new waterway. The appeal court affirmed the trial court's decision and maintained the injunction against the Fishermen (D).

Rule of Law

Canals built on private land with private funds are private things subject to the control of the owner, who may exclude the public from using the canals.

Chapter 3

Movables and Immovables; Corporeals and Incorporeals

1. **Immovables.**

   a) "**Tracts of land and their component parts** are immovables." La. C.C. art. 462.

      i. **Component parts** of a tract of land are "[b]uildings, other constructions permanently attached to the ground, standing timber, and unharvested crops or ungathered fruits... when they belong to the owner of the ground." La. C.C. art. 463.

      ii. "The transfer or encumbrance of an immovable includes its component parts." La. C.C. art. 469.

      iii. An immovable does not necessarily become legally movable by its physical removal. For example, topsoil — as a component part of land — is an immovable even after it has been physically removed by a third party and may only be alienated by written act. *Landry v. LeBlanc.*

      iv. **Buildings.**

         A. Buildings are immovables when they belong to the owner of the ground and "separate immovables" when they belong to another. La. C.C. arts. 463–4.

         B. What constitutes a "building" is not defined in the Code. It is instead determined by the prevailing notions of society. For example, a three-story-high, permanent steel structure destined for attachment to an oil platform as living quarters is a building and, therefore, an immovable. *P.H.A.C. Services v. Seaways International, Inc.*

      v. **Other constructions.**

         A. Constructions other than buildings that are permanently attached to the ground are immovables when they belong to the owner of the ground. *Bayou Fleet Partnership v. Dravo Basic Materials Co.*

         B. When determining whether a structure constitutes an "other construction" under article 463, courts will consider:
            - The size of the structure;
            - The degree of its integration or attachment to the soil; and
            - Its permanency.

23

C. **Accession.** "Unless otherwise provided by law, the ownership of a tract of land carries with it the ownership of everything that is directly above or under it." La. C.C. art. 490.

D. "Buildings, other constructions permanently attached to the ground, standing timber, and unharvested crops or ungathered fruits of trees... are presumed to belong to the owner of the ground, unless separate ownership is evidenced by an instrument filed for registry in the conveyance records of the parish in which the immovable is located." La. C.C. art. 491.

vi. **Component parts of buildings and other constructions.**

A. "Things incorporated into a tract of land, a building, or other construction, so as to become an integral part of it, such as building materials, are its component parts." La. C.C. art. 465.

B. "Things that are attached to a building and that, according to prevailing usages, serve to complete a building of the same general type, without regard to its specific use, are its component parts." La. C.C. art. 466. This class of component parts includes, doors, shutters, gutters, cabinets, plumbing, heating, cooling, electrical, and similar systems.

C. "Things that are attached to a construction other than a building that serve its principal use are its component parts." La. C.C. art. 466.

D. "Other things are component parts of a building or other construction if they are attached to such a degree that they cannot be removed without substantial damage to themselves or to the building or other construction." La. C.C. art. 466.

E. When determining whether an object is a component part of an immovable, a court will consider whether society expects the object to be part of the building and whether the object can be removed without substantial damage to the object or to the immovable to which it is attached.

   • For example, electrical installations that are permanently attached to a building by direct wiring are component parts of that building even though they can be removed without any damage to either the installation or the building. *Equibank v. U.S. IRS.*

   • Similarly, hard wired electrical fixtures and carpeting are component parts of a residence. *American Bank & Trust Company v. Shel-Boze, Inc.*

   • It is a question of fact whether alarm system control hardware bolted into racks that are themselves bolted to the floor of the building and connected to cables running through walls, ceilings, and underground conduit is a component part of the buildings of a development. *DeLage Landen Fin. Serv. v. Perkins Rowe Ass.*

vii. **Standing timber and crops.**

A. Standing timber, unharvested crops, and ungathered fruits are immovables when they belong to the owner of the ground. La. C.C. art. 463.

B. Standing timber is a "separate immovable[] when [it] belong[s] to a person other than the owner of the ground." La. C.C. art. 464. *See Brown v. Hodge-Hunt Lumber Co.*

C. Fallen timber is a movable, regardless of its owner.

D. Ownership of standing timber may be separated from the ownership of the ground by an act translative of title — e.g., sale, donation, or exchange. The transfer of standing timber must be made in accordance with the formal and substantive rules governing transfers of immovable property, and an instrument transferring standing timber must be recorded in the public records to affect third parties.

E. If the owner of the land and the owner of separate timber on that land cannot agree on a definite time period for the removal of the timber, the courts may set a reasonable time period. *Willetts Wood Products Co. v. Concordia Land & Timber Co.* If the timber is not removed in that time, its ownership reverts to the owner of the land.

F. Crops growing on leased land belonging to another person are not immovables. Instead, they are **movables by anticipation**. *Porche v. Bodin*. But when the lease calls for the payment of a portion of the crop as rent, "that part which the lessor is to receive is considered at all times the property of the lessor," regardless of delivery or tender by the lessee. La. R.S. 9:3204.

G. The owner of standing crops may sell, pledge, or dispose of his interest in the crop, and they may be seized separately from the land on which they are growing.

H. Standing crops encumbered with security interests of third parties are movables by anticipation with respect to the creditor, even when they are owned by the owner of the ground.

I. An owner of standing crops may always assert his ownership against the owner of the ground but may only assert his ownership against third parties if he has recorded his interest in the crops in the public records.

J. The sale or mortgage of immovable property includes the sale of standing crops and ungathered fruits unless they belong to someone other than the owner of the land. *See* La. C.C. art. 469. Similarly, where a landowner's general creditor seizes land, standing crops and ungathered fruits are included in the seizure only inasmuch as they belong to the debtor.

K. The sale of growing crops by the landowner is a sale of immovable property and must follow the form requirements for the transfer of immovables and be recorded to be effective against third parties.

L. The sale of growing crops by an owner who does not own the land is a sale of movable property and is not governed by any formal or recording requirements.

M. Gathered crops are always movables.

b) **Immovables by their object.**

    i. "Rights and actions that apply to immovable things are incorporeal immovables. Immovables of this kind are such as personal servitudes established in immovables, predial servitudes, mineral rights, and petitory or possessory actions." La. C.C. art. 470.

    ii. A principal beneficiary's interest in a trust holding immovable property is itself an incorporeal immovable. *St. Charles Land Trust v. St. Amant.*

c) **Immovables by declaration.** A declaration by an owner of an immovable that machinery, appliances, and equipment he owns has been placed "on an immovable other than his private residence for its service and improvement" are that immovable's component parts. The declaration must be registered in the conveyance records of the parish where the immovable is located. La. C.C. art. 467.

d) **Non-immobilization.**

   i. A method for preventing a movable from becoming a component part of an immovable or an immovable by destination in order to protect a third party's interest in that thing—e.g., a vendor's lien.

   ii. Non-immobilization can be achieved through several means, including:

      A. Recordation of separate ownership under La. C.C. art. 491 or

      B. Statutory provisions—e.g., La. R.S. 9:1106 provides that "[t]anks placed on land... by [someone] other than the owner of the land for the storage or use of... liquefied gases... [or] liquid fertilizer,... remain movable property, and the ownership of such tank or tanks shall not be affected by the sale, either private or judicial, of the land on which they are placed."

   iii. Equipment attached to an immovable does not necessarily lose its identity as a movable thing simply because it is attached to or incorporated into an immovable. Whether a particular item has become part of an immovable sufficiently to lose its separate identity is a question of fact. *In re Receivership of Augusta Sugar Co.*

   iv. As a procedural matter, a third person claiming ownership or security rights on seized property—e.g., fuel tanks or machinery incorporated into a factory—must assert his claim by filing a petition for intervention before the judicial sale of the seized property. La. C.C.P. art. 1092.

   v. Non-immobilization is distinct from de-immobilization in that a non-immobilized thing never loses its status as a movable, whereas a part of an immovable that is de-immobilized regains its classification as a movable upon de-immobilization.

e) **De-immobilization; Separate immovables.**

   i. Component parts of an immovable that have been damaged or have deteriorated to the point that they no longer serve the use of the immovable are de-immobilized and cease to be immovable component parts. La. C.C. art. 468.

   ii. When, from any cause, a movable ceases to be of service to a tract of land or is detached from a building to which it was attached as an accessory, it is de-immobilized and ceases to be an immovable. *Folse v. Triche.*

   iii. "The owner may de-immobilize the component parts of an immovable by an act translative of ownership and delivery to acquirers in good faith." La. C.C. art. 468.

   iv. "In the absence of rights of third persons, [e.g., mortgagees,] the owner may deimmobilize things by detachment or removal." La. C.C. art. 468.

2. **Movables.**

a) "Corporeal movables are things, whether animate or inanimate, that normally move or can be moved from one place to another." La. C.C. art. 471.

b) Incorporeal movables include "[r]ights, obligations, and actions that apply to a movable thing[s,]" including things like "bonds, annuities, and interests or shares in entities possessing juridical personality" like corporations. La. C.C. art. 473.

c) "Interests or shares in a juridical person that owns immovables are considered as movables as long as the entity exists; upon its dissolution, the right of each individual to a share in the immovables is an immovable." La. C.C. art. 473.

d) The category of movables is residual, *viz.*, things that are not immovable are movable. *See* La. C.C. art. 474.

e) Money, even if flowing from an immovable thing or right, is a movable thing. *Steinau v. Pyburn.*

f) "Materials gathered for the erection of a new building or other construction, even though deriving from the demolition of an old one, are movables until their incorporation into the new building or after construction." La. C.C. art. 472. *See Beard v. Duralde.*

3. **Corporeals and incorporeals.**

a) "**Corporeals** are things that have a body, whether animate or inanimate, and can be felt or touched." La. C.C. art. 461.

b) "**Incorporeals** are things that have no body, but are comprehended by the understanding, such as the rights of inheritance, servitudes, obligations, and right of intellectual property." La. C.C. art. 461.

c) "Rights and actions that apply to immovable things are incorporeal immovables. Immovables of this kind are such as personal servitudes established in immovables, predial servitudes, mineral rights, and petitory or possessory actions." La. C.C. art. 470.

d) "Corporeal movables are things, whether animate or inanimate, that normally move or can be moved from one place to another." La. C.C. art. 471.

e) Computer software is a corporeal movable because it is physically manifested on digital media. *South Central Bell Telephone Co. v. Barthelemy.*

f) Incorporeal movables include "[r]ights, obligations, and actions that apply to a movable thing[s,]" including things like "bonds, annuities, and interests or shares in entities possession juridical personality" like corporations. La. C.C. art. 473.

g) A bearer bond is an incorporeal immovable. *Succession of Miller.*

h) A person loses corporeal movables when someone cashes a fraudulent check through a third party check cashing service, even though the money physically paid out is not the same money on deposit at the bank. *Innovative Hospitality Systems v. Abraham.*

LANDRY V. LEBLANC

Lessor (P) v. Lessee (D)
416 So. 2d 247 (La. App. 3d Cir. 1982)

Facts & Procedure

The Lessor (P) brought suit against his Lessee (D) at the end of their farm lease to recover damages allegedly caused by the Lessee (D) removing the topsoil from some of the property during the lease. The Lessee (D) claimed that he had permission to do so from the Lessor's (P) brother in his capacity as the Lessor's (P) agent. The Lessor (P) and his brother both denied that they had given permission.

The trial court found in favor of the Lessee (D), and the Lessor (P) appealed.

Issue

Is topsoil an immovable thing subject to the writing requirements for transfer under the Civil Code?

Holding & Decision

Yes, topsoil is an immovable and, therefore, can only be alienated by written act. The appeal court reasoned that topsoil is a component part of a tract of land, which is itself an immovable. Under the civil code, any transfer of ownership of an immovable thing must be made in writing unless the adverse party admits under oath that he made the oral contract. The appeal court considered the Lessor's (P) testimony that he did not authorize the sale of the topsoil and the absence of a written contract concerning the transfer of the soil and held that the verbal sale of the topsoil was absolutely null.

The appeal court also considered the Lessee's (D) contention that the Lessor's (P) brother was a mandatary and consented to the sale. Under the Code, any contract of mandate authorizing the sale of immovable property must be in the same written form as a contract to sell that property. Here, there was no such contract, and the appeal court held that the trial judge erred in admitting parol evidence concerning the mandate.

Because the transfer of the topsoil was unauthorized by law, the appeal court reversed the trial court and rendered judgment for the Lessor (P).

Rule of Law

Topsoil, as a component part of land, is an immovable and may only be alienated by written act.

P.H.A.C. SERVICES v. SEAWAYS INTERNATIONAL, INC.

Subcontractors (P) v. General Contractor & Owner (D)
403 So. 2d 1199 (La. 1981)

Facts & Procedure

Two unpaid Subcontractors (P) who provided labor and materials for the construction of an offshore drilling platform's living quarters sued the General Contractor and the Owner of the platform (D) to assert a privilege on the living quarters. The Owner (D) contracted with the General Contractor (D) to build living quarters for the Owner's (D) offshore drilling platform. The platform was fabricated on land and transported out to the platform for attachment. The General Contractor (D) subcontracted some of the work to the Subcontractors (P). They performed the work but were not paid.

The Subcontractors sought to enforce their privilege under the Private Works act, which confers a privilege to suppliers of labor and material "for the erection, construction, repair, or improvement of immovable property." The defendants disputed that the living quarters were immovable property and argued that therefore the Private Works Act did not apply.

The trial court held that the living quarters unit was not a building because it was not being used as a building and because it rested on wooden blocks during construction. The appeal court reversed because there is no requirement in the Civil Code that a building be founded in the soil. Further, the appeal court asserted that the trial court's reliance on the building's actual use during the time the Subcontractors (P) were involved would undermine the Private Works Act because many buildings are not in use as buildings during their construction.

The General Contractor and Owner (D) petitioned for certiorari.

Issue

Is a large living quarters unit constructed on land and designed to be attached to an offshore platform an immovable?

Holding & Decision

Yes, such a unit is a building and, therefore, an immovable. Under the Civil Code, buildings are immovables and may be owned by someone other than the owner of the ground on which they rest. The Court held that the living quarters unit was a building, reasoning that a three story high steel structure with a helicopter landing pad designed to house offshore workers is a building under prevailing societal notions. The Court rejected the defendants' position that the structure could not be a building because it was designed to be moved offshore. Neither the factual mobility of the unit nor the owner's intent to move it could alter the structure's legal classification as an immovable.

The Court affirmed the appeal court's judgment.

Rule of Law

A three-story-high, permanent steel structure destined for attachment to an oil platform as living quarters is a building and, therefore, an immovable.

BAYOU FLEET PARTNERSHIP V. DRAVO BASIC MATERIALS CO.

Landowner (P) v. Former Lessee (D)
106 F. 3d 691 (5th Cir. 1997)

Facts & Procedure

A Landowner (P) sued a Former Lessee (D) for removing packed limestone working bases from the property while moving out. The Former Lessee (D) operated a aggregate yard on the property for many years and used the yard to store and sell loose limestone. The Lessee (D) created three packed limestone working bases by digging pits in the land, placing a liner in the pit, and filling the pits with loose limestone. Over time the weight of pile compressed the earth and the limestone into a solid base. The Lessee (D) then stored loose limestone in piles on top of these working bases.

The property was sold at sheriff's sale to Louisiana Materials, Inc., who then sold the property to the plaintiff in this case. The new Landowner (P) attempted to negotiate another lease with the current tenant, but the negotiations failed. The Former Lessee (D) began vacating the property and removed its loose limestone stock as well as the working bases.

The Former Lessee (D) petitioned the state court for a declaration that it owned all the limestone removed from the property. The Landowner (P) filed this lawsuit in federal court for damages and removed the state court action. The proceedings were consolidated, and the trial court held that the Former Lessee (D) was entitled to remove all the limestone that had not been incorporated into the land as a component part. It awarded the Landowner (P) $25,000.00 in damages for the removal of the limestone that had become component parts of the land.

Both parties appealed.

Issue

Are the limestone bases component parts of the land and, therefore, immovables?

Holding & Decision

Yes, the limestone bases are constructions other than buildings permanently attached to the ground, making them immovables under the Civil Code. Under article La. C.C. art. 463, the component parts of an immovable include constructions other than buildings that are permanently attached to the ground. What, exactly, constitutes an "other construction" under that article is determined by the courts. Louisiana courts generally apply three criteria to identify "other constructions:" the size of the structure, the degree of its integration or attachment to the soil, and its permanency.

The appeal court found that the bases were component parts under all three criteria and so classified them. First, the bases were massive in volume and holding capacity. Second, they were attached firmly to the property and had sunk into the batture to the point where they formed the surface level of the property. Third, the bases were placed there years before their removal and were never sold to customers in the course of business. Based on these factors, the appeal court held that the bases were component parts of the land and that they belonged to the Landowner (P) because no evidence of their separate ownership had been recorded.

The appeal court reversed the district court's judgment and remanded the matter for the entry of a judgment against the Former Lessee (D) in the amount of $263,222.22 plus interest as appropriate.

Test

Constructions other than buildings that are permanently attached to the ground are immovables under La. C.C. art. 463 and can be identified by three criteria:

1. The size of the structure,

2. The degree of integration between the structure and the soil, and

3. The permanency of the structure.

Rule of Law

Constructions other than buildings that are permanently attached to the ground are immovables when they belong to the owner of the ground.

EQUIBANK V. U.S. INTERNAL REVENUE SERVICE
Bank (P) v. IRS (D)
749 F. 2d 1176 (5th Cir. 1985)

Facts & Procedure

The parties have competing security interests in a house because the owners defaulted on their mortgage and failed to pay their income tax. The Bank (P) holding a mortgage on the house sought an injunction ordering the IRS (D) to return expensive chandeliers it had seized from the home. While the home was scheduled for sheriff's sale to satisfy the mortgages on it, the IRS (D) took physical possession of the residence and removed its contents, including its chandeliers and other light fixtures. The chandeliers were wired directly into the house's wiring and left open electrical boxes and disconnected wires in the ceilings and walls when removed. The Bank (P) sought the return of the fixtures in state court, and the IRS (D) removed the matter to federal court. The U.S. district court denied the injunction on the grounds that the fixtures were not component parts of the house and, thus, not subject to the Bank's (P) mortgage.

The Bank (P) appealed.

Issue

Are hardwired chandeliers component parts of a home?

Holding & Decision

Yes, hardwired chandeliers are component parts of a home. The appeal court determined that under La. C.C. art. 466, things permanently attached to a building are its component parts where there is a societal expectation that those things are part of the building. Additionally, certain other installations may be component parts if they cannot be removed without substantial damage to themselves or the immovable to which they are attached.

The court reasoned that an ordinary homebuyer would expect hardwired light fixtures to come with their new house. The court clearly distinguished between permanently hardwired light fixtures and lamps and other electrical devices that simply plug into an outlet. In the face of this strong societal expectation, the court was not persuaded that the chandeliers were not component parts simply because they could be removed without damage to themselves or the home. Accordingly, the chandeliers removed from the house were its component parts and burdened by the Bank's (P) mortgage.

The appeal court reversed the district court judgment and remanded the matter for the entry of judgment.

Rule of Law

Electrical installations that are permanently attached to a building by direct wiring are component parts of that building even though they can be removed without any damage to either the installation or the building.

AMERICAN BANK & TRUST COMPANY V. SHEL-BOZE, INC.

Bank (P) v. Subcontractors (D)
527 So. 2d 1052 (La. App. 1st Cir. 1988)

Facts & Procedure

American Bank & Trust Company (P) filed this lawsuit to recover the costs of replacing carpets, light fixtures, and associated electrical paraphernalia removed from two houses burdened by mortgages in favor of the Bank (P).

The Bank (P) financed the construction of two residences and secured its loans to the builder with mortgages on the properties. The builder subcontracted electrical and carpet installation to Shel-Boze, Inc. and Jenkins Tile Company, Inc., (D) respectively. After the homes were ready for occupancy, the builder defaulted on the loans and surrendered possession of the houses to the Bank (P). The Subcontractors (D) then removed all of the fixtures and carpet they had installed from the houses with the builder's permission. Neither Subcontractor (D) had been paid for its materials, and Jenkins Tile Company (D) had not been paid for labor.

The Bank (P) foreclosed on the houses and purchased them at sheriff's sale. The Bank then had light fixtures and carpet installed to replace those items removed by the Subcontractors (D).

The Bank sued the Subcontractors (D) and their principals to recover the costs of replacing the carpets, light fixtures, and associated electrical paraphernalia. The Bank (P) argued that the items removed by the Subcontractors (D) had become component parts of the houses and, therefore, were subject to the Bank's (P) mortgage. The trial court dismissed the Bank's (P) suit, and the Bank (P) appealed.

Issue

Are carpeting, light fixtures, and associated electrical paraphernalia component parts of a residence subject to a mortgage encumbering the residence?

Holding & Decision

Yes.

The appeal court held that the carpeting, light fixtures, and other electrical paraphernalia were component parts of the residences. The court found that all the electrical fixtures removed by the electrical Subcontractor (D) were hardwired into the electrical system, as opposed to being plugged in, and relied on the reasoning in *Equibank v. U.S. Internal Revenue Service* to conclude that those items were component parts. The court also applied *Equibank's* societal expectation test and concluded that the carpeting removed by the Subcontractor (D) was a component part because a reasonable homebuyer expects a residence to include finished floors, like carpet or other floor covering.

Under La. C.C. art. 469, the encumbrance of an immovable includes its component parts. The appeal court held that the Bank (P) had a security interest in the component parts of the residences burdened by its mortgages from the date those mortgages were recorded.

Finally, the appeal court reversed the trial court's judgment in part and affirmed it in part, rendering judgment against Shel-Boze, Inc., (D) for $2,550.57 and against Jenkins Tile Company (D) for $4,275.40. The appeal court affirmed the trial court's dismissal of the Bank's (P) claims against the Subcontractors' (D) principals in their individual capacities.

Rule of Law

Hard-wired electrical fixtures and carpeting are component parts of a residence and are encumbered by a mortgage on the residence.

DeLage Landen Financial Services v. Perkins Rowe Association

Equipment Lessor (P) v. Developers (D)
2011 WL 1337381 (U.S. Dist. Ct. M.D. La. 2011)

Facts & Procedure

This lawsuit arises out of the failure of the Developers (D) of mixed-use commercial and residential development to pay for the equipment controlling the development's fire and security systems from a central location. Cisco Corporation leased the equipment to the Developers (D) and assigned the lease to DeLage Landen Financial Services (P) who then installed and set up the system. Cisco retained a security interest in the equipment which was represented by a UCC-1 Financing Statement. Prior to the equipment lease and the recording of the Financing Statement, the Developers mortgaged the development, including all its structures and component parts, to Keybank National Association and Jones Lang LaSalle Americas, Inc.

When The Equipment Lessor (P) sued to collect the money due under its lease with the Developers (D), the banks intervened. The banks and the Equipment Lessor (P) filed cross-motions for summary judgment. The banks argued that the control system was a component part of the buildings and, therefore, subject to their mortgage, which was superior to the Equipment Lessor's (P) security interest. Conversely, the Equipment Lessor (P) argued that the system was not a component part of the development because it could be removed by unbolting the equipment from its racks, unbolting the racks from the floor, and pulling cables out of conduit and walls. The only damage to the building would be revealing the holes previously occupied by bolts and cables. All of the fire and alarm systems previously controlled by the leased equipment would function independently after the system's removal but could no longer be centrally managed.

Issue

Is alarm system control hardware that is bolted into racks bolted to the floor of the building and wired to cables running through walls, ceilings, and underground conduit a component part of the buildings of a development?

Holding & Decision

Maybe. The district court denied both motions for summary judgment because it could not determine whether the system was a component part of the development. It found that there were genuine issues of material fact concerning whether the central control system was a component part of the development under Louisiana law because the banks introduced evidence suggesting that removing the central control system would be inappropriate, impractical, and contrary to prevailing usage because such a system is practically necessary for overseeing the fire, security, and lighting systems of such a large mixed-use development.

Further, the court also found that there were genuine issues of material fact whether removing the control system would cause substantial damage to the system or the development. Specifically, the banks produced evidence that it was impossible to tell which wires were related only to the control system and whether removing those wires would damage other wires. Professionals would have to be hired to make these determinations.

The court denied both motions because it could not determine whether the system was a component part on summary judgment, which was required to decide the underlying issues.

Rule of Law

It is a question of fact whether alarm system control hardware bolted into racks that are themselves bolted to the floor of the building and connected to cables running through walls, ceilings, and underground conduit is a component part of the buildings of a development.

PORCHE V. BODIN
Lessee (P) v. Purchasers (D)
28 La. Ann. 761 (La. 1876)

Facts & Procedure

This is a dispute over the ownership of a crop standing on land leased to the plaintiff and subsequently sold at a foreclosure sale. The plaintiff leased farmland from a landowner and recorded the lease. The lease called for the Lessee (P) to give the lessor one quarter of his corn crop as the rent. During the term of the lease and before the corn was harvested, the owner of the land defaulted on his mortgage, and the defendants purchased the land at foreclosure sale.

The Purchasers (D) claimed the entire crop, arguing that the mortgage under which they purchased the property contained a clause prohibiting the owner from alienating any portion of the property, including the standing crop. This clause, they argued, operated to dissolve the lease, and the crop passed to them through the foreclosure sale. The mortgage certificate, on the other hand, specifically mentioned the recorded lease.

The Lessee (P) sued the original owner and the Purchasers (D) to be declared the owner of three-quarters of the corn crop and to enjoin the Purchasers (D) from gathering the crop. The matter went before a jury, and the trial judge entered a verdict dismissing the Lessee's (P) lawsuit.

The Lessee (P) appealed.

Issue

Does corn grown by a lessee on the land of another belong to the landowner or the lessee?

Holding & Decision

The corn belongs to the lessee, subject to the terms of the lease. The Court held that, even if the foreclosure sale had dissolved the lease, the mortgagor did not own the crop, so it could not have been transferred to the Purchasers (D) in a proceeding to which the Lessee (P) was not a party. Therefore, the corn, less the one-fourth owed as rent under the lease, belonged to the Lessee (P). The Court reasoned that crops raised on leased premises do not form part of the immovable. Since the corn had already been seized and disposed of by the Purchasers (D), the Court remanded the matter to the trial court to determine the value of the corn.

Dissent

Justice Morgan disagreed with the majority, stating that the mortgage under which the lessor purchased the land contained a non-alienation clause and that the lease violated this clause. Because the lease violated the non-alienation provisions of a recorded mortgage and act of sale, the Lessee (P) acted at his own peril. In the dissenter's opinion, the Purchasers (D) at the foreclosure sale purchased the land with everything growing on it.

Rule of Law

Crops growing on leased land belonging to another person are not immovables. Instead, they are movables by anticipation.

St. Charles Land Trust v. St. Amant

Trustees (P) v. Tax Collector (D)
253 La. 243, 217 So. 2d 385 (La. 1968)

Facts & Procedure

The trustees of the St. Charles Land Trust (P), a trust holding mineral rights in Louisiana, sought judicial instructions concerning the classification and disposition of a deceased beneficiary's interest in the trust and the taxes applicable to it.

The trust instrument stated that the purpose of the trust was to conserve the trust estate and distribute income to the beneficiaries. The trust held interests in several mineral leases in Louisiana. The trust instrument itself provided that the beneficiaries' interest in the trust consisted of movable property, even though the trust itself held immovable assets. It also empowered the trustees to require beneficiaries comply with the formalities associated with the transfer of immovable property when transferring interests in the trust.

Ella E. Watkins, a trust beneficiary, died in California, her domicile. The California court entered orders concerning her trust interest without any ancillary succession proceedings in Louisiana. Under Louisiana law, inheritance taxes would be due on all immovable property transferred as part of the succession but would not be due on intangible movable property because Mrs. Watkins was not domiciled in the state at the time of her death.

The Trustees (P) argued that Mrs. Watkins's interest should not be subject to estate tax because it was most like the interest of a corporate stockholder, which is classified as an incorporeal movable. The Tax Collector (D) argued that the trust instrument created a partnership or agency or, alternatively, that the beneficiary's interest was actually in a Louisiana immovable and, therefore, an immovable itself and subject to the estate tax.

The trial court found that the trust interest was an incorporeal immovable subject to Louisiana inheritance taxes and transferable only after ancillary succession proceedings in Louisiana. The appeal court reversed, and the Tax Collector (D) appealed.

Issue

Should a beneficiary's interest in a trust that holds mineral leases be itself classified as incorporeal immovable property?

Holding & Decision

Yes, the Court held that a principal beneficiary's interest in a trust that holds mineral leases is itself an incorporeal immovable subject to Louisiana inheritance taxes and ancillary succession proceedings.

First, the Court determined that the arrangement between the parties was a trust, as opposed a partnership or agency agreement. The beneficiaries were not a party to the trust instrument, so it could not be a partnership, and the trust property was titled in the names of the trustees directly, so they were not the principal beneficiaries' agents.

Next, the Court determined that the principal beneficiaries' interest in the trust was an incorporeal right. Under La. C.C. art. 470, incorporeal things are classified as either movable or immovable according to the object to which they apply. In this case, the Court reasoned, the beneficiaries' interest applied to mineral leases and servitudes held by the trustees. Such leases and servitudes are classified as immovables by law. Therefore, the object of their incorporeal right was an immovable, so the right itself should be classified as an immovable thing. The Court analogized the trust interest to a usufruct over immovables, which is also considered an incorporeal immovable.

Then the Court rejected the Trustees' (P) contention that the beneficial interest should be classified as a movable under Revised Civil Code article 474, which specifically classified shares in companies as movables. The Court concluded that the interest in the trust is not a share or interest in a bank or other commercial company and, therefore, not subject to article 474. The Court also declined to enforce the clause of the trust instrument classifying the beneficiaries' interest as movable property because it contravened the law to the prejudice of state tax agencies.

Finally, the Court held that the beneficiary's interest in the trust was an incorporeal immovable subject to Louisiana inheritance taxes. Consequently, the decedent's estate would be required to open ancillary succession proceedings in Louisiana to dispose of the trust interest. The Court reversed the appeal court's judgment and reinstated the trial court's judgment as its own.

Dissent

Justice Barham dissented and asserted that the majority improperly disregarded the legal personality of the trust. He analogized an interest in a trust to shares in a company and pointed out that Revised Civil Code article 474 merely uses the phrase "shares or interests in banks or companies" as an illustration of the types of incorporeal movables, not the only types to which the article applies. A trust beneficiary does not own any part of the mineral leases themselves. Instead, he owns an interest in a legal arrangement in which the trustees own the mineral leases. This interest, Justice Barham reasoned, is analogous to a share in a corporate entity and should be classified as an incorporeal movable under Revised Civil Code article 474.

He also relied on Civil Code article 475, which dictates that all things not designated as immovables are movables. Because a beneficiary's interest is not specifically designated by the law as an immovable, he reasoned, it should fall within article 475's catchall and be considered a movable. Accordingly, the character of the property owned by the trust should not affect its classification as an incorporeal movable.

Rule of Law

A principal beneficiary's interest in a trust holding immovable property is itself an incorporeal immovable.

IN RE RECEIVERSHIP OF AUGUSTA SUGAR CO.
134 La. 971, 64 So. 870 (La. 1914)

Facts & Procedure

The Augusta Sugar Company became insolvent and was placed in receivership. Payne & Joubert, one of the company's vendors, intervened in the receivership proceedings to assert their privilege on machinery sold to the insolvent company that had not been paid for. The intervenors requested that the receiver be ordered to sell the machinery to pay their claim.

The equipment in question had been placed on the plantation, and a metal building and wooden platform had been built around it. The receiver argued that the equipment became immovable by destination under La. C.C. arts. 466 and 467 upon its installation at the company's plantation.

The trial court found for the intervenors, and the receiver appealed.

Issue

Has equipment that has been installed in a sugar plantation for the production of sugar become so incorporated into the plantation as to have lost its identity as a movable subject to a vendor's privilege?

Holding & Decision

No, equipment attached to an immovable does not necessarily lose its identity as a movable thing simply because it is attached to or incorporated into an immovable. Whether a particular item has become part of an immovable sufficiently to lose its separate identity is a question of fact. The Court distinguished between materials and parts that lose their identity when used to repair or construct a building and a piece of machinery or equipment, like the machinery in question, that is merely installed on an immovable but remains distinct from the immovable to which it is attached.

The Court found that the machinery in question could be removed from the plantation by cutting an easily repaired hole in the side of one of the plantation buildings and disassembling a wooden platform built for the equipment. The Court held that the machinery did not lose its separate identity because a metal building and wooden platform had been built around it.

The Court affirmed the lower court's decision recognizing the intervenors' privilege on the equipment.

Dissent

Justice Monroe dissented against the recognition of the intervenors' privilege because the equipment could only be removed by removing the side of the factory containing it.

Rule of Law

Equipment attached to an immovable does not necessarily lose its identity as a movable thing simply because it is attached to or incorporated into an immovable. Whether a particular item has become part of an immovable sufficiently to lose its separate identity is a question of fact.

FOLSE V. TRICHE
Wife (P) v. Creditors (D)
113 La. 915, 37 So. 875 (La. 1904)

Facts & Procedure

This dispute arose over the disposition of damaged machinery and scrap materials left after a sugar house burned down. Mr. Folse's judgment Creditors (D) had seized the machinery and scrap and sought to have it sold in satisfaction of Mr. Folse's (P) obligations to them. Mrs. Folse, in her capacity as her husband's creditor and legal mortgagee, (P) sued to enjoin the sale of the machinery and other property separately from the immovable on which she held a mortgage. Neither party disputed that, prior to the fire, the equipment and materials in question had been immovables by destination.

The trial court concluded that the machinery and materials did not lose their character as immovables when the sugar house burned down, found for the Wife (P), and issued an injunction. The court reasoned that immovables by destination could only be de-immobilized by the act of their owner removing them or disposing of them in good faith.

The Creditors (D) appealed.

Issue

Do damaged machinery and other scrap materials remaining after the destruction of a building remain immovables by destination?

Holding & Decision

No, damaged machinery and other scrap materials remaining after the destruction of a building become movables. The Court so held because the machinery and other scrap no longer served or improved the recently destroyed sugar house. Under Revised Civil Code article 468, immovables by destination are things placed by the owner of the land upon it for its service or improvement. Since the building the equipment served was destroyed and the equipment itself was rendered useless as anything other than scrap, it became de-immobilized. The Court also cited Revised Civil Code article 476 , which stated that materials arising from the demolition of a building are movables until incorporated into a new building.

The Court held that Mrs. Folse (P) did not have a mortgage on the de-immobilized movables, dissolved the trial court's injunction, and dismissed her lawsuit. The Court reserved the Creditor's (D) right to seek damages in connection with the issuance of the injunction.

On rehearing, the Court confirmed the legal principals it applied but determined that it did not have sufficient facts before it to reach a final judgment. The Court remanded the matter for trial and the application of the rules set forth by the Court.

Rule of Law

When, from any cause, a movable ceases to be of service to a tract of land or is detached from a building to which it was attached as an accessory, it is de-immobilized and ceases to be an immovable.

BROWN V. HODGE-HUNT LUMBER CO.
Landowner (P) v. Lumber Company (D)
162 La. 635, 110 So. 886 (La. 1926)

Facts & Procedure

In this dispute over the ownership of standing timber, the Landowner (P) bought the land from a person who bought it at tax sale. The tax sale deed did not indicate that the timber on the land had previously been sold. But years before the tax sale, the then-owner (plaintiff's ancestor in title) purchased the land from Huie-Hodge Lumber Company (D), which reserved to itself the ownership of the merchantable timber on the land and the right to remove the timber. The company that owned the timber later changed its name to Hodge-Hunt Lumber Company (D).

The present Landowner (P) brought this lawsuit to recover the value of the timber cut and removed by the Lumber Company (D). The trial court awarded the plaintiff $750, and both parties appealed.

Issue

May a landowner reserve to himself the ownership of standing timber and sell the land on which it stands?

Holding & Decision

Yes. The Court recognized that standing timber is an immovable normally considered part of the land on which it stands but noted that, under the law, the ownership of the timber may be separated from the ownership of the ground by an act of the owner. Here, the Court concluded that the Lumber Company (D) reserved the ownership of the timber to itself when it sold the land to the Landowner's (P) ancestor in title. The Court held that title in the timber never vested in the Landowner (P) or his ancestor in title and that the various sale prices and tax assessments for the land did not include the value of the timber. The Court rejected the Landowner's (P) contention that, since the Lumber Company (D) had not been assessed taxes on the timber, its title in the timber should be forfeited.

The Court reversed and set aside the lower court's judgment and dismissed the Landowner's (P) lawsuit at his cost.

Rule of Law

Standing timber is an immovable that may be owned by someone other than the owner of the land on which it stands. In that case, it is a separate immovable.

WILLETTS WOOD PRODUCTS CO. v. CONCORDIA LAND & TIMBER CO.

Landowner (P) v. Lumber Company (D)
169 La. 240, 124 So. 841 (La. 1929)

Facts & Procedure

A Landowner (P) sued the Lumber Company (D) that owned the timber on the Landowner's (P) land to have the court fix a deadline for the Lumber Company (D) to remove its timber. At one point, the Lumber Company (D) owned both the land and the timber. The land was encumbered with a mortgage, and the Lumber Company (D) defaulted on the secured obligation. The land was foreclosed upon and passed to the plaintiff's ancestors in title. Each act transferring the ownership of the land specifically excluded the timber but did not provide for any specific period in which the timber was to be removed. There were no facts in dispute, only what time period would be reasonable for the removal of the timber.

The trial court ruled for the plaintiff and ordered the Lumber Company (D) to remove its timber from the Landowner's (P) land within four years from the date of the judgment. Ownership of any timber remaining on the land at the end of that period would revert to the Landowner (P).

The Landowner (P) appealed.

Issue

Is it reasonable for a court to fix a period of four years for the removal of timber from land owned by another?

Holding & Decision

Yes, timber standing on the land of another must be removed within the time period agreed upon by the parties or fixed by a court upon the application of one or both parties. Here, the Court found that a four year period was not manifestly erroneous.

The Court rejected the Lumber Company's (D) contention that the trial court lacked the authority to fix a period for the timber's removal because there was no contract between the parties to this lawsuit concerning the timber or the separation of the ownership of the timber from the land. The Court found that the Lumber Company (D) acquiesced in the separation of the two ownerships from one another when it allowed its mortgagee to sell the land separate from the timber in satisfaction of a debt and held that it had the same position with respect to the Landowner (P) as if the Landowner (P) had purchased the land directly from the Lumber Company (D).

The Court also rejected the Lumber Company's (D) argument that the Landowner (P) had no right to compel the timber owner to remove separately owned timber because it is an immovable equal in dignity to that of the land itself. The Court dismissed this argument as "legal heresy" and asserted its power to set a time for the timber owner to remove its timber.

The Court amended the time limit in the trial court's judgment to run from the date of the Supreme Court's judgment but affirmed it in all other respects.

Rule of Law

If the owner of the land and the owner of separate timber on that land cannot agree on a definite time period for the removal of the timber, the courts may set a reasonable time period.

STEINAU V. PYBURN
Heirs (P) v. Clerk of Court (D)
229 So. 2d 153 (La. App. 2d Cir. 1969)

Facts & Procedure

This is a dispute over the ownership of $8,000.00 placed in the registry of the court in a separate lawsuit. In that lawsuit, Murphy Oil Company placed the money in the registry of the court and sought specific performance from Lawrence T. Beck and Sybil Loewenberg Beck. The company claimed that the Becks agreed to execute an oil and gas lease on a tract of land they owned in Caddo Parish. The lawsuit was dismissed, but the oil company never withdrew its deposit.

Sometime later, Mrs. Beck died and left a New York will. That will recognized Mrs. Beck's mother, Minnie Loewenberg, as owner of one-third of the Caddo Parish Property but not of Mrs. Beck's movable property. When Mrs. Loewenberg died, her Heirs (P) filed this lawsuit claiming ownership of one-third of the $8,000.00 in the registry of the court and seeking a judgment ordering the Clerk (D) to pay them.

The Heirs (P) argue that the funds in the court were paid in connection with a mineral lease — which is an incorporeal immovable — and are therefore themselves incorporeal immovables. Since immovable property in Louisiana can only be disposed of by a Louisiana court, such a court should govern Mrs. Beck's interest in the money instead of Mrs. Beck's New York will. The Heirs (P) argued that they should inherit one-third of the money as an immovable connected to the Caddo Parish property they inherited part of.

The trial court found for the Clerk of Court (D), and the Heirs (P) appealed.

Issue

Is money paid in connection with a mineral lease an immovable?

Holding & Decision

No, money is a movable thing. The appeal court recognized that the law specifies that mineral leases give rise to real rights and incorporeal immovable property but noted that the law does not state that the proceeds from those arrangements are immovables. To the contrary, the Civil Code specifically states that money is movable. Accordingly, the appeal court held that the money, as a movable, was subject to disposition by Mrs. Beck's New York will.

The appeal court affirmed the trial court's judgment at the Heirs' (P) cost.

Rule of Law

Money, even flowing from an immovable thing or right, is a movable thing.

BEARD V. DURALDE

Plantation Owner (P) v. Creditor (D)
23 La. Ann. 284 (La. 1871)

Facts & Procedure

A Creditor (D) seized lumber and bricks from the plaintiff's plantation to sell to satisfy a debt. When the sheriff arrived to seize the materials, workmen were in the process of building a sugarhouse on the plantation. Some bricks had been laid as a foundation. The Sheriff seized only the lumber and bricks that had not yet been attached to the structure. Some of the seized lumber was still on the river landing where it had been delivered.

The Plantation Owner (P) filed this lawsuit to enjoin the sale of her materials, arguing that the materials were intended for the construction of a new sugarhouse on the plantation and that they were, therefore, immovables by destination not subject to seizure separate from the land.

The trial judge issued the requested injunction, and the Creditor (D) appealed.

Issue

Are lumber and bricks immovables by destination if they are intended for use in building a structure but not yet used?

Holding & Decision

No, lumber and bricks that have not yet been incorporated into a structure are separate movables. The Court distinguished materials that were intended for construction but that had not yet been used from those materials that are separated from a building with the intention of being replaced after repair or addition. Under La. C.C. art. 472, such materials that are removed maintain their status as immovables. On the other hand, the Court held that materials that are collected for erecting a new building are movables until they have been used in constructing that building.

The Court reversed the trial court's judgment, dissolved the injunction, and awarded the Creditors (D) damages and interest.

Rule of Law

Materials collected for the erection of a new building are movables until they have been incorporated into the new building.

SOUTH CENTRAL BELL TELEPHONE CO. V. BARTHELEMY

Telephone Company (P) v. Tax Collector (D)
643 So. 2d 1240 (La. 1994)

Facts & Procedure

This is a dispute over whether computer software is subject to the City of New Orleans's use taxes and whether related maintenance service payments are subject to the City's sales tax. The Telephone Company (P) licensed and installed telephone switching software for use in some of its central offices and accounting software for use in its data processing center. The switching software was delivered on magnetic tape and loaded onto the Company's (P) computers. The data processing software was delivered directly to the Company's (P) computers via modem.

After an audit, the City of New Orleans (D) notified the Company (P) that it had failed to pay the appropriate taxes on the software and related maintenance agreement. The City of New Orleans levied a tax on the sale or use of tangible personal property in the city and upon the sale of services within the city. The Telephone Company (P) paid the taxes under protest and filed this lawsuit to recover them. The Telephone Company contended that the software was not taxable because it was not "tangible personal" property, as defined by law and the City's tax regulations.

The parties filed cross-motions for summary judgment, and the trial court found for the Telephone Company (D), holding that the software and the services were not taxable. The City Tax Collector (D) appealed, and the appeal court affirmed the trial court's judgment. The appeal court found that the software was not taxable tangible personal property. Instead, it was intellectual property. Similarly, since the maintenance agreements concerned this intellectual property and not tangible property, they were not "repairs" and therefore not taxable.

The Tax Collector (D) applied for certiorari.

Issue

Is computer software tangible personal property taxable by the City of New Orleans?

Holding & Decision

Yes, computer software is tangible personal property. The Court noted that "tangible personal property" is synonymous with "corporeal movable property" as used in the Civil Code. Corporeal movable property includes all things that can be detected by the senses that are not immovables. The Court found that computer software is corporeal property because it is physically manifested in machine readable form on magnetic media. Because the information has a physical form recorded on magnetic tape, hard drive, or other device that can be perceived by the senses, it is a corporeal thing. The Court then concluded that, once the software was reduced to a physical form and came to rest in New Orleans, it was taxable under the law.

The Court specifically rejected the appeal court's conclusion that the software was incorporeal intellectual property. The Court distinguished the incorporeal right of copyright in the software from its physical manifestation. The Court also rejected a distinction between "canned" and custom software under which "canned" software is a taxable product purchased by a user and custom software is the untaxable end result of purchasing programming services.

The Court held that both pieces of software were taxable tangible personal property and reversed the appeal court in part, affirmed in part, and remanded the case for further proceedings.

Rule of Law

Computer software is a corporeal movable because it is physically manifested on digital media.

SUCCESSION OF MILLER
405 So. 2d 812 (La. 1981)

Facts & Procedure

Before her death, Ms. Miller purchased bearer bonds and gave them to Mrs. Meyer. Until Ms. Miller's death, Mrs. Meyer gave Ms. Miller the interest coupons from the bonds as they matured. Mrs. Meyer testified that the bonds were hers but that she would have returned them to Ms. Meyer if she had asked. Almost two years later, Ms. Miller closed a savings account in her name and transferred the money to a joint account with Mrs. Meyer. Mrs. Meyer testified that Ms. Miller told her she wanted Mrs. Meyer to have the money. Several months later, Ms. Miller was taken to the hospital. In the ambulance, she told Mrs. Meyer that she was about to die and instructed her to withdraw all the money from their joint savings account. Shortly after Mrs. Meyer made the withdrawal, Ms. Miller died.

During the succession proceedings, it came to light that Ms. Miller had written a will, but it was invalid because of its form. The succession administratrix listed the money withdrawn by Mrs. Meyer and the bearer bonds on the succession's inventory. Mrs. Meyer objected to the inclusion of those items on the succession inventory on the grounds that they were her property by manual gift made during Ms. Miller's life.

The trial court held that the items were correctly included in the succession, and the appeal court affirmed. Mrs. Meyer petitioned for certiorari. Upon its first hearing, the Supreme Court reversed the lower courts, finding that Mrs. Meyer received the money and the bonds as a valid manual gift. The Court reheard the matter.

Issue

Can a bearer bond be transferred by manual gift?

Holding & Decision

No, a bearer bond cannot be transferred by manual gift. The Court turned to the Civil Code, which defines a manual gift as "the giving of corporeal movable effects, accompanied by a real delivery." La. C.C. art. 1536 (1870). The Court held that the money withdrawn from the joint account was a corporeal movable actually delivered by manual gift even though Ms. Miller did not physically hand the funds to Mrs. Meyer. Mrs. Meyer's withdrawal of the funds at Ms. Miller's insistence constituted actual delivery for purposes of a manual gift.

The bonds, on the other hand, were incorporeal movables under La. C.C. art. 473. Because bonds are legally incorporeal, the Court held that they cannot be transferred by manual gift. Since they were not transferred by a notarial transfer and could not be transferred by manual gift, the Court held that the bonds belonged to Ms. Miller's estate.

The Court reversed the lower court's judgment with respect to the money withdrawn from the savings account and affirmed its judgment with respect to the savings bonds.

Dissent

Justice Watson concurred with the majority concerning the bonds but dissented with respect to the money from the savings account.

Justice Dixon dissented from the majority on both counts. He asserted that the civil code's classification of bonds as incorporeals should not be applied to commercial paper governed by commercial law. Instead, negotiable instruments are corporeal proof of incorporeal obligations and, by their own terms, sometimes modify those obligations. For instance, bearer bonds are instruments intended to be negotiable by delivery. He urged the Court to adopt the French doctrine insofar as it allows certain instruments like bearer bonds to be negotiated by manual gift.

Rule of Law

A bearer bond is an incorporeal immovable not transferable by manual gift.[1]

---

[1]Under Uniform Commercial Code Article 3, adopted as La. R.S. 10:3–202(1) subsequent to this decision, a bearer bond may be negotiated by delivery.

INNOVATIVE HOSPITALITY SYSTEM v. ABRAHAM
Fraud Victim (P) v. Check Casher & Insurer (D)
62 So. 3d 740 (La. App. 3d Cir. 2011)

Facts & Procedure

A Fraud Victim (P) sued the company (D) that cashed fraudulent checks drawn on its account and the company's commercial general liability Insurer (D). The plaintiff also sued the banks where the fraudulent checks were deposited, who then filed cross-claims against the Check Casher and its Insurer (D). The Insurer (D) moved for summary judgment, arguing that its policy did not cover losses from cashing fraudulent checks. The policy covered property damage, which was defined by the policy as either physical injury to tangible property or the "[l]oss of use of tangible property that is not physically injured." Money on deposit, the Insurer (D) argued, is not tangible property, only intangible rights, which are not covered by the policy.

The trial court held that the Check Casher (D) paid out cash, which was tangible and covered by the policy, and denied the motion. The appeal court denied supervisory writs. The Louisiana Supreme Court remanded the case to the appeal court for briefing, argument, and opinion. The appeal court denied the writ.

Issue

Does a person lose corporeal property when another cashes a fraudulent check through a third-party check cashing service?

Holding & Decision

Yes, a person loses corporeal property when another cashes a fraudulent check through a third party check cashing service, even though the money physically paid out is not the same money on deposit at the bank. First, the appeal court, noted that "tangible property" has the same meaning under Louisiana law as "corporeal property." The appeal court rejected the Insurer's (D) argument that the physical dollar bills paid out to the fraudsters were not covered by the insurance policy because the bills were not damaged and the Fraud Victim (P) had no right to use those particular physical bills, so could not claim loss of use of them.

The appeal court held that the insurance policy covered damages that arise from cashing a fraudulent check. It reasoned that the check was converted into cash upon presentation, that the cash was a corporeal movable, and that the Fraud Victim (P) suffered a loss of use of its cash money. The appeal court noted that the funds in the plaintiff's bank account were actual funds deposited at the bank.

Dissent

Judge Gremillion dissented because the Fraud Victim (P) had the use of its funds until the Check Casher (D) presented the check to the Victim's (P) bank and those funds were debited from its account. Therefore, he concluded, the Fraud Victim (P) did not lose cash, but lost the right to use its funds on deposit. The loss of intangible rights was not covered by the insurance policy. He also noted that the First Circuit Court of Appeal held that loss of use coverage, at issue here, did not cover an employee's embezzlement of funds and agreed with that analysis.

Rule of Law

A person loses corporeal movables when someone cashes a fraudulent check through a third party check cashing service, even though the money physically paid out is not the same money on deposit at the bank.

Chapter 4

Possession

1. **Possession.**

   a) **Possession** is "[t]he detention or enjoyment of a corporeal thing, movable or immovable, that one holds or exercises by himself or by another who keeps or exercises it in his name." La. C.C. art. 3421.

   b) *Cf.* **detention**, which is the physical control of a thing without intending to have it as one's own.

   c) *Cf.* **quasi-posession**, which is "the exercise of a real right, such as a servitude, with the intent to have it as one's own." La. C.C. art. 3421. "The rules governing possession apply by analogy to the quasi-possession of incorporeals." *Id.*

   d) "One who has possessed a thing for over a year acquires the **right to possess** it." La. C.C. art. 3422.

      i. **Right to Possess.** The phrase "right to possess" is effectively shorthand for saying that someone has acquired the right to bring a possessory action. *Todd v. State.*

   e) "A possessor is considered provisionally as owner of the thing he possesses until the right of the true owner is established." La. C.C. art. 3423.

      i. A legal possessor enjoys many of the benefits of the property as if he were its owner. For example, the possessor of movable property may recover damages for conversion of or damage to that property to the same extent as if he were its owner. *Peloquin v. Calcasieu Police Jury.*

   f) There are three ways of exercising possession: **corporeal, civil, and constructive possession**.

      i. **Corporeal possession** is "[t]he exercise of physical acts of use, detention, or enjoyment over a thing." La. C.C. art. 3425.

      ii. **Civil Possession** is the retention of possession by "the intent to possess as owner even if the possessor ceases to possess corporeally." La. C.C. art. 3431.

         A. "The intent to retain possession is presumed unless there is clear proof of a contrary intention." La. C.C. art. 3432.

         B. A buyer retains his seller's right to possess a thing whether the buyer continues that possession corporeally or civilly, even if the buyer has never personally resided on or used the land for any purpose. *Ellis v. Prevost.*

      iii. **Constructive possession.** "One who possesses a part of an immovable by virtue of a title is deemed to have constructive possession within the limits of his title. In the absence of title, one has possession only of the area he actually possesses." La. C.C. art. 3426. For example, establishing a pipeline on a portion of a tract of land is sufficient to establish corporeal possession over the whole tract of land. *Manson Realty Co. v. Plaisance.*

2. **Acquisition, exercise, retention, and loss of possession.**

    a) **Acquisition of possession.**

       i. "To acquire possession of a thing, one must intend to possess as owner and must take corporeal possession of the thing." La. C.C. art. 3424.

      ii. A person cannot establish the right to possess a thing without intending to possess it as its owner. *Harper v. Willis.*

      iii. One's constructive possession is insufficient to oust another's corporeal possession or corporeal possession followed by civil possession within natural or artificial enclosures. *Souther v. Domingue.*

      iv. "One may acquire possession of a thing through another who takes it for him and in his name. The person taking possession must intend to do so for another." La. C.C. art. 3428.

      v. "A juridical person acquires possession through its representatives." La. C.C. art. 3430.

    b) **Exercise of possession.** "Possession may be exercised by the possessor or by another who holds the thing for him and in his name. Thus, a lessor possesses through his lessee." La. C.C. art. 3429.

    c) **Loss of possession.** "Possession is lost when the possessor manifests his intention to abandon it or when he is evicted by another by force or usurpation." La. C.C. art. 3433.

      i. "The right to possess is lost upon abandonment of possession. In case of eviction, the right to possess is lost if the possessor does not recover possession within a year of the eviction. When the right to possess is lost, possession is interrupted." La. C.C. art. 3434.

      ii. The corporeal possessor of a tract of land continues in that possession until he divests himself of it, another expels him from it, or until he permits his possession to be usurped and held by another for a year without interfering with the usurper's possession. A possessor may possess quietly and without interruption for more than a year so as to be entitled to bring a possessory action, even though disturbances in fact or law have occurred during that year. *Liner v. Louisiana Land & Exploration Co.*

      iii. Mowing the grass of property possessed by another is not sufficient indication that the possessor's possession is endangered or that one intends to possess the property as owner. *Richard v. Comeaux.*

      iv. On the other hand, the act of building a fence around a parcel of land is a disturbance sufficient to interrupt another's right to possess that land. *Evans v. Dunn.*

3. **Transfer of possession.** "Possession is transferable by universal title[, as through succession to an heir,] or by particular title[, as by sale]." La. C.C. art. 3441.

4. **Tacking** is the cumulation of possession between a grantor and his successor. "The possession of the transferor is tacked to that of the transferee if there has been no interruption of possession." La. C.C. art. 3442. The possessions of both the grantor and his successor must be free from vice.

5. **Vices of possession.**

   a) "Possession that is violent, clandestine, discontinuous, or equivocal has no legal effect." La. C.C. art. 3435.

      i. **Violent possession** is "acquired or maintained by violent acts. When the violence ceases, the possession ceases to be violent." La. C.C. art. 3436. The vice of violence is relative, viz., only the person who is the victim of the violence can claim it to defeat the new possessor's possession. If the actual owner is a third party against whom no violence was perpetrated, the violent possessor may still gain the right to possess and eventually file a possessory action against the third-party owner.

      ii. **Clandestine possession** "is not open or public." *Id.*

      iii. **Discontinuous possession** "is not exercised at regular intervals." *Id.*

      iv. **Equivocal possession** occurs "when there is ambiguity as to the intent of the possessor to own the thing." *Id.* For example, acts of possession by a co-owner of property held in indivision could be ambiguous because they could be performed as part of that co-owner's partial ownership or as part of his intent to exert exclusive ownership.

6. **Precarious possession.** "The exercise of possession over a thing with the permission of or on behalf of the owner or possessor." La. C.C. art. 3437. A precarious possessor is not technically a possessor at all; he is exercising detention of the thing instead of possession.

   a) "A precarious possessor, such as a lessee or a depositary, is presumed to possess for another although he may intend to possess for himself." La. C.C. art. 3438.

   b) A person who uses land with the permission of the owner does not himself possess the land as owner and cannot gain the right to possess it for himself. *Falgoust v. Inness.*

   c) "A co-owner, or his universal successor, commences to possess for himself when he demonstrates this intent by overt and unambiguous acts sufficient to give notice to his co-owner. Any other precarious possessor, or his universal successor, commences to possess for himself when he gives actual notice of this intent to the person on whose behalf he is possessing." La. C.C. art. 3439.

   d) "Where there is a disturbance of possession, the possessory action is available to a precarious possessor, such as a lessee or a depositary, against anyone except the person for whom he possesses." La. C.C. art. 3440.

7. **Possessory action.**

   a) "The **possessory action** is one brought by the possessor of immovable property or of a real right therein to be maintained in his possession of the property or enjoyment of the right when he has been disturbed, or to be restored to the possession or enjoyment thereof when he has been evicted." La. C.C.P. art. 3655.

b) *Elements.* "To maintain the possessory action the possessor must allege and prove that:

   i. He had possession of the immovable property or real right therein at the time the disturbance occurred;

   ii. He and his ancestors in title had such possession quietly and without interruption for more than a year immediately prior to the disturbance, unless evicted by force or fraud;

   iii. The disturbance was one in fact or in law, as defined in Article 3659; and

   iv. The possessory action was instituted within a year of the disturbance." La. C.C.P. art. 3568.

c) To win a possessory action, a plaintiff must show that he at one time acquired the right to possess and that he has not lost the right in the year leading up to the disturbance. *Mire v. Crowe.*

d) **Disturbance in fact.** "An eviction, or any other physical act which prevents the possessor of immovable property or of a real right therein from enjoying his possession quietly, or which throws any obstacle in the way of that enjoyment." La. C.C.P. art. 3659.

e) **Disturbance in law.** "The execution, recordation, registry, or continuing existence of record of any instrument which asserts or implies a right of ownership or to the possession of immovable property or of a real right therein, or any claim or pretension of ownership or right to the possession thereof except in an action or proceeding, adversely to the possessor of such property or right." La. C.C.P. art. 3659.

f) **Ownership not at issue.** "In the possessory action, the ownership or title of the parties to the immovable property or real right therein is not at issue. No evidence of ownership or title to the immovable property or real right therein shall be admitted except to prove: (1) The possession thereof by a party as owner; (2) The extent of the possession thereof by a party; or (3) The length of time in which a party and his ancestors in title have had possession thereof." La. C.C.P. art. 3661.

g) **Relief.** "A judgment rendered for the plaintiff in a possessory action shall:"

   i. Recognize his right to possess the immovable and either restore his possession or maintain his possession, as appropriate;

   ii. Require the defendant to assert and prove his ownership via the petitory action within sixty days or be barred from asserting the ownership, if requested by the plaintiff; and

   iii. Award the plaintiff appropriate damages as demanded. La. C.C.P. art. 3662.

h) **Sequestration and injunctive relief.** Immovable property and real rights therein may be sequestered during the pendency of a possessory action. Further, injunctive relief under the applicable laws is available "to protect or restore possession of immovable property or of a real right therein, [for] (1) A plaintiff in a possessory action, during the pendency thereof; [or] (2) A person who is disturbed in the possession which he and his ancestors in title have had for more than a year of immovable property or of a real right therein of which he claims the ownership, the possession, or the enjoyment." La. C.C.P. art. 3663.

   i. A plaintiff must prove himself to be the legal possessor of the property to be entitled to injunctive or other relief to stop a factual or legal disturbance of possession where ownership may be a factual issue. *Gill v. Henderson.*

8. **Possessory action against the state.** A possessory action may be maintained against the State, but the State is not required to assert its adverse claim of ownership in a petitory action after another is adjudged the legal possessor of the disputed property. *Todd v. State.*

Peloquin v. Calcasieu Police Jury

Cat Owners (P) v. Parish Government & Neighbors (D)
367 So. 2d 1246 (La. App. 3d Cir. 1979)

Facts & Procedure

The plaintiffs had a pet cat named George. One of the plaintiffs found George as a kitten more than seven years before the events of this lawsuit. Their Neighbors (D) borrowed an animal trap from the Parish's animal control center (D) and trapped a cat, which was then returned with the trap to the animal control center and destroyed. George's Owners (P) maintain that their Neighbor (D) trapped George and that the Parish Government (D) killed him. They sued their Neighbors and Parish Government (D) for conversion of their cat; for the value of their cat; and for mental anguish, inconvenience, and humiliation.

The defendants filed exceptions of no right of action and no cause of action, arguing that the plaintiffs had no ownership interest in George and, therefore, they had no right to sue for damages. The trial court agreed, holding that the plaintiffs merely possessed George instead of owning him. The court sustained the defendants' exceptions and dismissed all the Owners' claims except for their claim for the value of the cat. The trial court also denied the Owners' request for a jury after determining the value of the cat did not meet the statutory minimum for a jury trial.

The Owners (P) appealed the dismissal of their claims.

Issue

May someone who possesses a cat sue for damages caused by its conversion?

Holding & Decision

Yes, the possessor of a movable has the same rights as its owner to sue for damages for conversion, including damages for mental anguish, inconvenience, and humiliation. The appeal court considered that George's Owners (P) would have acquired legal ownership of the cat upon taking possession of it if George had been a wild or abandoned cat but concluded that an owner and a possessor have the same rights to recover for damages to the property. Relying on French doctrine, the court concluded that, if the plaintiffs could prove they were George's owners or possessors, they would be entitled to proceed against the defendants for damages.

The appeal court reversed the trial court and remanded the case for further proceedings.

Rule of Law

The possessor of movable property may recover damages for conversion of or damage to that property to the same extent as if he were its owner.

ELLIS V. PREVOST
Landowner (P) v. Occupants (D)
19 La. 251 (La. 1841)

Facts & Procedure

This is a possessory action between a Landowner (P) and Occupants (D) who have occupied part of the disputed tract for several generations. The Landowner (P) purchased the tract of land in question in 1836 from John Hutchings. It included substantial acreage on both the east and west sides of bayou Grand Caillou. Hutchings, in turn, had purchased the land in 1829 and began working it. Hutchings placed an overseer and seven hands on the property to cultivate it, built cabins, girdled some trees, raised crops, and gave others permission to raise crops on the land. After purchasing the land, the Landowner (P) never resided there and abandoned Hutchings's improvements.

The Occupants (D) and their ancestors, on the other hand, resided on the west side of the bayou for many years. At various times, they occupied and cultivated substantial portions of both sides of the bayou. Shortly before this lawsuit, one of the Occupants (D) gave two people permission to reside on land on the east side of the bayou.

The Landowner (P) filed this possessory action against the Occupants (D), and the Occupants (D) reconvened to assert their own possessory action over part of the land. The trial court entered a jury verdict for the Occupants (D), and the Landowner (P) appealed.

Issue

May a person who purchased a tract of land from a seller who cultivated it for several years bring a possessory action against a third party residing on it, even though the purchaser has not resided on the land or used it for any purpose?

Holding & Decision

Yes, a purchaser who buys a tract of land from someone who has physically possessed it for more than one year enjoys the right to possess the land as if he had possessed it in place of the seller. At the outset, the Court distinguished between corporeal possession of a thing by physical detention and civil possession. Civil possession, simply put, is the continuation of corporeal possession by the mere intention to continue possessing it without the need for any actual use.

The Court concluded that the Landowner (P), although he never exercised corporeal possession of the property, acquired his vendor's several-year possession upon buying the property and possessed the property civilly to the boundaries described in his title. He was, therefore, entitled to bring a possessory action.

In so concluding, the Court rejected a literal reading of Code of Practice article 49, which stated that "a mere civil or legal possession is not sufficient" to support a possessory action. The Court reasoned that, if the article were construed literally, a person who was evicted from his home during a normal daily absence would not be entitled to bring a possessory action against the intruder. Instead, the Court stated that any possession that had its source in corporeal possession — even if it were not corporeal possession at the moment of the disturbance — would suffice.

After concluding that the Landowner (P) could bring his possessory action, the Court addressed the Occupants' (D) claims to possession of the land they had occupied. The Court cited precedent to the effect that an adverse possessor without a title must show his possession by enclosures. Here, the Court held, the Occupants (D) did not show possession over most of the land with any certainty. But they did show that they had enclosed and possessed a portion of land around their house for more than a year. The residents on the east side of the bayou, on the other hand, had not possessed any land for more than a year.

Accordingly, the Court held that the Occupants (D) were entitled to possess the portion of land they had enclosed and occupied for more than a year, that the Landowner (P) was entitled to possess the remainder of the land described in his title, and that the Occupants (D) were not entitled to any relief. The Court annulled the district court's judgment and substituted its own.

Rule of Law

A buyer retains his seller's right to possess a thing whether the buyer continues that possession corporeally or civilly, even if the buyer has never personally resided on or used the land for any purpose.

MANSON REALTY CO. V. PLAISANCE
Landowner (P) v. Occupant (D)
196 So. 2d 555 (La. App. 4th Cir. 1967)

Facts & Procedure

The Landowner (P), a real estate company, brought this lawsuit to enjoin the Occupant (D) from trespassing on its land and to force the defendant to remove shacks and fences he had constructed on the property. The Landowner (P) had granted a servitude and allowed a pipeline to be laid across part of his land. But the Occupant (D) claimed that he had been in possession of the disputed property for more than a year.

The trial court found that the Landowner (P) had not been in actual possession of the property for more than a year before filing its possessory action and that it was, therefore, barred from bringing a possessory action. The trial court also concluded that the Occupant (D) had not been in possession for more than a year either. The Landowner (P) appealed.

Issue

Are the granting of a pipeline servitude and the maintenance of the pipeline's right-of-way sufficient acts to establish corporeal possession over an entire tract of land?

Holding & Decision

Yes, a landowner granting a pipeline servitude and maintaining the pipeline's right-of-way is sufficient to constitute corporeal possession of the entire tract of land as described in its title. The court stated that, where a possessor has a title, even minor acts that show the intent to possess the land are sufficient to establish corporeal possession over the whole tract. In this case, where the land was undeveloped, the court held that continuous operation of the pipeline established the Landowner's (P) corporeal possession of the land. The court also reasoned that, even if the laying of the pipe was the only physical action taken by the Landowner (P), subsequent acts like paying property taxes and granting mineral leases would suffice to maintain its civil possession over the whole tract.

The court held that the Landowner (P) had been disturbed in its possession that it had enjoyed for more than a year before the disturbance and that it had timely brought its action. It reversed the trial court's judgment and rendered judgment enjoining the Occupant (D) from trespassing on the land and ordering him to remove the structures he had built.

Rule of Law

Establishing a pipeline on a portion of a tract of land is sufficient to establish corporeal possession over the whole tract of land to the extent of its title.

HARPER V. WILLIS

Rancher (P) v. Landowner (D)
383 So. 2d 1299 (La. App. 3d Cir. 1980)

Facts & Procedure

A cattle Rancher (P) filed this possessory action against a Landowner (D), asserting that he had the right to possess a parcel of land adjacent to parcels that the Rancher (P) owned. The disputed property was part of a development called the Old Pecan Orchard Subdivision. In the beginning, the owners of the development employed a caretaker to look after the property, but he quit in 1946 or 1947. At some point, lots in the development were sold for taxes, but none of the lot purchasers ever occupied or used the lots they acquired.

The Rancher (P) began running his cattle on the entire subdivision around 1939 and continued to do so. He began acquiring lots in the subdivision through tax sales. Just before the caretaker quit, he gave the Rancher (P) permission to run his cattle on the land rent free in exchange for looking after the property, keeping the brush down, and preventing fires. The Rancher continued to acquire lots in the subdivision and eventually came to own a substantial portion of it. He tried to purchase the lots over which he eventually sued, but the previous owner sold them to the defendant Landowner (D) instead. After the sale, the Rancher (P) sued to assert his right to possess the lots by virtue of having cared for them for several years. During his deposition, the Rancher (P) asserted that he never intended to possess the lots in question as their owner because he knew he did not own them.

The trial court granted the Landowner's (D) motion for summary judgment and dismissed the Rancher's (P) lawsuit.

The Rancher (P) appealed.

Issue

Can a person establish a right to possess a thing without intending to possess it as its owner?

Holding & Decision

No, in order to acquire the right to possess a thing, a person must intend to possess it as if he were the owner. Under La. C.C. art. 3424, in order to acquire possession of a thing, a person must have the intent to possess it as its owner and must corporeally possess it. The appeal court held that the Rancher (P) lacked the requisite intent to possess the lots as owner based on his testimony to that effect. Therefore, even assuming he could prove his corporeal possession, the Rancher (P) could not acquire possession of the lots. Acts on the property unaccompanied by the intent to possess the property as owner lack legal significance.

The appeal court affirmed the trial court's judgment dismissing the Rancher's (P) action.

Rule of Law

A person cannot establish the right to possess a thing without intending to possess it as its owner.

SOUTHER V. DOMINGUE
Landowner (P) v. Tenant (D)
238 So. 2d 264 (La. App. 3d Cir. 1970)

Facts & Procedure

The Landowner (P) filed a possessory action against neighboring landowners and their Tenant (D). The Landowner (P) purchased a tract of land in 1953 that contained highland on the eastern and western sides with a swamp in the center. The tract was bordered on the north, west, and south by the defendants' property and on the east by the Vermilion River. The Landowner (P) bridged the Vermilion to access the eastern highland portion of his property, which he used and developed significantly. The western portion of the tract remained unused and inaccessible to him because of the impassable swamp in the middle of the property.

This lawsuit concerns only the western end of the property. For about two years before this dispute arose, no one used the disputed land. Historically, the defendant landowners and their tenants pastured their cattle on the disputed property for at least thirty years and regularly cleared underbrush to allow their cattle to graze.

Markers indicated the boundaries of the disputed area. Before the dispute arose, no fences were erected on the western end of the Landowner's (P) property. The defendant landowners leased the premises to their Tenant (D), who began clearing the land with heavy equipment. The Landowner (P) had hired a surveyor to reestablish his northern boundary against nearby timber operations, and the surveyor noticed the clearing. At that time, the parties met on the disputed property to discuss boundaries and learned that they disagreed. The defendants then erected a fence on the property, and this lawsuit followed.

The trial court found for the Landowner (P) and ordered the defendants to place him back in possession of the disputed land. They suspensively appealed, arguing that the Landowner (P) never proved his corporeal possession of the land and, therefore, that he was not entitled to bring a possessory action. In the alternative, they contended that his possessory action was prescribed because it was not brought within one year of the disturbance of his possession.

Issue

Is one person's constructive possession of property by title sufficient to oust another's corporeal possession of a tract of unfenced land surrounded by natural boundaries, stakes, and tree blazes?

Holding & Decision

No, mere constructive possession is insufficient to oust another's corporeal possession or corporeal possession followed by civil possession within enclosures. Here, the neighboring landowner and his Tenant (D) had exercised corporeal possession over the disputed western tract. Further, the appeal court reasoned that a tract of land need not be fenced to be enclosed. Rather, as in this case, natural boundaries can be created by heavy wood lines, swamps, and other features of the land. Additionally, the natural boundaries in this case were supplemented by stakes and tree blazes sufficient to "enclose" the area the defendants possessed.

Because the neighboring landowner and his Tenant (D) corporeally possessed the disputed tract within natural and artificial boundaries for more than a year, the appeal court reversed the trial court and dismissed the Landowner's (P) lawsuit at his cost.

Rule of Law

One's constructive possession is insufficient to oust another's corporeal possession or corporeal possession followed by civil possession within natural or artificial enclosures.

LINER V. LOUISIANA LAND EXPLORATION CO.
Landowner (P) v. Land Company (D)
319 So. 2d 766 (La. 1975)

Facts & Procedure

A Landowner (P) brought a possessory action against the Land Company (D) that owned the marshland adjacent to his property. The disputed land was west of the boundary dividing Range 15 and Range 16. The Landowner's (P) title included only land in Range 16, and the Land Company's (D) title included all the land claimed by the Landowner (P) in Range 15. In short, the Landowner (P) claimed he owned the land up to the eastern bank of Bayou Dufrene, which was inside Range 15, but the Land Company (D) claimed that the line between Ranges 15 and 16 was the correct boundary.

While the Landowner (P) has no record title to the disputed property in Range 15, he asserted that he and his family possessed the land for about one hundred years. At the trial, the Landowner (P) testified that he had occupied and used the land for fifty-six years. He trapped, raised cattle, and raised his family on the land. For several months out of each year, his family occupied a camp on the bank of nearby Bayou DuLarge.

Before a severe storm in 1909, the Landowner's (P) grandfather and an aunt lived in houses on the bank of Bayou DuLarge. They maintained a fence on the north and south sides of the property running all the way from Bayou DuLarge to Bayou Dufrene. The family planted cotton, orange and pecan trees, and raised cattle on the land. The 1909 storm destroyed the fences and the houses, but the family continuously maintained the north and south boundaries with stakes. The Landowner (P) continued to use the land for his living, and his boundaries were recognized by other trappers in the area, including trappers employed by the Land Company (D).

In 1952, the Land Company (D) conducted a survey and placed concrete markers along the boundary line between Ranges 15 and 16. The Company (D) also set iron pipes and signs along the claimed boundary line. But in 1956, the Landowner (P) granted Tennessee Gas Transmission Company a pipeline servitude over all his land, including the disputed portion.

In 1958, the Land Company (D) marked the boundary it claimed with a ditch, monuments, and signs. The Landowner (P) appropriated the ditch to himself by constructing bulkheads and other improvements in the ditch and used it to water his cattle. The Land Company (D) removed the bulkheads in 1971, but the Landowner (P) replaced them.

In the 50s and 60s, the Land Company (D) alone gave seismograph crews permission to cross its land. It also sent crews to clean out the boundary ditch in 1965. Some of the Landowner's (P) stakes were removed as part of the cleanup. The Land Company (D) began cleaning the ditch again in 1971 and again removed the Landowner's (P) boundary stakes several times. Each time the stakes were removed, the Landowner (P) replaced them. The Landowner (P) then had his attorney notify the Company (D) that its employees had removed the stakes and requested that they stop. This lawsuit followed in 1972, several days after the Company (D) again removed the Landowner's (P) stakes.

The trial court found for the Landowner (P), and the appeal court reversed because the Tennessee Gas Transmission Company disturbed the Landowner's (P) possession of the disputed property by constructing and operating a gas pipeline across it.

The Landowner (P) appealed.

Issue

Is a person dispossessed of a tract of land when a usurper occasionally disturbs his possession without evicting him from it?

Holding & Decision

No, a person who has acquired corporeal possession of a tract of land continues in that possession until he divests himself of it, another expels him from it, or until he permits his possession to be usurped and held by another for a year without interfering with the usurper's possession.

The Court found that the Landowner (P) and his ancestors had exercised corporeal possession of the disputed property for many years; that the nature of the possession changed as the nature of the land changed; that the possession extended to visible boundaries; that it was neither precarious, violent, nor ambiguous; and that he possessed the disputed property as its owner. The Court held that the Land Company's (D) activities, while disturbing his possession, did not dispossess the Landowner (P). Specifically, neither the 1952 survey nor the Company's (D) seismic exploration dispossessed the Landowner (P), and he appropriated the ditch the Company (D) dug. Finally, the Tennessee Gas Transmission Company's pipeline ditch was dug with the Landowner's (P) permission, so it certainly did not dispossess him. Because the Landowner (P) protested against the Land Company's (D) invasions, continued to replace his boundary stakes, and did not acquiesce in the Company's (D) attempts to possess the disputed property, he remained in corporeal possession of the land and correctly brought the possessory action.

The Court reversed the appeal court and reinstated the trial court's judgment of possession. The Land Company (D) sought rehearing on the grounds that the Landowner's (P) possession had been disturbed in fact or in law, even though he was not evicted. The Court reasserted that a possessor does not lose possession against his consent unless he is forcibly expelled from the property or unless the usurper corporeally possesses it for more than a year and denied the request for rehearing.

Rule of Law

1. The corporeal possessor of a tract of land continues in that possession until he divests himself of it, another expels him from it, or until he permits his possession to be usurped and held by another for a year without interfering with the usurper's possession.

2. A possessor may possess quietly and without interruption for more than a year so as to be entitled to bring a possessory action, even though disturbances in fact or law have occurred during that year.

RICHARD V. COMEAUX
Heirs (P) v. Neighbor (D)
260 So. 2d 350 (La. App. 1st Cir. 1972)

Facts & Procedure

Seven Heirs (P) filed a possessory action against their Neighbor (D) seeking an injunction against him building a fence on their property and an order directing him to remove the fence he had already built. The Neighbor (D) erected a fence on what he believed to be the boundary dividing the parties' property. The Heirs (P) demanded he stop and filed this lawsuit when he did not.

The Heirs' (P) mother purchased the property at issue in 1916 and lived there until shortly before her death in 1966. For about a year on either side of the mother's death, no one lived in the house on the property, but the rest of the property was used by a tenant to grow sugarcane. Another tenant eventually moved into the house. Someone always maintained the property.

A partially filled-in ditch ran along what the Heirs (P) considered to be their western boundary. Before 1949, the Heirs' (P) father constructed a barbed wire fence along the eastern side of the ditch as a cattle enclosure. In 1970, the Neighbor (D) had a survey conducted, and it showed that his title included five to ten feet of land inside the Heirs' (P) old fence line along the ditch. He then began building a fence along the surveyed boundary. The Heirs (P), on the other hand, claimed possession of the land to the middle of the drainage ditch, well to the west of the Neighbor's (D) new fence.

When the Neighbor (D) purchased the property, the east side of the drainage ditch was overgrown, and he set out to clean it up by clearing undergrowth and removing stumps. Over time, the Neighbor (D) began including land east of the ditch in his regular lawn mowing and continued doing so after the Heirs' (P) mother died. But the Neighbor (D) did not place any construction or other sign of adverse possession east of the canal before building the fence that sparked this lawsuit.

The trial court entered judgment for the Heirs (P) and held that they had proved their possession up to the old fence line on the eastern bank of the ditch. The Neighbor (D) appealed.

Issue

Is mowing grass on the property possessed by another sufficient to disturb that possession?

Holding & Decision

No, mowing the grass on property possessed by another is not sufficient indication that a possessor's possession is endangered or that one intends to possess the property as owner. The appeal court held that the Neighbor (D) failed to demonstrate that he had established possession of the disputed property in a way sufficient to oust the Heirs (P) from their possession before building the fence. Because the construction of the fence almost immediately sparked this lawsuit, the Neighbor (D) could not show that the Heirs' (P) possession had been disturbed for more than a year.

The appeal court affirmed the judgment in part, reversed in part, and recast the judgment.

Rule of Law

Mowing the grass of property possessed by another is not sufficient indication that the possessor's possession is endangered or that one intends to possess the property as owner.

EVANS V. DUNN

Southern Landowner (P) v. Northern Landowner (D)
458 So. 2d 650 (La. App. 3d Cir. 1984)

Facts & Procedure

This lawsuit is a possessory action concerning a 36'x210' strip of land located along the northern side of the parties' joint property line. When Evans (P) purchased the southernmost property in 1951, there was an existing fence thirty-six feet north of the boundary described in his title. He mowed the disputed area and tended a flower garden on it.

Before Dunn (D) purchased the northernmost property in 1978, the fence was torn down, leaving no visible boundary between the properties. In May 1981, Dunn had the land surveyed and built a chain link fence on his southern boundary and excluded Evans (P) from the thirty-six foot strip he had previously used. Many of Evans's (P) plants were stranded north of the fence. In July 1982, Dunn (D) replaced the chain link fence with a barbed wire fence and destroyed the plants growing inside the fence. This lawsuit followed that fall.

The trial court heard Evans's (P) testimony that he never set foot on the disputed property again after Dunn (D) erected the chain link fence in 1981 and that Dunn (D) maintained the grounds north of the fence and allowed his cattle to graze on the disputed property. The trial court dismissed Evans's (P) petition, and he appealed.

Issue

Does a person lose possession of a tract of land by being evicted and having a fence erected around it?

Holding & Decision

Yes, the act of building a fence around a parcel of land is a disturbance sufficient to interrupt another's right to possess that land. Here, the appeal court found that, in May 1982, the property north of the boundary had been usurped and held for one year without any action by Evans (P). Accordingly, Evans (P) lost any right he had to the property and could not prevail on the possessory action.

The appeal court affirmed the trial court's judgment.

Rule of Law

The act of building a fence around a parcel of land is a disturbance sufficient to interrupt another's right to possess that land.

FALGOUST V. INNESS
Landowner (P) v. Tenant (D)
162 So. 429 (La. App. Orl. Cir. 1935)

Facts & Procedure

The Landowner (P) gave her son-in-law permission to build a garage and filling station on her land. He did so and had operated his business there for almost a year when the Landowner (P) served him with notice to vacate. The Tenant (D) refused to comply, and the Landowner (P) filed this lawsuit to compel him to do so, to remove all the buildings he had built there, and to impose a rental fee of $10 per month until he vacated and removed the buildings.

The Tenant (D) answered the lawsuit, admitting most of the allegations of the petition and maintaining that the had been given verbal permission to occupy the land for five years. He also filed a reconventional demand for damages equal to the cost of the buildings, stock on hand, expected profits, and the enhanced value of the property.

The trial court found for the defendant and ordered the Tenant (D) to vacate within forty days or have his buildings devolved by the Sheriff. The trial court rejected the Landowner's (P) claim for rent and the Tenant's (D) reconventional demand. The Tenant (D) appealed.

Issue

Does a person who is given permission to construct buildings on someone else's land and use the land for an indefinite term gain the right to possess the land?

Holding & Decision

No, a person who uses land with the permission of the owner does not himself possess the land as owner and does not gain the right to possess it for himself. The appeal court held that the Tenant (D) was not a possessor in good faith, or even a possessor at all, since he did not possess as owner. At best, the court held, the Tenant (D) had been granted the right to construct buildings and keep them there for a reasonable amount of time. Since they had been there for more than three years by the time the appeal was decided, he had had a reasonable amount of time.

The appeal court affirmed the trial court's judgment.

Rule of Law

A person who uses land with the permission of the owner does not himself possess the land as owner and cannot gain the right to possess it for himself.

MIRE V. CROWE

Possessor (P) v. Landowner (D)
439 So. 2d 517 (La. App. 1st Cir. 1983)

Facts & Procedure

Mr. Mire (P) purchased a parcel designated Lot 6 in the relevant section and township from Mr. Crowe (D) in 1968. Before the sale, the parties walked the boundaries of the property, and Mr. Crowe (D) indicated that the sale included a portion of land not in the property description of the sale but lying east of the lot being sold, between the lot being sold and a bayou. The land between Lot 6 and the bayou was part of Lot 7 by title.

Years later, Mr. Crowe (D) informed Mr. Mire's (P) tenant that Mr. Crowe (D) claimed ownership of Lot 7, including the property lying between Lot 6's boundary and the bayou. Mr. Mire (P) filed this possessory action against Mr. Crowe (D), claiming that he had disturbed his possession of the disputed property in Lot 7. Mr. Crowe (D) did not dispute Mr. Mire's (P) possession of Lot 6, but did not reconvene to assert his own right to possess the disputed property in Lot 7. Mr. Crowe (D) simply opposed Mr. Mire's (P) possession.

At the trial Mr. Mire (P) showed that he physically took possession of the disputed property, had it surveyed, and built a fence along the north boundary of Lot 6 all the way to the bayou along the north boundary of the disputed portion of Lot 7. He had a fence erected along the southern boundary to an area named the "gully," but did not complete the fence through the gully because the area was under water for part of the year. Mr. Mire's (P) family members and friends often hunted, fished, and conducted other activities — e.g., raising hogs and grazing cattle — with his permission on the disputed property, including a part of the disputed property called the "hill." Mr. Mire (P) himself raised a barn, grew a garden there for several years, and maintained the grass on the disputed property.

Mr. Crowe (D), on the other hand, lived on the disputed property as a child and conducted activities on the property before the 1968 sale. He also owned a camp south of the disputed property on the bayou, and he and his friends occasionally traveled across the disputed tract to reach the camp.

The trial court found for Mr. Mire (P) and maintained him in possession of the disputed area because he had been in open physical possession as owner of the property since the sale in 1968. The court also found that, upon the execution of the sale, Mr. Crowe (D) terminated his prior possession of the disputed property. Finally, the court found that Mr. Mire (P) had been in possession of the disputed property for more than a year before Mr. Mr. Crowe (D) disturbed his possession by informing Mr. Mire's (P) tenant of his claim to own the disputed property and that Mr. Mire (P) brought his possessory action within on year of the disturbance. The court held that Mr. Crowe's (D) friends' trespassing through the property to reach the camp was not a substantial enough disturbance to establish Mr. Crowe's (D) possession because they were unknown to Mr. Mire (P) and did not indicate to him that his possession was being challenged.

Mr. Crowe (D) appealed, arguing that Mr. Mire (P) did not establish his possession.

Issue

Will a person prevail on the possessory action when he shows that he acquired the right to possess property and that he had not lost the right to possess before the disturbance complained of in the action?

Holding & Decision

Yes, to win a possessory action a person must show that he at one time acquired the right to possess and that he has not lost the right in the year leading up to the disturbance. The appeal court agreed that Mr. Mire (P) acquired the right to possess the disputed property by performing acts of corporeal possession on the property and permitting others to do so from the date of the sale in 1968. These acts included building visible boundaries to complement the natural boundaries, building a barn, planting a garden, hunting, fishing, grazing cattle, raising hogs, and leasing out a portion of the disputed tract.

The appeal court noted that the areas of the disputed tract on which no corporeal activities took place were enclosed within the natural and artificial boundaries Mr. Mire (P) established. The court also agreed with the trial court's finding that Mr. Crowe (D) abandoned the use of the disputed property when the 1968 sale was executed. Even though Mr. Crowe (D) trespassed on the disputed property to reach his camp and occasionally hunted and fished on the land, these actions were insufficient to dispossess Mr. Mire (P).

Finally, the appeal court concluded that Mr. Mire (P) brought the possessory action well within one year of Mr. Crowe (D) disturbing his possession by informing Mr. Mire's (P) tenant that he was the owner of the disputed land.

Accordingly, the appeal court affirmed the trial court's judgment.

Rule of Law

To win a possessory action, a plaintiff must show that he at one time acquired the right to possess and that he had not lost the right prior to the disturbance.

GILL V. HENDERSON

Seeking Injunction (P) v. Failed Possessor (D)
269 So. 2d 571 (La. App. 1st Cir. 1972)

Facts & Procedure

Mr. Gill (P) filed this lawsuit seeking an injunction compelling Mr. Henderson (D) to remove his fence around a tract of land. Previously, Mr. Henderson (D) had filed and lost a possessory action concerning the fenced-in land. Mr. Gill (P) was the defendant in that lawsuit but did not reconvene or otherwise allege his own legal possession or ownership of the fenced in tract. Instead, in this proceeding, Mr. Gill (P) argued that Mr. Henderson (D) built the fence to force Mr. Gill (P) to bring his own action and bear the burden of proving his title.

The trial court dismissed Mr. Gill's (P) action for injunctive relief.

Issue

May a person who has not been legally recognized as the owner or legal possessor of a tract of land seek injunctive relief to protect his possession of that land?

Holding & Decision

No, injunctive or declaratory relief as sought by Mr. Gill is available only to a plaintiff in a possessory action or to one who is disturbed in his legal possession of property over which he claims ownership. Here, the appeal court reasoned, Mr. Gill did not claim ownership, possession, or enjoyment of the enclosed property. Accordingly, Mr. Gill could not avail himself of injunctive relief.

The appeal court affirmed the trial court's judgment.

Rule of Law

A plaintiff must prove himself to be the legal possessor of the property to be entitled to injunctive or other relief to stop a factual or legal disturbance of possession where ownership may be a factual issue.

TODD V. STATE
Possessor (P) v. State of Louisiana (D)
465 So. 2d 712 (La. 1985)

Facts & Procedure

The plaintiff filed a possessory action against the State of Louisiana (D). The trial court found for the plaintiff and ordered the State (D) to file a petitory action within sixty days or be barred for asserting ownership of the disputed land. The appeal court affirmed its decision, and the State (D) appealed to the Louisiana Supreme Court. In its initial opinion, the Court concluded that a possessory action could be maintained against the State (D) but that it was unconstitutional to require the state to file a petitory action subsequent to an adverse decision.

The State (D) sought rehearing, and the Court reversed itself and the lower courts' judgments. Upon rehearing, the Court concluded that no possessory action could be maintained against the State (D). The Court reasoned that the principal purpose of the possessory action is to protect possession while accruing time toward acquisitive prescription. Since the State's (D) property cannot be acquired by acquisitive prescription, the possessory action is useless with respect to the State (D). Further, public policy militates in favor of protecting the State's (D) resources against legal possession by others.

The Possessor (P) then sought a second rehearing, and the Court reinstated its first opinion.

Issue

1. Can a possessory action be maintained against the State of Louisiana when the object of possession is a private thing?

2. Is the State of Louisiana required to bring a petitory action after losing the possessory action or be barred from asserting its ownership of the disputed property?

Holding & Decision

A possessory action may be maintained against the State, but the State is not required to assert its adverse claim of ownership in a petitory action after another is adjudged the legal possessor of the disputed property. In reinstating its first opinion, the Court reasoned that the purpose of the possessory action is to protect possession itself, not simply to be a prelude to acquisitive prescription. The Court cited the Civil Code's explicit distinction between the ownership and the possession of a thing to support its conclusion. The Court dismissed the notion that the one year period of possession culminating in the right to possess is a type of prescription. Instead, it described the "right to possess" as shorthand for "acquired the right to bring a possessory action."

With respect to the public policy of protecting State resources, the Court noted that there are ample protections available to the State for protecting its property without contorting the law designed to resolve questions of possession and ownership. The Court allayed the State's fears about private profit using State lands by pointing out that fruits only belong to a good faith possessor and that many of the State's most valuable resources — e.g., timber and minerals — are not fruits and do not therefore belong to the possessor, good faith or otherwise.

Rule of Law

1. The possessory action may be maintained against the State of Louisiana when the object of possession is a private rather than a public thing.

2. After losing a possessory action, the State is not required to bring a petitory action or forfeit its right to assert its ownership of the disputed property.

Chapter 5

Ownership

1. **Content of ownership**.

   a) **Ownership** is "[t]he right that confers on a person direct, immediate, and exclusive authority over a thing. The owner of a thing may use, enjoy, and dispose of it within the limits and under the conditions established by law." La. C.C. art. 477.

   b) At Roman law, ownership had three component parts:

      i. **Usus**. The right to use and manage the thing in accord with the owner's will.

      ii. **Fructus**. The right to collect the fruits, revenues, and other benefits flowing from the thing.

      iii. **Abusus**. The right to alienate or otherwise dispose of the thing at will.

   c) The modern conception of ownership has several similar component parts, including the following:

      i. The right to use the property at will in any way that is compatible with its nature and to collect the profits, fruits, or other benefits that the thing can produce.

      ii. The right to physically dispose of the property and to perform all legal transactions of which it is susceptible, including the freedom to change the nature of the thing; burden it with servitudes, mortgages, or other charges; lease it; lessen its value; or destroy it.

         A. The right to alienate is of public order and, in principle, cannot be renounced by contract.

      iii. The right to exclude third parties from participation in any activity on the property.

   d) Ownership and its component parts may be modified by law or contract.

   e) The exercise of ownership rights is subject to restrictions imposed by the law and the public interest.

   f) Ownership rights must not be exercised so as to interfere with the property interests of others.

   g) "The ownership and the possession of a thing are distinct. Ownership exists independently of any exercise of it and may not be lost by nonuse. Ownership is lost when acquisitive prescription accrues in favor of an adverse possessor." La. C.C. art. 481.

      i. Possession is question of fact; ownership is a question of law.

h) "The right of ownership may be subject to a resolutory condition, and it may be burdened with a real right in favor of another person as allowed by law. The ownership of a thing burdened with a usufruct is designated as **naked ownership**." La. C.C. art. 478.

2. **Patrimony**.

   a) **Classical theory of patrimony**. Under classical French legal theory, **patrimony** is an attribute of personality that follows the following rules:

      i. *Only* natural and juridical persons may have a patrimony.

      ii. *Every* person has a patrimony, even if it contains only liabilities.

      iii. Every person has *exactly one* patrimony that is inseparable and indivisible.

   b) **Objective theory of patrimony**. Under some modern theories, a patrimony is an independent economic unit, a mass of assets and liabilities, tied inseparably until liquidation by the common destination and economic purpose of the elements that compose it. The objective theory of patrimony is incompatible with the Louisiana and French Civil Codes.

   c) **Patrimony in Louisiana**.

      i. The concept of patrimony in Louisiana relies on scattered provision of the Civil Code, including the following:

         A. "Whoever has bound himself personally, is obliged to fulfill his engagements out of all his property, movable and immovable, present and future." La. C.C. art. 3182 (repealed 2015).

         B. "The property of the debtor is the common pledge of his creditors, and the proceeds of its sale must be distributed among them ratably, unless there exist among the creditors some lawful causes of preference." La. C.C. art. 3183 (repealed 2015).

      ii. **Indivisibility**. A patrimony is a coherent mass of existing or potential rights and liabilities attached to a person for the satisfaction of his economic needs.

      iii. Every person has a patrimony, and only persons may have a patrimony.

      iv. **Multiple patrimonies**. A person may have multiple patrimonies when the law specifically allows it or may have distinct patrimonial masses that are subject to special rules for the purposes of administration and liquidation.

         A. Patrimonial masses are distinct from the patrimony of a person and consist of particular asses and liabilities destined for a special purpose. For example, where a married couple lives under the regime of community property, a spouse's separate property is a separate patrimonial mass.

      v. Except as specifically allowed by by law, patrimonial assets may only be transferred individually, execution may be made on particular assets only, and protection under the law of delictual obligations is available only to individual patrimonial rights.

      vi. But the patrimony as a whole may become the object of an obligation because the right of the credit is against the person of the debtor rather than his patrimony. *See* La. C.C. art. 3182 (repealed 2015).

      vii. **Transferability**.

         A. The entire patrimony is not normally transferable by *inter vivos* act. *See* La. C.C. art. 1498. Such an act would be invalid but might be a valid transfer of all of one's existing individual assets.

B. But the Civil Code expressly authorizes the transfer of a patrimony or a fraction of a patrimony by marriage contract.

C. Individual patrimonial assets are transferable by onerous and gratuitous title, subject to the relevant Code provisions and other laws.

D. Because patrimonial assets are transferred individually, the transferee does not normally acquire any personal obligations of the transferor without a contractual provision to that effect.

E. But where a person acquires all of a person's present assets there is jurisprudence to the effect that that person will also be held liable for his debts.

F. Upon death, the patrimony of a natural person is transmitted to his heir. The succession — the patrimony — of the deceased is not theoretically a distinct mass of rights and liabilities subject to administration but is an indistinguishable part of the heir's patrimony.

G. **Assets and liabilities**. The patrimony is composed of assets and liabilities that are susceptible of pecuniary evaluation. Assets include movable and real rights, credits, and accrued causes of action, whether or not they are exempt from seizure. Liabilities include personal and real obligations and claims of creditors against the patrimony of the debtor.

H. Practically, creditors are only concerned with the patrimonial assets they can seize at the time a judgment is rendered against the person. In theory, creditors may exercise all patrimonial rights and actions that the debtor has, except those that are strictly personal.

I. **Real Subrogation** is the substitution of one thing for another in a universality of assets and liabilities. The principle of real subrogation is not explicitly articulated in Louisiana law but underpins provisions of the Civil Code and other statutes. For example, real subrogation takes places when a spouse living under the community property regime purchases property with funds that are his separate property. The separate property forms a distinct patrimonial mass from the community property and, when separate funds are used to purchase a thing, that thing is substituted for the separate funds and maintains its identity as part of the separate patrimonial mass.

J. **Enterprise**. A mass of rights, interests, and relations destined for a determined purpose and organized as an economic unit by an entrepreneur. An enterprise is similar to a patrimonial mass because its elements form a universality that is not the object of a single right. It differs from a patrimonial mass because it includes interests and relations like good will, clientele, trade secrets, and the like as opposed to a patrimony that is comprised only of rights. An enterprise forms part of the patrimony of the entrepreneur. Accordingly, creditors may satisfy debts against the assets of the enterprise or the entrepreneur as they please.

3. Co-ownership.

a) **Ownership in indivision** is "[o]wnership of the same thing by two or more persons." La. C.C. art. 797. The right of each owner bears upon the whole of the thing held in indivision. The fundamental rules of co-ownership in indivision include:

i. Co-owners own the entire property with one another. Each co-owner's share does not have to be equal.

ii. Under Louisiana law, a co-owner is prohibited from unilateral acts concerning the property except for acts of use and acts of preservation. Other acts require unanimous consent or a court order.

   A. "The use and management of the thing held in indivision is determined by agreement of all the co-owners." La. C.C. art. 801.

   B. "When the mode of use and management of the thing held in indivision is not determined by an agreement of all the co-owners and partition is not available, a court, upon petition by a co-owner, may determine the use and management." La. C.C. art. 803.

   C. A co-owner may petition the court for an order regarding the use and management of co-owned property where the co-owners cannot agree and the property is already being offered for sale because the normal remedy — partition — is practically unavailable. *Succession of Miller*.

iii. "A co-owner may freely lease, alienate, or encumber his share of the thing held in indivision. The consent of all the co-owners is required for the lease, alienation, or encumbrance of the entire thing held in indivision." La. C.C. art. 805.

iv. A co-owner may freely use the entire property for its customary purpose but may not interfere with the other co-owners' right to use it similarly. La. C.C. art. 802. If the co-owners cannot agree on how to use the property, their remedy is partition.

   A. One co-owner may receive an injunction prohibiting another co-owner from deliberately denying her the equal and coextensive use of a part of the commonly held property. *LeBlanc v. Scurto*.

v. "A co-owner may without the concurrence of any other co-owner take necessary steps for the preservation of the thing that is held in indivision." La. C.C. Art. 800.

   A. Preservation implies a danger of decay, deterioration, or impending loss.

   B. The acts should be taken to preserve a thing rather than to alter it or its economic purpose.

   C. The necessity of the acts, their sufficiency, and their proportionality to the danger should be judged by an objective prudent-man standard.

   D. Acts of preservation may be taken without the consent of the other co-owners and over their objections.

   E. Acts taken under this article are taken in the actor's own name, and not in the name of his co-owners without their consent.

vi. A co-owner may not substantially change the property or devote it to a new use without the unanimous consent of the other co-owners. A co-owner's failure to object to an exceptional use or activity on the property after learning of it ordinarily constitutes his tacit consent to those activities. A co-owner who makes an unsanctioned use of the property may be liable to the other co-owners for any damage he causes — for example, diminution of the value of the property.

vii. "Co-owners share the fruits and products of the thing held in indivision in proportion to their ownership. When fruits or products are produced by a co-owner, other co-owners are entitled to their shares of the fruits or products after deduction of the costs of production." La. C.C. art. 798. But a co-owner is never liable for losses or expenses incurred by the other co-owners in connection with activities on the land in which he has not agreed to participate. In any case, a co-owner may not charge his co-owners for his personal services in producing or gathering the income.

viii. A co-owner must pay his proportionate share of the reasonable costs for maintaining and preserving the property.

ix. A co-owner may seek to partition the property at any time, and agreements to the contrary are valid only under certain circumstances and for limited times.

b) **Expenses**. "A co-owner who on account of the thing held in indivision has incurred necessary expenses, expenses for ordinary maintenance and repairs, or necessary management expenses paid to a third person, is entitled to reimbursement from the other co-owners in proportion to their shares." La C.C. art. 806.

i. **Necessary expenses** include expenses incurred for the preservation of a thing and for the discharge of private or public burdens, other than those incurred for ordinary maintenance and repairs — e.g., property taxes and assessments, indispensable repairs and maintenance costs, litigation costs for the preservation of the property, and insurance costs.

ii. *Cf.* **Useful expenses**, which are expenses that are not needed for the preservation of a thing but enhance its value — e.g., ordinary repairs.

iii. *Contrast* **Luxurious expenses**, which are expenses made to gratify one's personal predilections.

iv. **Unjust enrichment**. Article 806 does not override the doctrines of unjust enrichment or *negotiorum gestio*, and one co-owner may be able to recover the enhanced value of the thing from the others if the requirements of either doctrine are met.

A. There is some authority to suggest the doctrine of *negotio gestorum* does not apply between co-owners.

B. Some of the jurisprudence interpreting article 2297 reads it to require reimbursement only for expenses that are both "necessary and useful." But there is also jurisprudence to the contrary.

c) **Indirect rent**. "If the co-owner who incurred the expenses had the enjoyment of the thing held in indivision, his reimbursement shall be reduced in proportion to the value of the enjoyment." La. C.C. art. 806.

d) "A co-owner is liable to his co-owner for any damage to the thing held in indivision caused by his fault." La. C.C. art. 799.

e) "Substantial alterations or substantial improvements to the thing held in indivision may be undertaken only with the consent of all the co-owners. When a co-owner makes substantial alterations or substantial improvements consistent with the use of the property, though without the express or implied consent of his co-owners, the rights of the parties shall be determined by Article 496 [as if he were a good-faith possessor]. When a co-owner makes substantial alterations or substantial improvements inconsistent with the use of the property or in spite of the objections of his co-owners, the rights of the parties shall be determined by Article 497 [as if he were a bad-faith possessor]." La. C.C. art. 804.

f) Property held by spouses under a community property regime are subject to many special rules of co-ownership.

g) **Partition**. "No one may be compelled to hold a thing in indivision with another unless the contrary has been provided by law or juridical act. Any co-owner has a right to demand partition of a thing held in indivision. Partition may be excluded by agreement for up to fifteen years, or for such other period as provided" by law. La. C.C. art. 807. Partition may be made by agreement — a **conventional partition** — or judicially.

   i. **Conventional partition** is the partition by agreement of the co-owners. A conventional partition may be structured in any way that vests full ownership of the property in a single person.

      A. For example, two co-owners may divide a large tract of land in two and each convey his share in one part to the other, resulting in two separate, individually owned parcels where there was one co-owned piece before.

      B. An extrajudicial partition may be rescinded according to the rules of lesion, La. C.C. art. 814, and is subject to annulment for vices of consent like any other agreement.

   ii. **Judicial partition** is the result of an action brought by one or more co-owners against the others to have a court partition the property. Judicial partitions are made in two ways, in kind or by sale of the whole either at auction (called "by licitation") or at private sale.

      A. **Partition in kind**. The division of the co-owned property into several pieces, each of which becomes the individually owned property of a co-owner. Under the law, partition in kind is favored unless it is impractical to do so. Partition in kind is governed by many rules that, as interpreted by the courts, make it impractical in many cases. Specifically, the thing must be divided into "as many lots of nearly equal value as there are shares," the lots must be substantially equal in value, and "the aggregate value of all lots [must not be] significantly lower than the property in the state of indivision." La. C.C. art. 810.

      B. **Partition by licitation or by private sale**. A partition in which the thing is sold and the proceeds of the sale are distributed to the former co-owners in proportion to their shares. In a partition by licitation, the thing is sold at auction. In a partition by private sale, the thing is sold without auction on terms satisfactory the court.

      C. In the absence of an explicit agreement to privately sell or otherwise transfer property subject to partition, a court must order the property be sold at auction or partitioned in kind, as appropriate. *Thompson v. Celestain.*

      D. Where co-owners own several burial plots — some occupied and some not — they should be partitioned in kind as equally as feasible, and the remainder should be partitioned by licitation. *Ben Glazer Company, Inc. v. Tharp-Sontheimer-Tharp, Inc.*

   iii. **Real rights after partition**. "When a thing held in indivision is partitioned in kind or by licitation, a real right burdening the thing is not affected." La. C.C. art. 812.

   iv. **Indispensable use of a co-owned thing**. "Partition of a thing held in indivision is excluded when its use is indispensable for the enjoyment of another thing owned by one or more of the co-owners." La. C.C. art. 808.

   v. "The action for partition is imprescriptible." La. C.C. art. 817.

4. **Modes of acquiring ownership.**

a) The acquisition of property may be described along several axes:

  i. **Extent of the acquisition**. Transmission by **universal title vs. particular title**. Where a transferee acquires assets by universal title — either by acquiring an entire patrimony or a fractional portion of it — he also acquires a share of the transferor's obligations in proportion to his interest in the transferred mass. Where a transferee acquires assets by particular title, he does not acquire any of the transferor's liability, except those he agrees to acquire.

  ii. **Nature of the mode of acquisition**. Acquisition by **gratuitous act vs. onerous act**.

  iii. **Time at which the transfer occurs**. Transfer **inter vivos vs. mortis causa**.

b) **Sources of ownership**.

  i. **Methods of original acquisition**.

    A. **Occupancy** "is the taking of possession of a corporeal movable that does not belong to anyone. The occupant acquires ownership the moment he takes possession." La. C.C. art. 3412. In modern legal systems, title to unclaimed immovables is generally vested in the state, and property rights in unclaimed lands are generally acquired by license or grant from the state.

    B. **Finding lost things**. Lost things have an owner, but a person finding them can acquire title in them. "One who finds a corporeal movable that has been lost is bound to make a diligent effort to locate its owner or possessor and to return the thing to him. If a diligent effort is made and the owner is not found within three years, the finder acquires ownership." La. C.C. art. 3419.

    C. **Finding treasure**. "One who finds a treasure in a thing that belongs to him or to no one acquires ownership of the treasure. If the treasure is found in a thing belonging to another, half of the treasure belongs to the finder and half belongs to the owner of the thing in which it was found. A **treasure** is a movable hidden in another thing, movable or immovable, for such a long time that its owner cannot be determined." La. C.C. art. 3420.

    D. **Accession**. "The ownership of a thing includes by accession the ownership of everything that it produces or is united with it, either naturally or artificially, in accordance with" law. La. C.C. art. 482. The ownership of land also generally includes the ownership of everything directly above and below it, subject to contrary law (e.g., the mineral code).

    E. **Acquisitive prescription**. "Acquisitive prescription is a mode of acquiring ownership or other real rights by possession for a period of time" with the intent to possess it as owner. La. C.C. art. 3446. The length of the necessary period varies depending on the nature of the thing as a movable or immovable and whether or not the possessor possesses it in good faith or bad.

    F. **Expropriation**. The taking of property with or without compensation by a government.

    G. **Privileges conferred by public authorities**. The creation of new property rights by a government conferring special privileges on certain persons. For example, intellectual property, grants for the exploitation of natural resources, and radio spectrum leases.

  ii. **Derivative methods of acquisition**.

A. **Sale**. "Sale is a contract whereby a person transfers ownership of a thing to another for a price in money. The thing, the price, and the consent of the parties are requirements for the perfection of a sale." La. C.C. art. 2439.

B. **Donation**. "A donation *inter vivos* is a contract by which a person, called the donor, gratuitously divests himself, at present and irrevocably, of the thing given in favor of another, called the donee, who accepts it." La. C.C. art. 1468. "A donation *mortis causa* is an act to take effect at the death of the donor by which he disposes of the whole or a part of his property. A donation *mortis causa* is revocable during the lifetime of the donor." La. C.C. art. 1469.

C. **Judicial sale**. A sale ordered by a court. Judicial sales are made for a number of purposes, including to satisfy obligations to a creditor, for partition by licitation, or as part of the administration of a succession.

D. **Intestate succession**. The transfer by operation of law of the property of a decedent to his legal heirs when he dies without a testament.

E. "The ownership of an immovable is voluntarily transferred by a contract between the owner and the transferee that purports to transfer the ownership of the immovable. The transfer of ownership takes place between the parties by the effect of the agreement and is not effective against third persons until the contract is filed for registry in the conveyance records of the parish in which the immovable is located." La. C.C. art. 517.

F. "The ownership of a movable is voluntarily transferred by a contract between the owner and the transferee that purports to transfer the ownership of the movable. Unless otherwise provided, the transfer of ownership takes place as between the parties by the effect of the agreement and against third persons when the possession of the movable is delivered to the transferee. When possession has not been delivered, a subsequent transferee to whom possession is delivered acquires ownership provided he is in good faith. Creditors of the transferor may seize the movable while it is still in his possession." La. C.C. art. 518.

iii. **Bona fide purchaser doctrine**. A jurisprudential doctrine in which the ownership of a movable is transferred to the person who was least negligent in its acquisition.

A. Take, for example, a sequence of transactions in which A transferred a movable to B, and B transferred it to C. Normally, La. C.C. art. 518 would apply if A owned the movable when he transferred it and B owned it when he did so. However, if B acquired the movable by defrauding A, he would not be the true owner, and article 518 would not apply to the transfer between B and C. In such a case, the relative innocence or negligence of A and C would be determined, and ownership would be awarded to the less negligent party.

B. Before its repeal, former La. C.C. art. 520 changed that rule substantially. It provided that "A transferee in good faith and for fair value acquires the ownership of a corporeal movable, if the transferor, though not the owner, has possession with the consent of the owner, as pledgee, lessee, depositary, or other person of similar standing." While article 520 was repealed, the exceptions and special rules and exceptions in the following articles remain intact, leaving the topic incompletely regulated.

C. A person who purchases stolen property from another in bad faith does not obtain title to that property. *Autocephalus Greek-Orthodox Church v. Goldberg & Feldman Fine Arts, Inc.*

D. Since former article 520 has been repealed, the previous jurisprudential negligence analysis should remain relevant where special rules do not override it.

E. "One who has possession of a lost or stolen thing may not transfer its ownership to another." La. C.C. art. 521.

F. "A transferee of a corporeal movable in good faith and for fair value retains the ownership of the thing even though the title of the transferor is annulled on account of a vice of consent." La. C.C. art. 522. A person is in good faith "unless he knows, or should have known, that the transferor was not the owner." La. C.C. art. 523.

G. "The owner of a lost or stolen movable may recover it from a possessor who bought it in good faith at a public auction or from a merchant customarily selling similar things on reimbursing the purchase price." But "the former owner of a lost, stolen, or abandoned movable that has been sold by authority of law may not recover it from the purchaser." La. C.C. art. 524.

H. These provisions do not apply to movables that are required by law to be registered, like motor vehicles. La. C.C. art. 525.

LeBlanc v. Scurto

Sister (P) v. Brother (D)
173 So. 2d 322 (La. App. 1st Cir. 1965)

Facts & Procedure

This case concerns an injunction against a co-owner blocking a common alleyway behind a building owned by three siblings in indivision. Mrs. Santa Scurto LeBlanc (P) owned a commercial building with her brother, Sam Scurto (D), and the widow of Charles Scurto. The widow was a party but did not participate in the dispute or the case.

The parties each owned one third of the building in indivision. The Brother (D) operated a shoe store in part of the building. An alley ran behind the building and opened onto a nearby street. The Sister's (P) husband individually owned an adjacent store that could be accessed from the alley, and his tenants often used the alley to load and unload merchandise. City garbage trucks also used the alley for trash collection. On the day this dispute began in earnest, the Brother (D) parked his car in the alley, effectively blocking it and denying everyone access to it.

The Brother (D) claimed he parked there simply to unload some parcels into his store, but the evidence supported his Sister's (P) claim that he did so to deny everyone else the use of the alley. The trial court found that the Brother (D) did so in an attempt to persuade the Sister (P) into selling him her interest in the building.

The trial court granted the Sister (P) an injunction prohibiting her Brother (D) from blocking the alley or interfering with the Sister's (P) right to use it as a means of passage. The Brother (D) appealed.

Issue

May an injunction issue in favor of one co-owner against another to prevent the latter from deliberately denying the other co-owners equal and coextensive possession of a certain part of the commonly held property?

Holding & Decision

Yes, one co-owner may receive an injunction prohibiting another co-owner from deliberately denying her the equal and coextensive use of a part of the commonly held property. The appeal court established that the best and customary use of the alley was as a passage along the back of the building rather than as a parking lot. The court reasoned that an injunction does lie between co-owners to prevent the waste of the property or the denial of equal and coextensive possession of the property by a co-owner. Here, the court found, the Brother's (D) use of the alley as a parking lot rather than a passage constituted waste of the property and conversion of the purpose of the property. If he wished to have exclusive use of the property, the court suggested, his remedy was in partition.

The appeal court affirmed the decision of the trial court.

Rule of Law

One co-owner may receive an injunction prohibiting another co-owner from deliberately denying her the equal and coextensive use of a part of the commonly held property.

SUCCESSION OF MILLER
674 So. 2d 441 (La. App. 4th Cir. 1996)

Facts & Procedure

Mrs. Edna Kuntz Miller died testate and was survived by seven of her eight children. The child who predeceased her was survived by four children, all of whom survived Mrs. Miller. Her husband predeceased her.

In her testament, Mrs. Miller named her son Martin O. Miller II as her executor. At the time of their mother's death, each of the surviving children already owned a one-sixteenth undivided interest in the family home and its contents from their father's succession. The children of the sibling who predeceased their mother each owned a quarter of their father's share, or one-sixty fourth of the total. The heirs did not take possession of the house and its contents because their mother had a usufruct over it as Mr. Miller's surviving spouse.

The heirs agreed to sell the house and its contents. But after Martin was confirmed as executor, he was concerned with his personal liability as executor for anything that was damaged or went missing from the home, because both the home and its contents were very valuable. He presented two suggested plans to the other heirs: (1) he would supervise and allow access to anyone who wanted to enter the house for a reasonable time and for a legitimate purpose, or (2) he would allow all the heirs unfettered access to the home if the heirs would all release him from personal liability for the potential loss. Some heirs declined to release him from liability, so he instituted a restricted-access plan.

Martin's brother Val Miller objected to the restriction of his access and filed for an injunction to forbid Martin from restricting his access as a co-owner of the residence. Martin filed a motion to have the court approve his management plan.

After a hearing on Martin's motion, the trial court ratified Martin's plan; placed him in control of the keys and alarm code to the residence; and decreed that the heirs could only have access to the residence if supervised, upon reasonable notice, for a reasonable time, and for a legitimate reason related to the administration of the succession. The trial court relied on La. C.C. art. 803, which provided for a court-ordered management plan in cases where partition is not available.

Val appealed.

Issue

May a co-owner petition the court for an order regarding the use and management of co-owned property when the co-owners cannot agree on the management and the property is already up for private sale?

Holding & Decision

Yes, a co-owner may petition the court for an order regarding the use and management of co-owned property where the co-owners cannot agree and the property is already being offered for sale because the normal remedy — partition — is practically unavailable.

The appeal court examined the civil code articles concerning ownership in indivision and, specifically, the articles dealing with use and management of co-owned property and the article providing for a court-ordered management plan in cases where partition was not available. The court found that, at the time of the trial below, he property was already on the market to be sold and no co-owner had sought partition. The court reasoned that a court's only other remedy would have been to order a partition by licitation, which would have placed the house on the market for sale. Since the house was already on the market, the court found that partition was "not available" because it would have been a needless expense and unnecessary judicial procedure.

Since partition was not available, the court had the authority under La. C.C. art. 803 to make a management determination. It also found that the trial court's management order was reasonable in light of the facts and testimony in the record.

The appeal court affirmed the trial court's ruling.

Rule of Law

A co-owner may petition the court for an order regarding the use and management of co-owned property where the co-owners cannot agree and the property is already being offered for sale because the normal remedy — partition — is practically unavailable.

Thompson v. Celestain
Former Girlfriend (P) v. Former Boyfriend (D)
936 So. 2d 219 (La. App. 4th Cir. 2006)

Facts & Procedure

The parties lived together as unmarried intimate cohabitants in a house they purchased together. Some time after moving out of their home, Ms. Thompson (P) filed to partition the house and all of the movable property they held in indivision, including household belongings and some credit card debt. Both parties filed detailed descriptive lists of assets and liabilities. The parties also testified at the trial on the partition, and their testimony differed considerably. The largest point of contention between the parties was the number of mortgage payments each had made and how much each had paid toward the down payment on the house.

After hearing the evidence, the trial court issued a judgment awarding Ms. Thompson (P) a credit for $24,042.50 for payments made on the house, improvements to the house, and payments against the couple's credit card bill. The court awarded Mr. Celestain (D) a credit in the amount of $48,0256.60, finding that Mr. Celestain (D) had made almost all of the mortgage payments on the house. The court assessed interest from the date of judicial demand, which had not been made, and conveyed Ms. Thompson's (P) undivided interest in the house to Celestain (D) to cover the difference between their credits. Ms. Thompson (P) appealed on the grounds that the court could not transfer her interest instead of partitioning the property and on other grounds.

Issue

In a partition action, may the court order one co-owner to transfer his or her interest in the co-owned property to another co-owner in lieu of ordering a partition in kind or by licitation?

Holding & Decision

No, in the absence of an explicit agreement to privately sell or otherwise transfer property subject to partition, a court must order the property be sold at auction or partitioned in kind, as appropriate. An agreement to sell property in lieu of partition must be definite and certain. Here, the appeal court found the parties might have extensively negotiated amongst themselves before the rendition of judgment, but their agreement did not appear on the record. Accordingly, the trial court was bound to follow the procedure outlined in the Code of Civil Procedure and cause a partition by licitation. The appeal court also held that the trial court's determination of reimbursements owed was premature.

The appeal court vacated the trial court's judgment and remanded the matter for further proceedings. Judge Murray concurred in the result but noted that, while the reimbursement calculations were premature, they were not necessarily erroneous. Accordingly, the trial court could reaffirm its calculations after following the appropriate procedures.

Rule of Law

In the absence of an explicit agreement to privately sell or otherwise transfer property subject to partition, a court must order the property be sold at auction or partitioned in kind, as appropriate.

BEN GLAZER COMPANY, INC. V.
THARP-SONTHEIMER-THARP, INC.
Siblings (P) v. Widower (D)
491 So. 2d 722 (La. App. 4th Cir. 1986)

Facts & Procedure

Meyer Glazer's (D) wife passed away, and he buried her next to his mother and father in a family burial plot. The family had seven plots together, two occupied by the parties' parents, one occupied by the Widower's (D) deceased wife, and four unoccupied. Shortly thereafter his three Siblings and the family company (P) sued to have the title to the burial plots recognized in the company, to have the Widower's (P) former wife exhumed, and for damages for improper burial.

The trial court ruled that the burial plots were owned in indivision by the party siblings (and not the family company), ordered a partition by licitation of all seven plots, and reserved a damage determination until after the ownership was sorted out. The Widower (D) appealed, contending that the partition should have been in kind rather than by licitation.

Issue

May co-owned burial plots — some of which are occupied — be partitioned among co-owners by licitation, in kind, or by a combination of both methods.

Holding & Decision

Where co-owners own several burial plots — some occupied and some not — they should be partitioned in kind as equally as feasible, and the remainder should be partitioned by licitation.

The appeal court noted that the sale of the burial plots to an unrelated party would likely necessitate exhuming the parties' parents and the Widower's (D) former wife. Exhumation is against public policy and should only be done on a showing of good cause. The appeal court found that the parties did not intend to partition the plots where their parents were buried and, in any case, that their partition was prohibited by Civil Code Article 1303 (La. C.C. art. 808) because their use is indispensable to all the co-owners for paying respect to their parents and for religious worship.

The court concluded that, given the strong public policy against exhumation, the remaining five plots should be partitioned in kind among the four siblings, with the plot in which the Widower's (D) former wife was buried going to him. Because there were five plots and only four siblings to divide them among, the fifth plot should be partitioned by licitation since it was insusceptible of division.

The appeal court remanded the matter for further proceedings in accordance with its opinion and on the issue of damages.

Rule of Law

Where co-owners own several burial plots — some occupied and some not — they should be partitioned in kind as equally as feasible, and the remainder should be partitioned by licitation.

Autocephalus Greek-Orthodox Church v. Goldberg & Feldman Fine Arts, Inc.

Church (P) v. Art Dealer (D)
717 F. Supp. 1374 (S.D. Ind. 1989)

Facts & Procedure

This case concerns the ownership of four ancient mosaics taken from a church in Cyprus during the Turkish occupation. An American Art Dealer (D) purchased the mosaics in Europe and returned them to the United States. When the Church of Cyprus (P) discovered the whereabouts of the mosaics, it requested their return and, when the Art Dealer (D) refused, sued.

The district court issued a decision that included a lengthy examination of the history of Cyprus before and during the Turkish occupation. In short, the court found that the mosaics had been created and installed in a church in Cyprus in the sixth century and had remained there until they were removed during the Turkish occupation. The court found that the Turkish occupational government was not the legitimate government of Cyprus and that the mosaics were removed without the Church's (P) permission after most of the Cypriots had been chased from the area.

According to the Art Dealer's (D) testimony and documents produced on her behalf, she purchased the mosaics in Europe for just over a million dollars during a trip there to purchase another piece of art. She purchased the mosaics from a seller who had allegedly found the mosaics in the rubble of a destroyed church in Cyprus. According to the seller and his agents who spoke to the Art Dealer (D), he had received all the appropriate permissions and paperwork to export the artifacts. The purported export documents were offered at trial, but the district court found that none of the documents mentioned the specific mosaics at issue. Goldberg also testified that she inquired with the appropriate authorities about whether the mosaics had been reported stolen or missing or if any law or treaty would prohibit the importation of the mosaics into the United States.

The Art Dealer (D) began trying to sell the mosaic, and the Church (P) caught wind of it. The Church (P) requested that the Art Dealer (D) return them, but she declined. The Church (P) then filed suit to force their return.

Issue

Does a person who purchases stolen property from another in bad faith obtain title to the property?

Holding & Decision

No, a person who purchases stolen property from another in bad faith does not obtain title to that property. The district court considered the question under two legal systems: the law of Indiana, where the art came to rest, and the law of Switzerland, where the sale actually took place.

The court held that, under Indiana law, a thief obtains no title to stolen property. Therefore, there was no title to transfer to the Art Dealer (D), and the mosaics should be returned to the Church (P).

The court also determined that Swiss law would apply if Indiana law did not, and analyzed the question under that system. The court noted that, under Swiss law, a purchaser of stolen property acquires title superior that of the original owner if he purchases in good faith, which is presumed. A bad faith purchaser never acquires title. To overcome the presumption of a good faith purchase, the Church (P) had to show that the sale occurred under suspicious circumstances that should have caused a reasonably prudent purchaser to doubt the seller's capacity to convey property rights. Here, the court held that the Church (P) had done so based on the facts adduced at trial.

Because the Art Dealer (D) did not acquire good title under the rules of either applicable legal system, the court ordered the mosaics returned to the Church of Cyprus (P).

Rule of Law

A person who purchases stolen property from another in bad faith does not obtain title to that property.

Chapter 6

Accession

1. **In general.**

   a) "The ownership of a thing includes by accession the ownership of everything that it produces or is united with it, either naturally or artificially." La. C.C. art. 482.

   b) Most of the accession provisions in the Civil Code are suppletive and can be modified by agreement between owners of the things that are joined together.

   c) There are three principal forms of accession:

      i. **Adjunction.** The union of two things belonging to different owners such that the things permanently form a single whole.

      ii. **Transformation.** The act of making a new thing with materials belonging to someone else.

      iii. **Commingling.** The mixture of two or more dry or liquid matters belonging to different owners in such a way that they cannot be separated without difficulty.

   d) "For purposes of accession, a possessor is in good faith when he possesses by virtue of an act translative of ownership and does not know of any defects in his ownership. He ceases to be in good faith when these defects are made known to him or an action is instituted against him by the owner for the recovery of the thing." La. C.C. art. 487.

2. **Fruits and products.**

   a) "In the absence of rights of other persons, the owner of a thing acquires the ownership of its natural and civil fruits." La. C.C. art. 483.

   b) "When fruits that belong to the owner of a thing by accession are produced by the work of another person, or from seeds sown by him, the owner may retain them on reimbursing such person his expenses." La. C.C. art. 485.

   c) "The young of animals belong to the owner of the mother of them." La. C.C. art. 484.

   d) "In the absence of other provisions, one who is entitled to the fruits of a thing from a certain time or up to a certain time acquires the ownership of natural fruits gathered during the existence of his right, and a part of the civil fruits proportionate to the duration of his right." La. C.C. art. 489.

   e) "A possessor in good faith acquires the ownership of fruits he has gathered. If he is evicted by the owner, he is entitled to reimbursement of expenses for fruits he was unable to gather. A possessor in bad faith is bound to restore to the owner the fruits he has gathered, or their value, subject to his claim for reimbursement of expenses." La. C.C. art. 486.

f) "Products derived from a thing as a result of diminution of its substance belong to the owner of that thing. When they are reclaimed by the owner, a possessor in good faith has the right to reimbursement of his expenses. A possessor in bad faith does not have this right." La. C.C. art. 488.

g) Oil, gas, and other minerals are not fruits under the law, so a good-faith possessor does not gain ownership of them by gathering them. *Elder v. Ellerbe*.

h) A possessor in good faith but without valid title who fells and removes timber from another's land is liable to the landowner for the timber's value. *Harang v. Bowie Lumber Co.*

3. **Accession in relation to immovables.**

a) Buildings, other constructions permanently attached to the ground, standing timber, and unharvested crops or ungathered fruits of trees may belong to a person other than the owner of the ground. Nevertheless, they are presumed to belong to the owner of the ground, unless separate ownership is evidenced by an instrument filed for registry in the conveyance records of the parish in which the immovable is located." La. C.C. art. 491.

b) "Things incorporated in or attached to an immovable so as to become its component parts under Articles 465 and 466 belong to the owner of the immovable." La. C.C. art. 493.1.

c) "Separate ownership of a part of a building, such as a floor, an apartment, or a room, may be established only by a juridical act of the owner of the entire building when and in the manner expressly authorized by law." La. C.C. art. 492.

d) "Buildings, other constructions permanently attached to the ground, and plantings made on the land of another with his consent belong to him who made them. They belong to the owner of the ground when they are made without his consent.

  When the owner of buildings, other constructions permanently attached to the ground, or plantings no longer has the right to keep them on the land of another, he may remove them subject to his obligation to restore the property to its former condition. If he does not remove them within ninety days after written demand, the owner of the land may, after the ninetieth day from the date of mailing the written demand, appropriate ownership of the improvements by providing an additional written notice by certified mail, and upon receipt of the certified mail by the owner of the improvements, the owner of the land obtains ownership of the improvements and owes nothing to the owner of the improvements. Until such time as the owner of the land appropriates the improvements, the improvements shall remain the property of he who made them and he shall be solely responsible for any harm caused by the improvements.

  When buildings, other constructions permanently attached to the ground, or plantings are made on the separate property of a spouse with community assets or with separate assets of the other spouse and when such improvements are made on community property with the separate assets of a spouse, this Article does not apply. The rights of the spouses are governed by Articles 2366, 2367, and 2367.1." La. C.C. art. 493.

e) Professor Symeonides suggests that "it would therefore appear more equitable if [article 493] were interpreted as simply being *silent* as to the question of the removal of improvements which neither party wants," despite there being no explicit distinction in the Code. "Such an interpretation would be consistent with the cardinal principle that ownership is presumed free of burdens and would allow the court to" find a tailored, equitable solution. C.L.P. at 280.

f) Where the parties are engaged in a lease of immovable property, the ownership of improvements made by the lessee is controlled first by the provisions of the lease and then by La. C.C. art. 2695, which allows the lessee to remove his improvements, provided he restores the leased thing to its former condition. If the lessee does not remove the improvements, the lessor may either appropriate them by paying the lessee for the lesser of the costs of the improvements or the enhanced value to the leased thing, or the lessor may require the lessee remove them within a reasonable time. If the lessee does not do so, the lessor may remove at the lessee's expense or appropriate the improvements without reimbursing the lessee.

g) **The space above and below.**

   i. "Unless otherwise provided by law, the ownership of a tract of land carries with it the ownership of everything that is directly above or under it. The owner may make works on, above, or below the land as he pleases, and draw all the advantages that accrue from them, unless he is restrained by law or by rights of others." La. C.C. art. 490.

   ii. **Minerals.**

      A. "Ownership of land includes all minerals occurring naturally in a solid state. Solid minerals are insusceptible of ownership apart from the land until reduced to possession. La. R.S. 31:5.

      B. "Ownership of land does not include ownership of oil, gas, and other minerals occurring naturally in liquid or gaseous form, or of any elements or compounds in solution, emulsion, or association with such minerals. The landowner has the exclusive right to explore and develop his property for the production of such minerals and to reduce them to possession and ownership." La. R.S. 31:6.

      C. "A landowner may use and enjoy his property in the most unlimited manner for the purpose of discovering and producing minerals, provided it is not prohibited by law. He may reduce to possession and ownership all of the minerals occurring naturally in a liquid or gaseous state that can be obtained by operations on or beneath his land even though his operations may cause their migration from beneath the land of another." La. R.S. 31:8.

h) **Artificial accession.**

   i. Buildings are susceptible of ownership separate from the land on which they are placed and remain the property of the person who owned them before their placement unless they are conveyed in accordance with law. *Marcellous v. David.*

   ii. A person who owns land but not the building on it can sell both to a third party without compensating the owner of the building if the separate ownership of the building is not recorded in the public records. *Graffagnino v. Lifestyles, Inc.*

   iii. A pipeline buried below ground becomes the property of the landowner at the termination of a pipeline servitude if the owner of the pipeline declines to remove it. *Guzzetta v. Texas Pipeline Co.*

i) **Reimbursement for expenses and improvements.**

   i. "One who has lost the ownership of a thing to the owner of an immovable may have a claim against him or against a third person in accordance with the following provisions." La. C.C. art. 493.2

      A. "When the owner of an immovable makes on it constructions, plantings, or works with materials of another, he may retain them, regardless of his good or bad faith, on reimbursing the owner of the materials their current value and repairing the injury that he may have caused to him." La. C.C. art. 494.

      B. "One who incorporates in, or attaches to, the immovable of another, with his consent, things that become component parts of the immovable under Articles 465 and 466, may, in the absence of other provisions of law or juridical acts, remove them subject to his obligation of restoring the property to its former condition.

         If he does not remove them after demand, the owner of the immovable may have them removed at the expense of the person who made them or elect to keep them and pay, at his option, the current value of the materials and of the workmanship or the enhanced value of the immovable." La. C.C. art. 495.

      C. "When constructions, plantings, or works are made by a possessor in good faith, the owner of the immovable may not demand their demolition and removal. He is bound to keep them and at his option to pay to the possessor either the cost of the materials and of the workmanship, or their current value, or the enhanced value of the immovable." La. C.C. art. 496.

        • A good faith possessor may be required to remove incomplete buildings or other constructions from land belonging to another if those buildings or constructions diminish the value of the land. *Britt Builders v. Brister*.

        • A possessor in good faith is not entitled to reimbursement for improvements that cross the boundary between his land and another's that do not enhance the value of the other person's land. *Sanders v. Jackson*. In such a case, the landowner may keep the improvements without reimbursement.

      D. "When constructions, plantings, or works are made by a bad faith possessor, the owner of the immovable may keep them or he may demand their demolition and removal at the expense of the possessor, and, in addition, damages for the injury that he may have sustained. If he does not demand demolition and removal, he is bound to pay at his option either the current value of the materials and of the workmanship of the separable improvements that he has kept or the enhanced value of the immovable." La. C.C. art. 497.

        • A landowner who demands any action of a bad-faith possessor other than demolition and removal of the possessor's improvements tacitly accepts the improvements and is bound to pay the bad-faith possessor for them under La. C.C. art. 497. *Broussard v. Compton*.

        • A possessor in bad faith may not recover from a landowner the value of unnecessary improvements made on the landowner's property. *Voiers v. Atkins Bros.*

        • But a possessor in bad faith might recover for expenses that were necessary for the preservation of another's property or for conducting the business of another as a *negotiorum gestor*.

j) **Accession in relation to movables.**

    i. **Adjunction.** "When two corporeal movables are united to form a whole, and one of them is an accessory of the other, the whole belongs to the owner of the principal thing. The owner of the principal thing is bound to reimburse the owner of the accessory its value. The owner of the accessory may demand that it be separated and returned to him, although the separation may cause some injury to the principal thing, if the accessory is more valuable than the principal and has been used without his knowledge." La. C.C. art. 510.

        A. An engine mounted on a drilling platform and connected to a pump by a drive device does not become part of the pump it is powering if it can be easily removed without damaging the engine, the pump, or the drive device. *Aetna Business Credit Corp. v. Louisiana Machinery Co.*

        B. Repair parts that are installed in equipment become the property of the owner of the repaired equipment by accession at the time they are installed. *International Paper Co. v. E. Feliciana School Board.*

    ii. "Things are divided into principal and accessory. For purposes of accession as between movables, an accessory is a corporeal movable that serves the use, ornament, or complement of the principal thing.

        In the case of a principal thing consisting of a movable construction permanently attached to the ground, its accessories include things that would constitute its component parts under Article 466 if the construction were immovable." La. C.C. art. 508.

    iii. "In case of doubt as to which is a principal thing and which is an accessory, the most valuable, or the most bulky if value is nearly equal, shall be deemed to be principal." La. C.C. art. 509.

    iv. **Transformation.** "When one uses materials of another to make a new thing, the thing belongs to the owner of the materials, regardless of whether they may be given their earlier form. The owner is bound to reimburse the value of the workmanship.

        Nevertheless, when the value of the workmanship substantially exceeds that of the materials, the thing belongs to him who made it. In this case, he is bound to reimburse the owner of the materials their value." La. C.C. art. 511.

        A. "When an owner of materials that have been used without his knowledge for the making of a new thing acquires the ownership of that thing, he may demand that, in lieu of the ownership of the new thing, materials of the same species, quantity, weight, measure and quality or their value be delivered to him." La. C.C. art. 515.

        B. "If the person who made the new thing was in bad faith, the court may award its ownership to the owner of the materials." La. C.C. art. 512.

    v. **Commingling.** "When a new thing is formed by the mixture of materials of different owners, and none of them may be considered as principal, an owner who has not consented to the mixture may demand separation if it can be conveniently made. If separation cannot be conveniently made, the thing resulting from the mixture belongs to the owners of the materials in indivision. The share of each is determined in proportion to the value of his materials. One whose materials are far superior in value in comparison with those of any one of the others, may claim the thing resulting from the mixture. He is then bound to reimburse the others the value of their materials." La. C.C. art. 514.

vi. "One who uses a movable of another, without his knowledge, for the making of a new thing may be liable for the payment of damages." La. C.C. art. 516.

ELDER V. ELLERBE

Heir (P) v. Co-owner (D)
135 La. 990, 66 So. 337 (La. 1914)

Facts & Procedure

The plaintiff claimed an undivided one-half interest in a large tract of land that she inherited from her father. Part of the tract belonged to one Co-Owner (D), and part was purportedly owned by a corporation that purchased it from the other defendant Co-owner (D). Before this lawsuit, the Co-owner (D) had granted a mineral lease to an oil company and had received substantial royalties and bonuses for oil produced under the lease. The Heir (P) also sued to collect half of these bonuses and royalties. The corporation that purchased the land demanded the return of its purchase price from the Co-Owner (D) vendor.

The trial court rendered judgment in favor of the Heir (P) recognizing her as the owner of one-half of the entire tract and awarding her damages against the Co-Owner (D) equal to half of the bonus and royalties already paid under the mineral lease. The court also awarded the corporate buyer damages against the Co-Owner (D) equal to half the purchase price. All the defendants appealed. The plaintiff answered the appeal and requested her damages be doubled.

Issue

Is a possessor in good faith of land entitled to keep the royalties and bonuses flowing from the production of oil and gas from the land under a mineral lease?

Holding & Decision

No, oil and minerals are not fruits, so a good-faith possessor does not gain ownership of them by gathering them. The Court reasoned that, under the Civil Code, a possessor in good faith acquires the ownership of fruits he has gathered. But minerals are not fruits because minerals are not produced and reproduced from time to time or in successive seasons. The Court analogized the collection of minerals by a possessor to cutting timber from land, and a possessor in good faith must account to the landowner for the value of timber he removes from the owner's land. Similarly, the Court reasoned that a usufructuary has no right to open mines or quarries on the land of another, so a possessor in good faith cannot have more rights.

The Court affirmed the trial court's judgment.

Rule of Law

Oil, gas, and other minerals are not fruits under the law, so a good-faith possessor does not gain ownership of them by gathering them.

HARANG V. BOWIE LUMBER CO.

Landowners (P) v. Lumber Company (D)
145 La. 95, 81 So. 769 (La. 1919)

Facts & Procedure

Two Landowners (P) sued a Lumber Company (D) to recover the value of timber the company cut on their land. The trial court found that the Landowners (P) owned the land in question and that the Lumber Company (D) did remove the timber as alleged. The trial court dismissed one Landowner's (P) claims as prescribed and granted the other judgment for less than he requested. The prescription judgment became final, and the Lumber Company (D) appealed the money judgment.

Issue

Is a possessor in good faith of land required to reimburse the landowner for timber it has removed from the land?

Holding & Decision

Yes, a possessor in good faith but without valid title who fells and removes timber from another's land is liable to the landowner for the timber's value. The Court accepted as undisputed fact that the Lumber Company (D) was a good-faith possessor and that it removed the timber as alleged. After consulting French sources, the Court concluded that a possessor in good faith need not account to a landowner for fruits that had been gathered, but timber is not a fruit under the law. Accordingly, the Lumber Company (D) had to account for the value of the timber it removed from the Landowners' (P) land.

The Court affirmed the trial court's judgment.

Rule of Law

A possessor in good faith but without valid title who fells and removes timber from another's land is liable to the landowner for the timber's value.

MARCELLOUS V. DAVID
Niece (P) v. Aunt (D)
252 So. 24 178 (La. App. 3d Cir. 1971)

Facts & Procedure

This is a lawsuit by a Niece (P) against her Aunt (D) for the return of a house. The Aunt (D) was old and living in her house in the country. She wanted to move to the city and made a deal with her Niece (P) that, if she would purchase a lot in the city, move the house there, install a cesspool, and let the Aunt (D) live there rent-free until her death, the Aunt (D) would leave the house to the owner of the lot.

The Niece (P) agreed and fulfilled her part of the bargain. She purchased lots that were acceptable to the Aunt (D), had the house moved and placed on brick pillars, installed a cesspool and had it attached to the house's plumbing, and her husband painted the house. At the time, the Aunt (D) executed a will leaving the house to her Niece (P). She lived in the house for two years before the parties' relationship soured. The Aunt (D) contacted her brother, who purchased a lot down the street and moved her house onto it. The Niece (P) filed this lawsuit shortly thereafter for the return of the house, arguing that the house had become part of the immovable property that she owned when it was placed on pillars and connected to the cesspool.

The trial court held that the Aunt (D) remained the owner of her house after the first move and entered judgment in her favor and against the Niece (P). The Niece (P) appealed.

Issue

Does a house owned by one person that is placed on pillars on a lot belonging to another person and connected to a cesspool on the land become the property of the landowner?

Holding & Decision

No, buildings are susceptible of ownership separate from the land on which they are placed and remain the property of the person who owned them before their placement unless they are conveyed in accordance with law. The appeal court reasoned that, while buildings are presumed to belong to the owner of the ground on which they stand, the presumption can be overcome. Here, the Aunt (D) showed that she owned the house before moving it to her Niece's (P) lot and rebutted the presumption. The appeal court rejected the Niece's (P) contention that the house was conveyed by an oral donation because donations of immovables like houses may only be made by written instrument. The will was not a written donation because the Aunt (D) was still alive, and the will had no effect until her death.

The appeal court affirmed the judgment of the trial court.

Rule of Law

Buildings are susceptible of ownership separate from the land on which they are placed and remain the property of the person who owned them before their placement unless they are conveyed in accordance with law.

GRAFFAGNINO V. LIFESTYLES, INC.
Landowners (P) v. Building Owners (D)
402 So. 2d 742 (La. App. 4th Cir. 1981)

Facts & Procedure

This suit began when new Landowners (P) requested an injunction prohibiting the putative owners of a building on their land from removing the building. The Building Owners (D) answered and claimed the ownership of the building. At some point during the litigation, the Landowners (P) had the building destroyed, and the Building Owners (D) claimed damages for their loss. The Building Owners (D) also made a third-party demand against the former landowners for the value of the building because the former owners had failed to inform the new Landowners (P) of the arrangement concerning the building.

At trial, testimony showed that the Building Owners (D) had the permission of the previous landowners to place the structure there as a demonstration model of the type of structures the company sells in return for cutting the grass on the property. The trial court found that the Building Owner (D) and the former landowners had an oral lease and that the lease had not been recorded in the public records. It also found that the act of sale between the former landowner and the new Landowners (P) transferred "all buildings and improvements" on the land. Therefore, the court concluded, the new Landowners (P) acquired the buildings along with the property free from the obligations of the unrecorded lease, regardless of their actual knowledge of any lease. The former landowners, on the other hand, knew that they did not own the building when they sold it, so the trial court awarded the Building Owners (D) damages equal to the value of the building. Since the building was destroyed, the Landowners' (P) request for injunctive relief was moot.

Issue

Can a person who owns land but not the building on it sell both to a third-party without paying the owner of the building for it?

Holding & Decision

Yes, a person who owns land but not the building on it can sell both to a third party without compensating the owner of the building if the separate ownership of the building is not recorded in the public records. The appeal court noted that the court record reflected that the former landowners had notified the new Landowners (P) that they did not own the building and the Building Owner (D) that the land was being sold. The appeal court concluded that the Building Owner's (D) failure to protect itself by recording the lease, removing the structure prior to the sale, or working out an agreement with the new Landowner (P) was the proximate cause of their loss.

The appeal court reversed and set aside the portion of the trial court's judgment awarding the Building Owner (D) damages and affirmed it in all other respects.

Rule of Law

A person who owns land but not the building on it can sell both to a third party without compensating the owner of the building if the separate ownership of the building is not recorded in the public records.

Guzzetta v. Texas Pipe Line Co.
Landowners (P) v. Pipeline Company (D)
485 So. 2d 508 (La. 1986)

Facts & Procedure

The plaintiffs owned a tract of land over which a pipeline right-of-way servitude had been granted in favor of the Pipeline Company (D) in 1955. The Pipeline Company (D) constructed a buried pipeline on the servitude and used it for years. In 1982, the Pipeline Company (D) discontinued using part of the pipeline. The Landowners (P) asked the Pipeline Company (D) to remove the pipeline or to pay for its removal, and the Pipeline Company (D) refused. The Landowners (P) then sued the Pipeline Company (D) for damages amounting to the cost of removing the pipeline.

The trial court ruled that the Landowners (P) had no cause of action and dismissed their suit. The Landowners (P) appealed, and the appeal court affirmed the trial court's decision. The Landowners (P) appealed again.

Issue

Does a pipeline buried below ground become the property of the landowner at the termination of a pipeline servitude if the owner of the pipeline declines to remove it?

Holding & Decision

Yes, a pipeline buried below ground becomes the property of the landowner at the termination of a pipeline servitude if the owner of the pipeline declines to remove it. The Court rejected the appeal court's holding that the servitude agreement was necessarily still in effect until extinguished by ten-year prescription of nonuse because it contained no applicable term or resolutory condition.

The purpose of an exception of no cause of action is to determine the legal sufficiency of the petition on the face of the pleadings. The Court found that the servitude agreement contained a clause that allowed for the Pipeline Company (D) to retain its rights under the agreement "so long as such pipelines[,] underground equipment[,] or appurtenances thereof are maintained." The Landowners' (P) petition alleged that the pipeline had been abandoned. Because the contract contained a resolutory condition and the plaintiffs alleged facts that would trigger the condition, the Landowners' (P) petition was legally sufficient to survive an exception of no cause of action.

But even though the Landowners (P) had made sufficient allegations to support a declaratory judgment terminating the servitude if proven, the Court held that the Landowners (P) could not claim damages. Under La. C.C. art. 493, at the termination of a servitude the Pipeline Company (D) would have the right to remove the pipeline subject to the obligation to restore the property to its former condition. If the Pipeline Company (D) did not remove them within ninety days of written demand, the Landowners (P) would become the owner of the pipeline.

The Court reversed the appeal court and remanded the case to the trial court for further proceedings.

Justice Lemmon concurred with the majority but noted that neither La. C.C. art. 493 nor the servitude agreement spoke to the costs of removing the pipeline. He reasoned that, in the absence of statutory or contractual provisions, it would be necessary to determine the intent of the parties by implication from the circumstances of the agreement and conditions prevailing at the time of the agreement. He concluded that there was nothing in this case to suggest that the parties ever intended to remove the pipeline or for the Pipeline Company (D) to pay for its removal.

Rule of Law

A pipeline buried below ground becomes the property of the landowner at the termination of a pipeline servitude if the owner of the pipeline declines to remove it.

BROUSSARD V. COMPTON
36 So. 3d 376 (La. App. 3d Cir. 2010)

Facts & Procedure

In this intra-family dispute, the Broussard branch of the family agreed to take care of Violetta Charles, Mrs. Broussard's grandmother, and her property in return for ownership of the property. Mrs. Broussard alleges that her mother Mrs. Compton (D) agreed to this arrangement. Within a few years, the house caught fire, and Mrs. Charles died in the house.

The plaintiffs alleged that Mrs. Compton (D) made them a second deal. She would provide some money from the house's insurance proceeds for the Broussards (P) to start building a new house on the property in return for them clearing the land of the destroyed house and some other items. The Broussards (P) would build a private bedroom and bathroom in the new house and allow Mrs. Compton (D) to live there whenever she pleased for the rest of her life.

The parties allegedly agreed that Mrs. Compton (D) would transfer the land to the Broussards (P) after the house was complete. Construction started in 1993 and finished in 1995. The Broussards (P) lived in the house and maintained the property even before it was fully completed, and they provided Mrs. Compton (D) with the promised suite. Mrs. Compton (D) did not transfer the property to them as promised. In 2001, Mrs. Compton (D) executed an act purporting to donate the land and the property to her other children.

In 2007, the Broussards (P) learned of the donation to Mrs. Broussard's (P) siblings and filed a petition to revoke the donation of the house and the land they were promised. They also sought to enforce their agreement with Mrs. Compton (D) or, alternatively, reimbursement for the cost of the materials and workmanship of the home or the enhanced value of the property under La. C.C. article 496. If such an award were due, they requested that they be maintained in possession of the home until they received it.

Mrs. Compton (D) and the children she donated the property to filed exceptions; an answer; and a reconventional demand for the rental value of the property, for a judgment recognizing their ownership of the property, and for an order that the Broussards (P) immediately vacate the premises and surrender the property.

The Broussards (P) then filed an amended petition alleging breach of contract and for reimbursement for the value of the house under a theory of unjust enrichment.

After trial, the court found that the Broussards (P) had shown no act translative of ownership and applied La. C.C. art. 497, which governs works made by possessors in bad faith. The court held that, as the owners of property improved by bad-faith possessors, the defendants could demand demolition of the improvements or keep them and pay either the current value of the materials and workmanship or the enhanced value of the improved immovable to the Broussards (P). The court found that the Comptons (D) had not demanded the demolition of the house; instead they demanded the Broussards (P) be evicted. This constituted a tacit acceptance of the improvements, so the Comptons (D) were bound to pay the Broussards (P) under article 497. The court also found that the facts at bar proved that the Comptons (D) had been unjustly enriched.

An appraiser determined that the house was worth $220,000. The court deducted $32,0000 Mrs. Compton (D) paid toward the construction from insurance proceeds from that price and determined that the Comptons (D) were unjustly enriched by $188,000.

The court found that the Compton siblings (D) had decreed to Mrs. Broussard (P) that $250 per month would be sufficient rent in 2007. Before then, there was no demand for or discussion of rent, so the court awarded the Comptons (D) $250 per month in rental value from August 6, 2007, until the Broussards (P) vacated the premises, to be credited against the Broussards' (P) award.

Both sides filed requests for a new trial. The Comptons (D) asserted that the court should have applied La. C.C. art. 493 instead of 497 because the Broussards (P) were good-faith possessors. As a result, they argued, the Broussards' (P) only recourse was to remove the house, and they were not entitled to damages. The Broussards (P) argued for a new trial because they should have been permitted to remain in the house until they were paid the awarded amount under La. C.C. art. 529.

The trial court denied the Comptons' (D) motion and granted the Broussards' (P), amending the judgment only to allow them stay in the house until the awarded amount had been paid. The court reasoned that the same results obtained under both articles 493 and 497 because article 493 explicitly recognized the Broussards (P) as the owners of the home. The court again took the Comptons' (D) failure to elect to make a demand under either articles 493 or 497 to suggest they tacitly accepted the presence of the house on their property.

The Comptons (D) appealed.

Issue

Does a landowner lose his right to have a bad-faith possessor remove a home built on the owner's property when he demands a payment for the occupancy of the home?

Holding & Decision

Yes, when a landowner demands anything other than demolition and removal of improvements by a bad-faith possessor, he tacitly accepts the improvements under La. C.C. art. 497 and is bound to pay the bad-faith possessor for them. The appeal court noted that the trial court determined that the Broussards (P) were bad-faith possessors because they did not have an act translative of title. The court also noted that the Comptons (D) demanded that the Broussards (P) pay money monthly toward their contribution to taxes and insurance in 2007. Because this was a demand for rent instead of a demand for demolition under La. C.C. art. 497, the appeal court reasoned, the Comptons (D) became bound to pay for the improvements. Addressing the Compton's (D) arguments first asserted in their motion for new trial, the appeal court agreed with the trial court that the same results would have obtained had the trial court applied La. C.C. art. 493 because the Comptons (D) demanded payment rather than removal of the structure.

The amended judgment was affirmed.

Rule of Law

A landowner who demands any action of a bad-faith possessor other than demolition and removal of the possessor's improvements tacitly accepts the improvements and is bound to pay the bad-faith possessor for them under La. C.C. art. 497.

BRITT BUILDERS V. BRISTER
Builder (P) v. Landowner (D)
618 So. 2d 899 (La. App. 1st Cir. 1993)

Facts & Procedure

The Landowner (D) purchased an unusually shaped lot with a large oak tree growing on it. Months later, the former owner of the lot sold it a second time to a Builder (P). The Builder (P) hired an attorney to perform a title search and, shortly after the title was found to be cleared, he felled the oak tree, poured a concrete slab, and began framing walls.

The Builder (P) then learned that the Landowner (D) owned the lot and stopped work on the home. The parties began negotiations to mitigate their damages, but they fell through, and the Builder (P) filed a lawsuit seeking damages for the enhanced value of the lot because of the slab he placed on it. The Landowner (D) filed a reconventional demand seeking damages for the cost of her lot, trespass, mental anguish, and attorney's fees.

After a trial, the district court dismissed the Builder's (P) demand, cast him for court costs, and awarded the Landowner damages for the destruction of the tree and for cleanup of the lot. The Landowner (D) appealed.

Issue

Can a good faith possessor be required to remove incomplete buildings or other constructions from land belonging to another if those buildings or constructions diminish the value of the land?

Holding & Decision

Yes, a good faith possessor may be required to remove incomplete buildings or other constructions from land belonging to another if those buildings or constructions diminish the value of the land. Under La. C.C. art. 496, a landowner may not demand the demolition and removal of constructions made on his land by a possessor in good faith. Instead, he is bound to keep them and to pay the good faith possessor either the cost of the materials and labor, their current value, or the enhanced value of an immovable.

The appeal court agreed with the trial court's conclusion that the Builder (P) was a good faith possessor because he relied on a title search. But the appeal court reasoned that article 496 is worded in such a way that it only applies to buildings and other constructions that enhance the value of the immovable. It does not apply to an incomplete construction like the one at issue here that actually decreases the value of the land because the redactors of the Civil Code did not intend for the article to burden landowners with partial constructions and other works that diminish the value of their land.

Since the slab and partially framed house diminished the value of the land, the appeal court held that the Landowner (D) had recourse to delictual law for damages for trespass. After determining the damages, the court reversed the trial court's judgment rejecting the Landowner's (D) claim for trespass and for removing the slab. It affirmed the trial court's judgment insofar as it awarded the Landowner (D) reimbursement for the destruction of the tree and the cleanup of the lot. Finally, the appeal court rendered judgment in favor of the Landowner (D) for additional damages for trespass and the removal of the slab.

Rule of Law

A good faith possessor may be required to remove incomplete buildings or other constructions from land belonging to another if those buildings or constructions diminish the value of the land.

VOIERS V. ATKINS BROS.
Landowner (P) v. Trespassers (D)
113 La. 303, 36 So. 974 (La. 1903)

Facts & Procedure

Trespassers (D) went on the Landowner's (P) land, dug ditches, cleared timber, cleared land, and dug and cemented three cisterns. The Landowner (P) sued to recover her property, and the Trespassers (D) reconvened to recover the value of the works they made on the land. The trial court found for the Landowner (P), recognized her ownership of the land, and awarded the Trespassers (D) the costs of the improvements they made on the land. At its first hearing, the Louisiana Supreme Court reversed the trial court's determination that the Trespassers (D) were entitled to compensation and affirmed it in all other regards. The Court granted a rehearing on the Trespassers' (D) claim for compensation.

Issue

May a bad-faith possessor recover from a landowner the value of unnecessary improvements made on the landowner's property?

Holding & Decision

No, a possessor in bad faith may not recover from a landowner the value of unnecessary improvements made on the landowner's property. The Court concluded that the Trespassers (D) were possessors in bad faith. After canvassing the relevant case law, the Court announced that, despite the general rule of equity that a person should not enrich himself at another's expense, the doctrine of unjust enrichment does not extend to allow a possessor in bad faith to recover for willfully doing what was not necessary for the preservation of the land of another.

But a possessor in bad faith is entitled to remove his improvements, if possible and if the landowner does not elect to keep them. The landowner may instead elect to keep the improvements by paying the possessor the amount the improvements enhance the value of the land. For improvements that are inseparable from the soil, like ditching and clearing the land, the possessor is not entitled to compensation. The Court also noted that a possessor in bad faith might recover for expenses that were necessary for the preservation of another's property or for conducting the business of another as a *negotiorum gestor*.

The Court found that the Trespassers' (D) expenditures for fencing were made for the preservation of the property. Accordingly, they were entitled to reimbursement for the fencing. If the Landowner (P) elected to keep the remaining buildings and other improvements, she would be required to compensate the Trespassers (D). Otherwise, they were to be removed. Finally, the Trespassers (D) were not entitled to reimbursement for the ditches or other earthen works made on the property.

The Court reinstated its earlier judgment with the exception of ordering the Landowner (P) to pay for the fencing and set out a schedule of values to be paid to the Trespassers (D) for the buildings on the land should the Landowner (P) elect to keep them.

Rule of Law

A possessor in bad faith may not recover from a landowner the value of unnecessary improvements made on the landowner's property.

SANDERS V. JACKSON

North Property Owner (P) v. South Property Owner (D)
192 So. 2d 654 (La. App. 3d Cir. 1966)

Facts & Procedure

The parties are adjacent landowners who petitioned the district court to set the boundary between their properties. The court ordered a survey and set the boundary in accordance with it. The North Property Owner's (P) south boundary was moved fifty feet into the South Property Owner's (D) property. The new line placed improvements made by the South Property Owner (D) inside the property line of the North Property Owner (P), including landscaping and a small portion of a dam and a pond. The South Property Owner (D) demanded reimbursement for the cost of the improvements or for the enhanced value of the North Property Owner's (P) land. The North Property Owner (P) denied that the improvements enhanced the value of the land and demanded damages because the dam built by the other property owner impeded the flow of water into his pond. The trial court denied both sets of claims. The South Property Owner (D) appealed, and the North Property Owner (P) answered.

Issue

May a possessor in good faith claim reimbursement for improvements made to the land of another that only slightly encroach on the other person's property and that do not enhance the value of the property?

Holding & Decision

No, a possessor in good faith who makes improvements that cross the boundary between his land and another's and that negligibly enhance the value of the other person's land is not entitled to reimbursement for either the cost of the improvements or the enhanced value to the other person's land.

The appeal court agreed that the South Property Owners (D) were possessing the land beyond their boundary in good faith because, while a formal survey had never been made and the North Property Owner (P) informed him that he was exceeding his boundary, the South Property Owner (D) was possessing up to an old fence to which his ancestors in title had possessed. Further, both parcels of land were divided from a much larger tract, and the fifty foot discrepancy was not discernible by the naked eye from the ground.

Because the South Property Owner (D) possessed in good faith, he would normally be entitled to reimbursement for the cost of the workmanship and materials and labor or for the enhanced value of the land. The appeal court noted that the work was largely performed at no cost to the South Property Owner (D) by a friend and that the record demonstrated that the portion of the improvements on the north property did not enhance its value. Therefore, the South Property Owner (D) was not entitled to any reimbursement.

The appeal court affirmed the trial court's judgment.

Rule of Law

A possessor in good faith is not entitled to reimbursement for improvements that cross the boundary between his land and another's that do not enhance the value of the other person's land.

Aetna Business Credit Corp. v. Louisiana Machinery Co.

Lender (P) v. Vendor (D)
409 So. 2d 1304 (La. App. 2d Cir. 1982)

Facts & Procedure

This is a dispute between a Lender (P) and a Vendor (D) who sold equipment that became attached to the property covered by the Lender's (P) chattel mortgage. The borrower purchased two drilling rigs and related equipment, including an industrial pump, from a third party and financed the sale with a loan from the Lender (P). The borrower gave the Lender (P) a chattel mortgage over all this equipment. The borrower then leased the equipment to a drilling company. The drilling company purchased an engine from the Vendor (D) and replaced the engine on the leased pump with it. The engine was mounted to the drilling platform with bolts and connected to the pump by a drive device.

After the drilling and leasing companies hit hard financial times, the Vendor (D) repossessed the engine, and the Lender (P) foreclosed on the two rigs and equipment, including the pump. The Lender (P) then sued the Vendor (D), claiming that the engine became part of the pump by accession and was, therefore, subject to the chattel mortgage burdening the pump. The Vendor (D) asserted a vendor's privilege over the pump.

The trial court granted the Vendor's (D) motion for summary judgment, finding that the engine had not become part of the pump by accession because it could easily by removed without damage to the pump, the drive device, or the engine itself. In short, it did not become part of the pump simply by being mounted next to and connected to the pump. The Lender (P) appealed.

Issue

Does an engine that is mounted on a drilling platform and connected to a pump by a drive device become, by accession, part of the pump it is powering if it can be easily removed without damaging the engine, the pump, or the drive device?

Holding & Decision

No, an engine mounted on a drilling platform and connected to a pump by a drive device does not become, by accession, part of the pump it is powering if it can be easily removed without damaging the engine, the pump, or the drive device. The appeal court noted that the lessee only leased the rig and the pump and owned the engine, which indicated that any attachment of the engine to the pump was only temporary for the duration of the lease. After reviewing La. C.C. arts. 482 and 510, the appeal court concluded that ownership of movables by accession requires a *permanent* union of the two things, as determined by the facts of the case.

Here, the court held that the connection between the pump and the engine through a drive device was an insufficient union to form a whole because the engine was easily disconnected from the drive device. Therefore, the union was temporary rather than permanent, and the law of accession did not apply.

The appeal court affirmed the judgment of the trial court.

Rule of Law

An engine mounted on a drilling platform and connected to a pump by a drive device does not become part of the pump it is powering if it can be easily removed without damaging the engine, the pump, or the drive device.

INTERNATIONAL PAPER CO. V. E. FELICIANA SCHOOL BOARD

Paper Company (P) v. School Board (D)
850 So. 2d 717 (La. App. 1st Cir. 2003)

Facts & Procedure

The Paper Company (P) sent equipment into East Feliciana Parish for repair. The Parish School Board (D) levied sales taxes on the parts and labor used to repair the equipment. After paying the taxes under protest, the Paper Company (P) sued for a declaration that the School Board could not collect taxes on the repair parts and moved for summary judgment. The Paper Company (P) argued that the repair parts were delivered to its mill in Mobile, Alabama, and, therefore, that Parish sales taxes could not be collected on items delivered outside of the Parish. The School Board (D) filed a cross-motion for summary judgment on its entitlement to collect sales tax on parts used in repairs.

The trial court denied the Paper Company's (P) motion, granted the School Board's (D) motion, and entered judgment in favor of the School Board (D).

The Paper Company (P) appealed.

Issue

Do repair parts that are installed in equipment become the property of the owner of the repaired equipment at the time of the installation?

Holding & Decision

Yes, repair parts that are installed in equipment become the property of the owner of the repaired equipment by accession at the time they are installed. Under the Parish tax ordinance, a "sale" for sales tax purposes, is a "any transfer of title or possession of tangible personal property, for a consideration." "Tangible personal property" is synonymous with "corporeal movable property" under the Civil Code. The appeal court reasoned that, under La. C.C. arts. 482 and 510, when two movable things are united, the owner of the principal thing gains ownership of the accessory thing. Here, the court held, the Paper Company (P) gained ownership of the repair parts upon their incorporation with the repaired equipment during the repairs made in East Feliciana Parish. Accordingly, the transfer of title occurred in the Parish, and the sale of the parts was subject to sales tax.

The appeal court affirmed the trial court's judgment.

Rule of Law

Repair parts that are installed in equipment become the property of the owner of the repaired equipment by accession at the time they are installed.

Chapter 7

Occupancy

1. **Occupancy** is "[t]he taking of possession of a corporeal movable that does not belong to anyone. The occupant acquires ownership the moment he takes possession." La. C.C. art. 3412.

   a) Acquisition by occupancy is limited to corporeal movable things. Immovables and incorporeal things cannot be *res nullius* (things belonging to no one) and therefore cannot be acquired by occupancy because La. C.C. art. 3412 requires that the thing "not belong to anyone."

2. **Ownership of wild animals.**

   a) "Wild animals, birds, fish, and shellfish in a state of natural liberty either belong to the state in its capacity as a public person or are things without an owner. The taking of possession of such things is governed by particular laws and regulations. The owner of a tract of land may forbid entry to anyone for purposes of hunting or fishing, and the like. Nevertheless, despite a prohibition of entry, captured wildlife belongs to the captor." La. C.C. art. 3413.

      i. The state, in its sovereign capacity as trustee of the animals for the common use and benefit of the people of the state, owns wild birds and quadrupeds in Louisiana but is not responsible for the damage they cause. *Leger v. Louisiana Dep't of Wildlife and Fisheries.*

      ii. State ownership of wildlife is a novel conception that does not fit in the traditional conceptual framework. Though a "public thing," wildlife is not subject to public use; moreover it is susceptible of private ownership.

   b) A landowner can recover damages for the destruction of wild animals and animal habitats on his land when trapping is the principal economic use of that land. *Harrison v. Petroleum Surveys, Inc.*

   c) "If wild animals, birds, fish, or shellfish recover their natural liberty, the captor loses his ownership unless he takes immediate measures for their pursuit and recapture." La. C.C. art. 3414.

   d) "Wild animals or birds within enclosures, and fish or shellfish in an aquarium or other private waters, are privately owned. Pigeons, bees, fish, and shellfish that migrate into the pigeon house, hive, or pond of another belong to him unless the migration has been caused by inducement or artifice." La. C.C. art. 3415.

e) "Tamed wild animals and birds are privately owned as long as they have the habit of returning to their owner. They are considered to have lost the habit when they fail to return within a reasonable time. In such a case, they are considered to have recovered their natural liberty unless their owner takes immediate measures for their pursuit and recapture." La. C.C. art. 3416.

f) "Domestic animals that are privately owned are not subject to occupancy." La. C.C. art. 3417.

3. **Abandoned things** are also called *res derelictae*.

a) "One who takes possession of an abandoned thing with the intent to own it acquires ownership by occupancy. A thing is abandoned when its owner relinquishes possession with the intent to give up ownership." La. C.C. art. 3418.

4. **Lost things.**

a) "One who finds a corporeal movable that has been lost is bound to make a diligent effort to locate its owner or possessor and to return the thing to him. If a diligent effort is made and the owner is not found within three years, the finder acquires ownership." La. C.C. art. 3419.

5. **Treasure.** "A movable hidden in another thing, movable or immovable, for such a long time that its owner cannot be determined." La. C.C. art. 3420.

a) "One who finds a treasure in a thing that belongs to him or to no one acquires ownership of the treasure. If the treasure is found in a thing belonging to another, half of the treasure belongs to the finder and half belongs to the owner of the thing in which it was found." La. C.C. art. 3420.

b) Gold certificates sewn into a mattress by its recently deceased owner are lost property, not treasure, and belong to the decedent's heirs, not the person who subsequently found them. *United States v. Peter.*

LEGER V. LOUISIANA DEP'T OF WILDLIFE & FISHERIES
Farmer (P) v. LDWF (D)
306 So. 2d 391 (La. App. 3d Cir. 1975)

Facts & Procedure

The Farmer (P) sued LDWF (D) for damages he sustained when wild deer ate his sweet potato crop. Upon first noticing the deer eating his crop, the Farmer (P) called a LDWF (D) agent and told him that he would need to kill the deer to save his crop. The agent told him that killing any of the deer would violate the law. The Farmer (P) did not shoot the deer, and he lost his sweet potato crop.

In his lawsuit, the Farmer (P) alleged that LDWF (D) owns all wild animals in the state, that it is responsible for the harm they do, and that its agent was at fault for refusing to let him kill the deer to save his crop. The trial court sustained the exception of no cause of action filed by LDWF (D) and dismissed the Farmer's (P) lawsuit. The Farmer (P) appealed.

Issue

Does the state own all wild quadrupeds in the state and, if so, is it responsible for the damage they cause?

Holding & Decision

Yes and no, respectively: the state, in its sovereign capacity as trustee of the animals for the common use and benefit of the people of the state, owns wild birds and quadrupeds in Louisiana but is not responsible for the damage they cause.

The appeal court concluded that the state owns wild animals in the state solely in its public capacity rather than in its proprietary capacity because the citizens of the state are allowed to appropriate the animals as regulated by the state. The appeal court also held that the state had no duty to control the actions of wild animals or to prevent them from damaging private property. Further, the state would not be liable for damage caused by wild animals under La. C.C. art. 2321 because that article only applies to the owner of an animal in his proprietary capacity.

The court noted that, if interpreted differently, the law would place on the state the impossible burden of preventing damage to private property by animals like crows, sparrows, rats, and squirrels. Further, under the law, the LDWF (D) agent had no authority to give the Farmer (P) permission to kill the deer or to exculpate him from criminal liability if the Farmer (P) had elected to do so. Accordingly, the court held that the agent's statements to the Farmer (P) were not the proximate cause of his loss.

The appeal court affirmed the trial court's judgment.

Rule of Law

The state, in its sovereign capacity as trustee of the animals for the common use and benefit of the people of the state, owns wild birds and quadrupeds in Louisiana but is not responsible for the damage they cause

HARRISON V. PETROLEUM SURVEYS, INC.
Trapper (P) v. Surveyors (D)
80 So. 2d 153 (La. App. 1st Cir. 1955)

Facts & Procedure

A Trapper (P) sued a company engaged in geophysical surveys for oil exploration because its Surveyors (D) accidentally wandered onto the Trapper's (P) marshland during a survey and damaged the marsh. The Surveyors (D) traversed the marsh in vehicles called "marsh buggies," which have four-foot-wide wheels and leave tracks between eighteen inches and four feet deep. Because of a boundary surveying error, the Surveyors (D) crushed two acres of the Trapper's (P) land with their buggies and sunk a pipe 190 feet deep into one corner of the property.

The Trapper (P) trapped muskrats on the land before it was damaged. Muskrats live in underground chambers they dig and feed on the roots of certain grasses. The trial court found that the land in question had been good muskrat land and could have produced about a hundred muskrats per year through trapping if it had not been damaged. The Trapper (P) would have made a net profit of 57–58 cents per pelt.

The Surveyors (D) argued that the Trapper (P) had no cause of action for damages because he had no property interest in untrapped muskrats because they were wild animals owned by the state, not the landowner. The trial court sustained the defendant's exception and dismissed the Trapper's (P) lawsuit. The Trapper (P) appealed.

Issue

Can a landowner recover damages for the destruction of wild animals and animal habitats on his land when trapping is the principal economic use of that land?

Holding & Decision

Yes, a landowner can recover damages for the destruction of wild animals and animal habitats on his land when trapping is the principal economic use of that land. The appeal court held that, while the Trapper (P) did not own the wild muskrats on his land, he did own the exclusive right to take muskrats from it.

Under La. C.C. art. 2315, the Surveyors (D) were responsible for compensatory damages for the damage they caused when they unintentionally trespassed on the Trapper's (P) land. The appeal court held that the appropriate measure of the damages is not only the value of the grass that was destroyed, but the damage to the property right representing the chief economic value of the land, namely the production of muskrat pelts.

The appeal court reversed the judgment of the trial court and entered a judgment awarding the Trapper (P) compensatory damages based on the loss of one hundred muskrats per year over a period of eight years at an average loss of 57 cents per pelt, for a total of $456.

Rule of Law

A landowner can recover damages for the destruction of wild animals and animal habitats on his land when trapping is the principal economic use of that land.

UNITED STATES V. PETER
Government (P) v. Claimants (D)
178 F.Supp. 854 (E.D. La. 1959)

Facts & Procedure

This is an interpleader action brought by the United States Government (P) against several Claimants (D) to $22,200 in gold certificates. Emily Baron, a recluse, died. Her heirs, some of the Claimants (D), were placed in possession of her property and sold her mattress to the Clelands, another set of Claimants (D). The Clelands sent the mattress to The Mattress Works, a company that specialized in refurbishing old mattresses. During the refurbishment process, a Mattress Works employee found the gold certificates sewn into the mattress.

The Government (P) claimed ownership of the gold certificates but agreed to pay their face value to the rightful owner. It filed this interpleader action to have the district court adjudicate who owned the certificates. The Clelands (D) argued that the certificates were a treasure found in their property and, therefore, belonged to them. The heirs (D), on the other hand, argued that the certificates were simply lost property belonging to their ancestor and that they owned them.

Issue

Are gold certificates sewn into a mattress by its recently deceased owner treasure or lost property for purposes of determining their owner?

Holding & Decision

Gold certificates sewn into a mattress by its recently deceased owner are lost property, not treasure, and belong to the decedent's heirs, not the person who subsequently found them. The district court found that it was likely that the gold certificates belonged to Miss Emily Baron, who opened the mattress covering to insert the certificates inside and sewed the mattress back up. It was conceivable that she forgot about them.

Under the Louisiana Civil Code, a treasure is a thing hidden in another thing that no one can prove is his property. The finder of treasure does not own it if someone can show who it belonged to. Here, the heirs (D) sufficiently proved that the certificates belonged to their ancestor, Emily Barron.

Therefore, the district court held that the certificates were lost property — not treasure — and ruled that the heirs (D) were entitled to the face value of the certificates.

Rule of Law

Gold certificates sewn into a mattress by its recently deceased owner are lost property, not treasure, and belong to the decedent's heirs, not the person who subsequently found them.

Chapter 8

Prescription — General Principles

1. **Notion and kinds of prescription.**

   a) "There is no prescription other than that established by legislation." La. C.C. art. 3457.

   b) **Acquisitive prescription** is a "mode of acquiring ownership or other real rights by possession for a period of time." La. C.C. art. 3446.

      i. Acquisitive prescription allows people to be sure that they will be legally recognized as owners, even though they cannot trace their title and the title of their ancestors-in-title back to antiquity. Instead, an owner need only prove that he and his ancestors-in-title have been in possession of the property for thirty years.

      ii. Acquisitive prescription can provide both an action and a defense (e.g., through the exception of prescription in a case seeking to evict the prescribing party) in favor of the prescribing party.

   c) **Liberative prescription** is a "mode of barring of actions as a result of inaction for a period of time." La. C.C. art. 3447. It includes both the loss of an action at law and the extinction of the unexercised right.

      i. Liberative prescription protects debtors from being forced to pay twice if they were to lose their receipt for payment of a debt or if the receipt were destroyed. After a certain time, the debt is prescribed, so a creditor cannot demand payment a second time, regardless of what happens to the records of payment.

      ii. Liberative prescription provides a defense against an action by means of the exception of prescription.

   d) **Prescription of nonuse** is a "mode of extinction of a real right other than ownership as a result of failure to exercise the right for a period of time." La. C.C. art. 3448.

   e) Prescription leads to legal stability.

   f) "Prescription must be pleaded. Courts may not supply a plea of prescription." La. C.C. art. 3452.

      i. But anyone with an interest can plead it: "Creditors and other persons having an interest in the acquisition of a thing or in the extinction of a claim or of a real right by prescription may plead prescription, even if the person in whose favor prescription has accrued renounces or fails to plead prescription." La. C.C. art. 3453.

g) Prescription does not confer a vested right until after it is completed. Consequently, a new statute can change the rules governing the running of prescription without any retroactive effect.

    i. Prescriptive statutes, like other procedural or remedial law, cannot apply retroactively to divest a person of a vested right.

    ii. A newly created prescriptive statute or one that shortens an existing prescriptive period does not violate the constitutional prohibition against divesting a person of a vested right if it allows a reasonable time for affected people to assert their rights.

h) **Computation of prescriptive periods.**

    i. The same rules govern the computation of prescriptive periods for both acquisitive and liberative prescription.

    ii. "In computing a prescriptive period, the day that marks the commencement of prescription is not counted. Prescription accrues upon the expiration of the last day of the prescriptive period, and if that day is a legal holiday, prescription accrues upon the expiration of the next day that is not a legal holiday." La. C.C. art. 3454.

    iii. "If the prescriptive period consists of one or more months, prescription accrues upon the expiration of the day of the last month of the period that corresponds with the date of the commencement of prescription, and if there is no corresponding day, prescription accrues upon the expiration of the last day of the period." La. C.C. art. 3455.

    iv. "If a prescriptive period consists of one or more years, prescription accrues upon the expiration of the day of the last year that corresponds with the date of the commencement of prescription." La. C.C. art. 3456.

i) **Things susceptible of prescription.**

    i. "Prescription runs against all persons unless exception is established by legislation." La. C.C. art. 3467.

    ii. "All private things are susceptible of prescription unless prescription is excluded by legislation." La. C.C. art. 3485.

    iii. "Prescription shall not run against the state in any civil matter, unless otherwise provided in this constitution or expressly by law." La. Const. art. 12 § 13.

        A. "Lands and mineral interests of the state, of a school board, or of a levee district shall not be lost by prescription." La. Const. art. 9 § 4.

        B. *Contra* A person may acquire ownership through acquisitive prescription of private things owned by the state or its political subdivisions in their capacity as private persons. *City of New Iberia v. Romero.*

    iv. Acquisitive prescription can only confer ownership of certain real rights. It cannot confer ownership of mortgage rights or discontinuous or nonapparent servitudes.

    v. Liberative prescription applies to creditors' rights, real rights other than ownership, and to actions other than revendication.

j) **Prescription and peremption.**

    i. **Peremption** is a "period of time fixed by law for the existence of a right. Unless timely exercised, the right is extinguished upon the expiration of the peremptive period." La. C.C. art. 3458.

      ii. Prescription bars the remedy sought to be enforced and terminates the right of access to the courts for enforcement of the existing right; peremption, on the other hand, totally destroys the right such that a cause of action or substantive right no longer exists to be enforced.

      iii. Peremption is a species of prescription that cannot be interrupted or suspended. Where a constitutional provision bars prescription, it also bars peremption as a form of prescription. *Pounds v. Schori*, 377 So. 2d 1195 (La. 1979).

      iv. "The provisions on prescription governing computation of time apply to peremption." La. C.C. art. 3459.

      v. "Peremption may be pleaded or it may be supplied by a court on its own motion at any time prior to final judgment." La. C.C. art. 3460.

      vi. "Peremption may not be renounced, interrupted, or suspended." La. C.C. art. 3461.

  k) **Contractual freedom.**

      i. "A juridical act purporting to exclude prescription, to specify a longer period than that established by law, or to make the requirements of prescription more onerous, is null." La. C.C. art. 3471.

2. **Commencement of prescription.**

  a) Acquisitive prescription commences the day after the day the possessor begins possessing the property.

  b) Liberative prescription begins to run as soon as a cause of action accrues. *Rieger v. Tierney.*Where the action depends on a suspensive condition, the prescription does not run until the condition happens.

  c) **Continuous tort.** When tortious conduct continues, prescription runs from the date of the last harmful act. If tortious behavior causes successive damage, prescription runs from the end of the wrongful conduct.

  d) Prescription on a demand note runs from the date the note is made. *Darby v. Darby.*

  e) When a sum is payable in fractions due at different times, prescription runs separately against each part of the debt from the date it becomes due.

  f) "Prescription runs against absent persons and incompetents, including minors and interdicts, unless exception is established by legislation." La. C.C. art. 3468.

  g) "Prescription runs during the delay the law grants to a successor for making an inventory and for deliberating. Nevertheless, it does not run against a beneficiary successor with respect to his rights against the succession. Prescription runs against a vacant succession even if an administrator has not been appointed." La. C.C. art. 3470.

  h) **Imprescriptible actions.** Certain actions are not subject to liberative prescription, including:

      i. Partition action,

      ii. Boundary action,

      iii. Action to establish the right of passage to an enclosed estate, and

      iv. The action to acquire rights in a party wall.

3. **Interruption of prescription.**

a) "If prescription is interrupted, the time that has run is not counted. Prescription commences to run anew from the last day of interruption." La. C.C. art. 3466.

b) **Civil interruption by filing suit.**

   i. "Prescription is interrupted when the owner commences action against the possessor, or when the obligee commences action against the obligor, in a court of competent jurisdiction and venue. If action is commenced in an incompetent court, or in an improper venue, prescription is interrupted only as to a defendant served by process within the prescriptive period." La. C.C. art. 3462.

   ii. "An interruption of prescription resulting from the filing of a suit in a competent court and in the proper venue or from service of process within the prescriptive period continues as long as the suit is pending. Interruption is considered never to have occurred if the plaintiff abandons, voluntarily dismisses the action at any time either before the defendant has made any appearance of record or thereafter, or fails to prosecute the suit at the trial." La. C.C. art. 3463.

      A. " An action is abandoned when the parties fail to take any step in its prosecution or defense in the trial court for a period of three years." La. C.C.P. art. 561.

   iii. A suit that is not prescribed when it is filed does not become prescribed by the subsequent dismissal of a previous suit on the same cause of action.

c) **Civil interruption by acknowledgement.**

   i. "Prescription is interrupted when one acknowledges the right of the person against whom he had commenced to prescribe." La. C.C. art. 3464.

   ii. A debtor's request for additional time to pay the debt is an acknowledgment of the debt that interrupts prescription. *Carraby v. Navarre.*

   iii. "A payment by a debtor of interest or principal of an obligation shall constitute an acknowledgement of all other obligations including promissory notes of such debtor or his codebtors *in solido* pledged by the debtor or his codebtors *in solido* to secure the obligation as to which payment is made." La. R.S. 9:5807.

d) "Acquisitive prescription is interrupted when possession is lost. The interruption is considered never to have occurred if the possessor recovers possession within one year or if he recovers possession later by virtue of an action brought within the year." La. C.C. art. 3465.

4. **Suspension of prescription.**

a) The same rules govern suspension of both liberative and acquisitive prescription.

b) "Prescription is suspended as between: the spouses during marriage, parents and children during minority, tutors and minors during tutorship, and curators and interdicts during interdiction, and caretakers and minors during minority. A 'caretaker' means a person legally obligated to provide or secure adequate care for a child, including a tutor, guardian, or legal custodian." La. C.C. art. 3469.

c) **Fugitive from justice.** "Prescription does not run against the action of a citizen of this state against a former citizen or resident of this state who is a fugitive from justice and is without a representative in this state upon whom judicial process may be served. Prescription begins to run from the day the fugitive returns to the state or from the day his power of attorney appointing a representative upon whom judicial process may be served is filed in the office of the clerk of court of the parish of his former residence." La. R.S. 9:5802.

d) **Adjudicated properties.** Where property is adjudicated or forfeited to the state for nonpayment of taxes and is then redeemed by a purchaser in good faith, "prescription shall not be interrupted or suspended during the period that title is vested in the state." La. R.S. 9:5803.

e) **Municipal corporations.** "Any municipal corporation owning alienable immovable property may prevent the running of [acquisitive prescription] against it in favor of any third possessor, by recording a notice with the clerk of court of the parish where the property is situated, or with the register of conveyances in the Parish of Orleans insofar as property in that parish is concerned. This notice shall contain a description of the property and a declaration that it is public property belonging to the municipality and the recording shall suspend the running of prescription during the time the ownership of the property shall remain vested in the name of the municipality. The recordation of the written act by which a municipal corporation shall acquire alienable immovable property likewise shall be deemed sufficient notice in order to suspend the term of prescription." La. R.S. 9:5804.

f) **Contra non valentem**. Under this doctrine, prescription generally does not run in certain circumstances, including:

   i. Where there was some legal cause that prevented the courts or their officers from taking cognizance of or acting on the plaintiff's action;

   ii. Where there was some condition coupled with the contract or connected with the proceedings which prevented the creditor from suing or acting;

   iii. Where the debtor himself has done some act effectively to prevent the creditor from availing himself of his cause of action; and

      A. E.g., Prescription does not run against a plaintiff who suffers injuries at the hands of a tortfeasor that prevent him from pursuing his cause of action. *Corsey v. State Department of Corrections*.

   iv. Where the cause of action is not known or reasonably knowable by the plaintiff, even though his ignorance is not induced by the defendant.

5. **Renunciation of prescription.**

   a) "Prescription may be renounced only after it has accrued." La. C.C. art. 3449.

      i. Private agreements cannot derogate from this principle because prescription is a matter of public policy.

   b) "Renunciation may be express or tacit. **Tacit renunciation** results from circumstances that give rise to a presumption that the advantages of prescription have been abandoned. Nevertheless, with respect to immovables, renunciation of acquisitive prescription must be express and in writing." La. C.C. art. 3450.

   c) The acknowledgment of a debt and partial payment of it do not renounce prescription that has accrued against the debt. *Succession of Slaughter*.

   d) *Cf.* An oral promise to pay a prescribed debt and partial payment of the debt constitute a renunciation of accrued prescription. *Harmon v. Harmon*.

e) Renunciation is never presumed.

f) "To renounce prescription, one must have capacity to alienate." La. C.C. art. 3451.

g) A creditor may annul an insolvent creditor's renunciation of prescription through the Paulian or revocatory action. *See* La. C.C. art. 2036.

6. **Effects of prescription.**

a) When acquisitive prescription accrues, the possessor becomes the owner of the thing retroactive to the date the prescription began to run.

b) Acquisitive prescription conveys only ownership; it does not extinguish any personal actions that the former owner may have concerning the property. For example, if the former owner leased the property to a lessee, and the lessee allowed the property to be acquisitively prescribed by a third party, the lessee is still obligated to return the property at the end of the lease.

c) Liberative prescription, when accrued, allows the debtor to defend himself against his creditor's action to collect the obligation via the exception of prescription.

d) A natural obligation remains after an obligation prescribes.

CITY OF NEW IBERIA V. ROMERO
City (P) v. Landowner (D)
391 So. 2d 548 (La. App. 3d Cir. 1980)

Facts & Procedure

The City of New Iberia (P) sued to evict its tenant, a neighboring Landowner (D). He (D) owned a lot in the city that was bounded on one side by an alley. The parties executed an instrument in 1972 purporting to lease a portion of the alley to the Landowner (D). The Landowner (D) filed an exception of prescription, claiming that he acquired the disputed portion of the alleyway by thirty-year acquisitive prescription prior to executing the lease. The City (P), on the other hand, argued that the Landowner (D) was a precarious possessor of the alley and, therefore, could not prescribe against the City (P).

The trial court found that the property in dispute had been acquired by the City (P) for use as a public street but that it had not been used as one in over thirty years and probably never had been. The only evidence of any use by the City was the lease in 1972. The trial court also found that the Landowner (D) had been in uninterrupted possession of the disputed alley since 1940 and sustained the Landowner's (D) exception.

The City (P) appealed.

Issue

Does acquisitive prescription run against the state or its political subdivisions as to things they own in their capacity as private persons?

Holding & Decision

Yes, a person may acquire ownership of private things owned by the state or its political subdivisions in their capacity as private persons through acquisitive prescription. The court distinguished between the state or its political subdivisions acting in their sovereign capacity and in their capacity as private persons. Where the state or its political subdivision owns a thing in its capacity as a private person, anyone may acquire the ownership of that thing via acquisitive prescription as he could acquire it from anyone else.

The appeal court rejected the City's (P) argument that the City (P) owned the alley in its sovereign capacity because part of the tract that included the alley was being used for public benefit. The court reasoned that, just as a private person could lose only a part of a piece of property through prescription, the City (P) could lose only the portion of the property that was being used privately while retaining ownership and the public character of the parts being used by the public at large.

In this case, the appeal court reasoned, the disputed property lost any character it had as a public thing when the City (P) neglected to put it to public use. The court noted that the City's (P) attempt to lease the disputed property to a private person clearly indicated that the City (P) intended to own and to use the disputed property as a private thing. Because the Landowner (D) showed that he had been in uninterrupted possession of the disputed property as owner for over thirty years, the court granted his exception of prescription.

Nor was the court persuaded that the Landowner (D) renounced prescription by signing the lease because renunciation must be express and unequivocal; here, the Landowner testified that he thought the lease was some sort of partition agreement, and the lease did not speak to the renunciation of prescription.

The appeal court affirmed the trial court's judgment.

Rule of Law

A person may acquire ownership through acquisitive prescription of private things owned by the state or its political subdivisions in their capacity as private persons.

DARBY V. DARBY
Manager (P) v. Heirs (D)
120 La. 847, 45 So. 747 (La. 1908)

Facts & Procedure

Coralie Darby died, leaving her son, who worked as the Manager (P) of her plantation; another child; and several grandchildren as Heirs (D). Instead of being paid in cash, the Manager (P) took interest-bearing promissory notes as payment for his services because they were a good investment. The three notes at issue in this case were payable on demand and were given in the Januaries of 1899, 1900, and 1901. After Mrs. Darby's death, her Heirs (D) refused to honor those notes they considered prescribed, and the Manager (P) sued them in November 1905. The Heirs (D) pleaded five-year liberative prescription as a defense.

The Manager (P) argued that his mother had acknowledged the debts represented by the promissory notes during her life so as to interrupt prescription. The Heirs (D) objected to the admission of this evidence because the Civil Code forbids the admission of such parol evidence. The trial court did not explicitly rule on the objection.

Further, the Manager (P) argued that he and the Heirs (D) entered into a written agreement after Mrs. Darby's death that should interrupt or suspend prescription. The agreement partitioned the decedent's estate among the heirs; paid all the estate's debts, except those contested; and deposited cash in a bank account to cover the disputed debts. The agreement provided that suit on the contested debts should be brought within six months of the agreement, and the Manager (P) argued that this provision prevents the running of prescription against him during that period. But the agreement explicitly provided that it would not affect the rights of the parties except as expressly stipulated. Finally, the parties entered into the agreement when the earlier two notes were already prescribed.

The trial court held that prescription on the three notes did not begin to run until the Manager (P) made his demand on them, ordered the Heirs (D) to pay the three notes, and entered judgment on other issues.

The Heirs (D) appealed the judgment as to the three notes. The appeal court affirmed the trial court's judgment, and the Heirs (D) appealed again.

Issue

When does prescription on a demand note begin to run: upon demand or from the date the note is made?

Holding & Decision

Prescription on a demand note runs from the date the note is made. The Court reasoned that prescription attaches from the moment a right may be exercised and that the holder of a demand note may make demand for its payment at any time after the note is made.

Therefore, the Court held that prescription began to run on the three notes at issue when each note was made Thus, the Manager's (P) claims were barred by five-year liberative prescription. Parol evidence of any acknowledgement by Mrs. Darby was inadmissible, and the agreement entered into by the heirs neither explicitly suspended or interrupted prescription against the one note that had not yet prescribed nor renounced prescription of the two that had.

The Court set aside the lower courts' judgments with respect to the three notes at issue in the appeal and dismissed the plaintiff's lawsuit as to those notes. In all other respects, the Court affirmed the lower courts' judgments.

Rule of Law

Prescription on a demand note runs from the date the note is made.

RIEGER V. TIERNEY
265 So. 2d 279 (La. App. 4th Cir. 1972)

Facts & Procedure

This is a dispute over the ownership of a house informally purchased together by the parties. In 1947, the Riegers (P) and Mrs. Rieger's mother were forced to move from their rented home and began searching for a home to purchase. The Riegers (P) could not afford to make a down payment on their own, so they orally agreed to purchase a double together in 1947 with Mrs. Rieger's brother, Mr. Tierney (D). The Riegers (P) put up $1,200.00 of the required down payment, and Mr. Tierney (D) used his G.I. Bill housing benefits to cover the other half.

Mr. Tierney took title to the house in his name, and both families moved into the double. The Riegers (P) paid half the mortgage note until the house was paid off. In 1954, Mrs. Rieger (P) requested through counsel that Mr. Tierney (D) execute a counterletter recognizing the Riegers (P) as co-owners of the house; no counterletter was executed. The Riegers (P) lived in the house until Mr. Tierney (D) evicted them in 1966.

The Riegers (P) sued Mr. Tierney (D) for recognition as owners of one-half of the house or, in the alternative, to be reimbursed for all payments they made on the house and for repairs. The trial court overruled Mr. Tierney's (D) exception of prescription, held that the monthly payments made by the Riegers (P) constituted rent, and ordered Mr. Tierney (D) to return the $1,200.00 the Riegers (P) put down on the house because of unjust enrichment. Mr. Tierney (D) appealed and re-urged his defense that the Riegers' (P) claim for reimbursement had prescribed.

Issue

When does liberative prescription begin to run?

Holding & Decision

Liberative prescription begins to run as soon as a cause of action accrues. Here, the appeal court found that the Riegers (P) knew that Mr. Tierney (D) refused to acknowledge their ownership of the house on or before February 22, 1954, when Mrs. Rieger's (P) attorney sent a letter to Mr. Tierney (D) requesting that he execute a counterletter.

The court held that ten-year acquisitive prescription on the Riegers' (P) claims for unjust enrichment with respect to the deposit began to run at that time. By the time the Riegers (P) filed suit in 1968, the action had prescribed.

The appeal court sustained Mr. Tierney's (D) exception of prescription, reversed the trial court's judgment in part, and affirmed it in part.

Dissent

Justice Lemmon dissented from the majority opinion. He categorized the parties' agreement as an oral contract for the transfer of immovable property. While the contract was unenforceable because it was not in writing, Mr. Tierney (D) could have fulfilled his side of the bargain at any time. The Riegers (P) would not have had a cause of action for breach of the contract until Mr. Tierney (D) refused to honor their arrangement. The Justice noted that there was no evidence in the record to suggest that the Riegers (P) should have known that Mr. Tierney (D) would not eventually recognize their ownership.

Accordingly, in Justice Lemmon's view, prescription would not have begun to run against the Riegers (P) until Mr. Tierney unequivocally refused to honor the agreement. Mr. Tierney (D) did not affirmatively refuse to execute a counterletter in 1954; to the contrary, he testified that he did not understand the request when he received the letter and that he did not even discuss the counterletter with the Riegers (P) until after the loan was paid off in 1965. The Riegers' (P) lawsuit was filed three years later, well within the ten-year prescriptive period.

Rule of Law

Liberative prescription begins to run as soon as a cause of action accrues.

CARRABY V. NAVARRE

Borrower (P) v. Lender (D)
3 La. 262 (La. 1832)

Facts & Procedure

In this action on a promissory note secured by a mortgage on the Borrower's (D) home, the Borrower (D) argued that the debt was prescribed. The trial court found for the Lender (P), and the Borrower (D) appealed.

Issue

Does a debtor requesting additional time to pay a debt constitute an acknowledgement of that debt sufficient to interrupt prescription?

Holding & Decision

Yes, a debtor's request for additional time to pay the debt is an acknowledgment of the debt that interrupts prescription.

The Court found that, under the terms of the contracts, the Borrower (D) was allowed to suspend payment of the debt for up to two years by making an interest-only payment every three months. The Borrower (D) did not make any interest payments and argued that this meant that the debt was prescribed. But the Court also found that an agent of the Lender (P) had frequently requested payments from the Borrower (D) and that the Borrower (D) had answered the demand by requesting patience and additional time in which to pay the debt.

The Court reasoned that, under the Civil Code, prescription is interrupted by the acknowledgment of the debt and that a promise to pay a debt can only be taken as an acknowledgment of that debt. The Borrower (D) countered that prescription could only be renounced after it had been accrued. But the Court dismissed that argument because, while prescription cannot be renounced before it accrues, it can certainly be interrupted before being completed. The Court held that the Borrower (D) interrupted prescription on the note through acknowledging the debt by requesting additional time to pay.

The Court affirmed the trial court's judgment.

Rule of Law

A debtor's request for additional time to pay the debt is an acknowledgment of the debt that interrupts prescription.

CORSEY V. STATE DEPARTMENT OF CORRECTIONS
Prisoner (P) v. Penitentiary (D)
375 So. 2d 1319 (La. 1979)

Facts & Procedure

A Prisoner (P) suffered physical injuries, including injuries to his brain that rendered him unable to function normally, while incarcerated in the State Penitentiary (D) in 1972 and did not receive adequate medical care. He made a demand against the Penitentiary (D) in 1974, more than one year after sustaining the injuries and outside Louisiana's one-year prescriptive period for tort claims. The trial court dismissed the Prisoner's (P) lawsuit as prescribed, and the Prisoner (P) appealed.

Issue

Does prescription run against a prisoner within the total control of a state agency when, due solely to the agency's negligence, the prisoner suffers physical and mental brain injuries that incapacitated him to the extent that he could not understand what had happened and what legal remedies were available to him until after the prescriptive period would have run?

Holding & Decision

No, prescription does not run against a plaintiff who suffers injuries at the hands of a tortfeasor that prevent him from pursuing his cause of action. In reaching its conclusion, the Court examined the doctrine of *contra non valentem* and found four general categories where it applies:

1. Where there was some legal cause that prevented the courts or their officers from taking cognizance of or acting on the plaintiff's action;

2. Where there was some condition coupled with the contract or connected with the proceedings which prevented the creditor from suing or acting;

3. Where the debtor himself has done some act effectively to prevent the creditor from availing himself of his cause of action; and

4. Where the cause of action is not known or reasonably knowable by the plaintiff, even though his ignorance is not induced by the defendant.

The Court also noted a distinction between the personal disabilities of the plaintiff (e.g., congenital mental incompetence) and the inability to bring suit because of an outside cause. The latter case — i.e., external causation — suspends the running of prescription, but the former does not.

After examining the facts of this case, the Court found that the Penitentiary's (D) tort caused the Prisoner's (P) mental and physical inability to file suit during the normal prescriptive period and held that, as a result, prescription did not run against the Prisoner (P). The Penitentiary's (D) action prevented him from knowing about and availing himself of his cause of action. The Court also noted that while *contra non valentem* traditionally applied where the defendant prevented pursuit of the claim, there was no rational basis to distinguish that from a case like this where the tortious conduct itself also prevented the plaintiff from seeking a remedy.

The Court reversed the trial court's judgment and remanded the case for further proceedings.

Dissent

Chief Justice Summers dissented, arguing that the Prisoner (P) here should be treated no differently than any other incompetent. Viz., prescription should have run against him until he was formally interdicted. Since the Prisoner (P) was not interdicted, prescription ran against him, and his claim was barred when filed.

Rule of Law

Prescription does not run against a plaintiff who suffers injuries at the hands of a tortfeasor that prevent him from pursuing his cause of action.

SUCCESSION OF SLAUGHTER
Lender (P) v. Succession (D)
108 La. 492, 32 So. 379 (La. 1902)

Facts & Procedure

During his lifetime, the decedent made three promissory notes to a Lender (P): one for $500 dated May 28, 1884, and due forty-five days later; a second for $200 dated May 1, 1885, and due sixty days later; and a third for $75 dated May 31, 1889, and due sixty days later.

The decedent made no payments on the notes, and they were all prescribed on July 28, 1900, when the decedent wrote a letter to his Lender (D). The decedent wrote, "And my memorandum book tells me I owe you money. That I can pay. Difficult to pay you constant, never-failing friendship. I must plead bankruptcy for that." Five months later, the decedent wrote his Lender (P) a check for $1,000.

After the decedent's death, the Lender (P) intervened in his succession, claiming that the letter and the payment constituted a renunciation of accrued prescription and that he was entitled to payment for the remaining balance of the notes out of the succession. The trial court found for the Lender (P), and the heirs appealed.

Issue

Does a written acknowledgment of an unspecified debt and expression of the ability to pay that debt, coupled with a partial payment, serve to renounce accrued prescription of those debts?

Holding & Decision

No, the acknowledgment of a debt and partial payment of it alone do not renounce prescription that has accrued against the debt. The Court held that the decedent's letter to the Lender (P) was only an acknowledgement of a debt and the expression of the ability of the decedent to pay some unspecified amount of money that he owed. Such an expression was not an express or tacit renunciation of prescription by the decedent. Accordingly, the Lender's (P) claims were prescribed.

The Court set aside the trial court's judgment and found for the Succession (D).

Rule of Law

The acknowledgment of a debt and partial payment of it do not renounce prescription that has accrued against the debt.

HARMON V. HARMON
Sister (P) v. Brother (D)
308 So. 2d 524 (La. App. 3d Cir. 1975)

Facts & Procedure

A Sister (P) made her Brother (D) four loans totaling $2,300 between February 8, 1967, and February 7, 1968, during his final year of medical school and the first year of his internship. After his Sister (P) called and asked for payment, the Brother (D) made five monthly payments of $50 each — $250 total — between May and October of 1972 but made no other payments.

After the October 1972 payment, the parties quarreled. In November, the Brother (D) wrote his sister a letter to the effect that he would continue paying on the debt if his Sister (P) would apologize to his girlfriend. The Brother (D) did not resume payments, and his Sister (P) filed this suit on July 5, 1973.

The trial court rendered judgment in the Sister's (P) favor for $1,770 — $2,350 minus the $250 of payments made and $330 for services rendered to the Sister (P) by the Brother (D).

The Brother (D) appealed.

Issue

Do an oral promise to pay a prescribed debt and partial payment of the debt constitute a renunciation of accrued prescription?

Holding & Decision

Yes, an oral promise to pay a prescribed debt and partial payment of the debt constitute a renunciation of accrued prescription. The court found that the Sister's (P) last loan would have prescribed in 1971 at the end of the three-year prescriptive period unless the period were interrupted or suspended. The Sister (P) did not contend that any such interruption or suspension occurred.

In order for a person to renounce prescription, he must make a new promise to pay an accrued debt. The court concluded that neither the partial payments made by the Brother (D) nor his letter to his sister renounced prescription because neither included a new promise to pay the debt. But the Sister (P) testified that her Brother (D) promised to pay $50 per month until the debt was paid during their 1972 telephone call just before he began making monthly payments on the debt. Her Brother (D) disputed that he made this promise.

The court concluded that the trial court, despite giving no written reasons for judgment, must have accepted the Sister's (P) testimony to support its conclusion that prescription had been renounced. Because the record contained evidence supporting the conclusion that there was a new promise to pay (even though it was disputed) the appeal court found that the trial court had not committed manifest error holding that such a promise was made and that the promise renounced the Brother's (D) prescription.

Accordingly, the appeal court affirmed the trial court's overruling the Brother's (D) exception of prescription and affirmed its judgment in favor of the Sister (P) with minor clerical amendments.

Rule of Law

An oral promise to pay a prescribed debt and partial payment of the debt constitute a renunciation of accrued prescription.

Chapter 9

Acquisitive Prescription

1. **Acquisitive prescription in general.**

   a) Acquisitive prescription is the mechanism by which a person comes to own an immovable or movable thing by possessing it as owner for the requisite amount of time. *Cf.* adverse possession in the common law.

   b) "All private things are susceptible of prescription unless prescription is excluded by legislation." La. C.C. art. 3485.

   c) **Possession.**

      i. "The possessor must have corporeal possession, or civil possession preceded by corporeal possession, to acquire a thing by prescription. The possession must be continuous, uninterrupted, peaceable, public, and unequivocal." La. C.C. Art. 3476.

      ii. **Defects of Possession** render the possession legally ineffective. La. C.C. art. 3435. Defects include

         A. **Discontinuity.** Possession "not exercised at regular intervals" or otherwise broken up in time.

         B. **Violence.** Possession acquired to maintained by violence. "When the violence ceases, the possession ceases to be violent."

         C. **Clandestine.** Possession that "is not open or public."

         D. **Equivocality.** Possession where "there is ambiguity as to the intent of the possessor to own the thing." La. C.C. art. 3436.

   d) **Possession as owner.** Acquisitive prescription requires that the possessor possess with the public and unequivocal intent to be the owner of the thing.

      i. Squatters may possess property as owner and thereby acquire it by thirty-year acquisitive prescription. *Theriot v. Bollinger.*

      ii. A person is presumed to possess as owner, but that presumption is rebuttable. *Humble v. Dewey.*

   e) **Precarious possession.** "Acquisitive prescription does not run in favor of a precarious possessor or his universal successor." La. C.C. art. 3477.

      i. A precarious possessor cannot become an adverse possessor without communicating his intention to do so by some unequivocal act of hostility brought to the owner's attention. *Cortinas v. Peters.*

ii. **From co-owner to adverse possessor** "A co-owner, or his universal successor, may commence to prescribe when he demonstrates by overt and unambiguous acts sufficient to give notice to his co-owner that he intends to possess the property for himself. The acquisition and recordation of a title from a person other than a co-owner thus may mark the commencement of prescription." La. C.C. art. 3478. *See Franks Petroleum, Inc. v. Babineaux.*

    A. Occupancy, use, payment of taxes, and other normal acts of a co-owner are not sufficient to give other co-owners notice of the intent to possess adversely.

    B. The recording of an instrument transferring title from a third party to a co-owner might be sufficient to mark the beginning of his adverse possession against his co-owners without additional action, but it is not necessarily sufficient. *Cockerham v. Cockerham.*

    C. A co-owner who redeems the property after a tax sale or even purchases the property at tax sale merely pays the taxes for the other co-owners. He does not begin an adverse possession.

iii. "Any other precarious possessor, or his universal successor, may commence to prescribe when he gives actual notice to the person on whose behalf he is possessing that he intends to possess for himself." La. C.C. art. 3478.

iv. "A particular successor of a precarious possessor who takes possession under an act translative of ownership possesses for himself, and prescription runs in his favor from the commencement of his possession." La. C.C. art. 3479.

v. **From adverse possessor to precarious possessor.** A possessor who acknowledges that he is possessing on behalf of another both interrupts prescription and renders his future possession precarious.

vi. Possession for the convenience of another gives the possessor neither legal possession nor the right to prescribe. *McKee v. Hayward.*

f) **Tacking of possession** is the cumulation of two or more possessors' possession into one whole in order to satisfy the duration requirement for ten- or thirty-year acquisitive prescription.

i. "The possession of the decedent is transferred to his successors.... A universal successor continues the possession of the decedent with all its advantages and defects, and with no alteration in the nature of the possession.... A particular successor may commence a new possession for purposes of acquisitive prescription." La. C.C. art. 936.

    A. **Successors.** "There are in law two sorts of successors: the universal successor, such as the heir, the universal legatee, and the general legatee; and the successor by particular title, such as the buyer, donee or legatee of particular things, the transferee." La. C.C. art. 3506(28).

ii. The transfer of an estate generally described can include the transfer of property not also included in the explicit description. *Noel v. Jumonville Pipe and Machinery Co.*

iii. A person may tack his possession onto his ancestor-in-title's possession of property beyond his title within visible bounds where there is a juridical link between the parties through succession or contract. *Brown v. Wood.*

iv. For two or more possessions to be cumulated toward ten-year acquisitive prescription, all the possessions must meet the statutory conditions required of ten-year prescription, including good faith. *Bartlett v. Calhoun.*

v. A person who takes possession on his own and not as a successor to another starts a new possession.

2. **Immovables: ten year prescription.** "Ownership and other real rights in immovables may be acquired by the prescription of ten years." La. C.C. art. 3473.

   a) "This prescription runs against absent persons and incompetents, including minors and interdicts." La. C.C. art. 3474.

   b) Ten-year acquisitive prescription requires "possession of ten years, good faith, just title, and a thing susceptible of acquisition by prescription." La. C.C. Art. 3475.

   c) **Just title.**

      i. "A just title is a juridical act, such as a sale, exchange, or donation, sufficient to transfer ownership or another real right. The act must be written, valid in form, and filed for registry in the conveyance records of the parish in which the immovable is situated." La. C.C. art. 3483.

      ii. "A just title to an undivided interest in an immovable is such only as to the interest transferred." La. C.C. art. 3484.

      iii. "An absolutely null tax title constitutes just title for purposes of ten-year acquisitive prescription." *Wilkie v. Cox.*

   d) **Good faith.**

      i. "For purposes of acquisitive prescription, a possessor is in good faith when he reasonably believes, in light of objective considerations, that he is owner of the thing he possesses." La. C.C. art. 3480.

      ii. Good faith requires that the possessor believed that his transferor owned the property at the time of the transfer and that this belief was objectively reasonable.

      iii. If a possessor reasonably believes that the person who transferred the property to him owned it, other defects in the act — e.g., the transferor's incapacity — do not impair his good faith for purposes of ten-year prescription.

      iv. "Good faith is presumed. Neither error of fact nor error of law defeats this presumption. This presumption is rebutted on proof that the possessor knows, or should know, that he is not owner of the thing he possesses." La. C.C. art. 3481.

         A. The possessor may make errors of fact — e.g., overlapping titles overlooked during a title search — or of law — e.g., ignorance of the intricacies of succession law — and remain in good faith.

      v. "It is sufficient that possession has commenced in good faith; subsequent bad faith does not prevent the accrual of prescription of ten years." La. C.C. art. 3482.

      vi. The purchase of multiple properties, some with title warranty and others without, in the same transaction should raise sufficient doubt in the purchaser's mind as to the vendor's title in the unwarranted property to overcome the presumption of good faith at the time of the acquisition. *Board of Commissioners v. S.D. Hunter Foundation.*

vii. Quitclaim language in a conveyance's property description, a very low sale price, and obvious chain-of-title issues preclude a person from maintaining good faith for acquisitive prescription purposes. *Malone v. Fowler.*

viii. A person who receives an incorrect title examination does not necessarily possess the acquired property in bad faith; instead the title examination and the information actually revealed by the examination are factors to be considered when determining whether the good-faith presumption has been overcome. *Phillips v. Parker.*

ix. A seller's bad faith is irrelevant to determining whether a buyer is in good faith for purposes of ten-year acquisitive prescription. *Lacour v. Sanders.*

3. **Immovables: thirty year prescription.**

a) "Ownership and other real rights in immovables may be acquired by the prescription of thirty years without the need of just title or possession in good faith." La. C.C. art. 3486.

b) "For purposes of acquisitive prescription without title, possession extends only to that which has been actually possessed." La. C.C. Art. 3487.

c) "The rules governing acquisitive prescription of ten years apply to the prescription of thirty years" insofar as they are compatible. La. C.C. art. 3488.

4. **Movables.**

a) "Ownership and other real rights in movables may be acquired either by the prescription of three years or by the prescription of ten years." La. C.C. art. 3489.

b) **Movables: three-year prescription.** "One who has possessed a movable as owner, in good faith, under an act sufficient to transfer ownership, and without interruption for three years, acquires ownership by prescription." La. C.C. art. 3490.

i. A donee who knows that the donor concealed the donation of community assets from his spouse does not possess that property in good faith. *Succession of Wagner.*

c) **Movables: ten-year prescription.** "One who has possessed a movable as owner for ten years acquires ownership by prescription. Neither title nor good faith is required for this prescription." La. C.C. art. 3491.

i. A person who openly and notoriously possesses spoils of war for more than ten years acquires ownership of them. *Lieber v. Mohawk Arms, Inc.*

WILKIE V. COX

Tax Sale Purchasers (P) v. Heirs (D)
222 So. 2d 85 (La. App. 3d Cir. 1969)

Facts & Procedure

The disputed tract was homesteaded by George W. Cox, the Heirs' (D) father, and the U.S. Government issued him a patent in 1909. But the property was adjudicated to the state of Louisiana for nonpayment of taxes in 1904. The property remained on the tax rolls under various version of George Cox's name (e.g., G. W. Cox) in the following years and was adjudicated to the state at least five other times between 1904 and 1937. At another tax sale in 1941, the property was sold to Howard L. Raphiel, who purchased on behalf of himself and W.J. Colbert. Plaintiff B.B. Wilkie purchased Raphiel's half-interest in the property in 1962. The property was redeemed by George W. Cox in 1965.

The plaintiff filed an action to quiet his title and confirm his ownership. The tax debtor's Heirs (D) opposed the action, sought to have the tax title invalidated, and claimed ownership of the property. Several additional parties, including Colbert, were impleaded, and the trial court treated the case as a petitory action at trial. Colbert's and Wilkie's interests are basically the same, although one is technically a plaintiff and the other a third-party defendant because of the case's procedural posture. Together they will be referred to as Tax Sale Purchasers (P).

The Tax Sale Purchasers (P) contended that they owned the land by virtue of a 1941 tax sale and, alternatively, by ten-year good-faith acquisitive prescription. The Heirs (D) argued that the 1941 tax sale was an absolute nullity because the property had been adjudicated to the state and the taxing authority therefore had no authority to assess taxes on it or sell it at tax sale. After trial, the court recognized the Tax Sale Purchasers (P) as the owners of the disputed property, confirmed their tax title, and enjoined the Heirs (D) from claiming title to the property.

The Heirs (D) appealed.

Issue

1. Does an absolutely null tax title constitute just title for purposes of ten-year acquisitive prescription?

2. Does acquisitive prescription run against property that is adjudicated or forfeited to the state while title to the property is vested in the state if the property is subsequently redeemed?

Holding & Decision

Yes, an absolutely null tax title constitutes just title for purposes of ten-year acquisitive prescription. The appeal court held the 1941 tax sale to be a nullity because the taxing authority had no authority to tax or sell the disputed property because it had previously been adjudicated to the state. After concluding that the evidence showed that the Tax Sale Purchasers (P) or their authors in title were in good faith when they attempted to acquire the disputed property, the court reasoned that an invalid tax sale deed constitutes "just title" for purposes of ten-year prescription.

The Heirs (D) also argued that prescription could not run against the property while it remained adjudicated to the state. The court addressed their argument with La. R.S. 9:5803, which provides that acquisitive prescription runs and is not interrupted or suspended while the state has the adjudicated property if it is subsequently redeemed. Therefore, the property belonged to the Tax Sale Purchasers (P) through ten-year acquisitive prescription and not because of the tax title.

The appeal court affirmed the portions of the trial court's judgment that recognized the Tax Sale Purchasers' (P) ownership of the disputed property and reversed the portions of the judgment that confirmed and quieted the tax title.

Dissent

In dissenting from the denial of an application for rehearing, Judge Culpepper argued that an absolutely nullity cannot form just title for purposes of acquisitive prescription. To support his assertion, he cited Planiol's view that relatively null titles could constitute just title, not absolute nullities, and several cases where pleas of prescription based on absolute nullities were denied.

Rule of Law

1. An absolutely null tax title constitutes just title for purposes of ten-year acquisitive prescription.

2. Acquisitive prescription runs and is not interrupted or suspended while the state has title to adjudicated or forfeited property if the property is subsequently redeemed.

BOARD OF COMMISSIONERS V. S.D. HUNTER FOUNDATION

Levee District (P) v. Hunter Foundation & Widow (D)
354 So. 2d 156 (La. 1977)

Facts & Procedure

The Levee District brought a petitory action to assert its title to certain disputed acreage lying between Twelve Mile Bayou and the traverse line delineating the area subject to Soda Lake's overflow.

In 1951, S.D. Hunter (D) purchased several tracts of land from the George Family. He purchased some of the Georges' land (the George Tract) with a guarantee and warranty of title; the Georges reserved half of the mineral rights to that tract. Mr. Hunter also purchased the land north of the traverse line of Soda lake (the Disputed George tract) from the Georges without any guarantee of its title; the Georges did not reserve any mineral rights in that tract. Mr. Hunter also acquired another disputed tract of land north of the traverse line from the Powell family. By the time this lawsuit began, Mr. Hunter had died, and his interest in the disputed properties, if any, belonged to the S.D. Hunter Foundation and Mr. Hunter's widow (D).

All disputed land north of the traverse line of Soda Lake originally belonged to the United States government but was transferred to the state in the late nineteenth century. The state conveyed the title to the Levee District (P) in 1901. The Levee District (P) was record owner of the disputed tract at the time of the sale to Mr. Hunter. Before 1951, no surveys or other records indicated that anyone other than the Levee District (P) owned the lands north of the traverse line of Soda Lake.

The Hunter Foundation and Widow (D) claimed to own the Disputed George Tract by ten year, good-faith acquisitive prescription starting in 1951. The trial court found for the Levee District (P) and recognized its ownership of all the disputed property. The appeal court reversed, holding that Mr. Hunter (D) had acquired the disputed properties by ten-year acquisitive prescription.

The Levee District (P) appealed.

Issue

Does one who purchases immovable property, some with a warranty as to its title and some without in the same act, purchase the unwarranted portion in good faith for purposes of acquisitive prescription?

Holding & Decision

No, the purchase of properties, one with a title warranty and another without, in the same transaction should raise sufficient doubt in the purchaser's mind as to the vendor's title in the unwarranted property to defeat his good faith for purposes of acquisitive prescription.

Good or bad faith of a particular purchaser must be determined by the facts of the case against a reasonable-man standard. The Court noted that a non-warranty sale by itself is not sufficient to overcome the presumption of good faith. But where the deed itself indicates that a seller may not own the entire property, the buyer is not presumed to be in good faith. Here, Mr. Hunter (D) purchased some property with a title warranty and some without. That circumstance was sufficient to raise doubt in his mind as to whether his vendor had good title to the property he did not provide a warranty for.

Because Mr. Hunter (D) had or should have had doubt as to his vendor's title to the Disputed George Tract, he was not in good faith and could not rely on ten-year acquisitive prescription. Not enough time had elapsed to place thirty year prescription at issue. Further, the Court Found that the

Hunters and the Foundation (D) did not acquire title to the other disputed tract because they lacked continuous possession of it.

The Court reversed the appeal court's judgment and reinstated the trial court's judgment, recognizing the Levee District's (P) title to the disputed properties.

Rule of Law

The purchase of multiple properties, some with title warranty and others without, in the same transaction should raise sufficient doubt in the purchaser's mind as to the vendor's title in the unwarranted property to overcome the presumption of good faith at the time of the acquisition.

MALONE V. FOWLER
Co-Owner (P) v. Purchaser (D)
228 So. 2d 500 (La. App. 3d Cir. 1969)

Facts & Procedure

Mr. Malone (P) filed a petition to partition a 15 acre tract of land near Alexandria and named Mr. Fowler (D) and some absent heirs as defendants. Mr. Fowler (D) countered that he owned the entire tract by ten-year acquisitive prescription.

Mr. Fowler (D) purportedly purchased the entire property for $100. The property description in the conveyance recited that it was the same property that was sold to Sallie Jones. Frances Tutt Howard and Evelina Fields West signed the conveyance as vendors in the summer of 1955. There were no succession proceedings or other transfers showing how the property passed from Sallie Jones to Fowler's (D) vendors.

At the trial, Mr. Fowler testified that he had attended two years of law school and was familiar with the law of successions and land matter. He denied that he prepared the deed at issue, but the record indicates that he did. He also corresponded with Mrs. Howard's attorney, saying that he had told Evalina West's attorney that he needed a letter stating that she and Mrs. Howard were the owners of the tract because he wanted to buy the entire property rather than an undivided interest. A letter was entered into evidence purporting to be from Mrs. West stating as much, but the handwriting and signature on the letter were markedly different than Ms. West's signature on the conveyance. Mrs. West's first name was also misspelled. Mr. Fowler (D) testified that he received this letter along with the deed, but another letter in the record dated about two weeks later indicates that the deed was still in the possession of Mrs. Howard's attorney, who would send it when he received Mr. Fowler's (D) payment.

In August 1955, Mr. Fowler (D) paid for the property, fenced it, and began possessing it without incident. This suit was brought in 1967. The trial court found that his acquisition was not in good faith and overruled his exception of prescription.

Mr. Fowler (D) appealed.

Issue

Does a person purchase property in good faith for purposes of acquisitive prescription when he prepares a quitclaim style property description, the land is sold for a very low price relative to its value, and the surname of the vendors does not match that of the last record owner?

Holding & Decision

No, factors like quitclaim language, a very low price, and obvious chain-of-title issues preclude a person from maintaining good faith for acquisitive prescription purposes. The appeal court identified three key facts that indicated that Mr. Fowler (D) did not purchase the property in good faith. First, he prepared a "quitclaim" type property description whereby the vendors transferred their entire interest in the property; they did not warrant that they owned the entire property. Second, the appeal court noted that the property was worth $250 in 1916, was located ten miles from a major city, fronted a major highway, and had ten acres of pasture land suitable for farming cash crops. The land must have been worth more than $100 in 1955. Finally, the appeal court held that the letter purportedly signed by Mrs. West could not establish Mr. Fowler's (D) good faith because it was written in a different hand than the signature on the deed and because the letter misspelled Mrs. West's name. The letter, coupled with the different surnames involved should have alerted Mr. Fowler (D) that succession proceedings or an affidavit of heirship were required. Finally, that Mr. Fowler (D) requested the letter indicated that he was aware of a title problem.

Because Mr. Fowler (D) lacked good faith when he acquired the property, his plea of acquisitive prescription was properly overruled. The appeal court affirmed the trial court's judgment.

Rule of Law

Quitclaim language in a conveyance's property description, a very low sale price, and obvious chain-of-title issues preclude a person from maintaining good faith for acquisitive prescription purposes.

PHILLIPS V. PARKER
483 So. 2d 972 (La. 1986)

Facts & Procedure

This is a boundary action between neighboring landowners sharing a common ancestor in title. G.R. Weaver owned a two and a half acre tract on which he built a camp. In August 1955, he agreed to sell two lakefront lots, one to the defendant and the other to the McCuller brothers, the plaintiff's immediate ancestors in title. Both lots were sold for the same price. When Mr. Parker (D) went to the property to mark its boundaries, he learned that the description in his sale covered the tract where Mr. Weaver had built his camp, not the tract he intended to purchase.

Mr. Parker (D) consulted an attorney and hired a surveyor to determine what property they intended to purchase and a title attorney to examine the title to that property. The attorney opined that Mr. Weaver had good title to the lot they intended to purchase, so in October 1955 Mr. Weaver and Mr. Parker (D) executed acts to return Mr. Weaver's land to him and to convey the surveyed lot to Mr. Parker (D). Mr. Parker (D) cleared the property, built a camp, and built a fence in accord with the survey. He remained in peaceful possession of the property until 1982.

The McCullers transferred their lot to Ms. Phillips (P) in 1972. In 1982, Ms. Philips (P) learned that the description in Mr. Parker's (D) October 1955 deed overlapped the property described in McCuller's August deed by thirteen feet. She requested that Mr. Parker (D) remove his fence on the overlap and later filed this boundary action.

Mr. Parker (D) filed an exception of prescription maintaining that he had acquired ownership of the thirteen foot overlap by ten-year acquisitive prescription. The trial court took evidence on Mr. Parker's (D) good faith, and the title examiner testified that he did not recall finding the August 1955 sale from Weaver to the McCullers. Mr. Parker (D) relied entirely on the examiner's written title opinion. The trial court overruled the exception, concluding that the defendants were in legal bad faith because they obtained a title examination that did not reveal the title defect and found for the plaintiff.

Mr. Parker (D) appealed. The appeal court affirmed, concluding that a purchaser who makes a title search is charged with the knowledge of the defects in the title that a reasonable person would acquire from such a search.

Mr. Parker (D) again appealed.

Issue

Does the receipt of an incorrect title examination that shows clear title to the property preclude a person from acquisitively prescribing in good faith?

Holding & Decision

No, a person who receives an incorrect title examination does not necessarily possess the acquired property in bad faith; instead the title examination and the information actually revealed by the examination are factors to be considered when determining whether the good-faith presumption has been overcome.

The Court began with a review of the public records doctrine and found that the law of registry does not influence acquisitive prescription. That is, good faith for acquisitive prescription should be determined by consideration of all the relevant factors, not by any mechanical application of the public records doctrine or a theory of constructive knowledge of public records. The Court noted that there is no reason to deny a purchaser the status of a good-faith possessor because he received a faulty title examination; at worst, the purchaser lacks good faith only insofar as defects were discovered by the examination.

Here, Mr. Parker (D) was presumed to possess in good faith under La. C.C. art. 3481. No evidence adduced at trial suggested that he should have doubted that Mr. Weaver owned the property. Further, the defect was a small overlap with a contemporaneous sale without a survey that a title examiner could have easily missed. Both the examiner and Mr. Parker (D) testified that they were unaware of the overlap. Finally, the public records in the parish were not it good condition at the time.

The Court the judgments of the lower courts and sustained Mr. Parker's (D) plea of prescription.

Rule of Law

A person who receives an incorrect title examination does not necessarily possess the acquired property in bad faith; instead the title examination and the information actually revealed by the examination are factors to be considered when determining whether the good-faith presumption has been overcome.

Lacour v. Sanders

Estate (P) v. Buyer (D)
442 So. 2d 1280 (La. App. 3d Cir. 1983)

Facts & Procedure

The Buyer (D) purchased a 30.3 acre tract of land from Robert Jett Jr., the widower of Mary Ellen Scott. Mrs. Scott died near the end of 1959, and Mr. Jett sold the property in the summer of 1960. The Buyer and his family moved a house onto the property and lived there for several decades. He also executed mineral leases on the property in 1970 and 1982.

The petitioner, Mrs. Scott's daughter and Administratrix of her succession, filed this action to recognize the Estate's (P) one-half ownership interest in the property and to partition it. The Buyer (D) claimed ownership of the entire property by ten-year acquisitive prescription and made other claims against various third-party defendants.

The trial court found that the Buyer (D) proved that he exercised uninterrupted possession of the property with legal title sufficient to transfer possession in good faith. The court rendered judgment recognizing the Buyer (D) as the sole owner of the disputed tract, and the Estate (P) appealed.

Issue

Did the Buyer (D) own the entire tract by ten-year acquisitive prescription even though his vendor only owned half of it at the time of the sale?

Holding & Decision

Yes, the Buyer (D) acquired the remainder of the property by ten-year acquisitive prescription because he purchased it in good faith. Good faith for purposes of acquisitive prescription requires that a buyer reasonably believe that the seller is the true owner of the property. Here, both courts noted that the buyer and seller were uneducated men ignorant of Louisiana community property law. Further, at the time of the sale, Louisiana's Head and Master rule was in effect, and a husband could transfer the full interest in community assets by onerous title without his wife's consent, so it was not necessarily unreasonable for a person to believe that a husband could dispose of his wife's estate.

The Estate (P) presented evidence that some of Mr. Jett's children — including the Estate's administratrix — had objected to the sale, but Mr. Jett told the Buyer (D) that they were willing to sell. The Estate (P) introduced no evidence to show that the Buyer (D) knew otherwise. The record also shows that the administratrix received her portion of the sale proceeds from her father at the time of the sale but did not tell the Buyer (P) she objected to the sale until filing this lawsuit twenty-two years later.

The appeal court reasoned that, while Mr. Jett may have been in bad faith because he knew that he did not own the entire property and that his children objected to the sale, legal bad faith of the seller is irrelevant to the issue of the buyer's good faith. Because the record contained no suggestion that the Buyer (D) knew or should have known of any defect in his title and he complied with the other requirements of ten-year acquisitive prescription, his title must be recognized.

The appeal court affirmed the lower court's decision.

Rule of Law

A seller's bad faith is irrelevant to determining whether a buyer is in good faith for purposes of ten-year acquisitive prescription.

BARTLETT V. CALHOUN
Heirs (P) v. Purported Owner (D)
412 So. 2d 597 (La. 1982)

Facts & Procedure

Stella Calhoun (D) purportedly purchased a 300 acre tract of land from the Thompson family in November 1949. Ten days later, the Purported Owner (D) sold the property to a third party. She purchased the property back from him less than two years later. The Purported Owner (D) remained in possession of the property from 1951 through the filing of this lawsuit in 1977.

The Thompsons' Heirs (P) filed a petitory action seeking recognition of their ownership of the property. They alleged that the Thompsons' signatures were forged on the initial sale to Mrs. Calhoun (D). She (D) filed a motion for summary judgment, arguing that there were no issues of material fact and that she had acquired the tract by ten-year acquisitive prescription.

The trial court ruled in favor of the Purported Owner (D), finding that it didn't matter whether she was in good faith when she purchased the property the second time because the intervening third-party owner was in good faith. Therefore, her second possession counted toward ten-year prescription regardless of her own bad faith.

The appeal court affirmed, and the Heirs appealed to the Louisiana Supreme Court.

Issue

May a person acquiring property by particular title tack his bad-faith possession to his good-faith author's possession to acquire ownership by ten-year acquisitive possession?

Holding & Decision

No, when a person acquires property by particular title he commences a new, distinct possession. The two possessions may be cumulated, but both must meet all the statutory requirements to result in ten-year acquisitive prescription.

The Court surveyed the Louisiana jurisprudence and historic French sources and overturned a line of cases that held that a bad faith possessor might tack his possession to a prior good-faith possession in order to successfully acquire property by ten-year acquisitive prescription. In doing so, the Court described the ground rules for tacking by universal successors and successors by particular title.

A universal successor's possession continues the deceased's possession, so he inherits the decedent's good or bad faith regardless of his own actions. One who acquires property by particular title, on the other hand, starts a new possession colored by his own good or bad faith.

Where two possessions are tacked together to accrue prescription, they both must meet the statutory requirements for the prescription. For example, if a vendor possesses in good faith, and the purchaser is in bad faith, the entire possession counts toward thirty-year prescription, but the bad-faith purchaser cannot tack his possession onto the vendor's good-faith possession perfect ten-year acquisitive prescription. If the vendor is in bad faith and the purchaser is in good faith, a similar result obtains. The entire possession may count toward thirty-year prescription, but the two possessions cannot be tacked together for ten-year prescription because the vendor possessed it in bad faith.

Because the Purported Buyer's (D) status as a good- or bad-faith possessor was a material fact and the trial court did not make any findings on the issue, the Court reversed the appeal court's judgment and remanded the matter to the trial court for further proceedings.

Rule of Law

1. A universal successor's possession is a continuation of the deceased's possession.

2. A person who acquires property by particular title commences a new possession.

3. For two or more possessions to be cumulated toward ten-year acquisitive prescription, all the possessions must meet the statutory conditions required of ten-year prescription, including good faith.

Theriot v. Bollinger

Putative Owner (P) v. Record Owner (D)
172 La. 397, 134 So. 372 (La. 1931)

Facts & Procedure

The Putative Owner (P) sued for recognition of his ownership of a nine acre tract of land. He purchased the land from squatters. The evidence showed that the squatters took possession of the property in question in 1892, more than thirty years before selling the property to the plaintiff here.

The Record Owner's (D) title was derived, through intermediate transfers, from a patent issued by Louisiana in 1849. The Record Owner (D) leased some of the property to a concern that built a gas well on a small part of the disputed property near its northern boundary, but the well was soon abandoned.

The district court ruled in favor of the Record Owner (D) and denied the Putative Owner (P) recognition of his ownership.

The Putative Owner (P) appealed.

Issue

Can squatters possess as owners and acquire property by thirty-year acquisitive prescription?

Holding & Decision

Yes, squatters possess in their own name since they do not possess in the name of or for another. As a result, they may acquire property through thirty-year acquisitive prescription. Here, the Court noted that the Record Owner (D) had allowed one or more lessees to build oil wells on part of the property but found that the interruption was small, affected an indeterminate area, and was insufficient to deprive the squatters of possession. Therefore, they acquired the entire property by acquisitive prescription of thirty years and subsequently sold it to the Putative Owner (P).

The Court reversed the lower court's judgment and recognized the Putative Owner (P) as owner of the property.

Rule of Law

Squatters may possess property as owner and thereby acquire it by thirty-year acquisitive prescription.

CORTINAS V. PETERS
Seller (P) v. Buyer (D)
224 La. 9, 68 So. 2d 739 (La. 1953)

Facts & Procedure

In May 1949, a Buyer (D) agreed to purchase five lots from a Seller (P) who purchased them fifteen days before the sale from Mr. Joseph Sheldon. When it came time to close, the Buyer (D) refused to proceed, maintaining that the Seller's (P) title was not valid and merchantable. Mr. Sheldon claimed to have acquired the five lots by thirty-year acquisitive prescription.

Witnesses at trial testified that the entire square — containing 24 lots — in which the five lots in question were situated had been enclosed by a fence before 1918. Quaker Realty Company owned 19 of the 24 lots and continuously used the entire square as a truck farm and for grazing pasture. In 1918, Interstate Bank & Trust Company of New Orleans purchased 19 of the 24 lots from Quaker Realty but did not purchase the five at issue. Mr. Sheldon, General Sales Manager of Interstate Bank & Trust, took possession of the whole square on behalf of his employee. In 1921, the bank sold the 19 lots to Mr. Sheldon, and his son testified that at that time Mr. Sheldon took possession of the entire square for himself.

The trial court found for the Seller (P) and ordered the defendant to purchase the lots. The Buyer (D) appealed.

Issue

When does a precarious possessor begin possessing instead for himself as owner?

Holding & Decision

A precarious possessor cannot become an adverse possessor without communicating his intention to do so by some unequivocal act of hostility brought to the owner's attention. The Court noted that Mr. Sheldon's son's testimony ruined the Seller's (P) case, holding that it showed that Mr. Sheldon's possession of the five lots in 1918 began on behalf of the bank and that he remained a precarious possessor. Further, the Court posited that, even if the possession had converted from precarious possession to adverse in 1921 when Mr. Sheldon purchased the other 19 lots, thirty years had not passed by the time the lawsuit began. Therefore, Mr. Sheldon failed to prove the acquisition of the five lots by prescription of thirty years, and the Seller's (P) title was indeed invalid.

The Court reversed the lower court's judgment and dismissed the lawsuit.

Rule of Law

A precarious possessor cannot become an adverse possessor without communicating his intention to do so by some unequivocal act of hostility brought to the owner's or other possessor's attention.

HUMBLE V. DEWEY
Owners (P) v. Possessor (D)
215 So. 2d 378 (La. App. 3d Cir. 1968)

Facts & Procedure

The record Owners (P) of a six acre tract of land filed a petitory action against T.J. Dewey to recognize their ownership of it. Mr. Dewey (P) defended the lawsuit by claiming thirty-year acquisitive prescription over the western 4.5 acres of the tract.

J.W. Duckworth purchased the property at issue in 1927, built a house, and moved in. The house burned down in 1931 and was not rebuilt. Duckworth sold the property to A.A. Fuller, the Owners' (P) father, in 1939. Mr. Fuller died in 1950, leaving the property to his widow and the plaintiffs here. They eventually became the sole record Owners (P) of the property.

At trial, Mr. Dewey (D) proved that he had lived on an adjacent tract of land for forty years and that he began using the subject property in 1932, a year or so after the Duckworth house burned down. He testified that he did not know who owned it, instead he "just went over there and went to plowing and nobody didn't tell me to get off, and I didn't ask nobody." Over the years, he raised corn, cotton, beans, and other crops on part of the property and grazed livestock on the rest.

The property was fenced when Mr. Dewey (D) took possession of it, but he testified that in 1932 he was "ordered" by the nephew of a former owner to remove the existing fence wire. He then replaced it with his own wire on the same posts. Eventually he fenced off the eastern quarter of the property because it was poor and used only the western part for crops and pasturage.

In 1959, the plaintiffs gave Hardee Myers verbal permission to use the eastern portion of the tract for grazing. Mr. Myers did not ask Mr. Dewey (D) for permission because he believed the plaintiffs owned the property. When Mr. Myers began using it, he told Mr. Dewey of his agreement with the plaintiffs, and Mr. Dewey consented by saying, "O.K., just fix a good fence." Mr. Myers used the property without objection by Mr. Dewey (D) from 1959 on.

In 1962, the plaintiffs attempted to sell the entire tract, and Mr. Dewey (D) refused to allow prospective purchasers onto the land. The plaintiffs demanded he lease the property from them or vacate. Mr. Dewey refused that as well and announced his intention to keep the land for himself. The plaintiffs also demanded that he remove his fences from the land, which Mr. Dewey also refused.

One of the Owners (P) testified that Mr. Dewey (D) had been a good friend of their father and that Mr. Dewey's (D) daughter had been her sister's best friend. She further testified that the plaintiffs had assumed their father had given Mr. Dewey (D) permission to use the land and that they had no reason to believe he intended to adversely possess the property until 1962 when he refused to allow prospective buyers onto the property.

The trial court found that Mr. Dewey (D) failed to prove he had possessed the property for thirty years as owner because his ownership claim was not known around the community until 1962. The court ruled in favor of the Owners (P) and recognized their ownership.

Mr. Dewey (D) appealed.

Issue

Is the presumption that a person possesses property as owner, rather that precariously, rebuttable?

Holding & Decision

Yes, while the law presumes that a person possesses property for himself as owner, that presumption is subject to rebuttal. Here, the appeal court held that the Mr. Dewey's (D) own testimony, taken along with the facts and circumstances also detailed at trial, overcame the presumption that he possessed the property at issue as owner. The court found that Mr. Dewey (D) began to use the property for small crops to feed his family until the landowner put him out. In other words, he possessed at the whim of the owner, not as an adverse possessor. At some point, the court found, his intentions changed, but the evidence did not support the conclusion that he had possessed adversely for over thirty years.

The appeal court affirmed the trial court's judgment.

Rule of Law

A person is presumed to possess as owner, but that presumption is rebuttable.

FRANKS PETROLEUM, INC. V. BABINEAUX
Operator (P) v. Claimants (D)
446 So. 2d 826 (La. App. 2d Cir. 1984)

Facts & Procedure

The plaintiff oil and gas Operator (P) initiated a concursus proceeding to have the court determine which set of rival Claimants (D) were entitled to the mineral production royalties for a tract of land purchased by John A. Colvin and C.C. Colvin in 1874. There are two sets of potential co-owners (D), "the Group A defendants" and "the Group B defendants." The Group A defendants are the heirs of C.C. Colvin and his wife. The Group B defendants are two grandchildren of John A. Colvin by way of one of his ten children. The widow and other heirs of John A. Colvin signed quitclaims transferring their interest in the subject property to the Group A defendants in 1937 and 1938. The quitclaim deeds indicated that John A. Colvin had previously transferred the property to C.C. Colvin for cash but that the deed had been lost and not recorded.

Several documents were entered into evidence. In 1899, C.C. Colvin alone sold timber off the land, and John A. Colvin signed as a witness to the transaction. In 1937, C.C. Colvin's heirs received a judgment of possession recognizing their ownership of the entire property, and that judgment was recorded in the conveyance records. Finally, in 1950 the Group B defendants were explicitly told by one of the Group A defendants that they did not own any interest in the property because of the transfer between John A. and C.C. Colvin. Even before that, they knew that C.C. Colvin's heirs had quitclaimed the property and were approached to sign.

The trial court found that the Group A defendants had acquired full title to the property in question by adverse possession for more than thirty years and that the Group B defendants or their ancestors had received notice more than thirty years before bringing suit. The Group B defendants appealed, arguing that they didn't receive actual notice until 1950 and that the recorded judgment of possession was insufficient to put them on notice.

Issue

Can a recorded instrument constitute notice to a co-owner that another co-owner is adversely possessing the property?

Holding & Decision

Yes, a recorded instrument can constitute sufficient notice to a co-owner that another co-owner is adversely possessing the property. The appeal court reviewed the facts adduced at trial and accepted them as unquestioned on appeal. The court then reviewed the civil code provisions governing adverse possession between co-owners, primarily articles 3439 and 3478. Under La. C.C. art. 3439 a co-owner or his universal successor begins possessing property for himself "when he demonstrates the intent by overt and unambiguous acts sufficient to give notice to his co-owner." Contrast this with precarious possessors who are not co-owners, who must give actual notice to the person for whom they previously possessed.

Under article 3478 the "recordation of a title from person other than a co-owner thus may mark the commencement of prescription." This example is illustrative. By analogy, the court reasoned, a recorded instrument is also sufficient to provide overt and unambiguous notice to other co-owners that one has begun possessing the property for himself. The instrument is objective evidence the co-owner is possessing exclusively for himself. Simultaneously, the court also noted that mere occupancy, payment of taxes, and similar physical acts alone are not sufficient to constitute notice of adverse possession against a co-owner without a recorded instrument purportedly conveying title. But even where the recorded instrument does not purport to convey title, it is sufficient to put the dispossessed co-owners on notice of the possessing party's intent.

The appeal court held that the recorded judgment of possession sending C.C. Colvin's heirs into possession of the whole property was sufficient notice of adverse possession to the other record co-owners. More importantly, however, the declarations in the quitclaim deeds serve as notice to the other co-owners that C.C. Colvin's heirs possessed for themselves under a missing deed between the Colvin brothers. Because the Group B defendants and their ancestors-in-title received notice more than thirty years before the filing of this lawsuit, the Group A defendants had acquired full title by acquisitive prescription.

As a side note, the appeal court rejected out of hand the Group B defendants' argument that the quitclaim deeds were null for want of consideration. The deeds themselves recite the payment made between the Colvin brothers as their consideration. The appeal court was not persuaded that this was insufficient consideration, especially considering the natural obligation of John A. Colvin's heirs to honor the agreement between him and C.C. Colvin.

The appeal court affirmed the lower court's judgment.

Rule of Law

A recorded instrument can constitute sufficient notice to a co-owner that another co-owner is adversely possessing the property for himself.

COCKERHAM V. COCKERHAM
Clarence (P) v. Junior (D)
16 So. 3d 1264 (La. App. 2d Cir. 2009)

Facts & Procedure

This is a dispute between members of a large family over an 80-acre tract of land acquired by their ancestor and passed down over the years. Over several generations, a large number of Cockerham family members came to own undivided interests in the property. At some point, Clarence Cockerham (P) discovered a recorded donation purporting to transfer the entirety of the tract from John Cockerham, his uncle, and his wife to John's son Junior (D) and his wife. Clarence (P) filed a petitory action 2003 to prevent Junior (D) from accruing ten-year prescription and to recognize his and his family members' interest in the property.

John moved his family onto the property in the 1950s. He inherited a 3/24 interest in the property in 1953. In 1963 he entered into an agreement with Rufus Lacy purporting to convey the entire property to John. Rufus Lacy did not own any portion of the land at that time.

Testimony at the trial indicated that the rest of the family knew John lived there but still considered the property family land. Clarence (P) used the property as his home address while at college and lived there during the summers. Over the years, various other family members had discussed building homes on the property. The family used the property for recreation, family reunions, and other purposes, and various members performed work on the property and contributed to its upkeep.

Family members received their first indication that Junior (D) believed he owned the property outright in 2003 when he distributed letters and checks detailing the property's history. He asserted that 60 acres of the land had been placed in his name in 1993 and that he owned the other 20 acres in his own name as well after a sale to and purchase from a third party.

Neither Junior (D) nor his wife testified at the trial, but they asserted that their ancestors in title, John and his wife, had acquired the entire property by cash sale in 1963. Alternatively, they argued that they had acquired the property by ten- or thirty-year prescription.

The trial court found for Clarence (P) and the other plaintiffs, recognized the undivided interest of each co-owner, and ordered that funds in the court's registry from an expropriation proceeding be distributed in accordance with the parties' ownership.

Junior (D) and Melissa appealed.

Issue

Will a co-owner necessarily begin possessing as owner for himself simply by recording an act purporting to transfer title to him?

Holding & Decision

No, in order to begin possessing property for himself, a co-owner must demonstrate his intent to do so by overt and unambiguous acts sufficient to give his co-owners notice. The recording of an instrument might be sufficient but is not necessarily sufficient on its own.

After a brief review of the facts, the appeal court rejected Junior's (D) contention that his father acquired the entire property by ten-year acquisitive prescription based on the purported purchase from Rufus Lacy. The court noted that John — as a co-owner already — should have know that Rufus Lacy did not have any interest in the property to convey. Therefore, his possession was not in good faith and could not support ten-year acquisitive prescription. The court then turned to thirty-year acquisitive prescription.

The court detailed the testimony by Clarence (P) and Patricia, Junior's (D) niece, showing that the family believed the property belonged to all of them at all the relevant times and that neither Junior (D) nor his father ever gave any indication that they were possessing it for themselves until Junior (D) distributed letters to that effect at a family reunion in 2003. This lawsuit followed shortly thereafter. Because Junior (D) and his father did not demonstrate their intent to possess for themselves, prescription never began to run against their family members until 2003, at the earliest.

The appeal court held that the trial court was not manifestly erroneous in its conclusions and affirmed its judgment.

Rule of Law

The recording of an instrument transferring title from a third party to a co-owner might be sufficient to mark the beginning of his adverse possession against his co-owners without additional action, but it is not necessarily sufficient.

NOEL V. JUMONVILLE PIPE AND MACHINERY CO.
Possessor (P) v. Record Owner (D)
245 La. 324, 158 So. 2d 179 (La. 1963)

Facts & Procedure

The Jumonville Pipe and Machinery Company (D) filed this petitory action to be recognized as the owner of a 38.8 acre tract of land adjacent to the McManor Plantation. Frank S. Noel (P) responded by filing a jactitory action, alleging his ownership and possession for more than 30 years. The actions were consolidated.

Frank S. Noel (P) was the son of Robert E. Noel, who purchased McManor Plantation in 1914, sold it in 1920, and bought it back later that same year. The title to McManor Plantation included a specific description that did not include the 38.8 acres in dispute. Robert E. Noel died in 1937, and his estate passed to his widow and eight children.

From the time of his father's death, Frank S. Noel (P) operated the plantation and the disputed acreage as one piece on behalf of his family. By virtue of several transactions, Frank S. Noel (P) came to own the entirety of McManor Plantation in 1945. He subsequently sold an undivided one-half interest to a family member. In 1953, Frank S. Noel (P) re-purchased the undivided interest in the plantation and was the sole owner by the time this lawsuit was filed.

The trial court ruled in favor of Frank S. Noel (P), finding that Robert E. Noel and Frank S. Noel (P) continuously possessed the disputed property for over thirty years, starting from 1920. Over the years, they built fences on the disputed property, grazed cattle, and requested that others not hunt on it. The trial court reasoned that Frank S. Noel's (P) possession continued his father's possession without interruption because he was his father's successor. The court was persuaded that the actual title conveyed included the disputed portion because the title included the phrase "A certain sugar plantation known as McManor Plantation," and the Noels all believed that the plantation included the disputed tract.

The Record Owner (D) appealed. The appeal court reversed the trial court's judgment because there was no privity of contract between Frank S. Noel (P) and his ancestors in title. Consequently, he could not tack his possession onto theirs and, therefore, had possessed for less than thirty years. On rehearing, the appeal court reinstated its original decree and rejected some newly raised arguments made by Frank S. Noel (P).

He (P) appealed.

Issue

Can the transfer of an estate generally described include the transfer of property not also specifically described in the title?

Holding & Decision

Yes, the transfer of an estate generally described can include the transfer of property not also included in the explicit description. The Court accepted the trial court's recitation of the facts, including the finding that the Noel family all believed the McManor Plantation included the disputed tract. Because they believed they owned the disputed land as part of their plantation and intended to transfer it to Frank S. Noel (P), the language in their transfers describing McManor Plantation generally was sufficient to transfer it to him.

Robert E. Noel's heirs were able to continue their father's possession of the disputed property as his legal successors. Frank S. Noel (P) possessed the disputed tract as owner since his father's death, initially on behalf of himself and his co-owners. After he acquired the entire ownership of the plantation, his family members gave up their undivided interest in possessing the disputed property, but Frank S. Noel (P) did not.

Because he remained in control of the whole property at all relevant times, he possessed the disputed property as owner until the trial. This possession plus his father's possession from 1920 lasted more than thirty years and was sufficient to support the plea of thirty-year acquisitive prescription.

The Court reversed the appeal court's judgment and affirmed and reinstated the trial court judgment.

Dissent

Justice McCaleb dissented, arguing that Frank S. Noel (P) could not have acquired more than a 1/12 interest in the disputed property because he succeeded only to an undivided 1/12 interest in his father's possession. The instruments transferring his co-owners' interests in the plantation to him did not include any interest they may have had in the disputed tract, so they could not provide any juridical link for Frank S. Noel (P) to tack his co-owners' possession onto his own.

Justice Sanders also dissented for similar reasons. He asserted that there is no juridical link sufficient to tack the former co-owners' possession onto Frank S. Noel's (P) possession. He specifically rejected the majority's finding that the descriptions in the conveyances between the Noel family included the disputed property by general reference to the McManor Plantation. He also rejected the notion that the language transferring "all rights, ways, servitudes, privileges, and advantages" belonging to the plantation could operate to transfer an interest in the disputed property because that language pertains to servitudes, not ownership or possession.

Rule of Law

The transfer of an estate generally described can include the transfer of property not also included in the explicit description.

BROWN V. WOOD

Record Owner (P) v. Possessors (D)
451 So. 2d 569 (La. App. 2d Cir. 1984)

Facts & Procedure

In this petitory action, the Record Owners (P) of a disputed parcel of land sued to have their ownership recognized. The disputed parcel is bordered on the south by the Possessor's (D) land and on the north by a river. The disputed parcel is divided by a highway running East and West.

The plaintiffs are indisputably the Record Owners of the property in question and traced their title to the sovereign. The defendants purchased the land to the south of the disputed tract from Ernest "Buddy" Oliveaux in 1956. From then on they corporeally possessed the disputed tract. In 1981, while this controversy was brewing, they received a quitclaim deed from Mr. Oliveaux for the portion of the disputed tract lying between the highway and the river. Both Mr. Oliveaux and the defendants enclosed a portion of the disputed property within a fence running along the South side of the highway. The property on the North side of the highway remained unfenced, but they used it to grow crops and for grazing.

The trial court ruled in favor of the Record Owners (P) and ordered the Possessors (D) to surrender possession of the entire disputed property to the Record Owners (P).

The Possessors (D) appealed.

Issue

May a person who purchases property tack his possession to that of his ancestor in title where they both possessed property beyond the title but within visible bounds?

Holding & Decision

Yes, where there is a juridical link between two people — whether through succession or contract — a person may tack his possession onto his ancestor's possession of property beyond his title within visible bounds. The appeal court found that Mr. Oliveaux had possessed beyond his title to the fence running along the south side of the highway. The court ruled that the Possessors (D) were able, under La. C.C. art. 794, to tack their possession of disputed property south of the highway onto Mr. Oliveaux's possession because they enjoyed privity of contract. Because their possession from 1956 to 1982 and Mr. Oliveaux's prior possession lasted more than thirty years, they had successfully acquired the southern part of the disputed property through prescription.

But the Possessors (D) were not able to prove at trial that they continuously possessed the property between the highway and the river. Because of the contradictory evidence in the record, the appeal court deferred to the trial court and held that the Possessors (D) did not prove their possession of the north part of the disputed property.

The appeal court rejected the Possessors' (D) argument that the 1981 quitclaim deed to the northern portion of the disputed property from Mr. Oliveaux supported their claim to it. The court held that, at the time the quitclaim was signed, Mr. Oliveaux did not have possession's to transfer to the defendants. Mr. Oliveaux and the Possessors (D) did not enjoy any juridical link with respect to the northern portion of the disputed tract, presumably because it was not possessed within visible bounds. The court ruled that possession could not be retroactively transferred through privity of contract or estate.

The appeal court affirmed the trial court's judgment with respect to portion of the disputed property north of the highway and recognized the Record Owners' (P) ownership of that property. But the appeal court reversed the trial court's judgment with respect to the portion of the disputed property lying south of the highway, and recognized the Possessors' (D) ownership of it by acquisitive prescription. Finally, the court remanded the matter to the trial court for the entry of an order according to the decision.

Rule of Law

A person may tack his possession onto his ancestor-in-title's possession of property beyond his title within visible bounds where there is a juridical link between the parties through succession or contract.

MCKEE V. HAYWARD

Niece (P) v. Uncle (D)
710 So. 2d 362 (La. App. 1st Cir. 1998)

Facts & Procedure

In this family dispute over heirlooms, Joan Renken McKee (P) sued her uncle, Douglas Hayward (D), seeking to recover two paintings, the leaves to a table in her possession, and a watch chain and fob — all of which belonged to her mother before her death. Joan was her mother's only heir and inherited this property. Joan's (P) mother herself inherited the table and paintings but in approximately 1959 sent them to be stored at the family plantation house when Joan's (P) family moved into a smaller house.

Her Uncle (D) claimed that he owned the paintings and table leaves because his mother left him all the furnishings in the family plantation house, and the items in question were among the house's furnishings. He further maintained that his mother acquired them by acquisitive prescription because they had been in her possession for years.

The Uncle (D) did not dispute his Niece's (P) ownership of the watch chain and fob but claimed ignorance of their whereabouts. About a week before Joan's (P) mother's died, she requested that her mother and brother (D) visit her deathbed and bring the watch chain and fob to her. The Uncle (D) did as asked, showed the chain and fob to Joan's (P) mother, and returned them to his pocket before leaving. Joan (P) never saw them again.

The trial court rejected the Uncle's (D) plea of prescription and held that the items belonged to his sister. Therefore, they could not be bequeathed to him by his mother. The trial court ordered the Uncle (D) to give the table leaves and paintings to his Niece (P) within sixty days of the judgment. If he did not do so, the court ordered that Joan be allowed to search the family plantation house at a time of her choosing. The court also ordered that the Niece (P) be allowed to search the plantation house at a time of her choosing for the watch chain and fob.

The Uncle (D) appealed.

Issue

Can a person who possesses movable property for the convenience of another acquire that property by prescription?

Holding & Decision

No, possession for the convenience of another gives the possessor neither legal possession nor the right to prescribe. Here, the appeal court declined to overturn the trial court's factual determination that Joan's (P) mother sent the table leaves and paintings to be stored at the family's plantation house. As a result, any possession by Joan's (P) grandmother was for the convenience of Joan's (P) mother and insufficient to support acquisitive prescription. Joan's (P) grandmother could not be bequeath items she did not own to Joan's Uncle (D) and, therefore, they still belonged to Joan (P).

But the appeal court did take issue with part of the trial court's judgment. Specifically, the appeal court held that contempt was the appropriate remedy if the Uncle (D) refused to give his Niece (P) the paintings and table leaves, not the equitable remedy allowing her to search the house. On the other hand, there was no such remedy at law where the watch chain and fob were concerned, so the equitable search remedy was appropriate.

Rule of Law

Possession for the convenience of another gives the possessor neither legal possession nor the right to prescribe.

SUCCESSION OF WAGNER
993 So. 2d 709 (La. App. 1st Cir. 2008)

Facts & Procedure

Louis and Leila Wagner died within nine months of one another, leaving two children: Warren and Faye. Louis's testament left his entire estate to Warren and named him executor. Leila's testament left a bequest to a grandchild and the remainder of her estate to Fay, who she named executrix. The successions were administered separately but judicially consolidated for purposes of classifying certain property in the estates as separate or community.

Just under two years before his death, Louis donated $450,000 of gold coins to Warren by written act. The record revealed that Warren himself wrote the check for his father from a joint bank account. Nevertheless, Warren testified that his father told him he purchased the coins with separate funds. Louis did have substantial separate assets that he inherited from his brother. Finally, Louis concealed the donation from his wife and asked Warren to do the same. He complied, not admitting that he had received the coins until compelled to do so by discovery requests in the succession proceedings.

Faye disputed that the coins were her father's separate property and demanded that they be split between the two estates. Under Louisiana law, unusual donations of community property must be made with the concurrence of both spouses to be valid. Warren maintained that, even if the coins had not been his father's separate property to donate, he had acquired them by three-year good-faith acquisitive prescription.

The trial court found that the coins were purchased with community property and, therefore, could not be donated without Leila's consent. Further, the court rejected Warren's prescription claim, concluding that he did not act in good faith, particularly when he conspired with his father to conceal the donation from Leila. This determination went up on appeal along with other issues.

Issue

Is a donee possessing property in good faith when he knows that the donor concealed the donation of community assets from his spouse?

Holding & Decision

No. The donation of community property requires the consent of both spouses, so a donee is not in good faith when he knows such a donation was concealed from one spouse. The appeal court accepted the trial court's factual findings. Because Warren knew that the coins were paid for — at least in part — by community funds and he conspired with his father to conceal the donation, there was no manifest error in the trial court's holding rejecting good-faith acquisitive prescription.

Rule of Law

A donee who knows that the donor concealed the donation of community assets from his spouse does not possess that property in good faith.

LIEBER V. MOHAWK ARMS, INC.
Soldier (P) v. Collector (D)
64 Misc. 2d 206, 314 N.Y.S. 2d 510 (Sup. Ct. of N.Y. 1970)

Facts & Procedure

The plaintiff's Army unit occupied Munich during the second world war. He returned home to Louisiana with spoils of war, including Hitler's uniform jacket, cap, some decorations, and personal jewelry. The collection was well known and publicized. Some of the articles were also occasionally displayed to the public.

Decades later, the plaintiff's chauffeur stole the collection and sold it to a dealer in New York. The dealer sold it in turn to the Collector (D) in this case. The Collector (D) purchased the items in good faith. Shortly thereafter, the Soldier (P) tracked the collection down. He demanded the return of the property and filed this lawsuit when the Collector (D) refused.

Both parties filed motions for summary judgment. The Collector (D) resisted summary judgment and filed a cross-motion for summary judgment, arguing that the Soldier (P) never acquired good title of his own and that the items properly belonged to the Bavarian Government instead.

Issue

Does a person who openly and notoriously possesses spoils of war for more than ten years acquire ownership of them through acquisitive prescription?

Holding & Decision

Yes, a person who openly and notoriously possesses spoils of war for more than ten years acquires ownership of them. The trial court noted that this defense — title in a third party — was no longer sufficient under New York law. Instead, chattel is to be returned to the party who proves the superior right of possession. The court held that the Collector (D) had no title because its possession was derived from a thief. The Soldier's (P) possession was public and unquestioned from 1945 to 1968. Under Louisiana law, a person acquires ownership of movables by ten-year acquisitive prescription, regardless of his good or bad faith.

Rule of Law

A person who openly and notoriously possesses spoils of war for more than ten years acquires ownership of them.

Chapter 10

Protection of Ownership; Real Actions

1. "The **petitory action** is one brought by a person who claims the ownership of, but who does not have the right to possess, immovable property or a real right therein, against another who is in possession or who claims the ownership thereof adversely, to obtain judgment recognizing the plaintiff's ownership" or other real right. La. C.C.P. art. 3651.

   a) **Parties**. The following people may be parties to a petitory action:

      i. One claiming full ownership of the immovable.

      ii. One claiming an undivided interest in the immovable or real right therein.

      iii. One whose claim to ownership is limited to a certain period that has not yet lapsed or that may be terminated by a future event.

      iv. As a defendant, a lessee or other person enjoying use of the property or real right through an agreement with the person claiming ownership against the plaintiff. La. C.C.P. art. 3652.

   b) The petitory action is not available to a party in possession of the immovable.

   c) **Proof of ownership.** The burden of proof placed on a plaintiff in the petitory action depends on whether the defendant possesses the disputed immovable or neither party possesses it. La. C.C. art. 531; La. C.C.P. art. 3653.

      i. **Defendant in possession: ownership good against the world.** When the defendant possesses the disputed property the plaintiff must prove that he has acquired ownership from a previous owner or by acquisitive prescription. If both titles derive from a common ancestor, that person is presumed to be the previous owner.

         A. In a petitory action against a defendant in possession, the plaintiff must make out his title good against the world to the property claimed and must recover upon the strength of his own title rather than the weakness of the defendant's. The defendant's title is not at issue until the plaintiff has proved valid title in himself. *Deselle v. Bonnette.*

         B. A plaintiff in a petitory action where the defendant is in possession of the disputed property must make out a perfect chain of record title or show that he acquired title by acquisitive prescription. *Pure Oil Company v. Skinner.*

         C. A plaintiff can demonstrate perfect record title by showing acquisition from a previous owner, which either means proving perfect record title back to the sovereign or to the a common author, where the defendant has a title. *Weaver v. Hailey.*

155

    D. It is not sufficient for a petitory action plaintiff to trace his title back to a judicially recognized tax sale purchaser because a tax sale indicates that there has been prior private ownership, so it is not a chain of title back to the sovereign. *Baker v. Romero.*

    E. **Publican action.** The standard set out in *Pure Oil Company v. Skinner* and by statute is very harsh and can cause injustice. For example, if a person has an imperfect title containing a gap in its history, he or she can be permanently dispossessed without recourse by a squatter who possesses for a year. Roman law recognized the publican action to avoid injustice in such a case by permitting a former possessor who had accrued some time toward acquisitive prescription to prevail over a squatter. In essence, the action allowed a person to prove better possession instead of perfect title where justice required. The Louisiana State Law Institute has declined to introduce similar provisions in Louisiana Law, so the *Pure Oil* rule remains in force.

  ii. **Neither in possession: better title.** A plaintiff in a petitory action must show that he has a title and that his title is better than the other claimant's title if neither party is in possession of the disputed property. *Kelso v. Lange.*

    A. "Better title" is a nebulous concept, but some factors that might give one title an edge include

- A more ancient title,
- A more precise description,
- A relevant plat attached to the title,
- Extrinsic evidence referenced in the titles, e.g. references to roads or other monuments that lend specificity,
- A history of paying taxes on the property, or
- References to the property that demonstrate a connection to the parties in documents like succession proceedings, other titles, financial documents, or other articles. *See Griffin v. Daigle*

  iii. **Common ancestor in title.** A plaintiff in a petitory action who traces his title back to an author in common with the defendant need only prove his title back to the common author. *Nelsen v. Cox.*

  d) **Imprescriptibility.** The petitory action is imprescriptible because "[o]wnership exists independently of its exercise and may not be lost by nonuse. Ownership is lost when acquisitive prescription accrues in favor of an adverse possessor." La. C.C. art. 481.

2. **Revendicatory action** The revendicatory action is an innominate real action brought by the owner of a corporeal movable in another's possession for its return and for the recognition of his ownership or other real right. La. C.C. art. 526

  a) There is no distinct possessory action for movables. *Cf.* petitory vs possessory actions for immovables.

  b) "The possessor of a corporeal movable is presumed to be its owner. The previous possessor of a corporeal movable is presumed to have been its owner during the period of his possession." La. C.C. art. 530.

  c) **Lost or stolen movables.**

i. The prior possessor may bring the revendicatory action against the current possessor of a lost or stolen movable.

ii. "The owner of a lost or stolen movable may recover it from a possessor who bought it in good faith at a public auction or from a merchant customarily selling similar things on reimbursing the purchase price." La. C.C. art. 524. *See also* La. C.C. art. 520.

    A. A good-faith buyer who buys a stolen item on consignment with a merchant who customarily sells similar items is entitled to the reimbursement of the purchase price by the true owner, even though the item was never transferred to or from the merchant. *Southeast Equipment Co. v. Office of State Police.*

iii. The revendicatory action is not available when a lost or stolen thing is sold by authority of law; the former owner no longer has the right to the return of the movable. La. C.C. art. 524.

iv. A movable transferred as a result of fraud is not stolen, and the perpetrator may convey the movable to another. La. C.C. art. 521. Assuming the ultimate receiver acquires the movable in good faith and for a fair price, the original owner will have no right to the return of the movable. Fraud could vitiate the conveyor's consent for the first transaction but it is irrelevant to the second transaction. La. C.C. art. 522.

v. A thief, finder, or usurper of a movable may not bring an action against subsequent possessor.

d) **Burden of proof and presumptions.** The plaintiff bears the burden of proving ownership by proving a transfer from a previous owner, by accession, or by acquisitive prescription. The defendant may rely on the presumption that he, as possessor, is the owner of a corporeal movable, but this presumption is ineffective if the plaintiff was dispossessed by loss or theft. La. C.C. art. 530. In that case, the burden shifts to the defendant to prove the plaintiff was not the movable's owner or that he lost ownership. Precarious possessors like lessees do not benefit from the presumption of ownership.

e) **Defenses.** A defendant who has a real right to retain the movable will prevail, e.g., if the defendant is owner, usufructuary, or the transferee of the object.

f) A prevailing plaintiff is entitled to the recognition of his ownership, an order for the delivery of the movable, and for the fruits of the movable. The owner must reimburse the possessor for expenses incurred in producing the fruits before regaining the movable. La. C.C. art. 486.

g) **Imprescriptibility.** The revendicatory action is not subject to liberative prescription because it is a real action rather than a personal action. *Songbyd v. Bearsville Records, Inc.*

3. **Boundary action.** The boundary action is a nominate action for a court to fix the boundary between two contiguous parcels of land. A judgment in the boundary action both recognizes the prevailing party's ownership of the land and identifies the boundary between the parties' lands.

    a) "The boundary may be fixed upon the demand of an owner or of one who possesses as owner. It may also be fixed upon the demand of a usufructuary but it is not binding upon the naked owner unless he has been made a party to the proceeding." La. C.C. art. 786.

    b) The boundary action may be cumulated with other actions, including the petitory action.

c) If neither party proves ownership, the boundary is fixed by the limits of possession, and the judgment should not determine ownership.

d) Where both parties rely on titles only (as opposed to acquisitive prescription) the boundary is fixed by title.

e) If either party proves acquisitive prescription, the boundary is fixed by prescription over titles.

f) **Imprescriptibility.** The boundary action is imprescriptible.

g) **Res judicata.** A final judgment fixing the boundary is *res judicata* and may not be attacked for error. It may be attacked for fraud within one year of rendition.

h) **Surveys, descriptions, and calls.**

   i. A court in a boundary action may appoint an impartial surveyor to inspect the lands, prepare surveys, and give an opinion concerning the location of the boundary between contiguous estates. *Alcus v. Elliser.*

   ii. Disputed boundaries are determined in light of the parties' intention by the following calls in their titles, in order:

      A. Natural monuments,

      B. Artificial monuments,

      C. Distances,

      D. Courses, and

      E. Quantities. *Skillman v. Harvey.*

   iii. Where titles and surveys conflict, the court should consider all the evidence to determine the correct place to fix the boundary. In general, conflicts between a written description and a survey are resolved in favor the survey unless the survey is obviously wrong. And where two parties share a common ancestor in title, the more ancient title prevails. *Roy v. Belt.*

i) Under La. C.C. art. 794, a purchaser may tack its possession onto that of its vendor to prove acquisitive prescription beyond the limits of the title to visible bounds and to fix the boundary accordingly. *Loutre Land and Timber Company v. Roberts.*

4. **Boundary agreement.** A boundary may also be fixed extrajudicially by agreement. Such an agreement operates either as a confirmation of an existing boundary or as a conveyance of ownership up to the line between the landowners. It is effective against third parties when filed for registry in the public records.

   a) The placement of markers on the ground by contiguous landowners without a written agreement is not a boundary agreement and does not legally fix the boundary. But the markers may give one owner grounds to claim thirty-year acquisitive prescription after sufficient time passes.

   b) An agreement that makes reference to boundary markers on the ground and contains an error concerning the location of the boundary or of the markers may be a relative nullity. This error suffices for rescission. A party to the agreement may seek to annul the agreement within five years from the discovery of the error.

   c) Other errors may give rise to a ten-year liberative prescription for the reformation of the agreement to correct errors in the agreement.

DESELLE V. BONNETTE
Alleged Owner (P) v. Possessor (D)
251 So. 2d 68 (La. App. 3d Cir. 1971)

Facts & Procedure

The subject of this petitory action is a 65' strip of land between an abandoned highway and its replacement. The parties are neighbors who share a common ancestor in title. Their common ancestor in title sold a 36 acre tract in 1911, dividing it into two tracts, one on either side of the highway. The plaintiff's ancestors in title owned the part east of the highway, and the defendants' ancestors in title owned the part west of the highway. The highway was abandoned around 1920, and a new highway was built about 65' west of the old highway. The plaintiff claims ownership of the strip between the old and new highways, but the defendant is in possession of it.

Plaintiff's ancestor Marius acquired the 12 arpents lying east of the old highway. In 1926, after the old highway had been abandoned, Marius transferred "12 arpents and being all the land belonging to the vendor on the east side of the public road ... being the same acquired by the vendor," to the plaintiff's father without any mention that the highway had moved since Marius acquired the land. The plaintiff eventually acquired half of the property from his mother's estate and the other half directly from his father. His father transferred "12 acres, more or less, bounded ... [on the] west by public road" to him in 1945.

The trial court held that the defendant had no title to the disputed strip because his deed described the property as "located on the ... blacktopped highway" and the old highway was not blacktopped. The trial court reasoned that, since the plaintiff's 1945 property description was bounded by the public road, presumably the new highway, the plaintiff's title was better. The trial court rendered judgment in favor of the plaintiff, and the defendant appealed.

Issue

Has the plaintiff in a petitory action met his burden of proof against a defendant in possession of disputed property if he proves a better title than the defendant without proving valid title against the world?

Holding & Decision

No, when a plaintiff in the petitory action is not in possession of the disputed property, he must make out his title against the entire world before the defendant's title becomes an issue.

The appeal court noted that the trial court based its decision on old law that had been overruled by the Code of Civil Procedure. The Code of Civil Procedure joined the previous Code of Practice's petitory action (used to assert title when the plaintiff was not in possession) with the jurispruden-tially created action to establish title (used when neither party was in possession). Under the Code of Civil Procedure, the burden of proof is determined by the defendant's possession of the disputed property. If the defendant is not in possession of the disputed property, the plaintiff need only prove better title than the defendant. But as here, when the defendant is in possession, the plaintiff needs to "make out his title" good against the whole world. Prior law distinguished between a defendant possessing with and without an act translative of title; that distinction was abandoned in the Code of Civil Procedure.

Applying the Code of Civil Procedure, the appeal court held that the plaintiff did not make out his title against the whole world, reasoning that his ancestors in title had no right to expand their titles beyond the old highway that formed the boundary of the first transfer from the parties' common author.

Thus the appeal court reversed the trial court's decision.

Rule of Law

In a petitory action against a defendant in possession, the plaintiff must make out his title good against the world to the property claimed and must recover upon the strength of his own title rather than the weakness of the defendant's. The defendant's title is not at issue until the plaintiff has proved valid title in himself.

PURE OIL COMPANY V. SKINNER
Oil Company (P) v. Concursus Claimants (D)
294 So. 2d 797 (La. 1974)

Facts & Procedure

The Pure Oil Company (P) deposited oil, gas, and mineral lease royalties attributable to a piece of disputed property into the registry of the court in a concursus proceeding. The claimants filed a boundary action against one another over the disputed property, and the parties all stipulated that the judgment in the concursus proceeding would determine the boundary issues as well.

The Concursus Claimants (D) claimed the property under two chains of title. The lower courts determined that no party had a valid record title to the property in dispute. One party, the relators in the Louisiana Supreme Court, had been in possession of the property since 1947.

The Second Circuit appeal court held that a party in a petitory action need only prove better title in order to be recognized as owner of disputed property. The Louisiana Supreme Court reviewed the decision because it conflicted with the Third Circuit's decision in *Deselle v. Bonnette*, which held that a plaintiff in a petitory action against a defendant in possession must make out his title against the world without regard for the weakness of the possessor's title.

Issue

May a plaintiff in a petitory action against a defendant in possession of the disputed property prove his title by showing that his title is better than the possessor's?

Holding & Decision

No, a plaintiff in a petitory action against a defendant in possession of the disputed property must prove valid record title against the world, without regard to the title of the possessor. The Supreme Court quoted the Louisiana Code of Civil Procedure and the differing burdens of proof depending on whether the defendant was in possession of the property. The Court rejected the respondents' argument that they had acquired title by acquisitive prescription before the relators took possession of the disputed tract because it was unsupported by the record and not part of the judgments below. The Court then held that the relators failed to establish their title in the property in dispute. The Court also explicitly overruled *Hutton v. Adkins*, 186 So. 908 (La. App. 2d Cir. 1939), a case relied upon by the Second Circuit that held that relators were only required to prove better title.

The Supreme Court reversed the appeal court's decision.

Dissent

Justice Summers noted that the only defect in the Relator's chain of title is a missing link between the U.S. Government's grant to one person and his transfer to another person sixteen years later, in 1874. Since 1874 the chain of title is flawless, and there was no question of ownership until the respondents enclosed the disputed land with a fence in 1947.

The Justice noted that the requirement that a plaintiff out of possession show a perfect title when the defendant has no better title to assert is nearly impossible in cases like this one and unfair. He concluded that the relators made out a good, valid, and perfect title against every title opposed to it, despite the small break in the title chain due to lost records. The majority opinion, he argued, will create many problems and seriously impair the stability of titles in Louisiana.

Rule of Law

By statute, a plaintiff in a petitory action where the defendant is in possession of the disputed property must make out a perfect chain of record title or show that he acquired title by acquisitive prescription.

WEAVER V. HAILEY

Putative Owner (P) v. Possessors (D)
416 So. 2d 311 (La. App. 3d Cir. 1982)

Facts & Procedure

In this petitory action, the Putative Owner (P) filed a lawsuit seeking recognition of his ownership of a single acre he possessed out of a 40 acre tract. The Possessors (D) were in possession of the entire 40 acre tract, including the disputed one acre. They filed an answer to the lawsuit alleging that they owned the one acre in dispute by both 10 and 30 year acquisitive prescription but did not file a reconventional demand seeking recognition of their ownership.

At trial, the Putative Owner (P) proved his record title back to a 1946 transfer to one of his ancestors. He did not prove his title back to the sovereign, back to a author in common with the defendants, or by acquisitive prescription.

The trial court recognized the Possessors' (D) ownership of 39 of the 40 acres and recognized the plaintiff as the owner of the disputed acre.

The Possessors (D) appealed.

Issue

1. Can a person prevail on a petitory action by proving his record title back over thirty years if he does not prove it back to the sovereign, to an author in common with a possessor's title, and by acquisitive prescription?

2. Can a defendant be recognized as the owner of property if he only alleged acquisitive prescription as a defense rather than filing a reconvention demand praying for the recognition of his ownership?

Holding & Decision

1. No, under the 1980 revision of Civil Code article 531, a plaintiff in the petitory action in which the defendant possesses the disputed property "must prove that he has acquired ownership from a previous owner or by acquisitive prescription." The Third Circuit analyzed the 1980 amendment and concluded that the legislature did not intend to legislatively overrule the controlling jurisprudential rule set out in *Pure Oil Company v. Skinner*. Thus, the phrase "must prove that he acquired ownership from a previous owner" was meant by the legislature to retain the Pure Oil Company rule, viz., that a plaintiff must prove perfect record title to the sovereign. Civil Code article 532 provides that a common author of disputed titles is presumed to be a previous owner, so in that case a plaintiff need only prove perfect record title back to the common author. Because the Putative Owner (P) only proved his title back to a previous owner who was not a common author, he failed to prove his title sufficiently to prevail on the petitory action.

2. Yes, Louisiana courts are empowered to render any relief to which a party proved it would be entitled, whether or not they explicitly requested it because Louisiana is a fact-pleading state and does not require any technical pleading. After concluding that the plaintiff failed to make his case, the court held that it could render judgment recognizing the defendants' ownership of the disputed property if they proved it. The court recognized that the Possessors (D) had the good faith required to prove acquisitive prescription of ten years when they acquired the property, despite eventually learning that the Putative Owner (P) claimed one acre. The appeal court noted that there was no proof in the record sufficient to accurately describe the one acre in dispute even if they were to render a judgment concerning it. Finally, the court noted that

the 39 acres not in dispute were not the subject of this litigation, so the trial court lacked the authority to render a judgment concerning it.

Thus, the appeal court reversed the trial court's judgment and rendered judgment in favor of the defendants against the plaintiffs dismissing their lawsuit.

Rule of Law

1. A plaintiff in the petitory action in which the defendant possesses the disputed property must prove that he has acquired ownership by acquisitive prescription or from a previous owner, which means either proving perfect record title back to the sovereign or to a common author.

2. Louisiana courts are empowered to render any relief to which a party proves it is entitled, including the recognition of ownership by acquisitive prescription without an explicit demand, because Louisiana is a fact-pleading state.

BAKER V. ROMERO

Record Owner (P) v. Neighbors (D)
55 So. 3d 1035 (La. App. 3d Cir. 2011)

Facts & Procedure

In this petitory action, the Record Owner (P) purchased a forty-foot strip of property from six of her relatives for a purchase price of $10. She then notified the Neighbors (D) of her purchase, and this lawsuit followed when they refused to allow her surveyors to access land they claimed to own.

This lawsuit began as a request for injunctive relief, and the Neighbors (D) eventually allowed the requested survey. It revealed that the disputed property was not within their title, and the Record Owner (P) amended her petition to a petitory action. The Neighbors (D) filed a reconventional demand asserting that they had possession of the disputed property for more than a year and that they owned the disputed property.

At trial, the court found that the Record Owner (P) failed to make out her title to the disputed property, that the neighbors (D) had possessed the property since 1988, and that the Record Owner's (P) motion for summary judgment had converted the Neighbors' (D) reconventional possessory action to a petitory action. Along the way, the Neighbors (D) abandoned their ownership claims and maintained only their possessory action. The trial court rendered judgment in favor of the Neighbors (D) against the Record Owner (P) dismissing her petitory action and granting their possessory action.

The Record Owner (P) moved for a new trial, arguing that her burden of proof changed from proving better title than the Neighbors (D) when they asserted the petitory action to proving title good against the world when they abandoned that action in favor of the possessory action. The court granted a retrial to allow the introduction of new evidence to meet the higher burden. After, the court again found that the Record Owner (P) failed to meet her burden of proof on the petitory action and maintained its prior judgment.

The Record Owner (P) appealed the judgment.

Issue

1. Does a party waive the possessory action when it files a reconventional demand asserting ownership of disputed property?

2. Must a plaintiff in the petitory action prove his title against the world when the disputed property is in the defendants' possession?

3. In a petitory action, is it sufficient to prove title back to a former owner recognized by a court after a tax sale purchase?

Holding & Decision

1. Yes, when a person pleads the petitory and possessory actions in the same suit or pleads them in the alternative, he waives the possessory action. Similarly, if a plaintiff brings the possessory action and later institutes the petitory action in the same suit, the possessory action is abated. The Record Owner (P) argued on appeal that the trial court erred by allowing the Neighbors (D) to maintain the possessory action after asserting ownership of the disputed property.

   The appeal court noted that the Neighbors (D) initially claimed ownership of the disputed property but acknowledged that the property was outside their title after the survey and maintained only a claim of possession. Their reconventional demand prayed for the court to recognize their right to possess the disputed property, and they stipulated that they did not have title to the Property. The appeal court held that the Neighbors (D) did not claim ownership so they did not waive their possessory claims.

Further, the Record Owner (P) failed to argue in the court below that the burden of proving ownership should have been on the Neighbors (D) as plaintiffs in a petitory action. Thus the issue was not properly before the appeal court.

2. Yes, a plaintiff in the petitory action must prove his title against the world when the defendant is in possession of the disputed property. The appeal court reaffirmed that the *Pure Oil* standard applied to this case and noted that the it had already reaffirmed that holding in *Aymond v. Smith*, 476 So.2d 1081 (La. App. 3d Cir. 1985).

    The court distinguished this case from *Badeaux v. Pitre*, 382 So.2d 954 (La. 1980) (a Louisiana Supreme Court opinion issued after *Pure Oil* in which a petitory action plaintiff was only required to prove better title than the possessor) because that case involved a precarious possessor possessing the property with the owner's permission. Here, the Neighbors (D) believed they had purchased a tract that included the disputed strip, which was unmarked, and had no indication that anyone else claimed the disputed property until the Record Owner's (P) letter that precipitated these proceedings.

3. No, it is not sufficient for a petitory action plaintiff to trace his title back to a judicially recognized tax sale purchaser. The appeal court approvingly cited the trial court's reasoning that a tax sale indicates previous private ownership so is not a chain of title back to the sovereign as required by law. There could be no common ancestor because the Neighbors (D) did not claim ownership, only possession, and the Record Owner (P) did not claim to have accrued acquisitive prescription of the property.

Therefore the appeal court found that the trial court properly applied the law and affirmed the trial judgment in its entirety.

Rule of Law

1. When a person pleads the petitory and possessory actions in the same suit or pleads them in the alternative, he waives the possessory action. Similarly, if a plaintiff brings the possessory action and later institutes the petitory action in the same suit, the possessory action is abated.

2. A plaintiff in the petitory action must prove his title against the world when the defendant is in possession of the disputed property.

3. It is not sufficient for a petitory action plaintiff to trace his title back to a judicially recognized tax sale purchaser because a tax sale indicates that there has been prior private ownership, so it is not a chain of title back to the sovereign.

KELSO V. LANGE

George-Felonese Kelsos (P) v. George-Marie Kelsos (D)
421 So. 2d 973 (La. App. 3d Cir. 1982)

Facts & Procedure

In this petitory action, no party possessed the disputed tract of approximately 165 acres of marshland. The defendants did not file a reconventional demand for recognition of their ownership. Nevertheless, both plaintiffs and defendants claimed ownership of the disputed tract through a George Y. Kelso who purchased the property in 1876, but neither set of parties could definitively trace their title to him. No party proved ownership by acquisitive prescription, and it seems that the property was never legally possessed or used by anyone at all because it is completely enclosed by other landowners' property and has a bayou splitting it diagonally.

The plaintiffs descend from the George Y. Kelso who married Felonese Kelso in 1887. The defendants descend from the George Y. Kelso who married Marie Baillio in 1869. It appeared that the two George Y. Kelsos were different people rather than the same person who married twice during his lifetime.

In 1876, a George Y. Kelso purchased the tract. The transfer does not list his marital status, and there is no recorded transaction from the purchaser to anyone else. Neither group of parties presented any evidence to show that their ancestor George Y. Kelso was this purchaser.

The George-Felonese Kelsos (P) presented evidence that a family member of theirs remembered helping survey the disputed property in 1944. A family member also testified that she remembered her father telling her that her grandfather purchased the disputed property. And several members of the George-Felonese Kelsos (P) attempted to or did pay the taxes on the property several times over the years, but they stopped after learning someone else was paying them. No succession in the George-Felonese Kelso (P) family ever listed the property as an asset.

But the George-Marie Kelsos (D) showed that the disputed property was listed as an asset in their ancestor's succession. Their record title begins in the Succession of Marie A. Mitchell, who was the daughter of George and Marie Kelso. Since the 1920s, the tax notices for the disputed property have been sent to members of the George-Marie Kelso family (D), and the George-Marie Kelsos have transferred and encumbered the property over the years through timber sales, mineral leases, rights-of-way, and succession transfers.

The trial court found in favor of the George-Felonese Kelsos (P) because they established the best claim to the property. The defendants appealed.

Issue

Can a plaintiff in a petitory action where neither party possesses the disputed property prevail if he has shown no evidence of a record title?

Holding & Decision

No, a plaintiff in a petitory action must show that his title is better than the other claimant's title if neither party is in possession of the disputed property. This burden of proof implies that the plaintiff must show some title.

Here, the appeal court found that the George-Felonese Kelsos (P) did not prove any title to the disputed property, let alone better title than the defendants. The court noted that the plaintiffs have no record title to the property and that they presented no evidence to suggest that the George Y. Kelso who purchased the property in 1876 was their ancestor. Finally, the George-Felonese Kelsos (P) failed to show that the George Y. Kelso married to Felonese ever considered the property to be his or that he ever treated it so. The court considered it most damaging that none of their ancestors listed the property in their successions. Therefore, the George-Felonese Kelsos (P) failed to demonstrate any title to the property.

Because the plaintiffs failed to prove any title and because the defendants did not reconvene for recognition of their ownership, the appeal court did not consider whether the George-Marie Kelsos (D) proved better title or were entitled to ownership of the property. But the court did note that the defendants' ancestors had seen fit to claim and treat the property as their own since at least 1916.

The appeal court reversed the trial court's judgment and rendered judgment in favor of the defendants to reject the plaintiffs claims.

Rule of Law

A plaintiff in a petitory action must show that he has a title and that his title is better than the other claimant's title if neither party is in possession of the disputed property.

GRIFFIN V. DAIGLE

Western Landowner (P) v. Eastern Landowner (D)
769 So. 2d 720 (La. App. 1st Cir. 2000)

Facts & Procedure

The parties in this petitory action share a common ancestor in title because their properties were partitioned from a larger tract. The lots were partitioned in 1941 along the "public road" dividing them north to south. In the 1930s, a road called the New Hope-Whitaker Springs Road ran through the properties. It was reworked and renamed Morris Road between 1932 and 1935. Morris Road generally follows the same roadbed as the New Hope-Whitaker Springs Road but abandoned the old roadbed to jog to the west in one area. The area between the old roadbed and the present Morris Road is claimed by both the Western Landowner (P) and the Eastern Landowner (D).

The Western Landowner's (P) chain of title includes a clarifying parenthetical introduced in a 1955 transfer that describes his property as bordered on the east by the "public road (New Hope-Whitaker)," and in all the transfers leading to his acquisition.

The Western Landowner (P) petitioned for declaratory judgment recognizing his ownership of the disputed property, setting the eastern boundary of his property as the center of the old roadbed, and reforming the Eastern Landowner's (D) recorded title to reflect the judgment. The parties converted the lawsuit to a petitory action by stipulation.

At trial, the Eastern Landowner (D) testified that he assumed Morris Road was his western boundary. He also testified that there was an old fence and a drainage area between the fence and Morris Road.

The court heard testimony from Helen Spillman Miller, the Eastern Landowner's (D) direct ancestor in title, who claimed that she historically crossed the disputed portion of the property to access other property and that, after the Western Landowner (P) purchased his land, her family members crossed the disputed property to go hunting. She identified the gap in the fence where they crossed, but it appeared that the gap was not in the disputed area. She also testified that she had timber harvested from her property. When the logging trucks pushed through the fence onto the disputed property, the Western Landowner (P) confronted her and demanded she sign a servitude agreement. She did not sign it and had the fence reinstalled in the same place along with a gate south of the disputed area directly on Morris Road. Ms. Miller's children testified that they had crossed the disputed area a dozen or two times but not for a few years before the trial, opting instead to use the new gate on Morris Road.

Ms. Miller's brother testified that he advised his sister not to sign the servitude because she owned the disputed land, that the fence had been inside the old road for as long as he could remember, and that the old roadbed was more like a ditch. Her brother would burn the property all the way to Morris Road when it became overgrown, and the Western Landowner (P) would complain. During one burn, an old barn burned down, and the brother pushed it to the middle of the old roadbed, to which the Western Landowner (P) also objected. The brother responded that he "didn't push it but half way" and that the property did not belong to the Western Landowner (P) anyway.

The Western Landowner (P) testified that he did not know of any acts of possession by the Eastern Landowner (D) or his ancestors in title other than the use of the disputed area to move logging trucks. He recorded a survey showing the old roadbed as the eastern boundary of his property in 1998, before the Eastern Landowner (D) purchased the property and recorded his survey.

The trial court rendered judgment setting as Morris Road as the boundary between the properties, and Western Landowner (P) appealed.

Issue

How does the plaintiff in a petitory action prove better title when the parties derive their titles from a common author?

Holding & Decision

The plaintiff in a petitory action can prove better title traced to a common author in several ways: by showing that his title is more ancient, that his property description is more precise than his opponent's, that a plat of survey attached to his title shows he owns the disputed property, or that extrinsic evidence supports his ownership claim.

The appeal court noted that the trial court did not follow the procedural or substantive law of petitory actions in reaching its decision, found legal error in the decision, and conducted a *de novo* review of the matter.

Initially, the court found that the Eastern Landowner (D) and his predecessors possessed the property up to the fence along the old roadbed. The evidence did not suggest anyone crossed the disputed land. The court also noted that Ms. Miller's brother's burning of the disputed property seemed more likely a result of his inability to control the burn than an intentional act of ownership and that pushing the burned barn only halfway into the old road suggested that he recognized the Western Landowner's (P) claim to the other half and the disputed property.

The court found that the Western Landowner (P) challenged everyone else's acts of possession in the disputed property and publicly asserted his claim of ownership to the disputed property by recording the survey showing the old roadbed as his eastern boundary in 1998.

The court found that the Eastern Landowner (D) and his predecessors failed to establish continuous, uninterrupted, public, and unequivocal possession of the disputed area. Since the defendant was not in possession, the Western Landowner (P) bore the burden of proving better title to the disputed area to carry his petitory action.

The court noted several factors that suggest one title traced from a common author is better than another. First, the more ancient title is the better title. This factor did not apply here because the transfers to the parties' ancestors in title happened simultaneously in a partition. Second, the more precise title is the better title. This approach did not apply here because both titles used the same ambiguous reference to the "public road." Third, if there are differences between the textual description and a plat of survey, the survey controls. Again, this rule of thumb was not dispositive because the partition contained a rough sketch without enough precision to determine which "public road" was the boundary in the disputed area.

Because the partition description was ambiguous, the court looked to extrinsic evidence to determine the parties' intent. First, the court noted that the "public road" forming the majority of the boundary was the old road because it was an existing boundary that could not be altered by the partition and concluded that it would be logical to conclude that the old road formed the entire boundary. The partition sketch depicted only a straight line without a second roadbed or a jog near the disputed area. Second, the court noted that the parenthetical equating "public road" with "New Hope-Whitaker" in a subsequent transfer between parties to the original partition suggested that the original partition meant to use that as its boundary. Finally, the court noted that the partition used historical road names generally, because "State Highway No. 258" in the description had already been re-designated State Highway 421 at the time the instrument was executed. This description matched that in prior transfers before the partition and before the roads were renamed, suggesting that the parties intended to transfer according to the old boundaries.

The appeal court concluded that the Western Landowner (P) met his burden to establish better title and reversed the trial court's judgment. The court rendered judgment in favor of the Western Landowner (P) and declared the center of the old roadbed the boundary between the parties' properties.

Rule of Law

The plaintiff in a petitory action can prove better title traced to a common author in several ways: by showing that his title is more ancient, that his property description is more precise than his opponent's, that a plat of survey attached to his title shows he owns the disputed property, or that extrinsic evidence supports his ownership claim.

NELSEN V. COX
Heirs (P) v. Possessors (D)
2012 WL 2154253 (La. App. 1st Cir. 6/13/2012) (Unpublished)

Facts & Procedure

Henry Burton Nelsen's Heirs (P) filed this petitory action against an individual and two limited liability company defendants who claimed to have purchased a piece of property from Henry Nelsen's wife Elvira.

The Heirs (P) claim to be record owners of property by virtue of a judgment of possession in Henry Nelsen's succession recorded in 2009. That judgment declared the Heirs (P) to be the sole owners of the property, identified as Henry Nelsen's separate property that he acquired in 1942 before his marriage to Elvira.

The Possessors (D) answered the Heirs' (P) petitory action and filed a reconventional demand asserting their ownership of the property by both ten- and thirty-year acquisitive prescription. They claimed to own the property by virtue of a 2007 quitclaim deed from Elvira Nelsen Simmons, who purportedly acquired it from her husband Henry's succession in 1989. The Possessors (D) subsequently transferred the property amongst themselves. Documents submitted during the trial indicated that the Possessors (D) had tried to purchase the property from the Heirs (P) to address their claims of ownership. In correspondence, one of the Possessors (D) noted that Elvira had no interest in the property.

The Heirs (P) filed a motion for summary judgment, and the trial court granted their motion, recognizing them as the owners of the property and directing the Clerk of Court to annotate the public records accordingly. The Possessors (D) appealed.

Issue

Does a petitory action plaintiff who traces his title back to an author in common with the defendant need to make out title good against the world?

Holding & Decision

No, a plaintiff in a petitory action who traces his title back to an author in common with the defendant need only prove his title back to the common author. The appeal court noted that both sets of parties traced their titles back to Henry Nelsen and held that the Heirs (P) established their title through Henry Nelsen back to his direct ancestor in title from whom he purchased the property in 1942. They demonstrated that Elvira never acquired an interest in the property, and Henry's succession judgment showed that she only acquired an interest in Henry's community property, not the separate property at issue. Therefore, the Possessors (D) could not establish their title back to the common author.

The court also noted that the Possessors (D) could not prove possession sufficient to establish that they owned the property by acquisitive prescription. In order to acquire the property in ten years, they would have had to possess the property in good faith (in addition to tacking their possession onto Elvira's), and the record shows that the Possessors (D) knew the Heirs were the rightful owners of the property. Therefore, their possession did not commence in good faith. Similarly, in order to establish thirty-year acquisitive prescription, they would have had to tack their possession onto both Elvira's and Henry's, but there was no juridical link between their possession and Henry's.

Thus, the appeal court affirmed the trial court's judgment.

Rule of Law

A plaintiff in a petitory action who traces his title back to an author in common with the defendant need only prove his title back to the common author.

SONGBYRD V. BEARSVILLE RECORDS, INC.
Musician's Successor (P) v. Recording Company (D)
104 F. 3d 773 (5th Cir. 1997)

Facts & Procedure

Henry Roeland Byrd, more commonly known by his stage name "Professor Longhair," was a prominent New Orleans jazz musician. His popularity increased after he became a fixture at the then-new New Orleans Jazz and Heritage Festival in the early 1970s. Soon after Professor Longhair's first Jazz Fest performance, his manager Quint Davis and attorney Parker Dinkins arranged for him to make several master recordings at a recording studio in Baton Rouge.

Albert Grossman, a music producer operating Bearsville Records, Inc., (D) heard demo tapes made from these master recordings and arranged for Professor Longhair and another New Orleans musician to travel to a studio in Woodstock, New York, to record a session. For some reason, those recordings were not satisfactory. But Davis and Dinkins wanted Grossman to be able to demonstrate the master recordings from the Baton Rouge session, so they sent them to Grossman, according to their affidavit, "as demonstration tapes only, without any intent for either Albert Grossman or Bearsville Records, Inc. [(D)] to possess [them] as owner."

The tapes remained in Grossman's possession for several years before Dinkins wrote to the Recording Company (D) in 1975 to request the return of the master recordings on behalf of himself, Professor Longhair, and Davis. No one responded to either of Dinkins's requests, and no one pressed the request further.

Grossman died in the mid 1980s, and Bearsville Records, Inc., (D) dissolved. Nevertheless, Grossman's estate continued to do business as "Bearsville Records" by operating a recording studio and licensing recordings. Bearsville Records (D) licensed the master recordings of the Baton Rouge sessions to Rounder Records, which released an album including 11 tracks made from those recordings in 1987, and to Rhino Records, which released an album including 7 tracks made from those master recordings.

In 1993, SongByrd, Inc., (P) was incorporated and commenced operating as the successor-in-interest to the intellectual property of Professor Longhair and his deceased widow. Songbyrd (P) filed this lawsuit in state court in 1995 to assert its ownership of the master recording, to secure their return, and for damages. Bearsville Records (D) removed the lawsuit to federal court and moved to dismiss on the grounds that SongByrd's (P) claims were barred by liberative prescription.

The district court dismissed the case, holding that the claims were barred by liberative prescription and rejecting SongByrd's (P) claims that Bearsville Records (D) was at all times only a precarious possessor.

The plaintiff appealed.

Issue

1. Is an action for the return of movable property subject to liberative prescription?

2. Can a precarious possessor who is not a co-owner end his precarious possession by ignoring two letters requesting the return of the property?

Holding & Decision

1. No, the revendicatory action is not subject to liberative prescription. The circuit court reasoned that the district court erroneously characterized SongByrd's (P) action as a personal action. Instead, a revendicatory action — i.e., an action for the return of property to its owner — is a real action whether it relates to immovable property or personal property. An

incidental demand for damages made alongside a revendicatory action, like in this case, does not alter its classification as a real action. Under the Louisiana Civil Code, liberative prescription only applies to personal actions because ownership cannot be lost by the failure to exercise it; it can only be lost by another acquiring ownership. Thus, the circuit court held that SongByrd's (P) action was not subject to liberative prescription and therefore not prescribed.

2. No, a precarious possessor who is not a co-owner can only begin to possess for himself when he gives actual notice to the owner of his intent to do so. The circuit court noted that the district court prematurely ruled on SongByrd's (P) contention that Bearsville Records (D) was more than a precarious possessor because a precarious possessor is presumed to continue in that capacity until it begins acquisitively prescribing in accordance with law. This is an affirmative defense, and Bearsville Records (D) did not raise it before the district court.

The circuit court reversed the district court's dismissal and remanded the case for further proceedings.

Rule of Law

1. A revendicatory action is not subject to liberative prescription because it is a real action rather than a personal action.

2. A precarious possessor who is not a co-owner can only begin to possess for himself when he gives actual notice of his intent to the owner.

SOUTHEAST EQUIPMENT CO. V. OFFICE OF STATE POLICE

Buyer (P) v. Police (D)
437 So. 2d 1184 (La. App. 4th Cir. 1983)

Facts & Procedure

Southeast Equipment Company (P) purchased a stolen 1979 Caterpillar Loader for $54,000 from C. Ogle through his agent, Hattaway International Inc. Hattaway customarily sells heavy equipment like the loader in question, but in this case Ogle had placed the loader on consignment with Hattaway. At the trial, the parties stipulated that the Buyer (P) did not know the loader was stolen at the time of the sale.

Two weeks after the sale, the Louisiana State Police (D) seized the machine under a search warrant. The Buyer (P) filed a mandamus action requesting that the court order the Police (D) to return the loader. The owner of the loader when it was stolen, J.W. Conner and Son Construction Company, intervened and requested possession.

The trial court ordered the Police (D) to return the machine to the Buyer (P) as a good-faith possessor until the true owner reimbursed Southeast for the purchase price. The trial court relied on La. C.C. art. 524, which provides that "the owner of a lost or stolen movable may recover it from a possessor who bought it in good faith … from a merchant customarily selling similar things on reimbursing the purchase price."

The true owner appealed, arguing in part that La. C.C. art. 524 does not apply because the Buyer (P) purchased the loader from Ogle, not a merchant regularly selling heavy equipment.

Issue

Is a good-faith buyer who purchases an item on consignment with a merchant who customarily sells similar items entitled to the return of his purchase price by the true owner if the item turns out to be lost or stolen?

Holding & Decision

Yes, a good-faith buyer who buys a stolen item on consignment with a merchant who customarily sells similar items is entitled to the reimbursement of the purchase price by the true owner, even though the item was never transferred to or from the merchant. The appeal court noted that La. C.C. art. 524 applies as long as the sale is conducted by a merchant who customarily sells similar items, even where the merchant is acting as an agent for another. The court noted that, even though Hattaway was an agent for an individual seller, the bill of sale gave the impression that Hattaway was the seller and warrantied the title. Because the Buyer (P) purchased in good faith from a merchant customarily selling similar items, the appeal court affirmed the trial court's judgment.

Dissent

Justice Redmann dissented. He noted that the Buyer (P) tried to re-sell the loader just six days after purchasing it and that the prospective buyer readily determined that it was stolen. He reasoned that the stipulation that the Buyer (P) did not now the loader was stolen at the time of the sale was not a stipulation that the Buyer (P) was in good faith. The Buyer (P) would not have been in good faith if it knew or should have known that the loader was stolen, and it appears that the Buyer (P) at least should have known, given how readily it was discovered by another. Justice Redmann would reverse and give judgment for the true owner.

Rule of Law

A good-faith buyer who buys a stolen item on consignment with a merchant who customarily sells similar items is entitled to the reimbursement of the purchase price by the true owner, even though the item was never transferred to or from the merchant.

ALCUS V. ELLISER
Swampland Owner (P) v. Highland Owner (D)
310 So. 2d 663 (La. App. 1st Cir. 1975)

Facts & Procedure

In this boundary dispute, the parties owned contiguous pieces of ground, both previously owned by a common owner. By title, Alcus (P) owned 35 acres, more or less, of swampland situated in a tract. Elliser (D), on the other hand, had title to 15 acres, more or less, of highland in the same tract plus a better defined strip of land not relevant to the issues at hand.

In 1967, years before this litigation, the Swampland Owner (P) hired Alex Theriot to locate and determine the property line between the parties' estates. The surveyor set the boundary at the two-foot contour line. He made this determination without inspecting the property; instead he consulted academics and other surveyors.

The Swampland Owner (P) sued the Highland Owner (D) to determine the boundary and for an accounting of revenues the Highland Owner (D) received from improvements erected on the disputed property. The trial court appointed Mr. Theriot, the surveyor who earlier made the survey for the Swampland Owner (P), to survey the land and report his findings. Mr. Theriot updated his earlier survey to reflect improvements made since he originally drafted it but left the boundary where he previously determined it to be. The trial court rendered a judgment recognizing the two-foot contour line as the boundary, ordered Mr. Theriot to mark the boundary on the ground, and ordered the Highland Owner (D) to account for revenues earned below the boundary line.

The Highland Owner (D) appealed.

Issue

Can a court rely solely on a survey made without inspecting the land to judicially fix a boundary?

Holding & Decision

No, a court in a boundary action may appoint an impartial surveyor to inspect the lands, prepare surveys, and give an opinion concerning the location of the boundary between contiguous estates.

The appeal court found that no boundary survey bound was made after the trial court appointed Mr. Theriot. Instead, the surveyor merely updated his old survey and gave testimony to justify the previously determined boundary he identified for the Swampland Owner (P) years before litigation. The appeal court held that it was procedurally improper for the trial court to judicially recognize the previously determined boundary and subsequently order Mr. Theriot to survey the land and mark the boundary. The appeal court also noted that it was improper to appoint Mr. Theriot surveyor when he had predetermined the boundary for the Swampland Owner (P), but discussion of defense counsel's objection was pretermitted since procedure had not been followed.

The court remanded the matter for the appointment of another surveyor and additional proceedings, including the trial of exceptions.

Rule of Law

A court in a boundary action may appoint an impartial surveyor to inspect the lands, prepare surveys, and give an opinion concerning the location of the boundary between contiguous estates.

SKILLMAN V. HARVEY
Skillman Family (P) v. Harvey Family (D)
898 So. 2d 431 (La. App. 1st Cir. 2004

Facts & Procedure

The Skillman Family (P) owned a tract of land that shared its eastern boundary with a tract owned by the Harvey Family (D). In the Skillman Family's (P) title, the southeast corner of the property was defined by a gate in a field, and the western boundary was defined by reference to the neighbor's property line without further elaboration. The title described a parcel containing "29 acres, more or less" but contained no courses or boundary lengths. Similarly the Harvey Family's (D) title described a tract containing "thirty ... acres, more or less" and contained no courses or boundary lengths.

By the time this dispute arose, the gate no longer existed, and the Harvey Family's (D) boundary was not clearly marked. Thus it was no longer clear where the Skillman Family's (P) southern or western boundaries were. The Skillman Family (P) hired an surveyor to survey the land and determine the location of the southern and western boundary lines. The surveyed boundary described the parties' tracts such that the Skillman Family (P) had 28.94 acres, and the Harvey Family (D) had 30.31 acres.

The parties could not agree on the joint boundary, so the Skillman Family (P) filed this boundary action to establish the boundary as surveyed. The Harvey Family (D) reconvened, asserting the parties' joint boundary was an existing fence, painted line, and an old railroad embankment, which placed the boundary line farther north than claimed by the Skillman Family (P). There were approximately nine acres in dispute, and the Harvey Family (D) sought treble damages for timber cut by the Skillman Family (P) on the disputed acreage.

The trial court found that the Harvey Family (D) proved ownership of the nine acres by possession and fixed the common boundary in accordance with their reconventional demand. The court also awarded the Harvey Family (D) money damages for the timber. The Skillman Family (P) appealed, arguing that the Harvey Family (D) failed to establish their boundary by title and to show sufficient activity to acquire the land by prescription and that the court erred by awarding the defendants damage for timber the Skillman Family (P) removed from their own property.

Issue

How can one determine the extent of a title when some references in the title no longer exist?

Holding & Decision

Disputed boundaries are determined in light of the parties' intention by the following calls in their titles, in order: natural monuments, artificial monuments, distances, courses, and quantities. In this case, since there were no remaining natural monuments, artificial monuments, distances, or bearings it was necessary to use the last call: quantity.

The appeal court noted that the surveyor spoke with Mr. Harvey and used information he provided to project the joint boundary southward to yield a configuration where the Skillman Family (P) would have 28.94 acres and the Harvey Family (D) would have 30.31 acres. This was very consistent with the parties' titles calling for 29 acres, more or less, and 30 acres, more or less, respectively. The appeal court found this method to be predicated on sound surveying principles and accepted it as proof that the Skillman Family (P) owned the disputed property on the strength of their title.

The appeal court also found that the trial court was manifestly erroneous in concluding that the Harvey Family (D) acquired the disputed tract by acquisitive prescription. The surveyor hired by the Harvey Family (D) testified that he found evidence of an old fence, painted trees, and angle irons that could indicated possession by the Harvey Family (D) to that boundary. But he also testified that those signs were not necessarily external boundary markings. To the contrary, the appeal court noted that the only evidence concerning the fence showed that it was built by tenants of the Skillman Family (P) to keep livestock rather than to establish a boundary. The Harvey Family (D) did not maintain the fence, and they only occasionally walked or rode horses on the disputed land. The appeal court concluded the evidence was insufficient to support thirty-year acquisitive prescription. Similarly, the Harvey Family (D) did not demonstrate just title of the disputed tract, so they were unable to prevail on a claim of ten-year acquisitive prescription.

The appeal court reversed the trial court's judgment setting the boundary, re-set the south and west boundaries according to the Skillman Family's (P) survey, and reversed the timber damage award. The Louisiana Supreme Court denied certiorari.

Rule of Law

Disputed boundaries are determined in light of the parties' intention by the following calls in their titles, in order: natural monuments, artificial monuments, distances, courses, and quantities.

LOUTRE LAND AND TIMBER COMPANY V. ROBERTS
Timber Company (P) v. Title Owner (D)
63 So. 3d 120 (La. 2011)

Facts & Procedure

The Morgan family and the Roberts family owned adjacent tracts of land. The Morgan's 20 acre tract was north of the Roberts' 20 acre tract, and title identified a section line as their shared boundary. A fence was erected south of and parallel to the title boundary inside the Roberts' tract, and the Morgan family corporeally possessed the land up to that fence for over thirty years. The parties did not dispute that the Morgans acquired approximately fifteen acres from the Roberts' tract by thirty-year acquisitive prescription up to the fence. In addition to the 20 acre tract they owned by title and the 15 acres they owned by acquisitive prescription, the Morgans also owned an adjacent 80 acre tract, giving them approximately 115 acres together.

After Marie Wilson Morgan's death, her succession sold the 100 acres they owned by title to Loutre Land and Timber Company (P) along with "all rights of prescription, whether acquisitive or liberative, to which" the succession may have been entitled for $75,000.

Edward Roberts (D) inherited his parents' interest in his family's land south of the Morgan tract. A survey confirmed the disputed 15 acre tract fell within his title, so he sought a quitclaim deed from the Morgan succession. The succession attorney informed him that the succession had nothing left to give after selling all its rights to the Timber Company (P) but eventually conveyed to Mr. Roberts (D) whatever rights the succession may have had to the disputed tract. Mr. Roberts (D) entered the property and bush hogged a path where he planned to place a fence along the title boundary, destroying the Timber Company's (P) pine seedlings and rutting the ground.

The Timber Company (P) sued for recognition of the fence line as the boundary because the company tacked onto the possession of its ancestor in title and for damages. Roberts (D) reconvened to establish his ownership of the disputed tract to the title boundary and for compensation for lost rental income.

The Timber Company (P) won a motion for summary judgment on the boundary issue and damages after hearing. Roberts (D) appealed, and the appeal court found there was an issue of material fact whether the succession and the Timber Company (P) intended to transfer the disputed acreage in their instrument. On remand, the trial court heard testimony and ruled in the Timber Company's (P) favor again. The parties appealed again.

The appeal court noted that the Succession of Morgan was ancestor-in-title to both parties and concluded that, as a result, the public records doctrine controlled instead of the boundary articles of the Civil Code. Since Roberts's (D) quitclaim deed explicitly included the disputed tract in its title and the Timber Company's (P) title did not, the appeal court held that Roberts's (D) deed was superior. The appeal court reversed the trial court's judgment and remanded the matter for the trial court to fix the boundary in accordance with the parties' survey. The Timber Company (P) filed a writ of certiorari.

Issue

May a purchaser tack its possession onto that of its ancestor-in-title to prove acquisitive prescription beyond the limits of the title to visible bounds for boundary purposes?

Holding & Decision

Under La. C.C. art. 794, a purchaser may tack its possession onto that of its vendor to prove acquisitive prescription beyond the limits of the title to visible bounds and to fix the boundary accordingly. The Court held that La. C.C. art. 794 does not require particular title to convey acquisitive prescription rights to the land in question and that the Timber Company (P) owned the disputed tract via thirty-year acquisitive prescription through its conveyance from the succession.

The Court also noted that there were no legal grounds for the appeal court to rely on the public records doctrine in deciding this case rather than the Civil Code. But even if the sale were required to particularly describe the disputed tract in order to tract to transfer it to the Timber Company (P) the language conveying acreage "more or less" and all the succession's prescriptive rights was sufficiently particular to show that the succession was transferring all the rights it had to the disputed property. Further, the trial court's finding that the parties intended to transfer the disputed tract to the Timber Company (P) should not have been disturbed without a finding of manifest error or clear abuse.

The Court reversed the appeal court's judgment and remanded the case for hearings on issues pretermitted by the appeal court's ruling.

Rule of Law

Under La. C.C. art. 794, a purchaser may tack its possession onto that of its vendor to prove acquisitive prescription beyond the limits of the title to visible bounds and to fix the boundary accordingly.

ROY V. BELT
Private Owners (P) v. Sheriff (D)
868 So. 2d 209 (La. App. 3d Cir. 2004)

Facts & Procedure

The Roy family (P) filed suit against the Sheriff of Avoyelles Parish (D) alleging that the Parish's jail buildings encroached on their land. The Roys (P) sought a judicial determination of the parties' joint boundary and inverse condemnation damages.

The parties shared a common ancestor in title. In short, J. Clifton Cappel sold parcels to Pierre Poret and Louis Coco. The Sheriff's (D) title descended from the Poret transactions. The Roys (P), on the other hand, derived their title from Coco. The Roys (P) argue that their northern boundary was a line north of the bayou, and the Sheriff (D) maintained that the boundary was the center of the bayou.

The trial court heard substantial evidence from parties and surveyors concerning the many transfers, property descriptions, and surveys conducted over the years between Mr. Cappel's ownership and the parties' ownership. None of the transfers from Mr. Cappel to Messrs. Poret and Coco in the early 1900s identified the bayou as a boundary. Rather, Mr. Poret's conveyances contained language like "bounded on the south by vendor." Likewise, the conveyances to Mr. Coco did not reference the bayou as a boundary and contained reciprocal language like "bounded on the north by Pierre L. Poret."

In 1964, a judgment of possession was signed in the succession of Pierre and Eliza Poret that identified the bayou as part of the southern boundary of the individual lots at issue. But the survey prepared by Ralph Gagnard in conjunction with the judgment depicted a line along fences and trees north of the bayou and labeled the land south of the bayou "Van L. Roy." The property between the bayou and the fence and tree line was not labeled.

In 1976, the Poret heirs sold Lot 6, which was held in indivision by the five heirs, to two others. Four of the five conveyances described the property as bounded "on the south by the Estate of Van Roy (formerly Ernest Coco), on the East by Estate of Van Roy (formerly Ernest Coco) and T & P Railway." The fifth conveyance only referenced the 1964 survey.

Those buyers later optioned six acres of Lot 6 to Avoyelles Parish with a description "bounded on the south by Van L. Roy." But the sale of the six acres included another Gagnard survey showing the bayou as the southern boundary. In the years following, Mr. Gagnard produced other surveys concerning Lot 6 that depicted the boundary as in his 1964 survey, i.e., north of the bayou.

In 1989, the Sheriff (D) purchased 11 acres of the Poret tracts with a survey showing the boundary north of the bayou. This parcel is east of Government Street. The same surveyor, Mr. Lachney, also surveyed the jail facilities west of Government Street and depicted the bayou as the boundary. The Sheriff (D) erected buildings with this boundary in mind.

At trial, Mr. Lachney testified that he took the line on Mr. Gagnard's 1964 survey and others as a traverse line rather than a boundary line and concluded that the bayou was the boundary because it was depicted as such on a later Gagnard survey.

The trial judge recused himself after the trial, and an *ad hoc* judge decided the case on the record. The judge determined that the boundary was the center of the bayou.

The Roys (P) appealed.

Issue

Where titles and surveys conflict, how can boundaries be determined?

Holding & Decision

Where titles and surveys conflict, the court should consider all the evidence to determine the correct place to fix the boundary. In general, conflicts between a written description and a survey favor the survey. And where two parties share a common ancestor in title, the more ancient title prevails.

Noting that boundaries can be fixed either by ownership or possession, the appeal court found that neither party could show sufficient acts of possession to support a boundary action or acquisitive prescription. Therefore, the appeal court considered decades of titles and surveys to determine ownership and concluded that the best evidence of the boundary contained in the parties' title was Mr. Gagnard's 1964 survey, which depicts the boundary running north of the bayou.

The appeal court found several facts particularly persuasive in selecting that survey over the other conflicting surveys and titles:

- No titles before the Poret succession identify the bayou as a boundary.

- The conveyances to the Poret heirs and the Parish's option describe the Roys as the southern boundary.

- Mr. Gagnard did not identify the disputed line as a traverse line.

- The acreage is correct using the boundary north of the bayou and incorrect otherwise.

- There is no defensible reason the surveys of parcels on either side of Government Street should have different southern boundaries.

Accordingly, the appeal court set the boundary as depicted on the 1964 Gagnard survey and found that the Sheriff's (D) buildings encroaching on the Roys' land constituted inverse condemnations for which the Roys were entitled to damages. The matter was remanded to the trial court for determination of the quantum of damages.

Rule of Law

Where titles and surveys conflict, the court should consider all the evidence to determine the correct place to fix the boundary. In general, conflicts between a written description and a survey favor the survey. And where two parties share a common ancestor in title, the more ancient title prevails.

Part II

Dismemberments of Ownership

Chapter 11

Predial Servitudes — General Principles

1. **Dismemberments of ownership.**

   a) Patrimonial rights are either real or personal.

      i. A **personal right** pertains to another person and is governed by the law of obligations.

      ii. A **real right** pertains to a thing and is governed by the law of property.

   b) "An obligation is a legal relationship whereby a person, called the obligor, is bound to render a performance in favor of another, called the obligee. Performance may consist of giving, doing, or not doing something." La. C.C. art. 1756.

   c) Real rights are not legislatively defined, but the Louisiana Supreme Court declared that "the term 'real right' under the civil law is synonymous with proprietary interest, both of which refer to a species of ownership." *Harwood Oil & Mining Co. v. Black*, 124 So. 2d 764, 767 (La. 1960). By this, the Supreme Court intended to follow Louisiana's line of cases providing for the dismemberment of ownership into three parts — the use of a thing, the right to enjoy a thing, and the right to dispose of a thing.

   d) Typical characteristics of real rights:

      i. Correlative to real obligations. *See* La. C.C. art. 1763.

      ii. Relating to deriving an economic advantage from a thing.

   e) Some rights appear to be personal but exhibit real-right characteristics. For example:

      i. The owner of a servient estate is bound to make necessary works at his expense to support the exercise of a servitude. While this appears, at first glance, to be a personal obligation enforceable against the owner of the servient estate and his entire patrimony, La. C.C. art. 746 allows the owner of the servient estate to "exonerate himself by abandoning the servient estate or the part of it on which the servitude is granted to the owner of the dominant estate."

      ii. According to doctrinal writers, when a person acquires an immovable subject to mortgage, the acquirer's liability is limited to the immovable and is discharged by a forced sale.

   f) Still other personal rights have acquired real-right characteristics over time:

      i. A lease may be asserted against the lessor's successor-in-title.

      ii. A creditor in possession of a debtor's property may retain it until the debt is paid.

g) Real rights frequently mix with personal rights:

    i. Abusive exercise of ownership rights may create the obligation to repair damage suffered by the neighbors.

    ii. Exercise of ownership may create an obligation for compensation, e.g., an owner owes a good faith possessor reimbursement under La. C.C. art. 486.

h) Parties to a contract, subject to judicial scrutiny in the public interest, may create new real rights beyond those enumerated in the Civil Code. This is explicit in La. C.C. art. 476: "One may have various rights in things: 1. Ownership; 2. Personal and predial servitudes; and 3. Such other real rights as the law allows."

    i. The phrase "other real rights as the law allows" provides for the creation of real rights only in keeping with legislation and custom.

    ii. The most important novel real rights created by contract include mineral rights, limited personal servitudes, and building restrictions.

2. **Predial servitudes.**

a) "A **predial servitude** is a charge on a servient estate for the benefit of a dominant estate. The two estates must belong to different owners." La. C.C. art. 646.

    i. The servitude is a real right burdening an immovable, the servient estate.

    ii. The phrase "for the benefit of a dominant estate" should be read metaphorically to mean that the benefit of the servitude accrues to the owner of the dominant estate, whoever it might be, rather than to a particular person.

b) **Content of predial servitudes: negative rights.** "The owner of the servient estate is not required to do anything. His obligation is to abstain from doing something on his estate or to permit something to be done on it." La. C.C. art. 651.

    i. In general, the law does not specify the activities that can be made the subject of predial servitudes. This is generally left to the parties.

    ii. Examples of activities on the servient estate that may be tolerated under a servitude:

- Rights of way.
- Support of structures.
- Removal of quantities of materials like timber or stone. *But Cf.* to the removal of oil and gas, which are generally the subject of *sui generis* real rights akin to limited personal servitudes.

    iii. Examples of activities that might be prohibited by servitude:

- Prohibition against building on a vacant lot.
- Building in a style or height other than the one agreed.
- Use of the servient estate as a pasture or industrial facility.
- Prohibition against draining water onto a lower estate.
- Prohibitions against emitting reasonable amounts of smoke or noise.

    iv. Restrictions on the use of property may take the form of *sui generis* real rights like building restrictions or of predial servitudes. Public law in the form of zoning and building ordinances also affect the right to use and build on property.

v. Predial servitudes may not prohibit the performance of juridical acts affecting the servient estate like alienation or partition. It is not clear whether a predial servitude may be used to prohibit a competing business from being operated on the servient estate.

c) A predial servitude may not impose an affirmative duty on the owner of a servient estate. La. C.C. art. 651.

    i. *Exception.* The owner of the servient estate "may be required by convention or by law to keep his estate in suitable condition for the exercise of the servitude due to the dominant estate." La. C.C. art. 651. Examples of this sort of requirements include

- The owner of a servient estate subject to the servitude of support is bound to keep the wall fit for the dominant estate to rest buildings or other constructions on it.
- The owner of the servient estate subject to the servitude of drain may be required to remove underbrush impeding the flow of drainage.
- The owner of a riparian servient estate may be required to cut trees on the bank to keep the channel deep enough for navigational servitudes.

    ii. The owner of a servient estate may bind himself to perform affirmative duties as a personal obligation in connection with the establishment of a predial servitude. Such an obligation is heritable but is not transferred to his successor-in-title without express stipulation.

    iii. A servitude that purports to create an affirmative duty on the servient estate beyond that permitted by law is a servitude *in faciendo* and is prohibited.

d) **Nature of predial servitudes.**

    i. Predial servitudes are immovable real rights on land belonging to another.

    ii. "Predial servitudes are established by all acts by which immovables may be transferred. Delivery of the act of transfer or use of the right by the owner of the dominant estate constitutes tradition." La. C.C. art. 722.

    iii. "Apparent servitudes may be acquired by title, by destination of the owner, or by acquisitive prescription." La. C.C. art. 740.

    iv. "A. A predial servitude is inseparable from the dominant estate and passes with it. The right of using the servitude cannot be alienated, leased, or encumbered separately from the dominant estate. B. The predial servitude continues as a charge on the servient estate when ownership changes." La. C.C. art. 650.

    v. The owner of the dominant estate does not own the servitude because incorporeal things may not be owned.

    vi. A predial servitude does not grant the owner of the dominant estate any ownership in any part of the servient estate.

    vii. Predial servitudes may be lost through a sufficient period of nonuse.

e) **Things susceptible of predial servitudes: immovables.**

    i. "Predial servitudes are established on, or for the benefit of, distinct corporeal immovables." La. C.C. art. 698.

      A. Here the phrase "distinct corporeal immovables" precludes granting a predial servitude on the component parts of an immovable, with certain limited exceptions, namely timber estates and individual apartments.

B. Buildings can be subject to predial servitudes in the same way that they are separate immovables.

   ii. Incorporeal immovables, e.g., other servitudes, cannot themselves be subject to predial servitudes.

f) **Servitudes on public property.**

   i. Predial servitudes may be established on property owned by or for the benefit of the state and its political subdivisions.

   ii. **Private things.**

     A. Predial servitudes on private immovables owned by the state and its subdivisions may not be established by acquisitive prescription but may be conventionally established.

     B. Predial servitudes may be established on private immovables owned by municipalities by acquisitive prescription.

   iii. **Public things.**

     A. Predial servitudes on private immovables owned by the state and its political subdivisions may not be established by acquisitive prescription but may be established by contract.

     B. A private person dedicating a thing to public use may reserve a servitude for the use or enjoyment of that thing to himself.

g) **Essential features of predial servitudes.**

   i. Two estates, one **servient** and one **dominant**.

   ii. The estates must belong to different owners.

     A. If the estates belong to the same owner, the arrangement is a destination of the owner rather than a servitude. *See* La. C.C. art. 741.

     B. A co-owner of one estate in indivision may have a servitude on or for the benefit of an estate he owns as sole owner.

   iii. The servitude must benefit the dominant estate.

     A. This benefit may be economic, aesthetic, social, or of another kind.

     B. The benefit need not exist at the time the servitude is established and may be uncertain.

     C. If the benefit is for a particular person rather than the owner of the dominant estate, the servitude is a personal servitude instead of a predial one.

h) **Optional features of predial servitudes.**

   i. Servitudes are often established between contiguous or nearby estates but they need not be limited by geography.

   ii. Servitudes are often perpetual but may be for a term or conditional.

i) **Indivisibility of predial servitudes.**

   i. "A predial servitude is indivisible. An estate cannot have upon another estate part of a right of way, or of view, or of any other servitude, nor can an estate be charged with a part of a servitude. The use of a servitude may be limited to certain days or hours; when limited, it is still an entire right. A servitude is due to the whole of the dominant estate and to all parts of it; if this estate is divided, every acquirer of a part has the right of using the servitude in its entirety." La. C.C. art. 652.

ii. The division of a servient estate should not adversely affect the dominant estate's benefit, but which parts of the divided servient estate remain burdened by the servitude depends on the circumstances. E.g., a servitude of view might continue to burden all of the parts of the servient estate, but a servitude of passage might only burden the newly divided parcels through which the passage runs.

iii. The benefits of a servitude may be divided.

j) **Kinds of predial servitudes.**

  i. "Predial servitudes may be natural, legal, and voluntary or conventional. **Natural servitudes** arise from the natural situation of estates; **legal servitudes** are imposed by law; and **voluntary or conventional servitudes** are established by juridical act, prescription, or destination of the owner." La. C.C. art. 654.

    A. Some have criticized the classifications of servitudes as natural or legal as arbitrary because both arise by operation of law and are, therefore, literally legal.

    B. Other critics focus on the nature of natural and legal servitudes as limitations on ownership rather than true servitudes because it is often difficult to identify the dominant and servient estates and the beneficiary.

  ii. **Natural servitudes** include drainage and the obligation to return running water to its natural channel upon exiting one's estate. *See* LA. C.C. arts. 656–658.

  iii. "**Legal servitudes** are limitations on ownership established by law for the benefit of the general public or for the benefit of particular persons." La. C.C. art. 659. Examples include, requirements of keeping buildings in repair, preventing roofline drip from falling on a neighbor's property, and similar principles of good order.

Chapter 12

Natural Servitudes

1. **Natural drainage.** "An estate situated below is the servient estate and is bound to receive the surface waters that flow naturally from a dominant estate situated above unless an act of man has created the flow." La. C.C. art. 655.

   a) **No more burdensome.** "The owner of the servient estate situated below may not do anything to prevent the flow of the water. The owner of the dominant estate situated above may not do anything to render the servitude more burdensome." La. C.C. art. 656.

      i. The Civil Code grants a natural servitude of drain in favor of a higher estate against a lower estate requiring the lower estate to allow the water to drain across it so long as the proprietor of the dominant estate does not inappropriately increase the burden of the servitude on the lower estate or cause the water to run someplace it normally would not. *Broussard v. Cormier*.

   b) **Injunctive relief & damages.**

      i. The owner of property subject to a natural servitude of drain is not entitled to an injunction restricting drainage by a dominant estate where the damage caused by the drainage is negligible and can be easily compensated in money. *Adams v. Town of Ruston*.

      ii. The owner of the servient estate subject to a natural servitude of drainage is not liable for damage caused to the dominant estate and its owners by naturally occurring conditions that prevent water from draining from the dominant estate onto the servient one like beaver dams. *Bransford v. Int'l Paper Timberlands Operating Co.*

   c) A conventional servitude of drainage into a neighbor's canal can be acquired by contract or through acquisitive prescription as a result of thirty years of continuous, apparent use. *Poole v. Guste*.

2. **Running Water.** "The owner of an estate bordering on running water may use it as it runs for the purpose of watering his estate or for other purposes." La. C.C. art. 657.

3. **Diversion.**

   a) "The owner of an estate through which water runs, whether it originates there or passes from lands above, may make use of it while it runs over his lands. He cannot stop it or give it another direction and is bound to return it to its ordinary channel where it leaves his estate." La. C.C. art. 658.

b) "No person diverting or impeding the course of water from a natural drain shall fail to return the water to its natural course before it leaves his estate without any undue retardation of the flow of water outside of his enclosure thereby injuring an adjacent estate." La. R.S. § 38:218. Such an action can be punishable by criminal penalties.

BROUSSARD V. CORMIER
Southern Landowner (P) v. Northern Landowner (D)
154 La. 877, 98 So. 403 (La. 1923)

Facts & Procedure

In this dispute over the drainage servitude, the parties own adjacent rice farms. Both properties are low and marshy and have little natural drainage. The parties used artificial irrigation and drainage techniques for years to grow rice without any disputes over drainage. But 1918 saw a tremendous amount of rainfall.

The Northern Landowner (D) built up an old levee on the southern border of his property with the Southern Landowner's (P). A manmade ditch runs along the levee and through the Northern Landowner's (D) land, draining it away to the northwest.

The Southern Landowner (P) sued to enforce the natural servitude of drain owed to his estate by the Northern Landowner's (D) lower estate, alleging that the Northern Landowner's (D) estate was bound to receive all the surplus waters from the southern estate and that the levee blocked their natural flow. The Northern Landowner (D), on the other hand, argued that he did not owe any servitude of drain and that the plaintiff's land generally drained to the west instead of to the north.

The trial court found for the Southern Landowner (P), recognized the servitude of drain, and issued an injunction directing the sheriff to make openings in the levee to permit water from the Southern Landowner's (P) property to drain into the Northern Landowner's (D) ditch.

The Northern Landowner (D) appealed.

Issue

Can the proprietor of an estate situated below another block the normal drainage from the higher estate?

Holding & Decision

No, the Civil Code grants a natural servitude of drain in favor of a higher estate against a lower estate requiring the lower estate to allow the water to drain across it, with certain limitations. The Court noted that the proprietor of the dominant estate can do nothing to make the servitude more burdensome for the lower estate, except insofar as the owner of the dominant estate makes works required for cultivation and agricultural uses of his estate. This exception itself has an exception: even when cutting ditches and making other works for agricultural purposes, the owner of the dominant estate may not do so in a way that diverts the waters and concentrates them so that they flow onto the servient estate someplace other than their normal destination.

Even though the two estates are roughly the same elevation, the northern estate is a few inches lower. The Court held that the trial court reasonably found that unimpeded rainfall tends to drain northward from the Southern Landowner's (P) land onto that of the Northern Landowner (D). The Northern Landowner (D) did not dispute that he raised the levee or assert that receiving the water from the Southern Landowner (P) would unduly burden his estate. Instead he only asserted that he did not owe the Southern Landowner (P) any servitude of drain at all. The Court disagreed and affirmed the trial court's ruling recognizing the servitude and requiring removal or modification of the levee to allow drainage to the north.

Rule of Law

The Civil Code grants a natural servitude of drain in favor of a higher estate against a lower estate requiring the lower estate to allow the water to drain across it so long as the proprietor of the dominant estate does not inappropriately increase the burden of the servitude on the lower estate or cause the water to run someplace it normally would not.

ADAMS V. TOWN OF RUSTON
Landowner (P) v. Town (D)
193 La. 403, 193 So. 688 (La. 1940)

Facts & Procedure

A Landowner (P) whose property is near a swimming pool operated by the Town of Ruston (D) sued for an injunction restraining the Town (D) from draining the pool into a ditch that ran through the Landowner's (P) property. He alleged that the pool drainage made the natural servitude over his land more burdensome and irrevocably harmed his property by eroding the drainage ditch. He testified that the property was worth at least $10,000 and that the drainage had already caused at least $5,000 in damage. The Landowner (P) further testified that when he purchased the property about twenty years before the dispute, he could step across the ditch and that, at the time of the trial, it was six to eight feet wide due erosion.

The Town's (D) mayor testified that the Landowner (D) had not complained about any damage in the eight years the swimming pool had been in operation. An engineering professor testifying for the Town (D) opined that the pool's drainage flowing through the ditch is only one-tenth the amount of the rainfall flowing there. Further, he estimated that in a ten-year span only seventy-five cubic feet of soil would be carried off from the Landowner's (P) land as a result of the swimming pool's drainage. At trial, it was shown that the pool water remained confined to the ditch and did not overflow.

The trial court rejected the Landowner's (P) demand, and the Landowner (P) appealed.

Issue

Is the owner of property subject to a natural servitude of drain entitled to an injunction restricting drainage by a dominant estate where the damage caused by the drainage is negligible?

Holding & Decision

No, the owner of property subject to a natural servitude of drain is not entitled to an injunction restricting drainage by a dominant estate where the damage caused by the drainage is negligible and can be easily compensated in money. Citing several relevant cases, the Louisiana Supreme Court explained that, where a plaintiff can be adequately compensated for damages to his property, he is not entitled to an injunction. Relying on the record, the Court found that there was negligible damage the Landowner's (P) property and held that he was not entitled to an injunction or damages.

The Court declined to rule on the Town's (D) contention that the Landowner (P) was estopped from raising his claim because he had allowed the drainage without complaint for eight years because a ruling on that subject was not necessary to dispose of the case.

The Court affirmed the lower court's judgment at the Landowner's (P) costs.

Rule of Law

The owner of property subject to a natural servitude of drain is not entitled to an injunction restricting drainage by a dominant estate where the damage caused by the drainage is negligible and can be easily compensated in money.

BRANSFORD V. INT'L PAPER TIMBERLANDS OPERATING CO.

Individual Landowner (P) v. Timber Company (D)
750 So. 2d 424 (La. App. 2d Cir. 2000)

Facts & Procedure

The parties agreed on all relevant facts. The parties owned adjacent estates, and the Individual Landowner's (P) property drained onto the neighboring estate owned by the Timber Company (D). The Individual Landowner's (P) son discovered that beaver dams on her property were causing flooding in some areas of the property and removed them. He also found beaver dams on the Timber Company's (D) land that prevented drainage from his mother's tract but did not remove them.

The Individual Landowner (P) sued the Timber Company's (D), alleging that its failure to remove the beaver dams on its property flooded her property and damaged valuable timber. After removal to federal court and remand to state court, the state court heard the Timber Company's (D) motion for summary judgment.

For purposes of the motion, the Timber Company (D) acknowledged its servitude of drainage and that the beaver dams on its land had flooded the Individual Landowner's (P) property. But the trial court found that the Timber Company (D) had no affirmative duty to remove the beaver dams because they were a naturally occurring condition, granted the summary judgment, and dismissed the case.

The Individual Landowner (P) appealed.

Issue

Is the owner of a servient estate subject to a servitude of drainage liable for damage caused by naturally occurring conditions that reduce the flow of water draining onto the servient estate like beaver dams?

Holding & Decision

No, the owner of the servient estate subject to a natural servitude of drainage is not liable for damage caused to the dominant estate and its owners by naturally occurring conditions that reduce the flow of water draining onto the servient estate like beaver dams.

The appeal court began its analysis with the relevant Civil Code articles, noting that servitudes generally do not require the servient estate and its owner to do anything. Rather, they require the estate's owner to refrain from certain actions or to tolerate others taking certain actions. Nevertheless, the servient estate must be maintained in a way to allow for the exercise of the servitude.

As persuasive authority, the Individual Landowner (P) cited a Missouri case in which a railroad had a duty to keep a manmade culvert clear of beaver dams that caused flooding on a nearby farm. The Missouri court found the railroad negligent for failing to do so and awarded damages to the farmer for his crops. The Louisiana appeal court distinguished the cases because the Timber Company (D) did not build a structure or do anything else to modify or restrict drainage. Further, the record did not show that the Timber Company (D) was even aware of the dams before flooding occurred. Therefore, the Missouri case provided no precedential value. Finally, the court had only awarded damages before in cases where the owner of the servient estate actively obstructed drainage.

The Individual Landowner (P) also argued that the Civil Code provides an affirmative duty for the landowner to keep his land in a suitable condition to support the servitude. The appeal court noted that there are cases to that effect as well, but declined to rule on the contention because the

Individual Landowner (P) did not seek injunctive relief compelling the Timber Company (D) to remove the dams.

Because the Timber Company (D) did not obstruct the flow of water onto its lands, the appeal court held that it was not liable for any damage from flooding to the Individual Landowner's (P) property.

The appeal court affirmed the trial court's judgment.

Rule of Law

The owner of the servient estate subject to a natural servitude of drainage is not liable for damage caused to the dominant estate and its owners by naturally occurring conditions that prevent water from draining from the dominant estate onto the servient one like beaver dams.

POOLE V. GUSTE
Upper Owner (P) v. Lower Owner (D)
261 La. 1110, 262 So. 2d 339 (La. 1972)

Facts & Procedure

The parties own neighboring estates with the Poole (P) tract on the east side of a section boundary and the Guste (D) tract on the west side. Both tracts include thousands of acres. Previous owners of the two tracts agreed in writing in 1916 to construct a canal (known as the "Dedinger Canal") on what would become the Guste (D) tract to be used by Poole's ancestor-in-title to transport timber from his property. The canal flowed south into another canal and then into Lake Pontchartrain. Poole's (P) ancestor-in-title used the canal to transport timber for eight years, stopped, and did not renew the agreement.

Before the construction of the canal, the Poole (P) tract drained generally to the southeast and across the Guste (D) tract. The canal changed the flow of water by causing the Poole (P) tract to drain into the canal rather than across the Guste (D) tract. The drainage into the canal occurred largely at the part of the canal known as the "bridge site" or "the gap." The dirt dug from the canal was used to create a spoil bank on the side of the canal closest to the Poole (P) tract, but "the gap" allowed water to flow through the embankment into the canal.

After Guste (D) purchased the property, he built a seven foot high levee along the section line between the parties' property, filled the gap, and closed off the southern end of the canal that ran eventually to Lake Pontchartrain. He did so to stop tidal flow from the lake from inundating his property in order improve it for rice cultivation.

Pool (P) filed a lawsuit seeking recognition of his servitude of drain and for damages. The trial court found in Poole's (P) favor, awarded damages, and ordered Guste (D) to remove the levee in two places.

The appeal court affirmed, and Guste (D) appealed to the Louisiana Supreme Court.

Issue

Can an estate acquire a conventional servitude of drain into the canal of a neighbor through thirty-year acquisitive prescription?

Holding & Decision

Yes, a conventional servitude of drain into a neighbor's canal can be acquired by contract or through acquisitive prescription as a result of thirty years of continuous, apparent use.

The Court held that Poole's (P) tract enjoyed a conventional servitude of drain onto and through Guste's (D) tract through the Dedinger Canal. The estate acquired that servitude by acquisitive prescription after more than thirty years of continuous and apparent use.

The Court declined to rule on several related issues, including whether the prescription began at the inception of the 1916 agreement or at its end, whether the servitude might have been acquired by ten-years prescription, and whether the servitude is a natural servitude.

The Court also rejected Guste's (D) contentions that the timber floating servitude cannot be enlarged by prescription and that the Poole (P) tract cannot be the dominant estate with respect to the Guste (D) tract because it only drains onto the Guste (D) tract at some places along their lengthy boundary.

The Court affirmed the lower courts' judgments and the issuance of an injunction despite Guste (D) arguing that an injunction was inappropriate because the damage to Poole (P) could be compensated with money. Rather, the Court noted that injunctions have historically been used to protect property rights, including servitudes.

Dissent

Justice Summers offered a lengthy dissent. First, he argued that any servitude that may have been acquired was destroyed after the timber floating operation ceased because the canal became choked with brush and, by the time Guste (D) purchased the property, served no drainage function. He also noted that no court had determined which estate was dominant and which was servient overall. Rather, he argued, the courts had satisfied themselves with determining that there were isolated points of drainage along the parties' boundary.

He also argued that the result reached by the majority was deeply inequitable. Specifically, opening the levee system in the indicated places would render the entire levee useless, and the Guste (D) tract could only be protected from flooding by building another levee at a cost of $50,000. The Poole (P) tract, on the other hand, already contained canals and an unused levee system that could be opened relatively inexpensively to provide adequate drainage for the tract without impacting the neighbor.

Finally, Justice Summers surveyed French law to the effect that a landowner could take appropriate steps to protect his own land to prevent its flooding, even if that caused his neighbors to flood more. Practically, he concluded, drainage servitudes could not apply in flat, marshy swampland subject to tidal flooding because the waters flow in and out periodically. The law of drainage is built on the assumption that water generally flows in one direction; here it flows in each direction at different times. To apply the law of drainage to tidal marsh means, effectively, that the land can never be protected to be improved for any agricultural or industrial use.

Rule of Law

A conventional servitude of drainage into a neighbor's canal can be acquired by contract or through acquisitive prescription as a result of thirty years of continuous, apparent use.

Chapter 13

Legal Servitudes

1. **Levees and river roads.**

    a) "Servitudes imposed for the public or common utility relate to the space which is to be left for the public use by the adjacent proprietors on the shores of navigable rivers and for the making and repairing of levees, roads, and other public or common works. Such servitudes also exist on property necessary for the building of levees and other water control structures on the alignment approved by the U.S. Army Corps of Engineers as provided by law, including the repairing of hurricane protection levees. All that relates to this kind of servitude is determined by laws or particular regulations." La. C.C. art. 665.

    i. La. C.C. art. 665 does not apply to lakes, only navigable rivers or streams.

    ii. Lands that were riparian at the time they were severed from the sovereign remain subject to the article 665 servitude even if they cease to be riparian (e.g., by the movement of the river to a new course).

    iii. Under *Delaune v. Board of Commissioners*, 87 So.2d 749, 230 La. 117 (La. 1956), and its progeny, lands that were not riparian when severed from the sovereign but subsequently became riparian are not subject to the article 665 servitude. These lands could be expropriated for levee construction but could not be appropriated under La. C.C. art. 665. *See also Deltic Farm and Timber Co. v. Board of Commr's.*

    iv. Property appropriated under La. C.C. art. 665 need not be directly adjacent to the river but must be within a reasonable distance of the river. Landowners bear the burden of demonstrating that the construction should be placed elsewhere.

    b) **Levees.**

    i. Under the Louisiana Constitution of 1974, lands and improvements used or destroyed for levees muse be "paid for as provided by law," except for batture or property controlled by the state or a state subdivision for commercial purposes. Land other than batture appropriated from private landowners must be paid for at fair market value. Batture may be taken without compensation.

    ii. "Batture" as used in Louisiana law can mean three things:

    • "Accretion formed successively and imperceptibly on the bank of a river or stream." *See* La. C.C. art. 499.

    • Land formations on the bed of a river.

- The natural bank of a river between its ordinary low and high water stages. *See* La. C.C. art. 456. This is the most commonly used definition used by Louisiana law and has been adopted by the United States Supreme Court.

   iii. The owner of batture may sue for recognition of his ownership of the batture free from public servitudes where the batture is not necessary for public use. Courts determine the necessity of the servitude on a case-by-case basis.

   iv. The construction of a levee or flood bulkhead frees land on the inside of the levee from all public servitudes because the property is not batture once segregated from the river.

   v. *Mayer v. Board of Commissioners for Caddo Levee District*, 177 La. 1119, 150 So. 295 (La. 1933) charts the evolution of levees and related law from their roots as small earthworks raised directly alongside the river and paid for by the proprietors whose lands fronted the river to the massive works that are today often publicly constructed far from the bank of the river. This practical change drove changes to the laws defining a river's bank because it no longer made sense to define a river's bank as extending to its levee where the levee was not built several miles away.

c) **River roads.**

   i. *Replacement.* The owner of property bordering a river or stream must give additional property, without compensation, to replace a river road that has been destroyed or inundated to the point it is impassible. La. C.C. art. 666.

   ii. In *Hebert v. T.L. James & Co.*, 224 La. 498, 70 So. 2d 102 (La. 1953), the state tried to expand an existing river road to 75 feet wide and pave it without compensating the owner for taking additional land because the estate was burdened by the river road servitude. The Louisiana Supreme Court disagreed because such a large road was greater than that contemplated by the article.

2. **Obligations of neighborhood.**

a) "Although a proprietor may do with his estate whatever he pleases, still he cannot make any work on it, which may deprive his neighbor of the liberty of enjoying his own, or which may be the cause of any damage to him. However, if the work he makes on his estate deprives his neighbor of enjoyment or causes damage to him, he is answerable for damages only upon a showing that he knew or, in the exercise of reasonable care, should have known that his works would cause damage, that the damage could have been prevented by the exercise of reasonable care, and that he failed to exercise such reasonable care. Nothing in this Article shall preclude the court from the application of the doctrine of *res ipsa loquitur* in an appropriate case. Nonetheless, the proprietor is answerable for damages without regard to his knowledge or his exercise of reasonable care, if the damage is caused by an ultrahazardous activity. An ultrahazardous activity as used in this Article is strictly limited to pile driving or blasting with explosives." La. C.C. art. 667.

   i. One may not use his property in a way that infringes on the right of a neighbor or, without such a right, may not use his property without benefit to himself in such a way that damages his neighbor. *Higgins Oil & Fuel Co. v. Guaranty Oil Co.*

b) "Although one be not at liberty to make any work by which his neighbor's buildings may be damaged, yet every one has the liberty of doing on his own ground whatsoever he pleases, although it should occasion some inconvenience to his neighbor." La. C.C. art. 668.

c) "If the works or materials for any manufactory or other operation, cause an inconvenience to those in the same or in the neighboring houses, by diffusing smoke or nauseous smell, and there be no servitude established by which they are regulated, their sufferance must be determined by the rules of the police, or the customs of the place." La. C.C. art. 669.

d) **Abuse of right.** *Higgins Oil & Fuel Co. v. Guaranty Oil Co.* underpins the modern understanding of the doctrine of abuse of right, which has been applied outside of the context of property ownership and the obligations of neighborhood to contract, tort, and other areas of the law. Subsequent cases have refined the doctrine. It may be applied when one of the following conditions exists:

　　i. "the exercise of rights exclusively for the purpose of harming another or with the predominant motive to cause harm;

　　ii. the non-existence of a serious and legitimate interest that is worthy of judicial prosecution;

　　iii. the use of a right in violation of moral rules, good faith or elementary fairness; or

　　iv. the exercise of the right for a purpose other than that for which it was granted." *Mascaro v. Hudson*, 496 So. 2d 428 (La. App. 4 Cir. 1986).

e) A landowner can be held liable as a proprietor under La. C.C. art. 667 for damage caused by the works and operations of his lessee, e.g., the nuisance of playing overly loud music. *Yokum v. 615 Bourbon Street, L.L.C.*

f) **Injunctive relief** may lie against those who perform activities constituting a legal nuisance, either a **nuisance *per accidens* (or nuisance in fact)** or **nuisance *per se* (or nuisance at law).**

　　i. A property owner may obtain injunctive relief against a neighbor whose activities on their own property pose a threat to the owner's property or their family's health. *Fuselier v. Spalding.*

　　ii. The operation of a business may constitute a nuisance *per accidens* or in fact when such activity is not a nuisance *per se* or at law if it causes unreasonable inconvenience or discomfort to neighbors through unsanitary conditions, excessive noise, bad smells, or other inconveniences. *Robichaux v. Huppenbauer.*

　　iii. The operation of a legal business, including a funeral home, is never a nuisance *per se*, and a prospective injunction may only lie against such a nuisance *per se*. *Frederick v. Brown Funeral Homes, Inc.*

　　iv. The storage of flammable materials, while lawful and not a nuisance *per se*, becomes a nuisance in fact when it creates a substantial hazard to adjoining property. *Hilliard v. Shuff.*

g) **Actions for damages.**

　　i. A plaintiff may recover damages from a neighbor who violates the obligations of neighborhood, including both general compensatory damages and specific damages for mental anguish, when the the neighbor's action or inaction caused the damages and the neighbor knew or should have known that his action or inaction would cause the damage. *Rizzo v. Nichols.*

ii. Liability under La. C.C. arts. 667, 668, or 669 does not require a showing of negligence. These articles would be redundant if they required fault, because such behavior is subject to La. C.C. art. 2315. Under certain circumstances, liability might be found under both articles 667–669 and 2315 simultaneously.

iii. La. C.C. arts. 667, 668, and 669 apply to constructions made on an estate as well as operations or acts undertaken on an estate. Louisiana courts have broadly interpreted the articles and rejected challenges seeking to limit their application only to physical constructions and exclude activities that cause damage.

iv. In general, one-year liberative prescription applies to actions for damages under La. C.C. arts. 667–669. But in some cases where it is impossible for a person to know who or what caused the damage, the period begins to run from the date the damage "becomes apparent." *Dean v. Hercules*, 38 So. 2d 69 (La. 1976).

h) **Encroaching buildings.**

i. "When a landowner constructs in good faith a building that encroaches on an adjacent estate and the owner of that estate does not complain within a reasonable time after he knew or should have known of the encroachment, or in any event complains only after the construction is substantially completed the court may allow the building to remain. The owner of the building acquires a predial servitude on the land occupied by the building upon payment of compensation for the value of the servitude taken and for any other damage that the neighbor has suffered." La. C.C. art. 670.

ii. A court may not grant a predial servitude allowing a person to maintain an encroachment on another's property where the encroachment could be easily moved without demolition, undue expense, or impairing the utility of the encroaching structure. *Thompson v. Hemphill.*

iii. A person granted a servitude for an encroaching building is still protected by the obligations of neighborhood, and the owner of the servient estate may not exercise his rights to damage the encroaching building. *Winingder v. Balmer*, 632 So.2 408 (La. App. 4 Cir. 1994).

iv. A person who builds a structure that encroaches on another's land with permission is not entitled to a servitude from a subsequent owner because the builder lacked good faith that he owned the land on which he built. *Hayes v. Gunn*, 115 So. 3d 1141 (La. App. 3d Cir. 2013).

v. La. C.C. art. 670 cannot be used to prevent the removal of a building addition built entirely on the builder's land but that does not comply with applicable building restrictions because such a building does not encroach on a neighbor's estate. *Lafargue v. Barron*, 90 So. 3d 555 (La. App. 1 Cir. 2012).

3. **Common enclosures.**

a) "A landowner who builds first may rest one-half of a partition wall on the land of his neighbor, provided that he uses solid masonry at least as high as the first story and that the width of the wall does not exceed eighteen inches, not including the plastering which may not be more than three inches in thickness." La. C.C. art. 673.

i. This right belongs to a landowner and any person acting under his authority, e.g., usufructuaries or lessees.

    ii. There are two requirements to exercise this right: the person building must be the first to build a wall on a tract of land, and the land must not be surrounded by masonry walls already.

    iii. The right may still be exercised by a landowner if his neighbor has built a fence or wooden wall on the property line, for example.

    iv. The existence of a masonry structure (e.g., a house or a brick wall) more than 9 inches from the boundary does not preclude a person from exercising this right. A brick or stone wall within nine inches of the boundary line will preclude the exercise of this right, but it is unclear if such a wall could be made common by the application of La. C.C. art. 676 below.

    v. If more than half of the wall rests on the neighbor's property, it is an encroachment and is subject to the remedies available in the case of encroachment.

    vi. Iron columns are not a wall for purposes of La. C.C. art. 673.

    vii. Louisiana decisions suggest that a person may enjoin his neighbor from building a wall under article 673 that is made of anything other than stones or bricks, but timbers may be used as part of the foundation of a masonry wall.

    viii. French courts have held that any form of solid construction satisfies the requirements of their analogous code articles, even if the materials were not available at the time the code was written, e.g., reinforced concrete. This line of reasoning may be persuasive to Louisiana courts applying this article.

    ix. The foundation of a wall placed on the boundary line may extend beyond nine inches on either or both sides of the wall in order to support it.

    x. Exercise of this right does not require the consent of the neighbor. A party seeking to build a wall may force entry onto his neighbor's land by injunction if necessary.

b) "The wall thus raised becomes common if the neighbor is willing to contribute one-half of its cost. If the neighbor refuses to contribute, he preserves the right to make the wall common in whole or in part, at any time, by paying to the owner one-half of the current value of the wall, or of the part that he wishes to make common." La. C.C. art. 674.

    i. Where a wall on a boundary has been paid for only by the owner of one of the properties, it is not a common wall and may be disposed of freely as private property. *Jeannin v. DeBlanc.*

    ii. The owner of the wall may demand reimbursement for half the value of the wall if his neighbor makes any use of the wall whatsoever.

    iii. *Cf.* La. C.C. art. 676, which requires that the person acquiring co-ownership of a common wall pay half the value of the soil as well as half the value of the wall. Here, the co-owner only pays for half the value of the wall because he already owns the soil on his side of the boundary.

    iv. Under current precedent, a neighbor who converts a wall into a common wall is required to pay half the wall's present value or half the cost of constructing it, if he can prove that cost.

c) "A wall that separates adjoining buildings and is partly on one estate and partly on another is presumed to be common up to the highest part of the lower building unless there is proof to the contrary." La. C.C. art. 675.

d) "When a solid masonry wall adjoins another estate, the neighbor has a right to make it a common wall, in whole or in part, by paying to its owner one-half of the current value of the wall, or of the part that he wishes to make common, and one-half of the value of the soil on which the wall is built." La. C.C. art. 676.

    i. This article distinguishes a wall built entirely on one person's property from the wall built on both adjoining properties contemplated in La. C.C. art. 673.

    ii. The foundation for such a wall built entirely on one person's property may nevertheless be dug into the neighbor's property.

    iii. French doctrine that may be persuasive in interpreting this article holds that establishing co-ownership of an adjoining wall is excluded (1) where the wall belongs to the public domain because such property is inalienable or (2) where the owner of the wall enjoys servitudes of light and view that would be incompatible with co-ownership of the wall.

    iv. If a wall is separated by any distance from the boundary, it may never become a common wall under this article.

e) The Civil Code provides default provisions for determining rights and obligations concerning common walls, fences, or ditches, but these provisions can be superseded by agreement or local ordinances. La. C.C. art. 677.

    i. "A landowner has the right to enclose his land." La.C.C. art. 684.

    ii. "Necessary repairs to a common wall, including partial rebuilding, are to be made at the expense of those who own it in proportion to their interests." La. C.C. art. 678.

    iii. "The co-owner of a common wall may be relieved of the obligation to contribute to the cost of repairs by abandoning in writing his right to use it, if no construction of his is actually supported by the common wall." La. C.C. art. 679.

    iv. "The co-owner of a common wall may use it as he sees fit, provided that he does not impair its structural integrity or infringe on the rights of his neighbor." La. C.C. art. 680.

    v. "The co-owner of a common wall may not make any opening in the wall without the consent of his neighbor." La. C.C. art. 681. *But See Jeannin v. DeBlanc*: a wall on a boundary that is not co-owned may be disposed of freely as private property, including by making holes.

    vi. "A co-owner may raise the height of a common wall at his expense provided the wall can support the additional weight. In such a case, he alone is responsible for the maintenance and repair of the raised part." La. C.C. art. 682.

    vii. "The neighbor who does not contribute to the raising of the common wall may at any time cause the raised part to become common by paying to its owner one-half of its current value." La. C.C. art. 683. *Cf.* La. C.C. art. 674.

f) *Presumptions.* In general, fences (La. C.C. art. 685); ditches (La. C.C. art. 686); trees, bushes, and other plants (La. C.C. art. 687) are presumed to be common absent proof to the contrary.

    i. "When adjoining lands are enclosed, a landowner may compel his neighbors to contribute to the expense of making and repairing common fences by which the respective lands are separated. When adjoining lands are not enclosed, a landowner may compel his neighbors to contribute to the expense of making and repairing common fences only as prescribed by local ordinances." La. C.C. art. 685.

ii. "Adjoining owners are responsible for the maintenance of a common ditch." La. C.C. art. 686.

iii. "An adjoining owner has the right to demand the removal of trees, bushes, or plants on the boundary that interfere with the enjoyment of his estate, but he must bear the expense of removal." La. C.C. art. 687.

iv. "A landowner has the right to demand that the branches or roots of a neighbor's trees, bushes, or plants, that extend over or into his property be trimmed at the expense of the neighbor. A landowner does not have this right if the roots or branches do not interfere with the enjoyment of his property." La. C.C. art. 688.

4. **Enclosed estates.**

   a) **La. C.C. art. 689 right of passage.**

      i. "The owner of an estate that has no access to a public road or utility may claim a right of passage over neighboring property to the nearest public road or utility. He is bound to compensate his neighbor for the right of passage acquired and to indemnify his neighbor for the damage he may occasion. New or additional maintenance burdens imposed upon the servient estate or intervening lands resulting from the utility servitude shall be the responsibility of the owner of the dominant estate." La. C.C. art. 689.

         A. An estate is "enclosed" when government action, such as expropriation and the construction of a controlled-access highway, cuts it off from other means of sufficient ingress and egress. *Rockholt v. Keaty.*

         B. This article expressly only grants the right of passage from the enclosed estate to the nearest public road, not to a nearby parcel or other destination an owner prefers. *Rockholt v. Keaty.*

         C. A court should generally grant a right of passage via the shortest route to the nearest public road, but a court may change the route if circumstances warrant another route. Nevertheless. the owner of the servient estate may later demand relocation of the servitude to a more convenient location at his own expense. *Dickerson v. Coon.*

         D. The owner of a servient estate is entitled to damages where a servitude of passage is granted, but these damages are in the nature of indemnity for loss rather than compensation for a taking as in an expropriation. *Dickerson v. Coon.*

      ii. "The right of passage for the benefit of an enclosed estate shall be suitable for the kind of traffic or utility that is reasonably necessary for the use of that estate." La. C.C. art. 690.

      iii. "The owner of the enclosed estate may construct on the right-of-way the type of road, utility, or railroad reasonably necessary for the exercise of the servitude. The utility crossing shall be constructed in compliance with all appropriate and applicable federal and state standards so as to mitigate all hazards posed by the passage and the particular conditions of the servient estate and intervening lands." La. C.C. art. 691.

      iv. "The owner of the enclosed estate may not demand the right of passage or the right-of-way for the utility anywhere he chooses. The passage generally shall be taken along the shortest route from the enclosed estate to the public road or utility at the location least injurious to the intervening lands. The location of the utility right-of-way shall coincide with the location of the servitude of passage unless an alternate location providing access to the nearest utility is least injurious to the servient estate and intervening lands. The court shall evaluate and determine that the location of the servitude of passage or utility shall not affect the safety of the operations or significantly interfere with the operations of the owner of the servient estate or intervening lands prior to the granting of the servitude of passage or utility." La. C.C. art. 692. *See Dickerson v. Coon* and *Rockholt v. Keaty.*

b) **La. C.C. art. 694 right of passage.**

    i. "When in the case of partition, or a voluntary alienation of an estate or of a part thereof, property alienated or partitioned becomes enclosed, passage shall be furnished gratuitously by the owner of the land on which the passage was previously exercised, even if it is not the shortest route to the public road or utility, and even if the act of alienation or partition does not mention a servitude of passage." La. C.C. art. 694.

        A. The right to demand passage under this article is a legal servitude that travels with the land and may be asserted by subsequent acquirers of the land, not only the first acquirer of the parcel that became enclosed. *See Patin v. Richard.*

        B. The Louisiana Supreme Court has held that a purchaser of an enclosed estate is precluded by the public records doctrine from asserting a claim for the creation of a conventional servitude of passage under this article against the successors of the vendor. In Professor Yiannopoulos's opinion, the public records doctrine does not apply to legal servitudes and legal obligations to grant servitudes. While the conventional servitude of passage to fulfill the obligations of La. C.C. art. 694 must be written and recorded per the public records doctrine to be fully effective, the obligation to grant that conventional servitude does not.

c) **The La. C.C. art. 693 exception.**

    i. "If an estate becomes enclosed as a result of a voluntary act or omission of its owner, the neighbors are not bound to furnish a passage to him or his successors." La. C.C. art. 693.

    ii. La. C.C. art. 693 only applies where the enclosed estate's owner has caused the estate to become enclosed by selling off property that previously provided access; it does not apply to partitions because those are governed by La. C.C. arts. 694 and 689.*LeBlanc v. Thibodeaux.*

d) **The relationship between La. C.C. arts. 689 and 694.** While La. C.C. art. 694 typically applies when a property is enclosed by its alienation from a larger, unenclosed tract, the owner of an enclosed estate may seek a servitude under La. C.C. art. 689 over a neighbor's land if passage over the vendor's land would be impractical or prohibitively expensive and if, on balance, the burden on the neighbor is outweighed by the benefits and public policy concerns. *Stuckey v. Collins.*

DELTIC FARM AND TIMBER CO. V. BOARD OF COMMR'S
Landowner (P) v. Levee District (D)
368 So. 2d 1109 (La. App. 2d Cir. 1979)

Facts & Procedure

In 1970, the Levee District (D) appropriated the Landowner's (P) riparian land to construct, maintain, and repair a levee, asserting that the land was subject to La. C.C. art. 665's levee servitude. The Landowner (P) sued, arguing that the property was not subject to appropriation because, while it was riparian at the time of the taking, it was not riparian when transferred from the public domain by patent. The Landowner (P) sought damages for the land's fair market value or, alternatively, its assessed value.

The property was in a section that did not front on the river at the time it was severed from the public domain. The sections fronting the river at that time were transferred to others. Since then, the river changed course, and the river then abutted part of the Landowner's (P) property.

The parties submitted the matter on the record and stipulations, and the issues were decided under the 1921 Louisiana Constitution and the statutes in force at the time of the taking. (Louisiana adopted a new constitution in 1974 while this lawsuit and its appeals were pending.) The trial judge found that the property was not subject to the levee servitude and, therefore, not subject to appropriation. The court rendered judgment for the Landowner (P) and awarded it the property's fair market value. The Levee District (D) appealed.

Issue

Does the levee servitude under La. C.C. art. 665 burden property that was not riparian at the time it was severed from the public domain but subsequently became riparian?

Holding & Decision

No, for the La. C.C. art. 665 levee servitude to burden property, the property must have been riparian when it was severed from the public domain.

The Levee District (D) argued that all riparian lands were burdened by the servitude based on the *Wolf v. Hurley*, 46 F.2d 515 (W.D. La. 1930), line of decisions. But the appeal court noted that this line of cases was effectively overruled by *Delaune v. Board of Commissioners*, 109 So. 2d 441 (La. 1959), which provided a two-pronged test for determining whether a property was subject to the levee servitude: "(1) The property must have been riparian when severed from the public domain; and (2) The property taken must be within the range of the reasonable necessities of the situation as produced by the forces of nature unaided by artificial causes."

The appropriation for levee purposes under La. C.C. 665 does not violate the takings clause because the levee servitude was reserved to the public by law upon the property's severance from the public domain. Lands that were not riparian at that time were severed without any such reservation. Therefore, the appeal court held that imposing the levee servitude on the Landowner's (P) land without compensation would violate both state and federal constitutions because the property was not riparian at the time it left the public domain and, therefore, not burdened by the levee servitude.

The appeal court affirmed the trial court's judgment.

Rule of Law

For the La. C.C. art. 665. levee servitude to burden property, the property must have been riparian when it was severed from the public domain.

HIGGINS OIL & FUEL CO. V. GUARANTY OIL CO.

Oil Producer (P) v. Neighbor (D)
145 La. 233, 82 So. 206 (La. 1919)

Facts & Procedure

Higgins Oil & Fuel Co. (P) leased a tract of land, sunk an oil well, and began producing around 124 barrels of oil per day. Then its Neighbor (D) sunk its own well on the adjoining tract. The Neighbor's (D) well did not produce but did allow air to flow into the ground, which significantly diminished the production from the Oil Producer's (P) well. The Neighbor (D) refused to plug its dry well, which would restore the other well's previous production without significant expense to the Neighbor (D).

The Oil Producer (P) sued the Neighbor (D) to compel it to close its unproductive well and for damages it suffered as a result of reduced production. The Neighbor (D) filed an exception of no cause of action, which the lower court sustained.

The Oil Producer (P) appealed.

Issue

May a person maintain an unproductive well on his property that reduces the amount of oil his neighbor can pump from a well on his land?

Holding & Decision

No, one may not use his property in a way that infringes on the right of a neighbor or, without such a right, may not use his property without benefit to himself in such a way that damages his neighbor.

The Court initially reviewed the civil code articles governing the disposition of one's property and the obligations of neighborhood, viz., Revised Civil Code articles 477, 490, and 659 and Civil Code Articles 667, and 668. Based on the articles, the Court initially suggested the line of demarcation for the allowable use of property might be whether the use causes damage or merely inconvenience to the neighbor but rejected this simple formulation on the grounds that it would violate the core legal principle that the exercise of a right cannot constitute fault. The Court then turned to French commentators for guidance.

The commentators noted that according to Laurent, "The right of an owners is limited only in so far as it comes in conflict with some equal right of another owner. ... If [the owner] does not infringe some right of the neighbor, though he causes damage, he is not held to any reparation." But this formulation is limited: where the owner acts with malice — with the purpose of causing injury and without benefit to himself — this is an abuse of right and may be penalized.

The Court reviewed cases from the French courts: one where the court ordered the removal of a dummy chimney constructed to cut off light to his neighbor's window and another where an owner diminished the volume of water available to a neighbor from a spring by installing a pump. The French Court ordered damages for wasting the pumped water but did not order the removal of the pump because the owner had the right to pump water from the spring for his benefit.

Based on Louisiana law and French texts, the Court concluded that each case must be weighed on its facts subject to the principle that an owner must not injure his neighbor's rights and, even absent such a right, must not damage the neighbor without benefit to the owner.

Turning back to the case at hand, the Court found that the Oil Producer (P) had a right to operate an oil well on its land and that the Neighbor's (D) well provided no benefit to the Neighbor (D) while interfering with the Oil Producer's (P) rights.

Since the Neighbor's (D) well only hindered the Oil Producer's (P) rights, the Court overruled the lower court's judgment, overruled the exception, and remanded the case for trial.

Rule of Law

One may not use his property in a way that infringes on the right of a neighbor or, without such a right, may not use his property without benefit to himself in such a way that damages his neighbor.

YOKUM V. 615 BOURBON STREET, L.L.C.

Neighbors (P) v. Landowner (D)
977 So. 2d 859 (La. 2008)

Facts & Procedure

A married couple (P) sued 615 Bourbon Street, L.L.C. (D), the owner of a building in which its lessee operated a bar called The Rock, alleging that the noise emanating from The Rock's live music constituted a nuisance and unreasonably interfered with their quiet enjoyment of their property.

The Landowner (D) leased the property to O'Reilly Properties, L.L.C., which operated The Rock. Before filing suit, the Neighbors (P) sent certified letters to both the Landowner (D) and the manager of The Rock complaining of the excessive noise, requesting that the noise be abated, and informing them of their intent to sue if the noise were not reduced. The Neighbors (P) ultimately filed suit alleging that the defendants had violated various noise ordinances, that they constituted a nuisance, that they had violated provisions of Louisiana's alcoholic beverage control statutes concerning noise levels, and that they violated La. C.C. arts. 667 and 669.

The trial court granted the Landowner's (D) motion for summary judgment and dismissed the claims against the Landowner (D) without written reasons but presumably on the grounds that a landowner cannot be held liable for its lessee's conduct under nuisance law. The appeal court affirmed the judgment, and the Neighbors (P) appealed to the Louisiana Supreme Court.

Issue

Can a lessor or landowner be held liable for their lessee's actions that create a nuisance on neighboring property under La. C.C. art. 667?

Holding & Decision

Yes, a lessor or landowner can be held liable for the actions of their lessee that cause damage to their neighbors in violation of La. C.C. art. 667. That article provides that a "proprietor ... cannot make any work on [his estate], which may deprive his neighbor of the liberty of enjoying his own, or which may be the cause of any damage to him."

The Court noted that the definition of "proprietor" had grown to encompass both landowners and those whose rights derived from the owner, like agents or lessees. Therefore, a landowner could be responsible for damage caused by his lessee's works. Similarly, the Court noted that the phrase "make any work" now encompasses more than simply constructing buildings or earthen works; instead it includes general activities that may cause damage.

The Court held that causing excessive noise to emanate from the premises constituted a "work" under the law. The Court stopped short of declaring the Landowner (D) responsible for the noise because that question was not before the court. Instead, the Court noted that the Landowner (D) had not met the burden to carry its motion for summary judgment and remanded the matter for further proceedings.

Rule of Law

A landowner can be held liable as a proprietor under La. C.C. art. 667 for damage caused by the works and operations of his lessee.

FUSELIER V. SPALDING
Neighbor (P) v. Kiln Owner (D)
2 La. Ann. 773 (La. 1847)

Facts & Procedure

A residential Neighbor (P) sought and obtained an injunction to prevent a Kiln Owner (D) from burning a brick kiln he had constructed close to the Neighbor's (P) home. The Neighbor (P) alleged that burning the kiln would endanger both her property and the health of her family. The lower court maintained the injunction, and the Kiln Owner (D) appealed.

Issue

May a person obtain an injunction restraining a neighbor from conducting activities on his or her property that endanger the objecting person's property or the health of his or her family?

Holding & Decision

Yes, a property owner may obtain injunctive relief against a neighbor whose activities on their own property pose a threat to the owner's property or their family's health. The Court found that the Neighbor (P) was entitled to protection because the evidence showed that burning the kiln would endanger her wooden buildings by increasing the risk of fire and would likely impair her family's health. Accordingly, the Court affirmed the lower court's judgment making the injunction permanent.

Rule of Law

A property owner may obtain injunctive relief against a neighbor whose activities on their own property pose a threat to the owner's property or their family's health.

FREDERICK V. BROWN FUNERAL HOMES, INC.
Homeowners (P) v. Funeral Home (D)
222 La. 57, 62 So. 2d 100 (La. 1952)

Facts & Procedure

Homeowners (P) sought to enjoin a Funeral Home (D) from establishing and operating an establishment in their neighborhood, which they alleged to be an exclusively residential area. The Funeral Home (D) had not yet started operating at the time they filed suit.

The trial court granted a preliminary injunction, and the Funeral Home (D) appealed. The Louisiana Supreme Court reversed the trial court and remanded for trial on the merits. On rehearing, the Court set aside the preliminary injunction and again remanded the matter for trial.

Issue

Is a funeral home a nuisance *per se*? If not, can it be enjoined from operating before it has opened for business?

Holding & Decision

No and no, respectively. The operation of a legal business is never a nuisance *per se*, and a prospective injunction may only lie against such a nuisance *per se*.

The Court considered La. C.C. arts. 667–669 and concluded that, taken together, the articles establish that the owner of an estate may do as he pleases with his property unless he damages his neighbor or interferes with his neighbor's enjoyment of his own property. Because a funeral home is a lawful business, it cannot be considered a nuisance *per se*. Instead, in the absence of any zoning laws to the contrary (as in this case), it may be located in a residential area so long as its operation doesn't cause physical damage or become a nuisance in fact. Here there could be no evidence of actual damage or nuisance, since the funeral home was not yet in operation. Therefore an injunction was improper.

The Court dissolved the injunction and remanded the matter for trial on the merits consistent with its opinion.

Dissent

Justice Hawthorne dissented, noting that the sole issue before the Court was whether a funeral home's location in a residential neighborhood constituted, in itself, a nuisance. He argued that, while not a nuisance *per se*, a funeral home in a residential area is a nuisance *per accidens* or in fact, since it causes such a significant negative emotional impact and inconvenience that nearby residents would necessarily be deprived of the full enjoyment of their property. Therefore, Justice Hawthorne argued that the injunction should be maintained if the Homeowners (P) showed that the neighborhood was, in fact, exclusively residential.

Rule of Law

The operation of a legal business, including a funeral home, is never a nuisance *per se*, and a prospective injunction may only lie against such a nuisance *per se*.

ROBICHAUX V. HUPPENBAUER
Neighbors (P) v. Stable Owner (D)
258 La. 139, 245 So. 2d 385 (La. 1971)

Facts & Procedure

Neighbors (P) living near a horse stable sued the Stable Owner (D) to enjoin its operation. The horses stabled there pulled carriages for hire in the French Quarter, and the stable had been operating for longer than anyone could remember. After he purchased the stable and horse lot, the City charged the Stable Owner (D) with violating sanitation ordinances, but the charges were dismissed upon correcting the violations.

The Neighbors (P) filed this suit soon after. They alleged that the stable created noxious odors, attracted flies and rodents, and disturbed their peace with noise from the horses and carriages. The trial court granted the total injunction, the appeal court affirmed, and the Louisiana Supreme Court granted certiorari to consider whether the appeal court should have required the Stable Owner (D) to limit the scope and manner of his operations rather than fully enjoining them.

Issue

Is a horse stable operated in a residential neighborhood in an unsanitary manner a nuisance *per accidens*?

Holding & Decision

Yes. While a horse stable is not a nuisance *per se* or at law, the Court held that the operation of the stable at issue here was a nuisance *per accidens* or in fact because it was located so close to residences and was operated in an unsanitary manner. To reach this conclusion, the Court reviewed La. C.C. arts. 667–669, concluded that the plain language of article 669 only encompassed smoke and smells, and that it was not an illustrative list of nuisances. The 1808 version of article 669 was broader and included "other inconveniences." Because the then-current text of La. C.C. art. 669 did not sufficiently cover the facts at bar, the Court resorted to common law notions of nuisance to guide its judgment.

The record reflected that the stable emitted noxious odors and effluent consistently over long periods of time, that it harbored vermin and incubated bugs that swarmed nearby homes, and that the comings and goings of vendors disturbed neighbors at all hours. Nevertheless, the Court held that the stable could continue operations if certain mitigations were made, including limiting the number of horses, removing manure daily, covering feed bins, and regularly spraying disinfectant and deodorizers.

The Court remanded the case to the trial court to issue an injunction outlining the stable's permitted operations.

Justice Barham concurred in the judgment but argued that the result should have been based exclusively on the civil law, specifically, La. C.C. art. 669. He contended that the French text of the 1825 Code article was unchanged from its 1808 version and included the phrase "other inconveniences." The majority opinion had interpreted the redactors of the 1870 Code to have omitted that phrase purposely, but Justice Barham argued that their absence was an error of translation, rather than a change of substance.

Dissent

Justice Tate dissented, arguing that the injunction was proper and should not be modified because the operation of the stable in such a thickly settled neighborhood would continue to bother the Neighbors (D) despite the operational changes.

Rule of Law

The operation of a business may constitute a nuisance *per accidens* or in fact when such activity is not a nuisance *per se* or at law if it causes unreasonable inconvenience or discomfort to neighbors through unsanitary conditions, excessive noise, bad smells, or other inconveniences.

HILLIARD V. SHUFF
Resident (P) v. Truck Stop Operator (D)
256 So. 2d 127 (La. 1971)

Facts & Procedure

A Resident (P) sued to enjoin the Truck Stop Operator (D) next door from maintaining four aboveground diesel and gasoline fuel storage tanks on the property because they were a hazard to his property that deprived him of its use.

The Truck Stop Operator (D) leased the four-acre tract on which he operated his truck stop, service station, restaurant, and car wash. The operation stored almost sixty thousand gallons of fuel in the above-ground tanks at issue, which were located five feet inside the parties' joint property line and approximately 150 feet from the Resident's (P) house. Because the tanks were originally designed to store crude oil and not much more volatile products like diesel fuel and gasoline, they had to be vented to prevent pressure buildup. The vented fumes were flammable out to a radius that extended well into the Resident's (P) property.

The Resident (P) contended that the tanks deprived him of the use of 45 feet of his property and posed a threat to his residence. He sued to have the tanks moved elsewhere or placed underground. The trial court denied injunctive relief, finding the Resident (P) failed to prove the tanks and their fumes were a nuisance. The appeal court affirmed. The Supreme Court granted certiorari.

Issue

Does the storage of fuel in aboveground tanks that cause a substantial fire hazard to the adjoining property constitute a legal nuisance?

Holding & Decision

Yes, the storage of flammable materials, while lawful and not a nuisance *per se*, becomes a nuisance in fact when it creates a substantial hazard to adjoining property. The Court noted that courts should consider factors like the tanks' location and proximity to the adjoining property, their structure, the quantity of fuel stored, and the defendant's operational procedures.

After reviewing the record, the Court held that using tanks built for storing crude oil to store volatile fuel close to the Neighbor's (P) property constituted a nuisance under La. C.C. arts. 667–669. The Court reversed the appeal court and granted the Resident (P) an injunction on terms to be determined by the trial court after further proceedings to determine whether another corrective action short of removal or burial of the tanks would sufficiently mitigate the hazard.

Dissent

Justice Barham dissented, arguing that the Court should have based its decision on La. C.C. art. 667 rather than article 669. He argued that Civil Code article 667 provides a landowner with a servitude over his neighbors' land allowing him to require the neighbor to cease activities that might deprive him of enjoyment or damage him. That article, he argued, requires only an objective test of the probability that the owner of the dominant estate will suffer harm or lose enjoyment of his property. It does not require actual damage or an actual disturbance. Justice Barham continued his analysis, explaining that Civil Code article 668 limited the servitude of article 667 to only apply to "real damage" rather than "inconveniences," which are themselves regulated by article 669.

The justice concluded that the dangers posed by the gas tanks and flammable vapors were not mere inconveniences as would be regulated by the law of nuisance. Therefore, the Resident (P) was not entitled to relief under article 669 and the law of nuisance; instead he was entitled to a full, permanent injunction immediately under Civil Code article 667.

Rule of Law

The storage of flammable materials, while lawful and not a nuisance *per se*, becomes a nuisance in fact when it creates a substantial hazard to adjoining property.

RIZZO V. NICHOLS
Homeowners (P) v. Builder (D)
867 So. 2d 73 (La. App. 3d Cir. 2004)

Facts & Procedure

The parties owned adjacent properties. When the Rizzos (P) moved into their home the lot next door owned by Mr. Nichols (D) was vacant. Rainwater flowed from the Homeowners' (P) lot and adjoining properties through a lower area on Mr. Nichols's (D) vacant lot and drained into the street. Mr. Nichols (D) began building a duplex apartment on the lot, and the Rizzos' (P) property began to flood. Mr. Rizzo (P) spoke with Mr. Nichols (D) about the flooding several times, and Mr. Nichols (D) agreed to "look into it." Mr. Nichols (D) subsequently consulted with two plumbers about the drainage issue but took no action to correct it.

The drainage issues caused The Rizzos' (P) lot to collect standing water during rainstorms. This standing water damaged the shed in the Rizzos' (P) yard, caused the yard to be unusable at times, and gave mosquitoes a place to breed. The Rizzos (P) subsequently installed a catch basin to mitigate the drainage problem.

The Rizzos (P) filed suit against Mr. Nichols (D) for damages, including reimbursement for the installation of the catch basin, damage to the shed, mental anguish, and loss of use of the shed and yard. The trial court found that Mr. Nichols (D) had notice that the construction would cause drainage problems and that the construction of the duplex caused the drainage issues and associated damage. The trial court awarded the Rizzos (P) damages for the catch basin installation, shed repairs, inconvenience, and mental anguish.

Mr. Nichols (D) appealed.

Issue

Is a successful plaintiff in an action under La. C.C. arts. 667–669 entitled to damages, including mental anguish, for violations of the obligations of neighborhood or vicinage?

Holding & Decision

Yes, a plaintiff may recover damages from a neighbor who violates the obligations of neighborhood, including both general compensatory damages and specific damages for mental anguish, when the neighbor's action or inaction caused the damages and the neighbor knew or should have known that his action or inaction would cause the damage.

The appeal court reviewed the record and noted that Mr. Rizzo (P) informed Mr. Nichols (D) of the drainage problem and that he did nothing to correct it. The court further noted that the new duplex was built to a higher elevation than the surrounding lots and concluded that the trial court did not commit manifest error in concluding that the construction disrupted drainage, caused the plaintiffs' damages, and that Mr. Nichols (D) knew that the damage would occur.

Mr. Nichols (D) also took issue on appeal with the damages awarded to the plaintiffs. The appeal court noted that the trial judge has vast discretion when awarding damages in an action such as this and held that the court did not abuse its discretion in awarding the amounts it awarded. The appeal court specifically noted that mental anguish damages are appropriate under certain circumstances, including where property is damaged by acts of continuous nuisance.

The court affirmed the trial court's decision.

Rule of Law

A plaintiff may recover damages from a neighbor who violates the obligations of neighborhood, including both general compensatory damages and specific damages for mental anguish, when the the neighbor's action or inaction caused the damages and the neighbor knew or should have known that his action or inaction would cause the damage.

THOMPSON V. HEMPHILL
438 So. 2d 1124 (La. App. 2d Cir. 1983)

Facts & Procedure

In this lawsuit between brothers-in-law over encroachments, Thompson (P) and Hemphill (D) purchased adjacent commercial tracts from their in-laws and parents, respectively. Thompson (P) also purchased a third tract on the opposite side of Hemphill's (D) tract from an unrelated party (see the diagram on page 607 of the text). A building containing two stores straddled the parties' tracts with a common wall roughly (but not quite) on the property line.

Thompson (P) operated a gas station and store on his side of the building, but the tanks for his gas pumps were located underground on Hemphill's (D) tract. Additionally, Hemphill (D) placed an old truck body on a concrete slab or blocks partly on his tract and partly on the tract Thompson (P) purchased from the third party. He used this truck body as a shed. A corner of Hemphill's (D) store also encroached on the same lot encroached on by the trailer.

The parties disagreed over the continued use of the gas tanks, and Thompson (P) sued for injunctive relief prohibiting Hemphill (D) from interfering with the use of the gasoline tanks under Hemphill's (D) property, removal of the encroaching trailer and truck shed, and damages. The trial court initially issued a temporary restraining order, but Thomson (P) abandoned his claim for injunctive relief after building new storage tanks on his property. After trial, the court granted Hemphill (D) a predial servitude for both the building and trailer encroachments and awarded Thompson (P) $150 compensation for the servitudes and damages.

Thompson (P) appealed.

Issue

May a court encumber property with a predial servitude to accommodate an encroachment by a temporary structure unconnected to the ground?

Holding & Decision

No, a court may not grant a predial servitude allowing a person to maintain an encroachment on another's property where the encroachment could be easily moved without demolition, undue expense, or impairing the utility of the encroaching structure. The appeal court noted that La. C.C. art. 670 allows a court to grant a predial servitude for an encroachment if a landowner constructs a building encroaching on an adjacent property in good faith if it would be unduly expensive to remove the encroachment. The article provides for an equitable result where the encroachment is slight and the servient estate can be compensated for the servitude.

The appeal court avoided the question whether the trailer in this case was a "building" for which a servitude could be granted under La. C.C. art. 670, and found that the trial court abused its discretion because granting a servitude was not warranted for a trailer that could easily be moved. While the servitude granted for the corner of the store encroaching on the adjoining lot was not at issue on appeal, Thompson (P) argued that the $150 compensation was not reasonable. The appeal court disagreed because of the small encroachment.

The appeal court reversed the trial court's judgment insofar as it created a servitude for the trailer encroachment and amended the judgment accordingly.

Rule of Law

A court may not grant a predial servitude allowing a person to maintain an encroachment on another's property where the encroachment could be easily moved without demolition, undue expense, or impairing the utility of the encroaching structure.

JEANNIN V. DEBLANC
Neighbor (P) v. Builder (D)
11 La. Ann. 465 (La. 1856)

Facts & Procedure

The Builder (D) constructed a wall on the boundary line between her property with the Neighbor (P). The Neighbor (P) did not contribute to the cost of its construction. One half of the wall rested on the Neighbor's (P) property, as allowed by the Civil Code (now La. C.C. art. 673). Subsequently, the Builder (P) had windows cut into the wall on the second story and vents cut into the wall at crawlspace level. The Neighbor (P) objected and sued, maintaining that the Builder (D) usurped the right of view upon his property by opening the windows and caused him damage.

The trial court found in favor of the Builder (D), and the Neighbor (D) appealed.

Issue

May the builder of a wall resting on the boundary between two properties open apertures in the wall without his neighbor's consent if the neighbor did not contribute to the wall's construction?

Holding & Decision

Yes, where a wall on a boundary has been paid for only by the owner of one of the properties, it is not a common wall and may be disposed of freely as private property. The court noted that the Neighbor (P) did not contribute to the construction of the wall. Therefore, it could not be a wall in common and remained the Builder's (D) personal property to do with as she would, subject only to city building codes and other regulation. The court suggested that the Neighbor (P) could make the wall common (and therefore close its openings) at any time by contributing half of its value. Barring that, the court cited a latin maxim to support its suggestion that the Neighbor (P) could erect another wall without openings on his property opposite the wall in question, to wit: "A man may make windows in his own wall, even against the will of his neighbor; a neighbor may obscure them by building against them."

Rule of Law

Where a wall on a boundary has been paid for only by the owner of one of the properties, it is not a common wall and may be disposed of freely as private property.

ROCKHOLT V. KEATY

Landlocked Owners (P) v. Neighbor (D)
256 La. 629, 237 So. 2d 663 (La. 1970)

Facts & Procedure

The Landlocked Owners' (P) 35-acre, L-shaped tract was split into two parcels by the expropriation of a strip of land for the construction of Interstate 12 (See the diagram in the text on page 618). The northern parcel became landlocked despite bordering the interstate because the government denied the Landlocked Owners (P) permission to access the interstate.

As a result, the Landlocked Owners (P) sued their Neighbor (D) for a right of passage over his adjacent property. The Landlocked Owners (P) demanded a fifty foot strip parallel to and adjacent to I-12, not to connect to the nearest road, but to connect the northern parcel to the other parcel that had been severed by expropriation. The demanded passage would have ended 746 feet from a public road. Plaintiffs argued that this route, though not directly to a public road, was the "shortest legally permissible and feasible passage" considering cost, convenience, and practicality, as a shorter route across other neighboring residential properties was allegedly impeded by building restrictions.

The trial court sustained Neighbor's (D) exception of no cause of action and motion for summary judgment, dismissing plaintiff suit, holding that the property was not "enclosed" within the meaning of La. C.C. arts. 689 and 691 because it bordered the interstate. The appeal court affirmed, and the Landlocked Owners (P) appealed again.

Issue

1. Is an estate "enclosed" within the meaning of La. C.C. arts. 689 and 691 when it borders a controlled-access highway to which ingress and egress has been denied by the state?

2. Do La. C.C. arts. 689 and 691 grant a right of passage to an enclosed estate across a neighbor's property to reach another privately-owned parcel, which then provides access to a public road, even if a shorter, more direct route to a public road exists over other neighboring lands?

Holding & Decision

1. Yes, an estate is "enclosed" under La. C.C. arts. 689 and 691 when government action, such as expropriation and the construction of a controlled-access highway, cuts it off from other means of ingress and egress. The Court rejected the lower courts' reliance on *English Realty Company, Inc. v. Meyer*, 228 La. 423, 82 So.2d 698 (La. 1955), finding that, first, the case's holding should not be extended beyond its fact and, second, that subsequent legislation settled whether the state can deny neighboring landowners access to certain roads.

   The Court also reviewed doctrinal sources applicable to the French Civil Code article on which the Louisiana articles were based and found that the French also consider an estate enclosed if ingress and egress exist but are insufficient for the best use of the land. Finally, the Court held that public policy dictates strategic and desirable land should not be taken out of commerce.

   Therefore, the Court ruled that the Landlocked Owners' (P) land was enclosed for purposes of the Civil Code articles pertaining to rights of passage.

2. But the Court also ruled that La. C.C. arts. 689 and 691 expressly only grant the right of passage from the enclosed estate to the nearest public road, not to a nearby parcel or other destination an owner prefers. The Court found the route proposed by the Landlocked

Owners (P) was neither the shortest, most direct, nor most feasible route and that they did not seek passage to a public road at all.

Therefore, the Court held, the Landlocked Owners (P) were not entitled to the relief requested from the Neighbor (D) and suggested an action might lie against other neighboring landowners.

The Court affirmed the lower courts' judgments but replaced the lower courts' reasoning with its own.

Rule of Law

1. An estate is "enclosed" when government action, such as expropriation and the construction of a controlled-access highway, cuts it off from other means of sufficient ingress and egress.

2. La. C.C. arts. 689 and 691 expressly only grant a right of passage from the enclosed estate to the nearest public road, not to a nearby parcel or other destination an owner prefers.

DICKERSON V. COON
71 So. 3d 1135 (La. App. 2d Cir. 2011)

Facts & Procedure

The Dickersons (P) owned an enclosed estate with no access to a public road. Guyton Loop Road, partly located on Coons' (D) property, was the nearest public road. The Dickersons (P) filed sued for a right of passage over the Coons' (D) property to the public road, proposing two possible routes: one along an existing logging road and the other along the shortest route to the road. The Coons (D) argued that both routes would injure their property, as either would bisect a 55-acre tract, disturb a hunting club that leased the land, and make the best part of the property less desirable as a future homesite. They proposed an alternate route along the boundary of their property.

The trial court considered the proposed routes, heard expert opinions on the damage and effort involved in creating each passage, and granted the Dickersons (P) passage along the shortest route. The trial court did not address the Coons' (D) request for damages associated with granting the servitude.

The Coons (D) appealed.

Issue

1. Should a court generally grant a right of passage through the shortest route to the nearest public road rather than by some other route proposed by a party?

2. Is the owner of an estate burdened by a servitude of passage entitled to damages?

Holding & Decision

1. Yes, a court should generally grant a right of passage via the shortest route to the nearest public road, but a court may change the route if circumstances warrant another route. The appeal court noted that exceptions to the general rule are allowed when supported by "weighty considerations" after applying a balancing test of factors like distance, injury to the servient estate, practicability, and cost of developing the servitude.

   After weighing the logging-road option against the shortest route, the court opined that it might have chosen the logging route in the trial court's position but concluded that the trial court's judgment was not erroneous. The shortest route provided the most direct access to the public road and was significantly less expensive to develop than the Coons' (D) proposed boundary route.

   The appeal court dismissed the Coons' (D) concerns about future residential development and hunting club disruption, citing La. C.C. art. 695, which allows the servient estate to relocate the servitude at its own expense if it later interferes with property use.

2. Yes, the owner of a servient estate is entitled to damages where a servitude of passage is granted, but these damages are in the nature of indemnity for loss rather than compensation for a taking as in an expropriation. The Coons (D) presented expert testimony that valued their damages at nearly $17,000 by comparing the servitude to the sale of an easement and calculating the theoretical diminution of value to the land from it being used by the neighbor. The Dickersons' (P) expert, on the other hand opined that the value of the land was not affected by the servitude.

   The appeal court surmised that the trial court tacitly rejected the Coons' (D) expert testimony because it did not award damages. The appeal court agreed because this process is legally distinct from expropriation and not subject to the same kinds of damages. But the appeal court did hold that the trial court erred in ignoring the Dickerson's (P) expert testimony that approximately $300 of timber would need to be cleared to develop the servitude over the shortest route.

The appeal court affirmed the judgment insofar as it fixed the servitude of passage along the shortest route and amended the judgment to award the Coons (D) $291.43 in damages for the removal of timber along that route.

Rule of Law

1. A court should generally grant a right of passage via the shortest route to the nearest public road, but a court may change the route if circumstances warrant another route. Nevertheless, the owner of the servient estate may later demand relocation of the servitude to a more convenient location at his own expense.

2. The owner of a servient estate is entitled to damages where a servitude of passage is granted, but these damages are in the nature of indemnity for loss rather than compensation for a taking as in an expropriation.

PATIN V. RICHARD

So. 2d 879 (La. App. 3d Cir. 1974)

Facts& Procedure

The parties own adjacent camps near the Gulf of Mexico. Neither property has direct access to a public road, and historically both have crossed the estate of their northern neighbor, Mr. Savoie, to reach a public highway. All three properties were owned by a common ancestor in title until they were sold around the same time. Mr. Patin (P) historically crossed both Mr. Richard's (D) and Mr. Savoie's properties to reach the highway. After a dispute between the parties, Mr. Richard (D) built a fence across the driveway Mr. Patin (P) used to reach to his camp, cutting off his customary route.

Mr. Patin (P) sued Mr. Richard (D) to claim a servitude of passage across his land. The trial court dismissed the lawsuit, finding that the servitude would seriously inconvenience Mr. Richard, that passage could not be granted to a public road because Mr. Savoie was not a party, and that Mr. Patin (P) could (and during the trial actually did) use his brother-in-law's adjacent property to reach a public road without using Mr. Patin's (D) property.

Mr. Patin (P) appealed.

Issue

Can a purchaser assert a claim for a servitude of passage that arose from the sale of several lots held by one person even though he was not the original purchaser?

Holding& Decision

Yes, the servitude of passage burdens the land and is transmitted to subsequent owners even if the sale documents do not explicitly describe the servitude. The record reflected that the western side of both Mr. Savoie's and Mr. Richard's (D) property had been used to access the parties properties by different owners since they were sold from the common ancestor decades before. The appeal court noted that the trial court ignored the phrase "upon which the right of passage was before exercised" in La. C.C. art. 694.

Thus, the appeal court found that a servitude of passage existed under La. C.C. art. 694 burdening both the Savoie and Richard (D) estates. The court noted that Mr. Richard (D) relied on and recognized the same servitude on Mr. Savoie's land that Mr. Patin (P) asserted against Mr. Richard (D). The appeal court noted that the servitudes had existed by operation of law since the properties were sold from their common author. The appeal court rejected out of hand the notion that Mr. Savoie had to be a party because Mr. Savoie had all along recognized the servitude.

The appeal court reversed the judgment of the trial court and recognized a servitude of passage over Mr. Richard's (D) property in the place it had previously been exercised. The court fixed the servitude at twelve feet wide, the narrowest the court felt could safely fit automobile traffic.

Rule of Law

The servitude of passage burdens the land and is transmitted to subsequent owners even if the sale documents do not explicitly describe the servitude.

Dissent

Justice Domengeaux agreed with the fixing of the servitude but disagreed with the majority applying La. C.C. art. 694. He would have recognized the servitude under La. C.C. arts. 689 and 691. In his view, article 694 only applies where a landowner encloses his property through a transfer and reserves passage over the sold property. Here, the justice argued, the enclosure only arose after the sale and no passage was reserved. Therefore that article is inapplicable. Instead, articles 689 and 692 should have been applied to establish a new servitude granting passage to the nearest public road via the shortest route. In that case, Mr. Richard (D) would be entitled to indemnity. Under La.

C.C. art. 694, the servitude was wholly gratuitous.

Justice Domengeaux also disagreed that a judgment could be rendered without making Mr. Savoie a party because the path to the nearest road ran through his land. He would have remanded the case to the trial court to implead Mr. Savoie with instructions to fix the servitude as the majority did for different reasons and to calculate damages for the defendants.

LeBlanc v. Thibodeaux
615 So. 2d 295 (La. 1993)

Facts & Procedure

This is dispute between owners of properties that were partitioned from the same large tract. Generations before this lawsuit, five siblings inherited their parents' property by partitioning it into six pieces — one owned separately by each child and a 72 arpent parcel of swampland owned in indivision. The 72 arpent tract had no access to a public road, but the partition established a conventional servitude of passage over properties belonging to two of the siblings. A trial court eventually found that this servitude prescribed from nonuse.

In a separate lawsuit leading to this appeal, the LeBlancs (P) sued the Thibodeauxs (D) for a right of passage across their land for the benefit of the 72 arpent parcel. The trial court held that the LeBlancs (P) were not entitled to gratuitous passage under La. C.C. art. 694 because the 72 arpent tract was not partitioned or otherwise alienated; it instead remained owned in indivision both before and after the partition. But the trial court found that the LeBlancs (P) were entitled to passage under La. C.C. art. 689, which — as a legal servitude — did not prescribe.

The appeal court reversed the trial court's judgment, finding that the LeBlancs (P) were not entitled to a servitude under either article. The court concluded that the 72 arpent parcel did not become enclosed until the conventional servitude lapsed through nonuse. This loss, the court concluded, was a voluntary act or omission sufficient to relieve the neighbors of the obligation to provide passage under La. C.C. art. 693.

The LeBlancs (P) appealed.

Issue

Does La. C.C. art. 693 relieve neighbors from providing a servitude of passage to an enclosed estate if the partitioned estate previously enjoyed a conventional servitude of passage until it lapsed from nonuse?

Holding & Decision

No, La. C.C art. 693 only applies where the enclosed estate's owner has caused the estate to become enclosed by selling off property that previously provided access; it does not apply to partitions because those are governed by La. C.C. arts. 694 and 689. The Court held that the act of partition simultaneously created and enclosed the 72 arpent parcel, despite the existence of the conventional servitude. Because the estate was enclosed, it would be entitled to a servitude of passage under either La. C.C. art. 689 or 694, unless article 693's exception applied.

The Court reviewed the history of La. C.C. art. 693, transcripts related to its drafting, and Professor Yiannopoulos's treatise. The Court concluded that these materials demonstrated the article was created to address the situation in which a vendor sells property that he uses to access a public road without reserving passage. In that case, the vendee is not required to save the vendor from himself. The Court concluded that article 693 only applies to vendors who enclose themselves or, at the very least, does not apply to partitions.

The Court reversed the appeal court's judgment and affirmed the trial court's judgment, remanding the case to determine the location of the passage and the amount of indemnity the LeBlancs (P) owed.

Justice Lemmon concurred in the result but maintained that the parcel at issue became enclosed when the servitude lapsed, not upon its creation. Nevertheless, in his view allowing the servitude to lapse from nonuse was the kind of action or omission article 693 was designed to address, so the LeBlancs (P) were entitled to a servitude upon the payment of indemnity.

Rule of Law

La. C.C. art. 693 only applies where the enclosed estate's owner has caused the estate to become enclosed by selling off property that previously provided access; it does not apply to partitions because those are governed by La. C.C. arts. 694 and 689.

STUCKEY V. COLLINS
464 So. 2d 346 (La. App. 2d Cir. 1985)

Facts & Procedure

Mr. Stuckey (P) sued Mr. Collins (D) for a servitude of passage over his land to a nearby highway. Mr. Stuckey (P) purchased his residential lot from Mr. Willis, who developed and partitioned several residential lots from a large tract of land. This division enclosed Mr. Stuckey's (P) lot, and the title granted a servitude of passage over another lot Mr. Willis retained. But that lot did not itself reach the highway because Mr. Collins (D) owned a narrow strip between the encumbered lot and the highway. Mr. Willis cleared a road all the way from Mr. Stuckey's (P) lot to the highway over Mr. Collins's (D) strip without any objection, because Mr. Willis and Mr. Collins (D) intended to swap land so that Mr. Willis would own the strip between his land and the highway. This exchange never occurred.

Mr. Stuckey (P) used the passage over Mr. Collins's (D) strip before and after he purchased his lot. Initially he did not know Mr. Collins (D) owned the strip adjacent to the highway but he became aware when Mr. Collins (D) blocked the passage to assert his ownership. During the pendency of this dispute, the parties agreed to replace a fixed barrier with a cable that could be moved as needed. Mr. Stuckey (P) eventually removed the barrier, and Mr. Collins (D) replaced it.

The trial court awarded Mr. Stuckey (P) passage over the disputed strip of land, and Mr. Collins (D) appealed, in part on the grounds that Mr. Stuckey (P) should instead get a servitude of passage on a different route from Mr. Willis, his vendor.

Issue

If an enclosed estate is entitled to a servitude over the previous owner's property under La. C.C. art. 694, does this preclude the enclosed estate from receiving a servitude over an unrelated neighbor's land under article 689?

Holding & Decision

No, while La. C.C. art. 694 typically applies when a property is enclosed by its alienation from a larger, unenclosed tract, the owner of an enclosed estate may seek a servitude under article 689 over a neighbor's land if passage over the vendor's land would be impractical or prohibitively expensive and if, on balance, the burden on the neighbor is outweighed by the benefits and public policy concerns. Here, the appeal court found that the record showed that, while it would in theory be possible for Mr. Stuckey (P) to access a public road over property previously owned by his vendor Mr. Willis, building a road on that route would be nearly impossible because of the wet, boggy conditions.

After reviewing *Rockholt v. Keaty* and its survey of French sources, the appeal court concluded that the public policy against land locking property supported balancing the burden of the passage on a neighbor against the importance of maintaining land in commerce in exceptional cases like the one at issue. Here, passage under La. C.C. art. 694 was nearly impossible, and the burden on Mr. Collins (D) was minimal because the servitude would affect such a small piece of land at the far end of an unfenced property.

Therefore, the appeal court held that Mr. Stuckey (P) was entitled to a servitude of passage under La. C.C. art. 689 and that Mr. Collins (D) was prohibited from blocking the passage with a cable, as had been his practice. The court noted that this cable served no purpose other than to deny Mr. Stuckey (P) access. Finally, the court noted that Mr. Stuckey (P) was bound to indemnify Mr. Collins (D) for the damage the passage would cause but that it was not an issue in the lower court. Therefore, Mr. Collins (D) received the opportunity to make a claim for indemnification, if he wished.

The court amended the trial court's judgment to allow Mr. Collins (D) the opportunity to seek indemnification and affirmed the judgment as amended.

Rule of Law

While La. C.C. art. 694 typically applies when a property is enclosed by its alienation from a larger, unenclosed tract, the owner of an enclosed estate may seek a servitude under La. C.C. art. 689 over a neighbor's land if passage over the vendor's land would be impractical or prohibitively expensive and if, on balance, the burden on the neighbor is outweighed by the benefits and public policy concerns.

Chapter 14

Conventional Servitudes

1. **Contractual and testamentary freedom.**

    a) "Predial servitudes may be established by an owner on his estate or acquired for its benefit.
    The use and extent of such servitudes are regulated by the title by which they are created, and, in the absence of such regulation, by the Rules of the Civil Code." La. C.C. art. 697.

        i. The limitations on contractual freedom are a function of history. At Roman law, a predial servitude was a charge on an estate for the benefit of another estate. In medieval France, however, predial servitudes were a vehicle to enforce feudal obligations against lands and individuals, requiring certain positive duties from tenants and cementing tenants' position as social inferiors. The French Revolution and the authors of the Code Civil changed the law to eradicate feudalism.

        ii. The use and extent of a conventional predial servitude is regulated by the title rather than the default provisions of law, such as the duty under La. C.C. art. 745 to cause the least possible damage or potential duties arising under La. C.C. art. 667 concerning obligations of neighborhood, provided the agreement does not adversely affect the public interest. *Ryan v. Southern Natural Gas Company.*

    b) In general, modern property law respects individuals' contractual and testamentary wishes as long as they remain within the guardrails of public policy.

    c) **Imposition of services.** Generally, predial servitudes may not require performance of affirmative duties by the owner of the servient estate, except where specified by law. But predial servitudes do allow for the imposition by contract of incidental duties necessary to the exercise of the servitude, such as maintaining roads or other works on the servient estate to enable the exercise of the servitude. Nevertheless, law may impose substantial duties on the owner of a servient estate — e.g., riparian owners' duty to keep banks of waterways clear of vegetation.

    d) Predial servitudes are established in favor of the owner of a dominant estate, whoever it may be; they may not be established in favor of a named person.

    e) In order to form part of a predial servitude, the rights granted must have a direct relationship with the use of the dominant estate. All kinds of rights that have such a direct relationship with the use of the dominant estate — e.g., rights to take walks, collect fruits, or use the swimming pool on the property — may be predial servitudes.

f) It is unclear (and largely academic) whether fishing rights may form predial servitudes in Louisiana, but such rights may be part of a limited personal servitude.

g) In the opinion of Professor Yiannopoulos, prohibitions against competition should not be allowed to form the object of a predial servitude on public policy grounds. Louisiana courts have not addressed this issue directly, but French courts have found that such agreements may not form part of a predial servitude. Such agreements benefit a person, not an estate, and there is no direct relationship between the agreement and the use of a dominant estate. French courts have found that such non-competition agreements create rights other than predial servitudes, such as personal obligations.

   i. *But see RCC Properties, L.L.C. v. Wenstar Properties, L.P.* in which the Second Circuit found a servitude restricting the kinds of business that could be operated on the servient estate to be valid. The opposite result obtained in *SPE FO Holdings, LLC v. Retif Oil & Fuel, LLC*, 2008 WL 754716 (E.D. La. 2008), in which the court held that restrictions on competition contained in a recorded lease did not constitute a predial servitude or building restriction.

h) Agreements to purchase or sell quotas of agricultural or industrial products may not form predial servitudes because these agreements require substantial affirmative actions on the owner of the would-be servient estate. Instead, these agreements create personal obligations.

i) **Restraints on alienation of immovables.**

   i. Under traditional civilian doctrine, restraints on the alienation of immovables form personal obligations only. Under that understanding, universal successors would be bound not to alienate the property, but transferees who receive the property by particular title would not be so restrained.

   ii. In modern French doctrine, such a restraint may not form the object of a predial servitude because the restraint operates for the benefit of a person rather than an estate.

   iii. Under Louisiana law, a restraint on the alienation of an immovable may form a predial servitude. Absolute or perpetual restraints on the alienation of immovables are invalid, but restraints of limited duration imposed by parties with a substantial interest are valid against the original party as well as any acquirer of the property with notice of the restraint.

      A. An impending transfer contrary to the restraint may be enjoined.

      B. Remedies for a violation could include damages, resolution of the original transfer, or the annulment of the subsequent transfer.

      C. Annulment of the subsequent transfer should be the default remedy in cases where the impermissible transfer is a donation *inter vivos* or *mortis causa*.

2. **Kinds of servitudes.**

   a) "Predial servitudes are either affirmative or negative.
   Affirmative servitudes are those that give the right to the owner of the dominant estate to do a certain thing on the servient estate. Such are the servitudes of right of way, drain, and support.
   Negative servitudes are those that impose on the owner of the servient estate the duty

to abstain from doing something on his estate. Such are the servitudes of prohibition of building and of the use of an estate as a commercial or industrial establishment." La. C.C. art. 706.

    i. Classification of a servitude as affirmative or negative dictates the commencement of the prescription of nonuse for the servitude. Prescription begins to run against affirmative servitudes from their last use and against negative servitudes from the occurrence of an event contrary to the servitude. La. C.C. art. 754.

b) "Predial servitudes are either apparent or nonapparent.
Apparent servitudes are those that are perceivable by exterior signs, works, or constructions; such as a roadway, a window in a common wall, or an aqueduct.
Nonapparent servitudes are those that have no exterior sign of their existence; such as the prohibition of building on an estate or of building above a particular height." La. C.C. art. 707.

    i. Classification as either apparent or nonapparent depends on factual circumstances rather than the nature of the servitude. The same servitude could be either apparent or nonapparent, depending on how it is used. For example, a servitude allowing the installation of pipes across an estate would be apparent if the pipes are visible above ground or nonapparent if they are run below ground.

    ii. Classification of a servitude as apparent or nonapparent affects the rules for its creation. Nonapparent servitudes must be acquired by title; apparent servitudes may be acquired by title, by destination of the owner, or by acquisitive prescription.

c) Civilian tradition also classifies predial servitudes as either continuous or discontinuous. Louisiana law abandoned this classification with the 1977 revision of the Civil Code. The concept has no legal impact today.

3. **Acquisition of servitudes.**

a) **Acquisition by title.**

    i. "The establishment of a predial servitude by title is an alienation of a part of the property to which the laws governing alienation of immovables apply." La. C.C. art. 708.

    ii. "Predial servitudes are established by all acts by which immovables may be transferred. Delivery of the act of transfer or use of the right by the owner of the dominant estate constitutes tradition." La. C.C. art. 722.

      A. Conventional predial servitudes and personal servitudes affecting immovable property generally must be in writing to affect third parties, and that writing must contain sufficient information to identify the servient estate. But a verbal agreement will bind a grantor who admits to it under oath. *Langevin v. Howard*.

    iii. "A predial servitude may be established on a certain part of an estate, if that part is sufficiently described." La. C.C. art. 727.

      A. A stipulation to the effect that the purchaser of an estate and his successors and assigns may use a driveway on a neighboring estate owned by the vendor constitutes a predial servitude even though it does not style itself a servitude or describe the driveway in detail. *Burgas v. Stoutz*.

iv. "Doubt as to the existence, extent, or manner of exercise of a predial servitude shall be resolved in favor of the servient estate." La. C.C. art. 730.

    A. An act that clearly reflects the intention to create a predial servitude restricting the kinds of business that can be operated on the servient estate and lays out a formula for evaluating compliance is valid even though the procedure and timing for verifying compliance are unclear. *RCC Properties, L.L.C. v. Wenstar Properties, L.P. But see SPE FO Holdings, LLC v. Retif Oil & Fuel, LLC*, 2008 WL 754716 (E.D. La. 2008).

v. "A charge established on an estate expressly for the benefit of another estate is a predial servitude although it is not so designated." La. C.C. art. 731.

vi. "When the act does not declare expressly that the right granted is for the benefit of an estate or for the benefit of a particular person, the nature of the right is determined in accordance with the following rules." La. C.C. art. 732.

    A. "When the right granted be of a nature to confer an advantage on an estate, it is presumed to be a predial servitude." La. C.C. art. 733.

    B. "When the right granted is merely for the convenience of a person, it is not considered to be a predial servitude, unless it is acquired by a person as owner of an estate for himself, his heirs and assigns." La. C.C. art. 734.

vii. "Nonapparent servitudes may be acquired by title only, including a declaration of destination under [La. C.C. art.] 741." La. C.C. art. 739.

b) **Acquisitive prescription.**

i. "Apparent servitudes may be acquired by title, by destination of the owner, or by acquisitive prescription." La. C.C. art. 740.

    A. While a servitude of light and view is an apparent servitude that may be acquired by acquisitive prescription, a prohibition against building above a particular height is a nonapparent servitude that cannot be acquired by acquisitive prescription. *Goodwin v. Alexander.*

ii. "The laws governing acquisitive prescription of immovable property apply to apparent servitudes. An apparent servitude may be acquired by peaceable and uninterrupted possession of the right for ten years in good faith and by just title; it may also be acquired by uninterrupted possession for thirty years without title or good faith." La. C.C. art. 742.

    A. Servitudes of light and view can be acquired by acquisitive prescription either by peaceful possession for thirty years or by peaceful possession for ten years both in good faith and by just title that clearly expresses the nature and extent of the servitude. *Palomeque v. Prudhomme.*

    B. A servitude for the overhang of an air conditioner is an apparent, affirmative servitude and can therefore be acquired either by ten-year acquisitive prescription where there is just title and good faith or by thirty-year acquisitive prescription without those factors. *Ryan v. Monet.*

iii. "Mineral rights may not be established by acquisitive prescription." La. M.C. art. 159. *See Savage v. Packard*, 218 La. 637, 50 So. 2d 298 (La. 1950).

c) **Destination of owner.**

i. "Nonapparent servitudes may be acquired by title only, including a declaration of destination under Article 739." La. C.C. art. 739.

ii. "Destination of the owner is a relationship established between two estates owned by the same owner that would be a predial servitude if the estates belonged to different owners.

When the two estates cease to belong to the same owner, unless there is express provision to the contrary, an apparent servitude comes into existence of right and a nonapparent servitude comes into existence if the owner has previously filed for registry in the conveyance records of the parish in which the immovable is located a formal declaration establishing the destination." La. C.C. art. 741.

    A. Where an owner of two estates sells one with what would have been an apparent servitude had the estates been owned by separate owners, the retained estate is burdened by all apparent servitudes by operation of law so long as the title documents are silent as to the servitude. *Alexander v. Boghel.*

    B. An apparent servitude of light and view between adjoining estates owned by the same person is not extinguished by destination simply by boarding up the shutters for a long time. *Taylor v. Boulware.*

    C. A concrete driveway connecting an enclosed estate to a public road across an adjacent lot formerly owned by a common owner constitutes an exterior sign suggesting the establishment of a predial servitude by destination. *Phipps v. Schupp.*

d) **St. Julien doctrine.**

    i. *Judicial estoppel.* The St. Julien doctrine was a form of judicially created estoppel that allowed entities having the power of expropriation to acquire a servitude through the unopposed use and possession of another's property for some public purpose, for example, by building utility infrastructure on it. *See St. Julien v. Morgan La. & Tex. R.R. Co.*, 35 La. Ann. 924 (La. 1883). The doctrine was judicially overruled.

        A. *No prescriptive period.* Occupancy with the knowledge, consent, or acquiescence of the owner was sufficient to create a servitude. The servitude did not need to be exercised for any required period of time.

        B. *Consent required.* The St. Julien doctrine applied only with the consent of the owner.

        C. *Action for recovery.* The owner was entitled to recover the value of the servitude, and the action was subject to ten-year liberative prescription. The action was personal but could be assigned, e.g., to the subsequent owner of the property subject to expropriation.

        D. *Overruled.* The St. Julien doctrine was prospectively overruled by *Lake, Inc. v. Louisiana Power & Light Co.*, 330 So. 2d 914 (La. 1976).

    ii. *Subsequent legislation.* After the St. Julien doctrine was overruled, the legislature enacted R.S. 19:14, which creates a presumption that an owner waives his or her right to receive compensation before the taking when the state, its subdivisions, or other expropriating authority takes possession and constructs works on his or her immovable property for the public good, so long as the entity believed, in good faith, it had the authority to do so.

        A. *Remedy.* In such a case, the owner's only remedy is an action to determine whether the taking was for a public and necessary purpose and for compensation after the fact.

B. *Prescription.* It is not clear what prescriptive period applies. Some courts applied the two-year period under R.S. 19:14, but *Howard v. Louisiana Power & Light Co.* held that that period only applied to property that had been expropriated, not where it is "appropriated" under the St. Julien doctrine. R.S. 13:5111 provides a three-year prescriptive period for claims against the states for takings "other than through an expropriation proceeding" running from the discovery of the taking. This may be applicable to takings under R.S. 19:14.

C. *St. Julien doctrine.* R.S. 19:14 did not legislatively revive the St. Julien doctrine.

4. **Rights of the owner of the dominant estate.**

a) "The owner of the dominant estate has the right to make at his expense all the works that are necessary for the use and preservation of the servitude." La. C.C. art. 744.

b) "The owner of the dominant estate has the right to enter with his workmen and equipment into the part of the servient estate that is needed for the construction or repair of works required for the use and preservation of the servitude. He may deposit materials to be used for the works and the debris that may result, under the obligation of causing the least possible damage and of removing them as soon as possible." La. C.C. art. 745.

c) "If the act establishing the servitude binds the owner of the servient estate to make the necessary works at his own expense, he may exonerate himself by abandoning the servient estate or the part of it on which the servitude is granted to the owner of the dominant estate." La. C.C. art. 746.

d) "If the dominant estate is divided, the servitude remains due to each part, provided that no additional burden is imposed on the servient estate. Thus, in case of a right of passage, all the owners are bound to exercise that right through the same place." La. C.C. art. 747.

e) "The owner of the servient estate may do nothing tending to diminish or make more inconvenient the use of the servitude.
If the original location has become more burdensome for the owner of the servient estate, or if it prevents him from making useful improvements on his estate, he may provide another equally convenient location for the exercise of the servitude which the owner of the dominant estate is bound to accept. All expenses of relocation are borne by the owner of the servient estate." La. C.C. art. 748.

   i. A roof overhanging a servitude at a height that might impede the passage of equipment of any height impermissibly diminishes the dominant estate's servitude of ingress and egress. *Hymel v. St. John the Baptist School Board.*

f) "If the title is silent as to the extent and manner of use of the servitude, the intention of the parties is to be determined in the light of its purpose." La. C.C. art. 749.

g) "If the title does not specify the location of the servitude, the owner of the servient estate shall designate the location." La. C.C. art. 750.

5. **Extinction of servitudes.**

a) "A predial servitude is extinguished by the permanent and total destruction of the dominant estate or of the part of the servient estate burdened with the servitude." La. C.C. art. 751.

     i. A well that dries up and is reestablished and improved by digging deeper and recasing is not destroyed, so the servitude is not extinguished. *Vincent v. Meaux.*

b) "If the exercise of the servitude becomes impossible because the things necessary for its exercise have undergone such a change that the servitude can no longer be used, the servitude is not extinguished; it resumes its effect when things are reestablished so that they may again be used, unless prescription has accrued." La. C.C. art. 752.

c) "A predial servitude is extinguished by nonuse for ten years." La. C.C. art. 753.

d) "Prescription of nonuse begins to run for affirmative servitudes from the date of their last use, and for negative servitudes from the date of the occurrence of an event contrary to the servitude.
An event contrary to the servitude is such as the destruction of works necessary for its exercise or the construction of works that prevent its exercise." La. C.C. art. 754.

     i. A predial servitude of passage is established by title and subject to prescription of nonuse when the agreement reflects the parties' intent to create the servitude and use is possible, even if its exact location or other details are to be fixed later. *Tilley v. Lowery.*

     ii. Acts performed solely as mere gestures intended to interrupt prescription do not constitute sufficient use to interrupt the liberative prescription of nonuse; the servitude must be used in a manner consistent with the purpose or object for which it was granted, as determined from the title and surrounding circumstances. *Ashland Oil Company, Inc. v. Palo Alto, Inc.*

     iii. The prescription of nonuse is only interrupted by the use of a servitude by the owner of the dominant estate or someone acting under her authority or in her name for the ordinary, legitimate purpose for which the servitude was established. *Thompson v. Meyers.*

e) "If the owner of the dominant estate is prevented from using the servitude by an obstacle that he can neither prevent nor remove, the prescription of nonuse is suspended on that account for a period of up to ten years." La. C.C. art. 755.

f) "If the servitude cannot be exercised on account of the destruction of a building or other construction that belongs to the owner of the dominant estate, prescription is not suspended. If the building or other construction belongs to the owner of the servient estate, the preceding article applies." La. C.C. art. 756.

g) "A predial servitude is preserved by the use made of it by anyone, even a stranger, if it is used as appertaining to the dominant estate." La. C.C. art. 757.

     i. The use of a well is to draw water, so a plaintiff uses the servitude and interrupts prescription through his lessees when they draw water, even if they unnecessarily pay for it. *Vincent v. Meaux.*

h) "The prescription of nonuse does not run against natural servitudes.". La. C.C. art. 758.

i) "A partial use of the servitude constitutes use of the whole." La. C.C. art. 759.

j) "A more extensive use of the servitude than that granted by the title does not result in the acquisition of additional rights for the dominant estate unless it be by acquisitive prescription." La. C.C. art. 760.

k) "The use of a right that is only accessory to the servitude is not use of the servitude." La. C.C. art. 761.

    i. Using accessory rights like providing power to the servient estate, clearing vegetation, and providing clearance for an adjacent transmission line is insufficient to interrupt the prescription of nonuse where the power line servitude is not being used to transmit electricity. *Broomfield v. Louisiana Power & Light Company.*

l) "If the dominant estate is owned in indivision, the use that a co-owner makes of the servitude prevents the running of prescription as to all.
   If the dominant estate is partitioned, the use of the servitude by each owner preserves it for his estate only." La. C.C. art. 762.

m) "The prescription of nonuse is not suspended by the minority or other disability of the owner of the dominant estate." La. C.C. art. 763.

n) "When the prescription of nonuse is pleaded, the owner of the dominant estate has the burden of proving that he or some other person has made use of the servitude as appertaining to his estate during the period of time required for the accrual of the prescription." La. C.C. art. 764.

o) "A predial servitude is extinguished when the dominant and the servient estates are acquired in their entirety by the same person." La. C.C. art. 765.

p) "When the union of the two estates is made under resolutory condition, or if it cease by legal eviction, the servitude is suspended and not extinguished." La. C.C. art. 766.

q) "Until a successor has formally or informally accepted a succession, confusion does not take place. If the successor renounces the succession, the servitudes continue to exist." La. C.C. art. 767.

r) "Confusion does not take place between separate property and community property of the spouses. Thus, if the servient estate belongs to one of the spouses and the dominant estate is acquired as a community asset, the servitude continues to exist." La. C.C. art. 768.

s) "A servitude that has been extinguished by confusion may be reestablished only in the manner by which a servitude may be created." La. C.C. art. 769.

t) "A predial servitude is extinguished by the abandonment of the servient estate, or of the part on which the servitude is exercised. It must be evidenced by a written act. The owner of the dominant estate is bound to accept it and confusion takes place." La. C.C. art. 770.

u) "A predial servitude is extinguished by an express and written renunciation by the owner of the dominant estate." La. C.C. art. 771.

v) "A renunciation of a servitude by a co-owner of the dominant estate does not discharge the servient estate, but deprives him of the right to use the servitude." La. C.C. art. 772.

w) "A predial servitude established for a term or under a resolutory condition is extinguished upon the expiration of the term or the happening of the condition." La C.C. art. 773.

x) "A predial servitude is extinguished by the dissolution of the right of the person who established it." La. C.C. art. 774.

6. **Protection of servitudes.**

a) Servitudes may be asserted and recognized through the petitory action under La. C.C. arts. 3653–3654.

b) Likewise, quasi-possession of servitudes may be asserted and recognized through the possessory action under La. C.C. arts. 3655–3656.

   i. A person who possesses an apparent servitude for a period of one year beginning on or after January 1, 1983, may maintain a possessory action for that servitude, even though enough time has not passed to support acquisitive prescription. *Kizer v. Lilly*.

   ii. Injunctive relief maintaining a person in possession of an immovable, including a real right like a servitude, is only appropriate where the plaintiff has been in possession of the real right continuously for more than one year immediately prior to the disturbance. *Louisiana Irrigation and Mill Co. v. Pousson*.

c) See the chapters herein on *Possession* and *Protection of Ownership; Real Actions* for details on the possessory and petitory actions, respectively.

d) **The aftermath of Kizer.** Professor Symeonides examined some of the questions raised in *Kizer v. Lilly*:

   i. *Negatory action.* The plaintiff in the negatory action seeks "to determine the existence or nonexistence, validity, and scope of the claimed servitude."

      A. Professor Symeonides suggested that the plaintiff in the negatory action must show better title than the defendant exercising a claimed servitude. Since having title would extinguish any servitude over the immovable, the defendant will not have a title, so any title is better title.

      B. After demonstrating any title, the burden shifts to the defendant to prove that a servitude came into being.

   ii. Professor Symeonides reviewed two alternative procedures to keep the owner of the immovable from having to bring a second action to prove ownership in the case where a person acquires a judgment recognizing possession of a servitude in a possessory action.

      A. He rejected the merger of the confessory action into the possessory action because it would amount to a compulsory waiver of the possessory action and require proof of the servitude from the outset, thereby limiting its tactical application.

      B. He suggested that the defense of the possessory action be merged into the negatory action, allowing the owner to either defend the assertion of quasi-possession or convert it to a negatory action and force the possessor to prove the existence of the servitude in the same action.

BURGAS V. STOUTZ
141 So. 67, 174 La. 586 (La. 1932)

Facts & Procedure

This is a dispute over the use of a driveway between owners of neighboring lots purchased from a common author in title, Mrs. Pizzolata. She owned a lot that she subdivided into lots "A" and "B." Mr. Burgas (P) purchased lot "A," with a stipulation in the act of sale granting "the purchaser, its successors and assigns" the "privilege of using the paved driveway in the rear of the property hereinabove described, which paved driveway is part of Lot 'B' belonging to the vendors herein." The stipulation was recorded in the public records of Orleans parish with a slightly different wording, omitting the words "successors and assigns."

Mrs. Pizzolata later sold lot "B," and after several intermediate transactions, Mr. Stoutz (D) ultimately purchased it. Mr. Stoutz (D) notified Mr. Burgas (P) that he intended to build a fence that would obstruct Mr. Burgas's (P) use of the driveway, so Mr. Burgas (P) sued for an injunction. The trial court recognized Mr. Burgas's (P) right to use the driveway and granted a permanent injunction prohibiting Mr. Stoutz (D) from blocking it.

Mr. Stoutz (D) appealed.

Issue

Does a recorded stipulation in an act of sale granting the "purchaser, its successors and assigns ... the privilege of using of the paved driveway" located at the rear the vendor's adjacent lot create a valid predial servitude enforceable against a subsequent purchaser of the servient estate?

Holding & Decision

Yes, a stipulation to the effect that the purchaser of an estate and his successors and assigns may use a driveway on a neighboring estate constitutes a predial servitude even though it does not style itself a servitude or describe the driveway in detail. The Court held that the stipulation created a predial servitude, finding it significant (1) that the stipulation granted a right to the "purchaser" in his capacity as owner of the dominant estate rather than being directed to a named individual in his personal capacity and (2) that the right granted a real advantage to the dominant estate rather than conveying a personal convenience to an owner. To wit, the dominant estate enjoyed the advantage of using more of its surface area for things other than a driveway while maintaining the access a driveway provides. Under La. C.C. art. 733 a right is presumed to be a predial servitude, regardless of the words used to describe it, if it provides a real advantage to the dominant estate.

Additionally, the Court rejected Mr. Burgas's (D) contention that the right of passage was insufficiently described and ambiguous because there was no factual question concerning what driveway was meant by the parties. There was only one driveway on the property in question, and it could be seen with the naked eye. Finally, the Court held that the stipulation, even in the abbreviated form recorded in the public records, was sufficient to affect third parties and to give Mr. Stoutz (D) notice of the servitude, even though the servitude is not mentioned in Mr. Stoutz's (D) chain of title.

The Court affirmed the trial court's judgment.

Rule of Law

A stipulation to the effect that the purchaser of an estate and his successors and assigns may use a driveway on a neighboring estate owned by the vendor constitutes a predial servitude even though it does not style itself a servitude or describe the driveway in detail.

RCC PROPERTIES, L.L.C. v. WENSTAR PROPERTIES, L.P.

930 So. 2d 1233 (La. App. 2d Cir. 2006)

Facts & Procedure

This is a dispute over a predial servitude restricting the operation of a certain kind of business on the neighboring estate. Wenstar Properties, L.P. (D) (Wenstar) purchased a property from AZT Winnsboro La., Inc. (AZT) to operate a Wendy's restaurant. As part of the transaction, AZT granted Wenstar (D) a 20-year predial servitude on the adjacent property it retained prohibiting its use as a restaurant with a drive-thru whose primary business was selling hamburgers, hamburger products, or chicken sandwiches. The agreement defined "primary business" as having 15% or more of the operation's gross sales (excluding taxes, beverages, and dairy) across the prohibited food items. The servitude would terminate if the Wendy's ceased operation for three continuous months.

A few years later, AZT sold the servient estate to RCC Properties, L.L.C. (P) (RCC). RCC (P) received an offer from Hannon's Food Service to build a KFC restaurant, contingent on the release of the servitude. KFC sold chicken sandwiches, potentially in violation of the servitude. RCC (P) sued for a declaratory judgment to invalidate the servitude or find it inapplicable to RCC's (P) property. The trial court invalidated the servitude on the grounds that it was unclear and ambiguous because it was not explicitly defined how "primary business" was to be measured or over what time period it should be measured.

Wenstar (D) appealed.

Issue

Is a predial servitude acquired by title valid when the act establishing it describes the prohibited use and a formula for determining if that restriction is violated, even though the act does not specify a time period being measured or a procedure for verifying compliance with the restriction?

Holding & Decision

Yes, an act that clearly reflects the intention to create a predial servitude restricting the kinds of business that can be operated on the servient estate and lays out a formula for evaluating compliance is valid even though the procedure and timing for verifying compliance are unclear. The appeal court found that the trial court erred in invalidating the servitude and reviewed the matter *de novo*. The court held that, while ambiguities and doubts regarding a servitude should be resolved in favor of the servient estate, the parties clearly intended to create a predial servitude restricting the use of the servient estate. The act transferring the property was entitled "Act of Cash Sale and Servitude," the act clearly identified the prohibited use of the servient estate, and laid out a term and resolutory condition for the servitude.

Nevertheless, the appeal court also noted that it was unclear how to determine the "primary business" conducted on the servient estate. Because this measurement is related to the use of the servitude, the court evaluated the parties' intent reflected in the title document and found that the parties produced evidence below showing that KFC's chicken sandwiches were below the 15% threshold through the date of the trial. Therefore, the court concluded that the servitude did not prohibit the operation of a KFC on the property at issue. The appeal court did not opine on what should happen if KFC's chicken sandwich revenues crossed the threshold in the future or how compliance should be verified in the future.

The court reversed the trial court's judgment, instead finding that a valid servitude existed in favor of Wenstar's (D) estate and declaring that KFC did not violate the servitude.

Rule of Law

An act that clearly reflects the intention to create a predial servitude restricting the kinds of business that can be operated on the servient estate and lays out a formula for evaluating compliance is valid even though the procedure and timing for verifying compliance are unclear.

LANGEVIN V. HOWARD
363 So. 2d 1209 (La. App. 2d Cir. 1978)

Facts & Procedure

In this dispute over a driveway servitude, the parties owned adjacent lots that previously formed part of a larger parcel known as the Kent tract. That tract was partitioned in 1955 into six smaller tracts (lettered A-F), and the parties reserved a 50-foot wide strip running through the partitioned tracts to be held in indivision for the benefit of all the owners to access a public road. The owners of the 50 foot strip did not pay property taxes on it, and it was sold at tax sale in 1960.

Mr. Turk purchased Tract F in in 1969. In 1972, Mr. Howard (D) acquired the 50-foot strip and two other lettered tracts. In 1973, Mr. Howard (D) paid Mr. Turk $1,000 to build a driveway down the center of the 50-foot strip to access his (D) home. In 1975, Mr. Turk subdivided two small lots from Tract F and sold one to Mr. Langevin (P). He intended for Mr. Langevin (P) and the future purchaser of the other lot to use the driveway on the 50 foot strip for egress to the public road. Mr. Turk informed Mr. Howard (D) that he claimed an ownership interest in the 50 foot strip as a result of the Kent partition and gave him a check for $200 marked "use of driveway." Mr. Howard (D) accepted the check but was unaware Mr. Turk had sold one of the lots at the time the check was written.

Mr. Langevin (P) used the driveway until 1977 when Mr. Howard (D) blocked his access. Mr. Langevin (P) sued for recognition of a right of passage across the 50-foot strip, arguing a servitude was created by the 1955 partition or, alternatively, by the 1975 check transaction.

The trial court recognized the servitude, and Mr. Howard (D) appealed.

Issue

Can a servitude good against third parties be created by a verbal exchange and a check that contains only the phrase "use of driveway?"

Holding & Decision

No, conventional predial servitudes and personal servitudes affecting immovable property generally must be in writing to affect third parties, and that writing must contain sufficient information to identify the servient estate. Nevertheless, a verbal agreement will bind a grantor who admits to it under oath.

The appeal court first rejected Mr. Langevin's (P) claim that the $200 check with the notation "use of driveway" created a predial servitude because it did not describe the servient estate. The court declined to admit parol evidence to supply the missing description because the check did not sufficiently identify the property to justify a clarifying admission.

The court next rejected Mr. Langevin's (P) argument that the check created a personal servitude under the doctrine of stipulation *pour autrui* because a personal servitude affecting immovable property would also requires a writing describing the property. The check did not meet this requirement, and thus no personal servitude was created.

Finally, the appeal court addressed the plaintiff's contention that Messrs. Howard (D) and Turk had a verbal agreement to create a servitude. A verbal transaction can affect immovable property with respect to the grantor if he admits to the transaction under oath. Here, Mr. Howard (D) testified that he only agreed to Mr. Langevin's (P) use of the driveway for two years in return for the payment by Mr. Turk. That period had expired by the trial. The court refused to consider other parties' testimony on the subject because only the grantor's admissions are effective against him under the law.

The court amended the trial court judgment to hold that Mr. Langevin (P) had no right of passage on Mr. Howard's (D) property.

Rule of Law

Conventional predial servitudes and personal servitudes affecting immovable property generally must be in writing to affect third parties, and that writing must contain sufficient information to identify the servient estate. But a verbal agreement will bind a grantor who admits to it under oath.

PALOMEQUE V. PRUDHOMME
Doctor (P) v. Chef (D)
664 So. 2d 88 (La. 1995)

Facts & Procedure

A Doctor (P) owned a condominium unit on the second floor of a building that shared a common wall with the adjacent one-story building owned by a famous Chef (D). The buildings had initially been constructed together in 1834 as two buildings in a row of three. The Chef (D) planned to add a second story to his building, which would require bricking over windows in the exterior wall of the Doctor's (P) unit. The Doctor (P) sued for an injunction prohibiting the construction, arguing that he had acquired servitudes of light and view through the windows by acquisitive prescription.

The trial court denied the Doctor (P) a permanent injunction, holding that servitudes of light and view could not be acquired by acquisitive prescription. The appeal court affirmed the trial court's judgment, and the Louisiana Supreme Court granted certiorari.

Issue

Can servitudes of light and view be acquired by acquisitive prescription?

Holding & Decision

Yes, servitudes of light and view can be acquired by acquisitive prescription either by peaceful possession for thirty years or by peaceful possession for ten years both in good faith and by just title that clearly expresses the nature and extent of the servitude. The Court first determined that servitudes of light and view are apparent servitudes because the windows in the common wall are exterior signs perceivable from the outside and noted that apparent servitudes, unlike nonapparent servitudes, can be acquired by prescription. In rejecting the Chef's (D) argument that the servitude at issue was actually in the nature of a building restriction (and therefore nonapparent and not acquirable by acquisitive prescription), the Court distinguished a servitude of light and view from a servitude prohibiting building, finding the latter more onerous because it prevents any construction, while the former simply prevents some constructions that obstruct light and view.

The Court then addressed whether the Doctor (P) had, in fact, acquired a servitude by ten-year acquisitive prescription. The Court found that the Doctor (P) had possessed the servitude of light and view for more than ten years but the boilerplate language in his title was too ambiguous and imprecise to transfer a servitude. While this language did not reference the servient estate at all, even if it had been part of an agreement with that estate it would still be too vague to suffice as a title. Because the Doctor (P) lacked a just title, the Court rejected his acquisitive prescription claim without reaching the issue of good faith. The record clearly demonstrated that thirty-year acquisitive prescription was inapplicable because the windows had been in place less than thirty years.

Therefore, the Court affirmed the lower court's judgment.

Rule of Law

Servitudes of light and view can be acquired by acquisitive prescription either by peaceful possession for thirty years or by peaceful possession for ten years both in good faith and by just title that clearly expresses the nature and extent of the servitude.

Ryan v. Monet

666 So. 2d 711 (La. App. 4th Cir. 1995)

Facts & Procedure

Ms. Ryan (P) and Ms. Monet (D) owned adjacent properties in New Orleans. Both buildings were over 100 years old, and the foundation of Ms. Monet's (D) building was built on the properties' boundary. Four air conditioning units were installed in windows on the side of Ms. Monet's (D) residence and hung across the boundary over Ms. Ryan's (P) property. They were installed in 1971 or later. In 1958, the parties' ancestors in title signed an agreement styled as a servitude that recognized the overhang of the cornice and roof of Ms. Monet's (D) building onto Ms. Ryan's (P) property.

Ms. Ryan (P) filed suit seeking an injunction to remove the air conditioners and a gutter downspout draining onto her property. The trial court granted a preliminary injunction ordering Ms. Monet (D) to relocate the downspout but allowing her to maintain the air conditioners, holding that the overhang was a predial servitude acquired by acquisitive prescription.

Ms. Ryan (P) appealed the portion of the injunction regarding the air conditioners.

Issue

Can a landowner acquire a predial servitude for the overhang of window unit air conditioners by acquisitive prescription when there is no title supporting the servitude and the only evidence shows they were installed less than thirty years earlier?

Holding & Decision

No, a servitude for the overhang of an air conditioner is an apparent, affirmative servitude and can therefore be acquired either by ten-year acquisitive prescription if there is just title and good faith or by thirty-year acquisitive prescription without those factors.

The appeal court noted that an apparent, affirmative predial servitude like the one at issue could only be acquired by title, destination of the owner, or acquisitive prescription. The properties were never owned by a common owner, so it was not possible for the servitude to be created by destination. Similarly, the court found that the 1958 agreement between prior owners did not create a servitude for air conditioners because it unambiguously authorized only the overhang of the cornice and roof. The court likewise held that La. C.C. arts. 743 and 744 do not authorize the use of air conditioners as necessary or accessory rights for the use or preservation of the pre-existing servitude for the roof and cornice.

The appeal court then analyzed whether the air conditioner overhang could be considered a predial servitude acquired by acquisitive prescription. Acquisitive prescription of ten years requires good faith, just title, and peaceable and uninterrupted possession; prescription of thirty years requires only uninterrupted possession. While there was evidence that air conditioners had been present on the building since 1983 at the latest (though potentially replaced over time), there was no evidence of any title regarding the air conditioners, only the cornice and roof. Therefore, thirty-year prescription applied. Since thirty years had not elapsed between 1983 and the lawsuit filed in 1995, no servitude had been acquired by thirty-year acquisitive prescription.

Finally, the court rejected Monet's (D) estoppel argument based on Ryan's (P) alleged knowledge of the building's encroachment at the time of purchase. Estoppel is not a recognized method for creating predial servitudes, and equitable relief was inappropriate.

The appeal court amended the injunction to require Monet (D) to remove the air conditioners and remanded the matter for further proceedings.

Rule of Law

A servitude for the overhang of an air conditioner is an apparent, affirmative servitude and can therefore be acquired either by ten-year acquisitive prescription where there is just title and good faith or by thirty-year acquisitive prescription without those factors

GOODWIN V. ALEXANDER
105 La. 658, 30 So. 102 (La. 1901)

Facts & Procedure

Mrs. Goodwin (P) owned a house built just six inches inside the boundary between the parties' lot with a window facing Mrs. Alexander's (D) house. The window had blinds that, when opened more than six inches, passed into Mrs. Alexander's (D) property. The house and its blinds existed well over thirty years before this dispute. After disagreements between Mrs. Alexander (D) and Mrs. Goodwin's (P) tenant residing in the house, Mrs. Alexander (D) built a wooden screen on her property along the boundary line that blocked the view from the window between the houses and prevented the blinds from operating. The screen initially leaned slightly toward the Goodwin (P) house but was later straightened.

Mrs. Goodwin (P) sued, claiming a servitude of light and view by thirty-year acquisitive prescription and seeking damages and removal of the screen. The defendant filed an exception of no cause of action and a general denial.

The trial court rejected Mrs. Goodwin's (P) claims, and she (P) appealed.

Issue

Does a servitude of light and view acquired by acquisitive prescription includes a prohibition against building a structure to obstruct the light and view on a neighboring property?

Holding & Decision

No. While a servitude of light and view is an apparent servitude that may be acquired by acquisitive prescription, a prohibition against building above a particular height is a nonapparent servitude that cannot be acquired by acquisitive prescription. The Court noted that affirmative servitudes, such as rights of way or drainage, can be acquired by prescription, but negative servitudes, like the prohibition against building above a certain height or on a certain part of an estate, can only be established by title. The Court emphasized that the right to build on one's own property is inherent in ownership and is imprescriptible. Further, the Court distinguished the right of enjoyment of light and view from the separate right to prohibit acts on the neighboring property, holding that even if plaintiffs acquired a right to light and view, it would not include a right to prohibit the defendant's construction of the screen on her own property. Because Mrs. Goodwin (P) had no legal basis to claim a servitude, the Court also rejected her demand for damages.

The Court affirmed the trial court's judgment.

Rule of Law

While a servitude of light and view is an apparent servitude that may be acquired by acquisitive prescription, a prohibition against building above a particular height is a nonapparent servitude that cannot be acquired by acquisitive prescription.

ALEXANDER V. BOGHEL
4 La. 312 (La. 1832)

Facts & Procedure

Messrs. Alexander (P) and Boghel (D) owned adjacent lots derived from a common vendor. Mr. Boghel (D) purchased his lot first, and the lot included a house situated so that its roof extended over the adjacent vacant lot and dripped rainwater on it. Mr. Alexander (P) subsequently purchased the vacant lot and sued to enjoin Mr. Boghel (D) from allowing the rainwater to fall on his property. Mr. Boghel (D) asserted that he had a servitude of drip and pleaded prescription. The trial court ruled for Mr. Boghel (D) and recognized the servitude.

Mr. Alexander (P) appealed.

Issue

Is a predial servitude of drip established by destination of the owner where a common owner sells one of two estates on which an apparent servitude exists without mentioning the servitude in the act of sale?

Holding & Decision

Yes, where an owner of two estates sells one with what would have been an apparent servitude had the estates been owned by separate owners, the remaining estate is burdened by all apparent servitudes by operation of law so long as the title documents are silent as to the servitude. The Court held that when the common vendor sold the lot with the house to Mr. Boghel (D), a servitude was created in favor of that lot over the lot subsequently sold to Mr. Alexander (P) because the estates, as situated, bore apparent signs of the servitude.

The Court highlighted the Civil Code provision in force at the time which stated, "if the proprietor of two estates, between which there exists an apparent sign of service, sell[s] one of those estates, and if the deed of sale be silent respecting the service, the same shall continue to exist actively or passively, in favor of, or upon the estate, which has been sold." Because the common vendor's sale to Mr. Boghel (D) was silent with respect to the apparent servitude, it continued to burden the lot that the common vendor retained and subsequently sold to Mr. Alexander (P).

Therefore, Mr. Boghel's (D) estate enjoyed a predial servitude, and the Court affirmed the trial court's judgment.

Rule of Law

Where an owner of two estates sells one with what would have been an apparent servitude had the estates been owned by separate owners, the retained estate is burdened by all apparent servitudes by operation of law so long as the title documents are silent as to the servitude

TAYLOR V. BOULWARE
New Owner (P) v. Previous Owner (D)
35 La. Ann. 469 (La. 1883)

Facts & Procedure

Mr. Boulware (D) owned two adjacent lots, one with a two-story brick house and the other with a cottage a few feet from the brick house. To protect the privacy of the cottage and its tenant, he boarded up the venetian blinds (shutters) of the brick house from the outside, rendering them inoperable.

Fifteen years later, Mr. Boulware (D) sold the brick house and its lot to Mrs. Taylor (P) with the boards on its windows. After taking possession, the New Owner (P) demanded the Previous Owner (D) remove the boards. He refused, so she had them removed. The Previous Owner (D) then erected screens on his lot between the brick house and the cottage to block the view from the brick house's windows.

The New Owner (P) sued to have the screens removed and for damages, arguing the boarded-up windows demonstrated an apparent servitude of light and view in favor of the brick house that was impaired by the screens. In the alternative, she requested a reduction in the purchase price if the court found the windows should be closed or the screens maintained. She also complained of other minor encroachments that provided convenience to the cottage and its lot, including a water pipe attached to her property, sheds and a gutter just over the property line, and a clothesline affixed to her property with iron staples — all of of which she sought to have removed. The Previous Owner (D) claimed the New Owner (P) committed trespass by opening the windows, sought damages, and demanded the windows be boarded up again.

The trial court recognized the New Owner's (P) right to open and use the windows, ordered the screens removed, and rejected both parties' damage claims. It also rejected the New Owner's (P) claims regarding the minor encroachments.

Both parties appealed.

Issue

Is an apparent servitude of light and view established by destination between two neighboring buildings owned by a single owner extinguished simply by boarding up its shutters if the shutters and the windows would other wise be operable?

Holding & Decision

No, under Civil Code articles 728 and 769 (now La. C.C. arts. 707 and 741, respectively), an apparent servitude of light and view is not extinguished simply by closing the windows for a time, even fifteen years. The Court noted that when the New Owner (P) purchased the house the windows and blinds were still present and gave the appearance of intended use. The presence of these windows constituted an apparent sign of servitude. The mere act of nailing boards over them did not constitute a sufficiently permanent change to destroy the servitude because it was a trivially reversible process, unlike, e.g., bricking the openings up.

In the initial hearing, the Court held that the Previous Owner (D) also had the right to erect screens on his property to protect the cottage from view. The Court reasoned that the Previous Owner (D) would be allowed to block the view by constructing a second story; therefore a screen was not less permissible.

Initially, the Court affirmed the trial court's judgment in part with respect to rejecting the damage claims, rejecting the New Owner's (P) demand to remove the minor encroachments, and recognizing the New Owner's (P) right to use the windows. The Court reversed the judgment below in part insofar as it required the removal of the screens.

On rehearing, the Court clarified that the servitude did not extend to the unlimited right to open the shutters fully but only to open them to the degree they could have been opened if the boards had not been present and amended its judgment so that the screen opposite the window labeled "B" in the record must be removed.

Rule of Law

An apparent servitude of light and view between adjoining estates owned by the same person is not extinguished by destination simply by boarding up the shutters for a long time.

PHIPPS V. SCHUPP
45 So. 3d 593 (La. 2010)

Facts & Procedure

Richard Katz owned a parcel of land that he subdivided into two lots bearing street addresses 541 and 543 Exposition Boulevard. Exposition Boulevard is not a public street; it is a walking path that borders Audubon Park and prohibits vehicular traffic. Patton Street, a public road, runs alongside 543 Exposition Boulevard, and that lot has access to it. But 541 Exposition Boulevard is an enclosed estate.

At the time Mr. Katz sold 541 Exposition Boulevard, it had no access to a public road except through a concrete driveway that crossed 543 Exposition Boulevard. Mr. Phipps (P) purchased 541 Exposition Boulevard from an intermediate owner in 1982, and used the driveway to access Patton Street until the defendants fenced it off completely in 2006. The Schupps (D) partially blocked the driveway with a carport in 2003, at which point Mr. Phipps (P) stopped using it for vehicular traffic. But he continued to use it to access Patton Street on foot.

When the defendants began building a fence blocking the driveway, Mr. Phipps (P) filed a possessory action claiming a servitude of passage. The Schupps (D) filed for summary judgment. The district court granted it, holding the driveway's mere existence wasn't proof of the common owner's intent to create a servitude. The appeal court affirmed.

Mr. Phipps (P) appealed.

Issue

Does a concrete driveway connecting an enclosed estate to a public road across an adjacent lot owned by the same person, constitute an exterior sign suggesting the establishment of a predial servitude by destination?

Holding & Decision

Yes, a concrete driveway connecting an enclosed estate to a public road across an adjacent lot formerly owned by a common owner constitutes an exterior sign suggesting the establishment of a predial servitude by destination.

At the outset, the Court noted that La. C.C. art. 689 (providing for forced passage for enclosed estates) is relevant and raised material questions of fact on its own. Turning to the servitude issue, the Court also noted that an apparent servitude by destination comes into existence of right unless expressly disclaimed. The Court distinguished the case from *730 Bienville Partners v. First Nat. Bank of Commerce*, 596 So.2d 836 (La. App. 4th Cir.1992), where no exterior signs of a servitude by destination existed and the use of the property was contingent upon a separate agreement. Here, the Court found that the driveway itself could be considered a sign under La. C.C. art. 707. The lack of an express provision in the original sale disavowing the servitude, coupled with the possible existence of a key given to Mr. Phipps (P) by the previous owner to use the gate across the driveway at Patton Street further added to the factual dispute.

Finally, the Court addressed the Schupps's (D) argument that Mr. Phipps's (P) possessory action was prescribed because he did not file suit within one year of the defendants disturbance of possession in 2003 when they enclosed the carport and blocked vehicular traffic on the driveway. The Court found that Phipps's (P) continued pedestrian use of the driveway after vehicular access was blocked constituted use of the entire, indivisible servitude, thus interrupting prescription.

The Court vacated the summary judgment because material facts remained in dispute and remanded the case for further proceedings.

Rule of Law

A concrete driveway connecting an enclosed estate to a public road across an adjacent lot formerly owned by a common owner constitutes an exterior sign suggesting the establishment of a predial servitude by destination.

HYMEL V. ST. JOHN THE BAPTIST PARISH SCHOOL BOARD

Farmers (P) v. School Board (D)
303 So. 2d 588 (La. App. 4th Cir. 1974)

Facts & Procedure

The parties owned adjacent tracts derived from a common ancestor who reserved a 25 foot servitude over the northern tract (eventually owned by the School Board (D)) to allow the owner of the southern tract to use for ingress and egress. The southern property was at all relevant times used to farm sugar cane, and the School Board (P) built a school on the northern tract.

When the Farmers (P) purchased the southern tract and the servitude, their surveyor noted several encroachments on the servitude by the School Board (D), including a chain link fence across the servitude at the front, the overhang of the school roof by several feet along 70 feet of the servitude, and drain apparatus extending above ground level inside the servitude. Additionally, school automobiles regularly parked on the front of the servitude.

The Farmers (P) sued for an injunction preventing the School Board (D) from interfering with their use of the servitude. The School Board (D) denied that it impeded the Farmers' (P) use of the servitude. The Farmers (P) testified that the servitude was used sporadically to various extents according to the agricultural season. During harvest, they used the servitude for cane cutters (vehicles approximately 13 feet tall and 10 feet wide), cane haulers (about the same size), and various tractors (some 20 feet wide). Given the size of the equipment, the encroachments often prevented two vehicles from passing side-by-side.

The trial court found for the Farmers (P), recognizing their servitude and enjoining the School Board (D) from interfering with it. But the trial court ruled that the School Board (D) would not be required to remove the encroaching roof and that the Farmers (P) would not be allowed to use the servitude to have two cane cutters pass abreast. The trial court assessed each party with their own costs.

The Farmers (P) appealed the paragraph of the judgment regarding the roof encroachment and restraining them from using cane cutters abreast on the servitude, the paragraph of the judgment directing the School Board (D) to remove its drainage devices and replace it with a drainage ditch on its property alongside the servitude, and the assessment of costs.

Issue

Does a roof overhang encroaching over a right-of-way servitude, even minimally, violate the dominant estate owner's right to use the servitude for ingress and egress?

Holding & Decision

Yes, any encroachment that diminishes the use of a servitude, regardless of degree, violates La. C.C. art. 748. Though the overhang didn't fully block the large equipment, the court found it nevertheless reduced the usable width of the servitude. The court reasoned that a right-of-way includes the space above the ground, at least to a height sufficient for the kind of vehicles contemplated by the servitude's purpose — in this case, sugarcane farming. The court rejected the trial court's reasoning that removal was an unreasonable burden on the School Board (D), as no evidence supported this. The court also noted that while the servient estate can relocate a servitude if it becomes more burdensome, here the School Board was seeking to maintain an encroachment, not relocate the entire servitude.

The court reversed the trial court's judgment in part and affirmed it in part. The court amended the trial court's judgment to delete the paragraph pertaining to the roof encroachment in its entirety and ordered that the School Board (D) remove the encroachment. But the court affirmed the order to replace the drainage devices with a ditch.

Rule of Law

A roof overhanging a servitude at a height that might impede the passage of equipment of any height impermissibly diminishes the dominant estate's servitude of ingress and egress.

RYAN V. SOUTHERN NATURAL GAS COMPANY
Landowners (P) v. Gas Company (D)
879 F. 2d 162 (5th Cir. 1989)

Facts & Procedure

In 1956, the Gas Company (D) acquired a servitude from the ancestors of the Landowners (P) to construct a pipeline canal across their marshland. The written servitude agreement specifically required the Gas Company (D) to backfill the canal on the northern portion of the property but gave it the explicit option to leave the canal open on a southern portion and prohibited backfilling at a later time. The Gas Company (D) constructed the canals, leaving the southern canal open.

In 1978, the Landowners (P) complained about erosion widening the canal beyond the servitude and salt water intrusion deteriorating the surrounding marsh and demanded that the Gas Company (D) dam the canal. The Gas Company (D) refused.

In 1986, the Landowners (P) sued the Gas Company (D) for damages due to canal widening and marsh loss, alleging negligence, strict liability under La. C.C. art. 667, and breach of the servitude agreement. The district court found the contract claim had prescribed but held the Gas Company (D) liable under negligence for failing to dam the canal. It awarded damages for land loss and marsh stabilization costs.

The Gas Company (D) appealed.

Issue

Does a servitude agreement that explicitly grants the servitude owner the option to leave a canal open and prohibits backfilling absolve the servitude owner of any duty under general servitude law like La. C.C. art. 745 or obligations of neighborhood like La. C.C. art. 667 to subsequently dam the canal to prevent damage to the servient estate?

Holding & Decision

Yes, the use and extent of a conventional predial servitude is regulated by the title rather than the default provisions of law, such as the duty under La. C.C. art. 745 to cause the least possible damage or potential duties arising under La. C.C. art. 667 concerning obligations of neighborhood, provided the agreement does not adversely affect the public interest.

The Fifth Circuit reversed the district court, holding that the explicit terms of the servitude agreement controlled and relieved the Gas Company (D) of any duty to dam the canal. The court emphasized that under La. C.C. art. 697, the agreement creating a servitude regulates its use and extent and that default rules apply only in the absence of such regulation.

Here, the contract plainly gave the Gas Company (D) the option to leave the canal open and prohibited backfilling, which necessarily included the right not to dam it. The court reasoned that any general duty imposed by La. C.C. art. 745 (requiring the servitude owner to cause the least possible damage) is suppletive and subordinate to the specific agreement between the parties. Similarly, even assuming La. C.C. art. 667 (imposing duties on proprietors) could apply to a servitude owner, La. C.C. art. 729 allows parties to contractually alter that duty.

Therefore, the servitude agreement dispensed with any duty the Gas Company (D) might otherwise have had under La. C.C. arts. 745 or 667 to dam the canal. The court noted an internal Gas Company (D) memo from the time the servitude agreement was executed expressing surprise at the ancestor in title agreeing not to require damming. The court concluded this supported the Gas Company's (D) position by showing the issue was specifically negotiated.

Since the agreement relieved the Gas Company (D) of the duty to dam the canal, there was no basis for the negligence finding. The Fifth Circuit reversed and remanded the matter for the entry of a take-nothing judgment in favor of the Gas Company (D).

Rule of Law

The use and extent of a conventional predial servitude is regulated by the title rather than the default provisions of law, such as the duty under La. C.C. art. 745 to cause the least possible damage or potential duties arising under La. C.C. art. 667 concerning obligations of neighborhood, provided the agreement does not adversely affect the public interest.

VINCENT V. MEAUX
325 So. 2d 346 (La. App. 3d Cir. 1975)

Facts & Procedure

In 1941, a partition agreement created a predial servitude granting the owners of Lots 1, 2, and 3 the right to use a deep water well located on Lot 3 for irrigation on all the lots. In 1951, the original well dried up due to a falling water table. The father of the owners of Lot 2, the Abshires and Meauxs (D), deepened the well and replaced the casing. Mr. Vincent's (P) lessees regularly used the well almost continuously from 1941 onward. They used the water for free from 1941 until the deepening of the well, at which time they agreed to pay 1/5th of their crop for the water.

At the time of this decision, David Meaux, Jr., (D) husband and brother-in-law of the owners of Lot 1, claimed ownership of the well on Lot 3. Mrs. Agnes Hebert, the owner of Lot 3, testified that she had verbally given all her rights in the well to the father of the owners of Lot 2. Neither transfer was explained in the record.

Mr. Vincent (P), owner of Lot 2, sued for a declaratory judgment affirming his right to use the well. Mr. Meaux (D) asserted that the servitude on the original well was extinguished by its destruction when the well dried up and that the servitude was prescribed because agreeing to pay for the water was not using the servitude in the intended way. Mrs. Hebert, owner of Lot 3 (the servient estate), disclaimed interest and was not a party.

The trial court recognized Mr. Vincent's (P) right to use the well, and Mr. Meaux (D) appealed.

Issue

1. Was the predial servitude for use of the water well extinguished when the well dried up but was subsequently deepened and improved on the same site?

2. Does using a servitude in a way other than the explicitly intended way interrupt the running of the prescription of nonuse?

Holding & Decision

1. No, a well that dries up and is reestablished and improved by digging deeper and re-casing is not destroyed, so the servitude is not extinguished. The court reasoned that deepening the well shaft and replacing the casing on the same site constituted "works necessary to use and preserve the servitude" under La. C.C. arts. 772 and 773. This was a re-establishment or repair of the existing well, not the creation of a new well or the total destruction under La. C.C. art. 783. But the court did note that Mr. Vincent (P) would be unjustly enriched if he were allowed to continue using the improved well without contributing his pro rata share toward the improvements.

2. No, the use of a well is to draw water, so a plaintiff uses the servitude and interrupts prescription through his lessees when they draw water, even if they unnecessarily pay for it. The court found that the servitude was used whenever Mr. Vincent (P), through his lessees, drew water from the well for irrigation purposes. The fact that payment was required after 1951 did not negate the fact that the well, the object of the servitude, was used.

The court remanded the matter for the owner of the servient estate, Mrs. Agnes Hebert, to be made a party, noting that the servitude could not be divested separately from the servient estate.

Rule of Law

1. A well that dries up and is reestablished and improved by digging deeper and re-casing is not destroyed, so the servitude is not extinguished.

2. The use of a well is to draw water, so a plaintiff uses the servitude and interrupts prescription through his lessees when they draw water, even if they unnecessarily pay for it.

TILLEY V. LOWERY
511 So. 2d 1245 (La. App. 2d Cir. 1987)

Facts & Procedure

The parties and their ancestors in title own adjacent tracts separated by a bayou. The defendants' property fronts more than 200 feet on a public road. In 1974, Kemmerly (plaintiffs' ancestor in title) entered into a "Right of Way" agreement and counterletter with the defendants' ancestors in title granting the plaintiffs' property a 60 foot wide servitude of passage across the the defendants' property to Foster Road to build a bridge over the bayou for ingress and egress to his property. The agreement did not fix the servitude's exact location but provided that the parties would fix its location in the future. Kemmerly paid for the servitude, but no one ever used it, built the bridge, or fixed the servitude's location.

Over ten years later, Kemmerly's successors and assignees (P) filed suit to enforce the agreement. The defendants argued the servitude was created in 1974 and extinguished by ten-year prescription for nonuse. The plaintiffs, on the other hand, argued that the servitude was never actually established. Instead, the fixing of its location was a suspensive condition. Thus, prescription for nonuse could not have run.

The trial court held that the servitude was created in 1974 and extinguished by nonuse ten years later. The court dismissed the plaintiffs' suit, and they (P) appealed.

Issue

Does the prescription of nonuse begin to run against an unused servitude of passage when a title demonstrates the parties intention to create a servitude, even if the title does not fix its exact location?

Holding & Decision

Yes, a predial servitude of passage is established by title and subject to the prescription of nonuse when the agreement reflects the parties' intent to create the servitude, even if its exact location is to be fixed later. The appeal court reasoned that a servitude agreement is effective if it evidences that the parties intend to create a servitude, even if some details are left to be determined later. Further, a servitude of passage is subject the prescription of nonuse from the date the servitude is established and use is possible. Here, the 1974 agreement created the servitude, and use was possible immediately.

The appeal court noted that nothing in the record suggested the parties intended to suspend the creation of the servitude until the parties fixed its location. The court contrasted this case against some older cases in which the servitude agreement was accessory to another contract and the parties explicitly intended the servitude to come into existence later, e.g., when timber was ready for harvest. As an aside, the appeal court also remarked that any doubt regarding the servitude's creation date would be resolved in favor of the servient estate under La. C.C. art. 730.

Because the parties stipulated that the servitude was never used, the appeal court affirmed the trial court's judgment that the servitude had been extinguished by nonuse.

Rule of Law

A predial servitude of passage is established by title and subject to prescription of nonuse when the agreement reflects the parties' intent to create the servitude and use is possible, even if its exact location or other details are are to be fixed later.

ASHLAND OIL CO. V. PALO ALTO, INC.
Chemical Company (P) v. Landowner (D)
615 So. 2d 971 (La. App. 1st Cir. 1993)

Facts & Procedure

A Chemical Company (P) acquired a pipeline servitude across a Landowner's (D) property in 1980 granting the Chemical Company (P) the right to construct and operate an underground pipeline "for the transportation of carbon dioxide in either its gaseous or liquid state" through the Landowner's (P) land. The agreement also contained a clause stipulating that if the Chemical Company (P) failed to use the pipeline "for the purposes herein provided for a period of twelve consecutive months" after it was put into service, the servitude would terminate. The parties intended this clause to shorten the standard 10-year period for the prescription of nonuse.

Initially, the Chemical Company (P) intended to use the carbon dioxide transported in the pipeline to produce methane at its Allemania plant. Operations continued as planned until July 1984, when methanol production ceased due to market conditions. To prevent the servitude's termination under the 12-month clause, the Chemical Company (P) flowed carbon dioxide through the pipeline to the Allemania plant and vented it to the atmosphere. The Chemical Company (P) also pressurized the pipeline with nitrogen when not in use and conducted regular visual inspections and maintenance on the pipeline. After a handful of years maintaining and venting the pipeline, the Chemical Company (P) began to use the pipeline to transport gas for sale. In 1989, market conditions made methane production profitable again, so production using the pipeline resumed.

In litigation over the servitude, the Landowner (D) reconvened to terminate the servitude for nonuse for over 12 months, arguing that periodic transportation of carbon dioxide simply to vent it did not constitute "use" as contemplated by the agreement.

The trial court terminated the servitude, and the Chemical Company (P) appealed.

Issue

Does periodically flowing gas through a pipeline and venting it into the atmosphere, solely for the purpose of interrupting prescription, constitute use sufficient to prevent the extinction of a servitude when the original intent was to use the transported gas in an industrial manufacturing process at the pipeline's terminus?

Holding & Decision

No, acts performed solely as mere gestures intended to interrupt prescription do not constitute sufficient use to interrupt the liberative prescription of nonuse; the servitude must be used in a manner consistent with the purpose or object for which it was granted, as determined from the title and surrounding circumstances.

The appeal court noted that interrupting prescription requires the use of a servitude in the manner contemplated by the grant of the servitude as determined by reference to the context and language of the title. The Chemical Company (P) objected to the trial court using parol evidence to read into the servitude agreement the condition that the carbon dioxide be used in the production of methane. The appeal court rejected this position, finding that the intended use was sufficiently apparent from the circumstances and agreement. Therefore, it was unnecessary to rely on parol evidence to reach this conclusion.

The appeal court agreed with the trial court that the servitude at issue was granted for the transportation of carbon dioxide for use in the Allemania plant's methanol production process. Thus, simply transporting gas to vent it was a "mere gesture" that fell short of this intended use and failed to interrupt prescription.

The appeal court affirmed the trial court's judgment terminating the servitude.

Dissent

Judge Foil disagreed, observing that there was no requirement in any document that the Chemical Company (P) continue producing methane to maintain the servitude.

Rule of Law

Acts performed solely as mere gestures intended to interrupt prescription do not constitute sufficient use to interrupt the liberative prescription of nonuse; the servitude must be used in a manner consistent with the purpose or object for which it was granted, as determined from the title and surrounding circumstances.

BROOMFIELD V. LOUISIANA POWER & LIGHT COMPANY

Landowners (P) v. Power Company (D)
623 So. 2d 1376 (La. App. 2d Cir. 1993)

Facts & Procedure

In 1955, the Power Company (D) acquired a 16 foot wide power line servitude along a highway through eight separate instruments that gave the Power Company (D) the right to operate and maintain transmission lines, including poles, wires, and other appurtenances as well as the right to trim trees to keep wires clear. Several instruments also granted the Power Company (D) the right to fell trees that endangered the lines. Between 1956 and 1967, the Landowners (P) herein purchased property burdened by the servitude over several transactions.

The Power Company (D) initially installed a transmission line with poles located on the servitude. In 1968, the Power Company (D) installed a pole on the servitude to provide service to the Landowners' (P) house while also supporting the transmission line. In 1972, the Power Company (D) upgraded the line but needed additional servitude width to maintain safe clearance. The Landowners (P) refused to widen the servitude, so the Power Company (D) moved the entire transmission line and its supporting poles off the servitude area onto the adjacent highway right-of-way. The service pole remained on the servitude but no longer supported the transmission line, only the service line to the Landowners' (P) property. After 1972, no transmission line passed over or was supported by a pole in the servitude area.

In 1988, the Power Company (D) trimmed trees on the servitude area, triggering a dispute. The Landowners (P) sued for damage to their trees, and the Power Company (D) reconvened for an injunction and a declaration that its servitude remained valid. The trial court dismissed the Landowners' (P) damage claim and denied the Power Company's (D) reconventional demand, finding the servitude had not been used in more than 10 years.

The Power Company (D) appealed.

Issue

Is the prescription of nonuse interrupted for a power line servitude when the power company no longer uses the servitude to transmit electricity but does leave a single pole on the servitude to serve the servient estate and uses the servitude to trim trees and provide clearance for a transmission line off the servitude?

Holding & Decision

No, using accessory rights like providing power to the servient estate, clearing vegetation, and providing clearance for an adjacent transmission line is insufficient to interrupt the prescription of nonuse where the power line servitude is not being used to transmit electricity.

The appeal court noted that at the time of the decision a power line servitude was an affirmative servitude but that, under the law in effect when the servitude was created, the law considered it a discontinuous servitude that required regular physical acts to interrupt prescription by nonuse. In either case, though, nonuse would be measured from the last use. The servitude's primary use was to transmit electricity via transmission line across the servient estate.

The court held that, after moving the transmission line in 1972, the Power Company (D) did not exercise this principal right on the servitude. The remaining service pole and line served only the Landowners' (P) property and were no longer integral to the transmission function. Therefore, their presence did not constitute use of the servitude as contemplated by the grant. Similarly, the court held that trimming trees and maintaining clearance from the transmission line outside the servitude were accessory uses and therefore did not constitute use of the servitude. Since the servitude was not used to transmit electricity for more than 10 years, the court held that the servitude had prescribed.

The appeal court affirmed the trial court's judgment.

Rule of Law

Using accessory rights like providing power to the servient estate, clearing vegetation, and providing clearance for an adjacent transmission line is insufficient to interrupt the prescription of nonuse where the power line servitude is not being used to transmit electricity.

THOMPSON V. MEYERS
34 La. Ann. 615 (La. 1882)

Facts & Procedure

The plaintiffs filed suit in 1878 for recognition of a servitude of passage over an alley between their property and a nearby street. In 1841, both parties' properties were owned by a single owner who divided it into lots, established the alley for the use of those lots, and sold them to separate owners. There is no dispute that the plaintiffs' ancestor in title had a servitude on the alley in 1841 when she purchased the property and that she used the alley until at least 1863. But the defendants asserted that at least ten years of nonuse extinguished the servitude.

The trial court heard testimony that the alley was boarded up in 1864. The only testimony regarding subsequent use of the alley came from an unrelated neighbor who occasionally chased her son through the alley when he climbed the plaintiffs' fence to go to the grocery store.

Nevertheless, the trial court found for the plaintiffs and recognized the servitude. The defendants appealed.

Issue

Is the prescription of nonuse interrupted by an unrelated trespasser using the servitude without the owner of the dominant estate's knowledge or consent?

Holding & Decision

No, the prescription of nonuse is only interrupted by the use of a servitude by the owner of the dominant estate or someone acting under her authority or in her name for the ordinary, legitimate purpose for which the servitude was established. Here, the Court found that the plaintiffs had not advanced any evidence that the plaintiffs or anyone acting on their behalf had used the alley as intended after 1864. Therefore, the servitude had been extinguished by ten years' nonuse by the time this lawsuit was filed in 1878.

The Court reversed the trial court's judgment.

Rule of Law

The prescription of nonuse is only interrupted by the use of a servitude by the owner of the dominant estate or someone acting under her authority or in her name for the ordinary, legitimate purpose for which the servitude was established.

LOUISIANA IRRIGATION AND MILL CO. V. POUSSON

Irrigation Company (P) v. Landowner (D)
262 La. 973, 265 So. 2d 756 (La. 1972)

Facts & Procedure

An Irrigation Company (P) operated an irrigation canal across several parcels owed by many individuals, including the Landowner (D). The Irrigation Company (P) operated this canal for many years prior to 1967 to supply water to rice fields along the canal. In 1962, the Landowner (D) dug his own well and a second irrigation canal parallel to the Irrigation Company's (P) canal to supply his own fields with water.

In 1967, the Irrigation Company (P) did not use the canal because it had no contracts for water that year because the adjacent rice fields had been rotated to soybean crops that year to maintain the fertility of the land. That year, the Landowner (D) used the canal he dug to water his own soybeans, but that canal failed and flooded a neighbor's soybean field. So the Landowner (D) switched to using the Irrigation Company's (D) unused canal for the remainder of the season. In 1968, the Irrigation Company (P) used some of its canal for irrigation. The Landowner (D) also used a large portion of the Irrigation Company's (P) canal to carry water to irrigate his own crop. In 1969, the Irrigation Company (P) exclusively used its entire canal beginning in May.

Before this lawsuit began, the Landowner (D) began pumping water into the Irrigation Company's (P) canal in March 1970 and subsequently cut the levee along the canal. Shortly thereafter, the Irrigation Company (P) sued for an injunction prohibiting the Landowner (D) from interfering with is use of the "lateral aqueduct servitude" and the canal.

The trial court granted the Irrigation Company (P) a preliminary injunction. The appeal court reversed, holding that the Irrigation Company (P) lost the right to possess the canal when the Irrigation Company (P) failed to use the canal in 1967 and 1968 and the Landowner (D) usurped it.

The Irrigation Company (P) appealed.

Issue

Is a person who has used a servitude for less than a full year entitled to an injunction defending its right to continue using the servitude?

Holding & Decision

No, injunctive relief maintaining a person in possession of an immovable, including a real right like a servitude, is only appropriate where the plaintiff has been in possession of the real right continuously for more than one year immediately prior to the disturbance. The Court agreed with the appeal court that the Landowner's (D) use of the canal in 1967 and 1968 constituted a usurpation of the Irrigation Company's (D) possession. The Court noted that plaintiff regained possession on May 12, 1969, when it began using the canal again and excluding other users. But, the Landowner (D) again disturbed the Irrigation Company's (P) possession on March 20, 1970, less than one year after the company regained possession. Therefore, the Court reasoned, the Irrigation Company (P) was not entitled to injunctive relief because it lacked possession for a year or more. The Court expressly limited its holding to the procedural issue of possession for injunctive relief and declined to rule on the substantive nature of the servitude or its ownership.

Dissent

At the outset, Justice Barham noted that the record does not reveal the nature of the parties' right to the canal in question but only shows that the Landowner (D) used parts of the canal, "by sufferance," in 1967 and 1968. The record also reflects that it is common and customary for rice irrigation canals to go unused but maintained for years at a time because fields and crops are rotated. The Irrigation Company's (P) periodic use, the justice argued, is the customary, expected way the possession of irrigation canals is exercised under La. C.C. article 3421. Further, the justice noted, there is no evidence in the record that the Landowner (D) intended to possess the canal adversely as owner until damaging the canal levee in 1970. The justice would have found that the Irrigation Company (P) maintained continuous possession for over 50 years, including the year leading up to the lawsuit and would have maintained its action for an injunction.

Rule of Law

Injunctive relief maintaining a person in possession of an immovable, including a real right like a servitude, is only appropriate where the plaintiff has been in possession of the real right continuously for more than one year immediately prior to the disturbance.

KIZER V. LILLY
471 So. 2d 716 (La. 1985)

Facts & Procedure

Goldie Kizer (P) filed a possessory action claiming she and her lessees had possessed and used a servitude of passage over a twenty-foot gravel roadway on Fred Lilly Jr.'s (D) adjacent property since the 1930s. This road provided the only access from Ms. Kizer's (P) property to Louisiana Highway 412. On May 23, 1984, Mr. Lilly (D) erected a fence blocking the road at its junction with the highway. Mr. Lilly (D) filed an exception of no cause of action, which the trial court overruled. On appeal, the court ordered that Mr. Lilly's (D) exception be sustained.

Ms. Kizer (P) sought writs.

Issue

Can a person maintain a possessory action over an apparent servitude it has possessed for at least one year but not long enough to acquire it by acquisitive prescription?

Holding & Decision

Yes, a person who possesses an apparent servitude for a period of one year beginning on or after January 1, 1983, may maintain a possessory action for that servitude, even though enough time has not passed to support acquisitive prescription.

The Court acknowledged that under the 1870 Civil Code, the servitude of passage, though apparent due to the existence of a gravel road, was classified as discontinuous and could not be acquired by prescription. But the 1977 revision changed the law, allowing apparent servitudes, regardless of continuity, to be acquired by prescription. This change was not retroactive, so Ms. Kizer (P) could not have acquired the servitude by prescription in 1984 since less than 10 years had passed since the effective date. But the possessory action was available because she had possessed it for more than one year when she was disturbed in May 1984. The Court reasoned that that the rules governing possession apply by analogy to the quasi-possession of incorporeal rights like servitudes.

After reviewing the requirements for a possessory action, the Court concluded that Ms. Kizer (P) stated a valid cause of action for possessory protection of her quasi-possession of the servitude. The Supreme Court reversed the appeal court and overruled the exception of no cause of action.

Justice Lemmon concurred in the result. After reviewing the code articles and literature, the justice noted the right to possess is implicit in the recognition of the right to acquire by acquisitive prescription and that, arguably, an apparent servitude is possessed by its regular use. But upon further discussion, Justice Lemmon noted that the right to possess a servitude is different from the right to use it. Thus, the effect of a successful possessory action concerning a servitude is to shift the burden of proof to the owner of the servient estate to prove no servitude has ever been established. Here, the justice noted, the pleadings did not and could not make out a case for ownership of the servitude because it had been less than ten years since apparent servitudes had become susceptible of acquisitive prescription.

Dissent

Chief Justice Dixon dissented, arguing that Ms. Kizer (P) failed to state a cause of action either for possession of a servitude over the gravel road or for a legal servitude of passage for an enclosed estate. He argued that she lacked the requisite intent to possess the servitude as owner and that she failed to state as much in her pleadings.

Justice Blanche also dissented similarly, noting that Ms. Kizer (P) did not assert in her pleadings that she possessed as owner by title, destination, or acquisitive prescription. Acquisitive prescription would be impossible, he argued, because the requisite ten- or thirty-year periods had not passed since apparent servitudes became susceptible of prescription. He would not object to giving Ms.

Kizer (P) an additional attempt to amend her pleadings to state a cause of action, e.g., to show destination of the owner or some means to possess the servitude.

Rule of Law

A person who possesses an apparent servitude for a period of one year beginning on or after January 1, 1983, may maintain a possessory action for that servitude, even though enough time has not passed to support acquisitive prescription.

Chapter 15

Building Restrictions

1. **Building restrictions** are *sui generis* real rights that impose charges on an immovable "in pursuance of a general plan governing building standards, specified uses, and improvements." La. C.C. art. 775.

   a) Building restrictions typically regulate the future use of immovables, prohibit or require the erection of certain kinds of buildings, or define the value of buildings that may be erected on the land. They are often used to establish and regulate subdivisions.

   b) "The plan must be feasible and capable of being preserved." La. C.C. art. 775.

      i. Without a plan, agreements purporting to establish building restrictions cannot do so. Such agreements may create other kinds of rights and obligations instead, such as personal rights, limited personal servitudes, or predial servitudes, depending on the agreements' details and structure.

2. **Historical development**. Civil law jurisdictions, including Louisiana, have struggled to define the nature of the rights created by building restrictions.

   a) *Nonapparent servitudes*. An early line of cases under the Louisiana Civil Code of 1870 likened building restrictions to nonapparent predial servitudes under article 728 of the Code of 1870. This analysis is insufficient because servitudes cannot impose affirmative duties on the servient estate like building restrictions are intended to do.

   b) *Real obligations*. Another line of cases likened building restrictions to real obligations that travel with the land under article 2012 of the Code of 1870. This conceptual framework ignores the real rights created by building restrictions while recognizing only the real obligations they create.

   c) *Covenants running with the land*. A third line of cases adopted the common law terminology and concept of covenants running with the land. There is no reason for a civil law jurisdiction to force fit a common law concept into its framework when the civil code provides simpler solutions.

   d) *Other jurisdictions*. French courts reached comparable results to Louisiana through the lens of personal obligations. In Germany and Greece, "building restrictions may not be established by private persons[,]" only by public law. C.L.P. at 721.

3. **Nature of building restrictions**. The 1977 revision of the Louisiana Civil Code adopted the view that building restrictions are a *sui generis* real right similar to predial servitudes. "They

are regulated by application of the rules governing predial servitudes to the extent that their application is compatible with the nature of building restrictions." La. C.C. art. 777.

 a) Building restrictions are property rights in the same way predial servitudes are. But it is unclear to what extent the constitutional guarantees against takings apply to building restrictions.

 b) **Affirmative duties**. "Building restrictions may impose on owners of immovables affirmative duties that are reasonable and necessary for the maintenance of the general plan. Building restrictions may not impose upon the owner of an immovable or his successors the obligation to pay a fee or other charge on the occasion of an alienation, lease or encumbrance of the immovable." La. C.C. art. 778.

   i. Whether a duty is "reasonable and necessary for the maintenance of the general plan" is a question of fact. Duties established "on a mere caprice... [that] tie up property to the detriment of public interest" are unenforceable. C.L.P. at. 725.

4. **Establishment**. Building restrictions, like nonapparent servitudes, "may be established only by juridical act." La. C.C. art. 776.

 a) To be effective against third parties, the instruments creating building restrictions must be recorded in the conveyance records of the parish where the immovable is located. If no restriction is recorded when the subdivider sells a property, it is transferred free from restrictions and cannot be unilaterally subjected to building restrictions by the subdivider in the future.

 b) Past practice saw building restrictions inserted into each individual transfer's title documents. In modern practice, building restrictions are recorded as a separate notarial act or as an attachment to a recorded plat, and each individual transfer incorporates the act by reference.

   i. Restrictions contained in individual acts rather than in a separate plan must be uniformly and consistently applied in order to constitute a plan sufficient to create building restrictions. If not applied uniformly or in all (or at least almost all) of the applicable transfers, this might be evidence that there was no general plan and therefore the agreements did not create building restrictions.

     A. Provisions that allow for exceptions on a case-by-case basis at the developer's discretion may still constitute a general plan sufficient to create genuine building restrictions rather than personal or other rights and obligations. *Cosby v. Holcomb Trucking, Inc.*

     B. An area developed haphazardly without a plan is not subject to a general plan of building restrictions even though some titles contain restrictions. These restrictions are predial servitudes instead of building restrictions. *Richard v. Broussard.*

 c) Building restrictions are often established by land developers planning to subdivide a larger property into lots for a certain purpose, like a residential subdivision, commercial development, or industrial park.

   i. Because there is no dominant estate where a developer imposes a plan across property owned by one person or entity, this approach cannot inadvertently create predial servitudes.

d) Individual landowners who own all the affected property may establish building restrictions by agreement.

5. **Protection and enforcement**. Building restrictions give rise to both active real rights and passive real obligations.

   a) **Real right**. The owner of an immovable burdened by building restrictions has a real right to enjoy that property without the violation of the building restrictions. That owner may enforce this right through a variety of actions.

      i. **Injunctive relief**. "Building restrictions may be enforced by mandatory and prohibitory injunctions without regard to the limitations of Article 3601 of the Code of Civil Procedure." La. C.C. art. 779. Remedies might include ordering a person to cease some action or remove a structure that violates a restriction.

        A. Because the limitations of Code of Civil Procedure article 3601 do not apply to this action for injunction, a landowner does not need to prove irreparable harm.

        B. Where a person states that he does not object to the construction of a structure that violates a building restriction, he may be estopped from later filing an action to enforce the building restriction to have that structure removed.

        C. Injunctions will not issue to restrain or correct "minor, insignificant, or merely technical violations." C.L.P. at 724.

      ii. **Damages**. A landowner who suffers damage as a result of the violation of a building restriction may sue for compensation. Similarly, if the violation amounts to an abuse of right or a disturbance of peaceful possession, the injured person has recourse to the general general laws of delict, nuisance, and neighborhood.

      iii. **Contractual remedies**. Where building restrictions are created by contract, a party has recourse to the actions available for the enforcement of conventional obligations, including specific performance and dissolution.

   b) **Real obligation**. Owners of immovables burdened by building restrictions are obliged to do nothing that violates those restrictions.

   c) **Other rights and obligations**. Building restrictions established by agreement may also create personal obligations that are enforceable through the appropriate contractual or other actions.

      i. The action for "collection of assessments is a personal action subject to the ten-year liberative prescription." C.L.P. at 725.

6. **Interpretation**.

   a) **Strict interpretation**. "Doubt as to the existence, validity, or extent of building restrictions is resolved in favor of the unrestricted use of the immovable. The provisions of the Louisiana Condominium Act, the Louisiana Timesharing Act, and the Louisiana Homeowners Association Act shall supersede any and all provisions of this Title in the event of a conflict." La. C.C. art. 783.

   b) The instruments "establishing building restrictions are subject to the general rules governing the interpretation of juridical acts." Common words have their normal meanings, and terms of art have their received meanings. For example,

    i. An instrument establishing building restrictions that, read as a whole, makes clear that owners may only build single family residential buildings and incidental structures prohibits any business activity. *Oak Ridge Builders, Inc. v. Bryant.*

    ii. An instrument restricting the use of an immovable to residential purposes excludes the erection of a church or the use of a lot exclusively as a roadway to access property outside the subdivision.

    iii. A restriction that excludes commercial establishments prohibits the erection of a billboard or the use of a lot as a parking lot.

    iv. A restriction that that requires only single-family residences be constructed prohibits the construction of multiple dwellings on one lot or apartments.

    v. But a court held that a restriction to use property only for a "single family dwelling" did not prohibit the use of a house as a community home for mentally impaired people. The court relied on a statute that defined such community homes as "single family units."

7. **Amendment, prescription, and termination**.

    a) **Amendment and termination**. "Building restrictions may be amended, whether such amendment lessens or increases a restriction, or may terminate or be terminated, as provided in the act that establishes them. In the absence of such provision, building restrictions may be amended or terminated for the whole or a part of the restricted area by agreement of owners representing more than one-half of the land area affected by the restrictions, excluding streets and street rights-of-way, if the restrictions have been in effect for at least fifteen years, or by agreement of both owners representing two-thirds of the land area affected and two-thirds of the owners of the land affected by the restrictions, excluding streets and street rights-of-way, if the restrictions have been in effect for more than ten years." La. C.C. art. 780.

        i. Parties are free to design termination provisions so long as they comport with public order. Some examples might include termination after a period, upon the occurrence of an event, by some specified procedure for polling the landowners who benefit from the restriction, or some other condition.

        ii. Amendments and terminations must be recorded in the public records to affect third parties.

        iii. A provision that provides for perpetual restrictions or a fifty year duration if perpetual restrictions are not allowed by law is a contractual termination provision under La. C.C. art. 780 and precludes the application of the portions of that article applicable in the absence of termination provisions. *Diefenthal v. Longue Vue Foundation*

    b) **Two-year prescription**. "No action for injunction or for damages on account of the violation of a building restriction may be brought after two years from the commencement of a noticeable violation. A violation is noticeable when an apparent activity has occurred on the immovable in violation of the building restriction. The recordation of an instrument that provides for a violation of the building restriction does not constitute a noticeable violation. After the lapse of this period, the immovable on which the violation occurred is freed of the restriction that has been violated." La. C.C. art. 781.

        i. A violation that is "noticeable" is not secret or clandestine, and a violative activity conducted on a modest scale may not be noticeable (or a violation at all).

A. Liberative prescription will only begin to run under La. C.C. art. 781 where there is apparent activity occurring on the immovable property itself that is contrary to the restriction and not merely when the activity begins internally or is advertised elsewhere, such as on a website. *Bayou Terrace Estates Home Owners Assn, Inc. v. Stuntz.*

B. Conducting a part-time, unlicensed business sporadically serving one or two customers at a time in one's living room using limited special equipment is not sufficient conduct to begin running two-year prescription against building restrictions regarding commercial activity. *Oak Ridge Builders, Inc. v. Bryant.* In that case, the violation became noticeable once the commercial operation became full-time, formally registered, and publicly advertised.

C. The two-year prescriptive period under La. C.C. art. 781 begins to run only upon the occurrence of a noticeable violation of a requirement to keep an area neat and clean, like the accumulation of trash rather than questionable but defensible decorating choices like garish paint schemes and fluorescent lawn chairs. *Hidden Hills Community, Inc. v. Rogers.*

ii. Note that prescription in this case does not just bar action on a claim; it frees the immovable from the restriction permanently.

iii. Some Louisiana courts have held that the successful assertion of liberative prescription against a restriction on commercial activity frees the property from restrictions on all kinds of commercial activity, not just the activity giving rise to prescription. Under that logic, the owner could change businesses or enlarge his or her operation without violating the restrictions. Others have expressed doubt as to this conclusion.

iv. Personal actions for enforcing restrictions that qualify as personal obligations are not extinguished by two-year prescription; they are generally subject to the ten-year liberative prescription applicable to personal actions.

c) **Abandonment**. "Building restrictions terminate by abandonment of the whole plan or by a general abandonment of a particular restriction. When the entire plan is abandoned the affected area is freed of all restrictions; when a particular restriction is abandoned, the affected area is freed of that restriction only." La. C.C. art. 782.

i. Failure to take action against noticeable violations and the perfection of two-year prescription can support the conclusion that certain restrictions or an entire plan have been abandoned. But a small number of technical violations of a building restriction do not establish the general intent to abandon or substantially change the nature of an area subject to building restrictions. *Gwatney v. Miller.*

ii. A subversion of or significant change to the intended nature of part of a subdivision — e.g., by using it for commercial purposes and excluding subdivision residents from a lake created on it — over a long period demonstrates that the general plan of building restrictions has been abandoned and frees that part from restrictions contained in the plan. *Robinson v. Donnell.*

iii. The abandonment of one restriction does not affect other restrictions — e.g., the abandonment of residential-only restrictions would not affect setbacks.

iv. Changes to nearby areas outside the restricted area do not affect the restrictions' or the general plan's validity.

8. **Interaction with zoning ordinances**.

a) "Zoning ordinances neither terminate nor supersede existing building restrictions." Ordinances enacted after a building restriction plan is recorded "cannot interfere with that plan." C.L.P. art. 725.

b) Changes to zoning may be evidence tending to show that a building plan has been abandoned, e.g., the re-zoning of a residential area to commercial use may indicate that commercial use has displaced the residential character of the area.

c) But landowners may not subsequently create building restrictions that violate a properly enacted zoning ordinance that affects previously unrestricted property. E.g., a building restriction cannot be created to allow industrial use of an immovable in an area already zoned for residential use only.

d) Commercial zoning is a permissive ordinance because it allows that use rather than requires only that use. Landowners are free to derogate from permissive zoning laws and impose greater limitations on property use by contracts like building restrictions. *Oak Ridge Builders, Inc. v. Bryant.*

9. *Louisiana Homeowners Association Act (LHAA).* In 1999, the legislature created a special set of rules concerning building restrictions governing "residential planned communities," which are "real estate development[s] used primarily for residential purposes, in which the owners of separately owned lots are mandatory members of an association by virtue of such ownership." La. R.S. 9:1141.2(7) (1999). These rules were codified at La. R.S. 9:1141.1 *et seq.*

   a) Where the LHAA applies, it supersedes the Civil Code's general rules concerning building restrictions where the two conflict. La. C.C. art. 783.

   b) Unliked the Civil Code, the LHAA allows for the establishment, amendment, and termination of building restrictions without unanimous consent of all the owners. The following can be varied by agreement of the owners, but by default:

      i. Establishing a new building restriction requires the agreement of three-quarters of the owners.

      ii. Amending an existing restriction to increase it or make it more onerous requires the agreement of two-thirds of the owners.

      iii. Terminating a building restriction or amending it to reduce it or make it less onerous requires the agreement of one-half of the owners.

   c) Effective January 1, 2025, the Louisiana Planned Community Act governs "planned communities," which is defined differently than in the LHAA. *See* La. R.S. 1141.1 *et seq.* This is a largely prospective change to the law that displaces the Louisiana Homeowners Association Act and affects newly created communities and homeowners associations. It is modeled after the Uniform Common Interest Ownership Act.

COSBY V. HOLCOMB TRUCKING, INC.
Neighbors (P) v. Truck Owners (D)
942 So. 2d 471 (La. 2006)

Facts & Procedure

In the 1980s, the King family developed Wedgewood Acres Subdivision and adjacent property they referred to as the "Front Lots" and established recorded building restrictions on them. The restrictions designated the tracts as residential only, and limited construction to one single-family dwelling and appropriate outbuildings.

Restriction 7 in the instrument contained two parts. First, it provided that no commercial vehicle could be "kept, store[d], repaired, or maintained on any lot ... in a manner which would detract from the appearance of the subdivision." Second, it prohibited any temporary structure from remaining on a lot "for a prolonged period of time so as to detract from the appearance of the subdivision, unless approved by developer." Restriction 16 in the instrument prohibited the use of any structure or lot "to operate any commercial activity ... in [the] subdivision, unless approved by the developer."

In 1985, the Truck Owners (D) acquired a lot in Wedgewood Acres. That same year William M. King, Jr., one of the developers, gave the Truck Owners (D) permission to park one commercial truck on the lot, perform normal maintenance, and construct a building to house the truck, all subject to the requirement that the activities not detract from the appearance of the subdivision.

In 1992, the Truck Owners (D) exchanged the first lot for one of the Front Lots outside the subdivision but still subject to most of the same building restrictions. They built a home on their Front Lot and later raised a 40'x40' steel outbuilding for maintaining and servicing multiple trucks for their company. They conducted oil changes, lubrication, and brake adjustments on the property and regularly power washed trucks there.

In 2002, eight of the Truck Owners' (D) Neighbors (P) filed suit to enforce the building restrictions against commercial activities and alleged that they suffered damage contrary to the obligations of neighborhood and La. C.C. art. 667. The Truck Owners (D) filed peremptory exceptions of no right of action because the developer waived the restrictions in 1985 and of prescription because the alleged violations had continued for more than two years. The trial court overruled the exceptions, finding the violation wasn't noticeable until 2001, and granted a preliminary injunction against the commercial activity and truck maintenance. The appeal court reversed, finding the action prescribed because the violation was noticeable more than two years before suit was filed.

The Louisiana Supreme Court granted writs on the prescription issue and *sua sponte* requested briefing on whether the restrictions constituted a "general plan" sufficient to create building restrictions under La. C.C. art. 775, given the developer's discretion under several provisions. This was not at issue in the lower courts.

Issue

Do provisions that grant the developer discretion to approve some generally prohibited activities constitute a valid general plan under La. C.C. art. 775, making them genuine building restrictions?

Holding & Decision

Yes, provisions that allow for exceptions on a case-by-case basis at the developer's discretion may still constitute a general plan sufficient to create genuine building restrictions rather than personal or other rights and obligations.

Despite nodding to this statement of the law, the Court mostly avoided the issue here by finding that the violation driving the Neighbors' (P) complaint — viz., keeping, storing, repairing, and maintaining commercial vehicles in a manner detracting from the subdivision's appearance under the first sentence of Restriction 8 — was not subject to the developer's discretion. The Court also found that, while commercial activity generally might be allowed in the developer's discretion, the activity at issue was specifically and strictly prohibited. Thus, the Court disposed of the matter without addressing the larger question of whether the developer's discretion invalidated building restrictions for want of a general plan.

The Court also found that the trial court did not err in overruling the exception of prescription and that there was evidence to support the conclusion that the offending activity only became noticeable in 2001.

Accordingly, the Court reversed the appeal court's judgment, reinstated the trial court's judgment issuing the injunction, and remanded the matter to the appeal court for further proceedings consistent with the Court's opinion. On remand, the appeal court rejected the remaining assignments of error, including the Truck Owners' (D) waiver defense.

Dissent

Justice Knoll dissented, chastising the majority for skirting the larger issue regarding the developer's discretion undermining the general plan. He argued that this approach ignored La. C.C. art. 783's requirement that doubt regarding building restrictions be resolved in favor of unrestricted use.

Under La. C.C. art. 775, a general plan must be "feasible and capable of being preserved," otherwise the rights and obligations contained in the instrument cannot be building restrictions. "Failure to provide uniformity of the restrictions may vitiate a general development plan[,]" as it did in *LeBlanc v. Palmisano*, 43 So. 2d 263 (La. App. Orl. 1949), in which a restriction was found "contingent entirely upon the caprice of" a party. Here, Justice Knoll argued, the use of the Truck Owners' (D) property was dependent entirely on the caprice of the King family, and the same result should obtain as in *LeBlanc*.

He distinguished *LeBlanc* from *Oakbrook Civi Ass'n v. Sonnier*, 481 So. 2d 1008 (La. 1986), cited by the majority, because in that case committees of neighbors were empowered to make certain decisions; here, anyone purchasing the property would be on notice that a developer could at any time greenlight any property for commercial use, which undermines any finding of a general plan.

Because of this uncertainty, the doubt should be resolved in favor of unrestricted use, and Justice Knoll would have affirmed the appeal court's judgment, dismissed the Neighbors' (P) building restriction claims, and remanded the matter to the trial court for the consideration of the Neighbors' (P) damage and injunction claims under nuisance law.

Rule of Law

Provisions that allow for exceptions on a case-by-case basis at the developer's discretion may still constitute a general plan sufficient to create genuine building restrictions rather than personal or other rights and obligations.

OAK RIDGE BUILDERS, INC. V. BRYANT
Homeowners (P) v. Hairdresser (D)
252 So. 2d 169 (La. App. 3d Cir. 1971)

Facts & Procedure

Homeowners (P) in the Cherry Hill Subdivision sued a Hairdresser (D) who owned a home in the subdivision to enjoin her from operating a beauty parlor in her home. The Homeowners (P) alleged that this activity violated recorded building restrictions. The Hairdresser (D) admitted the subdivision's restrictions applied to her property but argued her activity was not prohibited because the restrictions only prohibited "noxious, offensive, unsanitary, unsightly, or unusually noisy activity or" businesses.

The Hairdresser (D) had been fixing hair part-time in her home since 1967 but obtained a state license and began operating full-time with full equipment in February 1970. This suit was filed shortly thereafter. She (D) argued that the action was prescribed because she had been conducting business for more than two years before the lawsuit was filed and that the restrictions were invalid because the area was zoned commercial by a 1956 city ordinance before the restrictions were established in 1964.

The trial court found the Hairdresser (D) violated the restrictions and issued a permanent injunction. She (D) appealed.

Issue

1. Do recorded building restrictions that allow only "one detached single family dwelling" and "outbuildings incidental to residential use" prohibit the operation of a home-based beauty parlor?

2. Does the two-year prescriptive period for violating such a building restriction begin to run when the homeowner operates an unlicensed, part-time business without much special equipment and that only serves one or two customers at a time?

3. Does a pre-existing zoning ordinance permitting commercial use prevent the establishment of building restrictions that limit the area to residential use?

Holding & Decision

1. Yes, an instrument establishing building restrictions that, read as a whole, make clear that owners may only build single family residential buildings and incidental structures prohibits any business activity. The appeal court rejected the Hairdresser's (D) narrow reading that the restrictions only prohibited certain unseemly businesses in favor of broader reading taking all the provisions into account. The court found that the clear intent of the instrument was to prohibit business activity as a whole by limiting the use of the land to residential purposes and held that the Hairdresser's (D) operation of a listed and licensed beauty parlor with full equipment was prohibited by the restrictions.

2. No, conducting a part-time, unlicensed business sporadically, serving one or two customers at a time in one's living room using limited special equipment, is not sufficient conduct to begin running two-year prescription against building restrictions regarding commercial activity. The trial court also noted that the Hairdresser (D) kept no business records, reported no taxable income, and maintained no business telephone listing before early 1970. The appeal court agreed with the trial court and held that prescription did not begin to run until she began operating a full-time business with a license, commercial listing, and specialized equipment in 1970, less than two years before the Homeowners (P) filed suit.

3. No, landowners are free to derogate from permissive zoning laws and impose greater limitations on property use by contracts like building restrictions. The court reasoned that a 1956 zoning ordinance allowing commercial activity in the area established a permissive use. Since individuals can derogate from a permissive ordinance by contract, the restrictions established and recorded in 1964 validly restricted the use of subdivision property.

Rule of Law

1. An instrument establishing building restrictions that, read as a whole, make clear that owners may only build single family residential buildings and incidental structures prohibits any business activity.

2. Conducting a part-time, unlicensed business sporadically serving one or two customers at a time in one's living room using limited special equipment is not sufficient conduct to begin running two-year prescription against building restrictions regarding commercial activity.

3. Landowners are free to derogate from permissive zoning laws and impose greater limitations on property use by contracts like building restrictions.

RICHARD V. BROUSSARD

Buyer (P) v. Developer (D)
378 So. 2d 959 (La. App. 3d Cir. 1979)

Facts & Procedure

The Buyer (P) of a lot sued the Developer (D) who initially divided a larger parcel of land for declaratory judgment that the Buyer's (P) parcel was not burdened by a restriction limiting it to residential use only. In 1968, the Developer (D) sold a lot to John Elmer Jagneaux with the residential restriction. Jagneaux sold that lot to the Buyer (P) here in 1972.

The Developer (D) owned a large tract from which be began selling differently sized lots over many years. Lots sold before 1954 had no restrictions. Starting in 1954, the Developer (D) inserted a clause in all titles stating the property "shall be and remain residential property" and binding the purchasers' successors. The Developer (D) and his family also maintained ownership of large, unrestricted parcels among the lots. No overall subdivision plat and restrictions was ever recorded; the restrictions appeared only in individual deeds after 1954.

At trial, the Buyer (D) asserted that no valid building restriction existed because the development lacked a general plan. The Developer (D) argued that either a valid building restriction under a general plan existed or the restriction constituted a predial servitude enforceable by him, as the owner of the dominant estate, against the owner of the Buyer's (P) property. The trial court held that the restriction was enforceable but explicitly declined to rule on whether a general plan existed, implying reliance on the predial servitude theory.

The Buyer (P) appealed.

Issue

Is the presence of uniform restrictions in some but not all of the lots in an area sufficient to establish a general plan of building restrictions when the subdivision and sales were conducted haphazardly and without an apparent plan of any kind?

Holding & Decision

No, an area developed haphazardly without a plan is not subject to a general plan of building restrictions even though some titles contain restrictions. These restrictions are predial servitudes instead of building restrictions. The court noted that the Developer (D) maintained ownership of large blocks of land in the area that were unrestricted, that lots were sold in various sizes as the opportunity presented itself, and that lots without restrictions were sprinkled among others with restrictions. These facts undermined any finding of a general plan and *a fortiori* a regime of building restrictions.

But the court found that the restriction in the 1968 Jagneaux deed constituted a conventional predial servitude because it was established by title; it imposed a charge on one estate limiting its use expressly for the benefit of another estate, the Developer's (D) retained property; and the deed stated the restriction was binding on successors. Such a predial servitude is enforceable by the owner of the dominant estate against subsequent owners of the servient estate, even without a general subdivision plan.

The appeal court affirmed the judgment below but specifically limited its judgment to affect only the two parties. It did not determine the rights between the parties and anyone else or between third parties.

Rule of Law

area developed haphazardly without a plan is not subject to a general plan of building restrictions even though some titles contain restrictions. These restrictions are predial servitudes instead of building restrictions.

DIEFENTHAL V. LONGUE VUE FOUNDATION
Neighbors (P) v. Museum (D)
865 So. 2d 863 (La. App. 4th Cir. 2004)

Facts & Procedure

Seven Neighbors (P) on Garden Lane sued Longue Vue Foundation (D), the owner of a historic house-turned-museum bordering Garden Lane. The dispute centered on restrictive covenants established in a 1931 Act by all the Garden Lane property owners, including the Museum's (D) ancestor in title. These restriction prohibited commercial use and stated that the restrictions were binding "without any limitation of time," but if perpetual restrictions were invalid, then for "fifty (50) years."

A series of disputes between the neighbors bore three lawsuits. In the 1960s, the owner of the Longue Vue property first converted the home into a museum and opened its gardens to the public. The other owners on Garden Lane sued in 1973, alleging the owner violated the 1931 Act. The parties signed an agreement in 1977 settling that lawsuit; the neighbors agreed to relax the commercial use prohibitions, and the owner of Longue Vue agreed to construct a new road to access the museum to keep Garden Lane private. In 1987, the Museum (D) began hosting raucous parties, and the neighbors again sued in 1988, this time alleging violations of both the 1931 and 1977 agreements. The Louisiana Supreme Court decided the first *Diefenthal* case in 1990 and decreed that the Museum (D) was not allowed to host such parties under the applicable restrictions.

Subsequently, the Museum (D) acquired an adjacent home on Garden Lane and became the owner of more than one-half of the land area subject to the restrictions. The Museum sought and received a City Ordinance allowing it demolish the newly purchased house, turn that area into a parking facility, and block off the end of Garden Lane because the Museum (D) owned the land on all three sides of it. The Neighbors (D) filed this lawsuit seeking to stop the demolition of the newly purchased house and the Museum's (D) expansion.

Meanwhile, the Museum (D) recorded an Act of Termination purporting to terminate all the 1931 and 1977 restrictions under La. C.C. art. 780. The Museum (D) averred that the Museum (D) owned over half the land affected and that the restrictions had been in effect over 15 years without the agreement providing a means for termination. The Neighbors (P) amended their petition to challenge the Act of Termination on the grounds that the restrictions were servitudes, not building restrictions, and therefore not terminable under article 780 and that, if they were building restrictions, the article could not be applied retroactively.

The trial court granted summary judgment for the Neighbors (P), holding that La. C.C. art. 780 could not be retroactively applied to impair vested contract rights.

The Museum (D) appealed.

Issue

Does a provision in an instrument establishing building restrictions that states that the restrictions are perpetual or for fifty years' duration, only if restrictions could only be established for a limited time, constitute a contractual termination provision under La. C.C. art. 780?

Holding & Decision

Yes, a provision that provides for perpetual restrictions or a fifty year duration if perpetual restrictions are not allowed by law is a contractual termination provision under La. C.C. art. 780 and precludes the application of the portions of that article applicable in the absence of termination provisions.

The Court disagreed with the trial court that the core issue was the retroactivity of article 780 and reviewed the matter *de novo*. The Court founded its decision of two issues: first, whether the restrictions were building restrictions or servitudes and, second, whether the duration stated in the agreements precluded the Museum (D) from unilaterally terminating the restrictions. The Court determined that the parties intended to create building restrictions and moved on to the second issue.

Under La. C.C. art. 780, building restrictions terminate "as provided in the act that establishes them" or, if there is no termination provision, terminate by agreement of landowners who own a majority of the covered area. The Court reasoned that the earlier *Diefenthal* court had implicitly rejected the unlimited duration in the agreement and held that the provisions were valid for fifty years, which started again upon the agreement's amendment in 1977. In addition, the Court reviewed doctrinal sources, legislative history, and comments associated with La. C.C. art. 780 and its predecessor La. R.S. 9:5622 to demonstrate that the default termination mechanism in the code forbids perpetual building restrictions.

Because the fifty-year term reset with the 1977 agreement, the building restrictions were binding until 2027. Since agreement contained termination provisions, the default mechanisms under La. C.C. art. 780 were not applicable, and the Museum (D) was unable to terminate the restrictions without the Neighbors' (P) consent.

The Court affirmed the trial court's judgment grating summary judgment for the Neighbors (P).

Rule of Law

A provision that provides for perpetual restrictions or a fifty year duration if perpetual restrictions are not allowed by law is a contractual termination provision under La. C.C. art. 780 and precludes the application of the portions of that article applicable in the absence of termination provisions.

HIDDEN HILLS COMMUNITY, INC. V. ROGERS

Homeowners Association (P) v. Slovenly Neighbor (D)
869 So. 2d 984 (La. App. 3d Cir. 2004)

Facts & Procedure

A Homeowners Association (P) sued one of its residents seeking a declaratory judgment that the property violated the subdivision's recorded restrictions requiring lots to be kept "reasonably neat and clean." The Association (P) sought enforcement and fines.

Testimony revealed that the Slovenly Neighbor (D) began decorating in quirky but inoffensive ways — e.g., pastel paint, some bones in trees, and striped sidewalks — in 1997–1998. The accumulation increased in 1999, and neighbors began complaining to the association board in late 2000. In this period, the Slovenly Neighbor's (D) property displayed many unconventional decorations, including toilets on the lawn, hundreds of plastic jugs strung between trees, political signs, banners, junk TVs, cash registers, and other objects, creating what the appeal court described as a "veritable junkyard." The board issued a notice of violation in early 2001 to little effect.

The Homeowners Association (P) filed suit in September 2001. The trial court overruled the Slovenly Neighbor's (D) exception of no right of action but found at trial that he had not violated the "reasonably neat and clean" restriction. The Homeowners Association (P) appealed. The Slovenly Neighbor (D) raised the exception of prescription on appeal, arguing that he had been decorating his house in the offending manner since 1998.

Issue

Does the two-year liberative prescriptive period to enforce building restrictions begin to run when initial, minor deviations from a subjective standard like "reasonably neat and clean" first appear, or when the cumulative effect of the deviations becomes significant enough to constitute a noticeable violation of the restriction?

Holding & Decision

The two-year prescriptive period under La. C.C. art. 781 begins to run only upon the occurrence of a noticeable violation of a requirement to keep an area neat and clean, like the accumulation of trash rather than questionable but defensible decorating choices like garish paint schemes and fluorescent lawn chairs. The appeal court found that the trial court was not manifestly erroneous in implicitly finding that prescription had not run, reasoning that the Slovenly Neighbor's (D) activities in 1998 (pastel paint, some bones, striped sidewalk, painted chairs) were not significant enough to constitute a noticeable violation of the "reasonably neat and clean" standard.

Although neighbors noticed these decorations, they did not rise to the level of violating the intent of the restriction. The court determined that the "massive accumulation of various objects" constituting a violation only became truly noticeable in the legal sense in late 2000, when neighbors began formally complaining to the board. Because the suit was filed in September 2001, it was within two years of the commencement of the noticeable violation. Therefore, the action was not prescribed under La. C.C. art. 781.

The court reversed the trial court on the merits, finding the property clearly violated the "reasonably neat and clean" restriction under every conceivable meaning of those words. It reversed the judgment and remanded the matter for the trial court to rule on the Homeowners Association's (P) imposition of and claim to collect penalties.

Rule of Law

The two-year prescriptive period under La. C.C. art. 781 begins to run only upon the occurrence of a noticeable violation of a requirement to keep an area neat and clean, like the accumulation of trash rather than questionable but defensible decorating choices like garish paint schemes and fluorescent lawn chairs.

Bayou Terrace Estates Home Owners Assn, Inc.
v. Stuntz
Homeowners Association (P) v. Art Teacher (D)
97 So. 3d 589 (La. App. 1st Cir. 2012)

Facts & Procedure

Bayou Terrace Estates is a residential subdivision governed by recorded building restrictions and managed by its Homeowners Association (P). The recorded restrictions include section 5.1.1, which allows for subdivision lots to be used "solely for single family residential purposes," and explicitly prohibits commercial uses. An Art Teacher (D) moved to the subdivision in October 2006. While she lived in the subdivision, she provided art lessons and hosted painting parties, both open to the public, in return for compensation under the name "Ink Girl Studios." She maintained a website advertising art-related services starting in 2002 and in the fall of 2009 she distributed postcards around the subdivision and placed a sign in her yard advertising her art lessons. Several subdivision residents took art lessons as early as 2009.

In March 2010, the Homeowners Association (P) notified the Art Teacher (D) that she was violating subdivision restrictions, including those related to signage, parking, and the section 5.1.1's commercial use restriction. In July 2010, the Homeowners Association (P) sued to enjoin the Art Teacher (D) from operating the Ink Girl Studio or any other commercial enterprise from her home, alleging the violation of section 5.1.1.

The trial court granted a temporary retraining order and then a permanent injunction, finding the art lessons constituted a prohibited commercial enterprise. The Art Teacher (D) appealed, arguing that her activities were not commercial and, for the first time on appeal, filed a peremptory exception of prescription under La. C.C. art. 781, asserting the Homeowners Association (P) filed its lawsuit over two years after she commenced the alleged violations in late 2006.

Issue

Is advertisement of commercial services or maintaining a website a sufficiently noticeable violation to commence liberative prescription against a building restriction that prohibits commercial activity without additional physical activity on the property governed by that restriction?

Holding & Decision

No, liberative prescription will only begin to run under La. C.C. art. 781 where there is apparent activity occurring on the immovable property itself that is contrary to the restriction and not merely when the activity begins internally or is advertised elsewhere, such as on a website.

The court cited Yiannopoulos's treatise for the doctrinal proposition that prescription commences when the violation is "neither secretive nor clandestine" and that small-scale activity "may not be noticeable or may not be a violation at all[,]" but could grow into a noticeable violation after expanding. The court specifically declined to hold that maintaining a website or advertising online constitutes a noticeable violation on the immovable property.

Based on the Art Teacher's (D) testimony, the court found that her commercial activities first became legally noticeable in the fall of 2009 when she distributed postcards in the subdivision and placed a sign in her yard. Though she had conducted lessons since 2006, there was insufficient evidence that this internal activity was noticeable enough to neighbors and the Homeowners Association (P) to commence prescription under article 781. Since the Association (P) filed suit in 2010, within two years from the fall of 2009, the action was not prescribed.

The court overruled the peremptory exception and affirmed the trial court's judgment granting permanent injunction.

Rule of Law

Liberative prescription will only begin to run under La. C.C. art. 781 where there is apparent activity occurring on the immovable property itself that is contrary to the restriction and not merely when the activity begins internally or is advertised elsewhere, such as on a website.

ROBINSON V. DONNELL
Residents (P) v. Developer (D)
374 So. 2d 691 (La. App. 1st Cir. 1979)

Facts & Procedure

In 1965 the Developer (D) herein recorded restrictive covenants designating a large tract of land residential and prohibiting the use of trailers and other temporary structures on the land. The next year, he recorded a plat subdividing part of this tract into 35 residential lots that composed the Beau Village Subdivision and left a larger, contiguous portion designated on the plat as "Tract 'A' (Unsubdivided)."

In 1967, the Developer (D) leased part of Tract A as a borrow bit for nearby construction, leaving an 8-acre artificial lake on Tract A. The Developer (D) then sold Tract A in 1969 to Donnel Industrial Maintenance, Inc., which became Titan Properties, Inc., another defendant herein. In 1974, Titan leased the lake to Cooper Marine Service, Inc. for use exclusively for the commercial purpose of testing and demonstrating boats. The general public and Beau Village Subdivision residents were entirely excluded from the use of the lake. Cooper erected a large advertising sign visible from the nearby Interstate and, in July 1977, placed a mobile home trailer on Tract A near the lake as an office.

Beau Village Subdivision Residents (P) filed suit in August 1977, alleging that the trailer violated a restriction prohibiting trailers as residences and seeking injunctive relief against current and future violations. Defendants reconvened for a declaration that Tract A was entirely free from all the 1965 restrictions due to abandonment of the original plan for that tract.

The trial court enjoined future violations and ordered the trailer removed. But the court permitted the continued commercial use of the lake for boat testing and the presence of the sign, effectively freeing Tract A only from some restrictions.

Defendants appealed, arguing the entire Tract A should be declared free of all restrictions due to abandonment of the general plan.

Issue

Does the use over years of an unsubdivided portion of a tract neighboring a subdivision that could not economically be divided into residential lots as a construction borrow pit, as a lake used exclusively for commercial purposes, and for the placement commercial billboards and an office trailer demonstrate the abandonment of the original residential development plan as to that tract and free it from those restrictions?

Holding & Decision

Yes, a subversion of or significant change to the intended nature of part of a subdivision — e.g., by using it for commercial purposes and excluding subdivision residents from a lake created on it — over a long period demonstrates that the general plan of building restrictions has been abandoned and frees that part from restrictions contained in the plan.

The court reasoned that abandonment occurs when ongoing violations of restrictions substantially alter the intended nature of the area. Assuming for the sake of argument that Tract A was subject to the restrictions without ruling on the question, the court identified key factors demonstrating abandonment of the residential plan with respect to Tract A: (1) the tract remained unsubdivided, unlike the rest of Beau Village; (2) much of Tract A was permanently altered into an 8-acre lake; (3) the lake was leased and continuously used for exclusively commercial purposes that excluded recreational use by subdivision residents; (4) a large, visible commercial sign advertised this use for years; (5) a mobile home was placed on the tract for commercial office use; and (6) evidence indicated that residential development of the remaining portion of Tract A was likely economically infeasible for want of access to municipal utilities.

These facts demonstrated in total a "subversion of and a significant change in, the original plan of development" regarding Tract A and showed that Developer (D) abandoned the intent to develop it residentially.

The appeal court reversed the trial court's judgment and held that the original plan to develop Tract A residentially had been abandoned, freeing Tract A from all the 1965 restrictive covenants.

Rule of Law

A subversion of or significant change to the intended nature of part of a subdivision — e.g., by using it for commercial purposes and excluding subdivision residents from a lake created on it — over a long period demonstrates that the general plan of building restrictions has been abandoned and frees that part from restrictions contained in the plan.

GWATNEY V. MILLER

Neighbors (P) v. Carny (D)
371 So. 2d 1355 (La. App. 3d Cir. 1979)

Facts & Procedure

Neighbors (P) in the Oakcrest Plantation Subdivision, sued Joseph Miller (D), another home-owner, to enjoin him from storing commercial "street fair" equipment on his lot in the subdivision. The parties all derived their titles from common owners, and all the parties' lots were subject to the same restrictive covenants. Restrictive covenant number 6 prohibited the use "of any house ... either directly or indirectly[] for trade or business of any form or for any purpose other than that of a residential purpose."

The Carny (D) used Lot 26, where his mobile home residence was also located, to store a variety of equipment and attractions needed for putting on a church or school street fair, including rides, concession stands, billboards, and trucks (including tractor-trailers) when not in use. He also maintained and repaired the equipment on the property.

At trial, the Carny (D) raised several defenses, arguing (1) that the plaintiffs lacked a right of action because the restrictions constituted a purely personal obligation toward the vendor rather than building restrictions enforceable by other owners; (2) that the restrictions did not prohibit his use, in part because it was not conducted from a house; and (3) that the restrictions were abandoned because several neighbors also used their property for commercial endeavors, including selling shrimp, tomato plants, and puppies; advertising a business using a home telephone number; and storing a school bus when not in use.

The trial court found the Carny's (D) use violated the restriction and issued a permanent injunction, implicitly rejecting his defenses.

The Carny (D) appealed.

Issue

Do several instances of minor, technical violations of a restriction by various homeowners within a subdivision (such as small-scale home-based sales, parking a commercial vehicle like a school bus, or advertising a business with a home phone number) demonstrate the abandonment of a building restriction limiting property use exclusively to residential purposes?

Holding & Decision

No, a small number of technical violations of a building restriction do not demonstrate a general intent to abandon or substantially change the nature of an area subject to building restrictions.

While acknowledging that building restrictions can be terminated by abandonment of the general plan, the appeal court noted that not every violation implies abandonment; insubstantial, technical, or infrequent violations that do not manifest the intent to subvert the original scheme will not suffice. The appeal court found the Carny's (D) evidence of commercial activities in the neighborhood showed they were minor, lacked significant outward manifestations of nonresidential use, and did not represent a general intent by the community to abandon the residential character of the subdivision. Thus, the restriction remained enforceable against the Carny's (D) significantly more intensive commercial storage and repair activities.

The appeal court also explicitly rejected the Carny's (D) other defenses. The court found that the restrictions were building restrictions rather than personal obligations because the Carny (D) failed to demonstrate that they were not uniformly imposed across the subdivision. To the contrary, the court found that the restrictions burdening all the lots at issue were identical and concluded that the restrictions were inserted to maintain a general plan of development for the subdivision. Finally, the appeal court also rejected the Carny's (D) assertion that the restriction number 6 only governed the commercial use of houses rather than the lots around them out of hand, finding that the subdividers' clear intent was to prohibit all but residential use of the property in the subdivision, land and structures alike.

The court affirmed the trial court's judgment.

Rule of Law

A small number of technical violations of a building restriction do not establish the general intent to abandon or substantially change the nature of an area subject to building restrictions.

Chapter 16

Limited Personal Servitudes

1. **General principles**. "A personal servitude is a charge on a thing for the benefit of a person.... Limited personal servitudes are real rights that confer on a person limited advantages of use or enjoyment over an immovable belonging to another person." C.L.P. at 782.

   a) *Cf.* with a predial servitude, which is a charge on an immovable, the servient estate, for the benefit of another immovable, the dominant estate, owned by a different person.

   b) The 1976 revision of the Civil Code discarded "use" as a nominate real right, replacing it with the general category of "rights of use," which are the subject of La. C.C. arts. 639–645.

   c) Use under previous codes and rights of use under the current code are distinct from usufruct. Limited personal servitudes are "an intermediate category between usufruct and predial servitudes." C.L.P. at 783.

   d) "Personal" in the case of servitudes indicates that the rights operate in favor of a person rather than an estate (as in the case of predial servitudes).

2. **Types of limited personal servitudes**.

   a) **Rights of use**. "The personal servitude of right of use confers in favor of a person a specified use of an estate less than full enjoyment." La. C.C. art. 639.

      i. A conventional right of passage established by an instrument specifying a servient estate and a person rather than a dominant estate is a right of use instead of a predial servitude and does not run with the land upon transfer of the land to a new owner. *Sustainable Forests, LLC v. Harrison*.

      ii. A charge that exhausts the utility of property is properly categorized as a usufruct.

      iii. "The right of use may confer only an advantage that may be established by a predial servitude." La. C.C. art. 640.

      iv. "A right of use may be established in favor of a natural person or a legal entity." La. C.C. 641.

         A. *Cf.* with habitation, which may only be established in favor of a natural person.

      v. "A right of use includes the rights contemplated or necessary to enjoyment at the time of its creation as well as rights that may later become necessary, provided that a greater burden is not imposed on the property unless otherwise stipulated in the title." La. C.C. art. 642.

     vi. "The right of use is transferable unless prohibited by law or contract. " La. C.C. art. 643.

       A. Rights of use do not run with the land upon transfer of the land to a new owner. They must be explicitly transferred instead. *Sustainable Forests, LLC v. Harrison.*

    vii. "A right of use is not extinguished at the death of the natural person or at the dissolution of any other entity having the right unless the contrary is provided by law or contract." La. C.C. art. 644.

       A. *Cf.* with usufruct, which may only operate in favor of a juridical person for 30 years or less.

   viii. "A right of use is regulated by application of the rules governing usufruct and predial servitudes to the extent that their application is compatible with the rules governing a right of use servitude." La. C.C. art. 645.

    ix. The Civil Code does not provide for automatic termination of a right of use servitude solely for failure to pay a periodic fee stipulated in the establishing title, especially when the timing for payment is unspecified. If the owner of the servient estate interferes with the holder's exercise of the right of use, the owner may lose the ability to demand payment for that period and preclude termination of the servitude based on non-payment for that period. *McCormick v. Harrison.*

b) **Habitation**. "Habitation is the nontransferable real right of a natural person to dwell in the house of another." La. C.C. art. 630.

     i. "The right of habitation is established and extinguished in the same manner as the right of usufruct." La. C.C. art. 631.

    ii. "The right of habitation is regulated by the title that establishes it. If the title is silent as to the extent of habitation, the right is regulated in accordance with Articles 633 through 635." La. C.C. art. 632.

   iii. "A person having the right of habitation may reside in the house with his family, although not married at the time the right was granted to him." La. C.C. art. 633.

   iv. "A person having the right of habitation is entitled to the exclusive use of the house or of the part assigned to him, and, provided that he resides therein, he may receive friends, guests, and boarders." La. C.C. art. 634.

    v. "A person having the right of habitation is bound to use the property as a prudent administrator and at the expiration of his right to deliver it to the owner in the condition in which he received it, ordinary wear and tear excepted." La. C.C. art. 635.

   vi. "When the person having the right of habitation occupies the entire house, he is liable for ordinary repairs, for the payment of taxes, and for other annual charges in the same manner as the usufructuary. When the person having the right of habitation occupies only a part of the house, he is liable for ordinary repairs to the part he occupies and for all other expenses and charges in proportion to his enjoyment." La. C.C. art. 636.

      A. The person having the right of habitation is not required to pay the debt secured by the mortgage on the property burdened by the right of habitation. *Succession of Firmin*, 938 So. 2d. 209 (La. App. 4th Cir. 2006). "Annual charges" in this code article refers to annual public charges only. There is no support in the code that a usufructuary or the person having the right of habitation must pay mortgage payments.

vii. "The right of habitation is neither transferable nor heritable. It may not be alienated, let, or encumbered." La. C.C. art. 637.

    A. *Contast* with rights of use, which are transferable.

viii. "The right of habitation terminates at the death of the person having it unless a shorter period is stipulated." La. C.C. art. 638.

ix. Where the cause of a contract granting the right of a habitation is to achieve a result prohibited by law or public policy (e.g., circumventing constitutional tax exemption requirements), the cause is illicit, and the contract and the habitation are absolute nullities. *Gonsoulin v. Pontiff*.

3. **Rules of interpretation**.

a) Acts that create servitudes are subject to the general rules of construction and interpretation and those specifically designed to address the creation of servitudes.

    i. The "intention of the parties governs." This intention is, as usual, determined from the entire act and, where an act itself is unclear, extrinsic evidence.

    ii. There are no magic or required words. The use or nonuse of words like "servitude" or "easement" or the like are not dispositive.

    iii. Doubts concerning a servitude are resolved against the existence of the servitude and in favor of the free use of the servient estate because Louisiana law presumes property is free from burdens.

    iv. Servitudes must be express and should not be created by implication. *See* C.L.P. at 798.

        A. At French, German, and Greek law, servitudes may be created by implication in exceptional cases where the parties necessarily contemplate their creation, such as when dealing with enclosed estates. *See* C.L.P. at 798.

b) The Louisiana Civil Code contains rules for interpreting what kind of right is created by an unclear instrument.

    i. "A charge established on an estate expressly for the benefit of another estate is a predial servitude although it is not so designated." La. C.C. art. 731.

    ii. "When the act does not declare expressly that the right granted is for the benefit of an estate or for the benefit of a particular person, the nature of the right is determined in accordance with the following rules." La. C.C. art. 732.

    iii. "When the right granted be of a nature to confer an advantage on an estate, it is presumed to be a predial servitude." La. C.C. art. 733.

    iv. "When the right granted is merely for the convenience of a person, it is not considered to be a predial servitude, unless it is acquired by a person as owner of an estate for himself, his heirs and assigns." La. C.C. art. 734.

    v. Even where a phrase like "his successors and assigns" is omitted, a servitude may be created by the intent of the parties and the facts of the case, e.g., where the right granted is of real utility to the property and the recipient is "the purchaser" in general rather than the particular named recipient.

    vi. Louisiana courts have long recognized limited personal servitudes in favor of persons rather than estates, e.g., public utility, utility, and government servitudes.

SUSTAINABLE FORESTS, L.L.C. v. HARRISON
Hunting Lessor (P) v. Landowner (D)
846 So. 2d 1283 (La. App. 2d Cir. 2003)

Facts & Procedure

A Hunting Lessor (P) sued the Landowners (P) of a nearby parcel to prevent them from interfering with the Hunting Lessor's (P) use of a road servitude across their land. The parcel owned by the Hunting Lessor (P) and leased to hunters was near but not adjacent to the Landowners' (D) land, but the forest road across their land was an important ingress to the Hunting Lessor's (P) property for the lessor and its lessees.

The Hunting Lessor (P) filed a possessory action, claiming that it had possessed a servitude created by 1963 "Grant of Roadway Easement" from the Landowners' (D) ancestor in title to the Hunting Lessor's (P) ancestor in title, International Paper Company (IP). This 1963 deed described the Landowners' (D) land as the servient estate and identified a 12-foot right-of-way for a "forest road," but crucially, it did not identify any dominant estate owned by IP.

In 1998, IP sold the land allegedly benefitting from the servitude (and other tracts) to the Hunting Lessor (P) via the instrument identified by the court as the "1998 Deed." But the 1998 Deed did not explicitly describe or convey the 1963 right-of-way servitude.

The Landowners (D) filed an exception of no right of action, arguing the Hunting Lessor (P) did not own the servitude because it wasn't transferred in the 1998 Deed. Instead the ownership remained with IP. The trial court overruled the exception but ruled on the merits that the servitude did not include use by hunters.

The Hunting Lessor (P) appealed.

Issue

Is a conventional right of passage established by an instrument that identifies a servient estate but identifies a party rather than a dominant estate, a right of use (and therefore a limited personal servitude) rather than a predial servitude?

Holding & Decision

Yes, a conventional right of passage established by an instrument specifying a servient estate and a person rather than a dominant estate is a right of use instead of a predial servitude and does not run with the land upon transfer of the land to a new owner. It must be explicitly transferred.

The appeal court held that the right created by the 1963 agreement was a personal servitude conferring a right of use, not a predial servitude, because the instrument failed to identify a dominant estate. The court reasoned that while a right of use is a transferable real right, it is distinct from a predial servitude that automatically is transferred with ownership of the affected estates. The 1998 Deed from IP to the Hunting Lessor (P) described the land being accessed but did not describe or convey the separate personal servitude over the Landowners' (D) land. Thus, ownership of the servitude remained with IP, and the Hunting Lessor (P) lacked the requisite legal interest to bring an action to enforce the servitude.

The appeal court sustained the peremptory exception of no right of action, reversing the trial court, and remanded the case to allow the Hunting Lessor (P) an opportunity to amend its petition to properly allege its title to the right of use servitude, if possible.

Rule of Law

A conventional right of passage established by an instrument specifying a servient estate and a person rather than a dominant estate is a right of use instead of a predial servitude and does not run with the land upon transfer of the land to a new owner. It must be explicitly transferred.

McCormick v. Harrison
Track Owner (P) v Horse Boarder (D)
926 So. 2d 798 (La. App. 2d Cir. 2006)

Facts & Procedure

The Owner (P) of a piece of land containing a private horse racetrack sued for a judicial declaration that a nearby Horse Boarder's (D) servitude allowing him to exercise horses at the track was extinguished.

In 1993, the Paynes acquired a two-acre tract along with a "non-exclusive servitude of usage" over a horse track located on adjacent property then owned by the Ciavaglias and Plum Hill Training Center, Inc. The servitude allowed exercising up to 15 horses stabled at the Paynes' barn, contingent upon paying the track owner a $100 monthly maintenance fee for any month the track was used. In 1995, the Paynes sold the property and assigned their servitude rights to the defendant in this case. He used the track and paid the Ciavaglias until 1999 when the Ciavaglias sold the track property to Lifeline Nursing Company. Lifeline objected to the Horse Boarder's (D) use, and he stopped using the track.

In September 2004, Lifeline sold the property to the plaintiff in this case. Neither the Track Owner's (P) title nor Lifeline's title mentioned the servitude in favor of the Paynes or the Horse Boarder (D). In October 2004, the Horse Boarder (D) attempted to resume using the track. His employee used it once successfully but was asked to leave on two subsequent attempts. The Horse Boarder (D) did not pay the $100 fee for October 2004.

The Track Owner (P) argued, among other things, that the servitude was extinguished because someone had plowed the track as a farm field and raised subsurface rocks, making it unsafe for use by horses, and because the Horse Boarder (D) failed to pay October 2004's $100 maintenance fee. The Horse Boarder (D) reconvened for damages caused by the refusal to let him use the track.

The trial court found the servitude was a personal servitude of right of use, that it still existed, and that the Horse Boarder (D) was entitled to use it upon advance payment of the $100 monthly fee. The court held that the Horse Boarder (D) did not owe the fee for October 2004.

The Track Owner (P) appealed.

Issue

Does a personal servitude of right of use that requires the holder to pay a monthly fee for any month the right is exercised terminate automatically upon the holder's failure to pay the fee for a month of use, particularly when the timing of payment is unspecified in the creating instrument and the owner of the servient estate interfered with the holder's use during that month?

Holding & Decision

No, the Civil Code does not provide for automatic termination of a right of use servitude solely for failure to pay a periodic fee stipulated in the agreement, especially when the timing for payment is unspecified. If the owner of the servient estate interferes with the holder's exercise of the right of use, the owner may lose the ability to demand payment for that period and preclude termination of the servitude based on non-payment for that period.

The appeal court agreed with the trial court that the right at issue should be categorized as a personal servitude of right of use under La. C.C. art. 639 because the instrument granted rights to specific persons rather than the owner of an estate. The court noted that such rights are transferable and governed by rules of usufruct and predial servitudes where compatible.

The appeal court quickly dismissed the Track Owner's (P) arguments that the servitude was extinguished because the track had been destroyed (finding it still usable for limited purposes) and because of nonuse (finding less than 10 years had elapsed since the Horse Boarder's (D) last use).

Addressing the Track Owner's (P) primary argument that the servitude was terminated for non-payment, the court found no specific Civil Code provision stating that a right of use servitude terminates for failure to pay a required fee. The agreement required payment for any month used but was silent regarding when payment was due. Based on the law of obligations, the court found an implied monthly term for payment, but when during the month payment was due was indeterminable. Critically, the appeal court found that the Track Owner (P) failed in his obligation to allow the Horse Boarder (D) to exercise his use right without interference in October. Because the Track Owner (P) failed to fulfill his obligation, he lost the right to demand payment from the Horse Boarder (D) for that month. Consequently, the Horse Boarder's (D) failure to pay a maintenance fee for October 2004 could not be grounds for extinguishing the servitude.

The appeal court affirmed the trial court's judgment.

Rule of Law

The Civil Code does not provide for automatic termination of a right of use servitude solely for failure to pay a periodic fee stipulated in the establishing title, especially when the timing for payment is unspecified. If the owner of the servient estate interferes with the holder's exercise of the right of use, the owner may lose the ability to demand payment for that period and preclude termination of the servitude based on non-payment for that period.

GONSOULIN V. PONTIFF
Homeowner (P) v. Occupant (D)
74 So. 3d 809 (La. App. 3d Cir. 2011)

Facts & Procedure

In 1992, the Occupant (D) of a home and her then-husband executed a *dation en paiement* transferring ownership of their home to Pontiff's (D) mother, making her the Homeowner (P). The Occupant (D) continued to live in the house after the transfer and after her divorce.

In 2010, the Homeowner (P) sought to evict the Occupant (D), and the Occupant (D) defended the eviction, claiming the Homeowner (P) had granted her a right of habitation entitling her to live in the house for life. The Occupant (D) could not produce a written, recorded document establishing the habitation but claimed the Homeowner (P) had executed such documents, which were now lost or destroyed. The Occupant (D) specifically claimed the Homeowner (P) had executed a form at the Lafayette Parish Assessor's office granting a "right of use of habitation" for the purpose of allowing the Occupant (D) to claim the homestead exemption on the property, a practice the assessor's office promoted until 2000.

The trial court found the Occupant (D) proved that the Homeowner (P) had executed the assessor's office form granting her a limited right of habitation. But the court held this document was an absolute nullity because its cause — allowing a non-owner occupant to claim the homestead exemption to unlawfully avoid paying property taxes — was illicit and contrary to public policy. The trial court granted the eviction.

The Occupant (D) appealed, arguing that the cause was lawful and that that the right of habitation should be recognized.

Issue

Is a purported right of habitation established for the specific purpose of allowing a non-owner occupant to claim the homestead exemption and avoid the payment of property taxes invalid as an absolute nullity due to an illicit cause?

Holding & Decision

Yes, where the cause of a contract, meaning the reason a party binds itself, is to achieve a result prohibited by law or public policy (e.g., circumventing constitutional tax exemption requirements), the cause is illicit, and the contract is an absolute nullity. While the Occupant (D) proved the existence of the lost assessor's form under La. C.C. art. 1832, the appeal court agreed that its purpose was clearly unlawful.

The court found that the sole purpose and effect of the assessor's form, as stated on the form itself and confirmed by testimony, was to allow the non-owner occupant, to claim the homestead exemption, which the owner not residing there was not entitled to claim under Louisiana law. An obligation requires a lawful cause, and a contract with an unlawful cause is absolutely null. A cause is unlawful if enforcing the obligation produces a result prohibited by law or public policy. The parties' attempt to circumvent tax law violated public order, making the cause illicit and the contract granting the right of habitation an absolute nullity. The appeal court rejected the Occupant's (D) arguments that alternate, valid causes existed, finding them unsupported and strained.

Because the purported right of habitation was an absolute nullity due to its illicit cause, the Occupant (D) had no legal right to remain in the house, and the appeal court affirmed the trial court's eviction judgment.

Rule of Law

Where the cause of a contract, meaning the reason a party binds itself, is to achieve a result prohibited by law or public policy (e.g., circumventing constitutional tax exemption requirements), the cause is illicit, and the contract is an absolute nullity.

Chapter 17

Usufruct

1. **General principles**.

   a) "Usufruct is a real right of limited duration on the property of another. The features of the right vary with the nature of the things subject to it as consumables or nonconsumables." La. C.C. art. 535.

      i. Note that usufruct is always a real right, whether the subject property is movable or immovable.

      ii. "Usufruct is an incorporeal thing. It is movable or immovable according to the nature of the thing upon which the right exists." La. C.C. art. 540.

   b) **Usufruct of consumables and non-consumables**.

      i. "Usufruct may be established on all kinds of things, movable or immovable, corporeal or incorporeal." La. C.C. art. 544.

      ii. "If the things subject to the usufruct are consumables, the usufructuary becomes owner of them. He may consume, alienate, or encumber them as he sees fit. At the termination of the usufruct he is bound either to pay to the naked owner the value that the things had at the commencement of the usufruct or to deliver to him things of the same quantity and quality." La. C.C. art. 538.

         A. If the usufructuary sells the consumables, the usufruct attaches to the proceeds.

         B. Similarly, if items subject to usufruct are sold to pay estate debts, the usufruct attaches to the remaining proceeds

         C. The proceeds flowing from an expropriation or involuntary liquidation of nonconsumables subject to usufruct are themselves subject to the usufruct.

         D. *But cf.* "when the usufructuary converts nonconsumables into money without right or authority... the usufructuary [does] not acquire ownership of the proceeds and his liability to the naked owner [is] not limited to the value of the things at the time of the conversion plus interest[.]" C.L.P. at 805. The usufruct may terminate for violating the obligation to preserve the thing, and the usufructuary may be liable for damages under La. C.C. art. 623.

         E. Company stock is a nonconsumable thing because it represents an investment intended to generate revenue. Accordingly, the usufructuary is entitled only to the fruits of the stock, namely dividends, and may not sell the naked owner's portion of the asset. *Leury v. Mayer*.

301

F. *But see Vivian State Bank v. Thomason-Lewis Lumber Co.*, 162 La. 660, 111 So. 51 (La. 1926), in which the Court held that a certificate of deposit (CD) was, in effect, money and therefore a nonconsumable. Thus a usufruct of a CD granted the usufructuary ownership of the CD and it could be pledged freely.

iii. "If the things subject to the usufruct are nonconsumables, the usufructuary has the right to possess them and to derive the utility, profits, and advantages that they may produce, under the obligation of preserving their substance. He is bound to use them as a prudent administrator and to deliver them to the naked owner at the termination of the usufruct." La. C.C. art. 539.

iv. *Classification under prior law*. Under the Louisiana Civil Code of 1870, the term "perfect usufruct" described the usufruct of nonconsumable things, and the terms "imperfect usufruct" and "quasi usufruct" described the usufruct of consumable things. These terms are not part of the revised Code.

c) **Contractual and testamentary freedom**.

   i. "Usufruct may be established in favor of a natural person or a juridical person." La. C.C. art. 549.

   ii. "Usufruct may be established by a juridical act either *inter vivos* or *mortis causa*, or by operation of law. The usufruct created by juridical act is called conventional; the usufruct created by operation of law is called legal." La. C.C. art. 544.

   iii. "A disposition *inter vivos* or *mortis causa* by which the usufruct is given to one person and the naked ownership to another is not a prohibited substitution." La. C.C. art. 1522.

   iv. "When the usufruct is established by an act *inter vivos*, the usufructuary must exist or be conceived at the time of the execution of the instrument. When the usufruct is established by an act *mortis causa*, the usufructuary must exist or be conceived at the time of the death of the testator." La. C.C. art. 548.

   v. "Usufruct may be established for a term or under a condition, and subject to any modification consistent with the nature of usufruct.
   The rights and obligations of the usufructuary and of the naked owner may be modified by agreement unless modification is prohibited by law or by the grantor in the act establishing the usufruct." La. C.C. art. 545.

      A. Parties may, by agreement, treat nonconsumables subject to usufruct as consumables.

      B. "The grantor may relieve the usufructuary of the obligation to preserve the substance of a" nonconsumable, e.g., by allowing the usufructuary to sell a home subject to usufruct and attach the usufruct to the proceeds. C.L.P. at 803.

d) **Partition of the usufruct and of the naked ownership**.

   i. "Usufruct is susceptible to division, because its purpose is the enjoyment of advantages that are themselves divisible. It may be conferred on several persons in divided or undivided shares, and it may be partitioned among the usufructuaries." La. C.C. art. 541.

      A. N.B. that in this case there is a single right shared by several co-usufructuaries.

   ii. "The naked ownership may be partitioned subject to the rights of the usufructuary." La. C.C. art. 542.

iii. "When property is held in indivision, a person having a share in full ownership may demand partition of the property in kind or by licitation, even though there may be other shares in naked ownership and usufruct.

A person having a share in naked ownership only or in usufruct only does not have this right, unless a naked owner of an undivided share and a usufructuary of that share jointly demand partition in kind or by licitation, in which event their combined shares shall be deemed to constitute a share in full ownership." La. C.C. art. 543.

 A. Naked owners cannot compel a usufructuary or an owner with perfect title to partition his interest by licitation. *Smith v. Nelson.*

e) "Usufruct may be established in favor of successive usufructuaries." La. C.C. art. 546.

 i. A testamentary provision like "all oil & gas royalty interest payments owned by me shall be paid to A for life and then divided between B, C, and D" demonstrates the testator's intent to create successive usufructs rather than a prohibited substitution because it identifies the payments separately from the underlying royalty interest and describes the intent for the fruits of the interest to be enjoyed by successive groups. Because the language is silent as to the naked ownership, it passes via intestacy. *Succession of Goode.*

f) "When the usufruct is established in favor of several usufructuaries, the termination of the interest of one usufructuary inures to the benefit of those remaining, unless the grantor has expressly provided otherwise." La. C.C. art. 547.

2. **Rights of the usufructuary**.

a) Generally

 i. "The usufructuary takes the things in the state in which they are at the commencement of the usufruct." La. C.C. art. 557.

 ii. "The usufructuary may make improvements and alterations on the property subject to the usufruct at his cost and with the written consent of the naked owner. If the naked owner fails or refuses to give his consent, the usufructuary may, after notice to the naked owner and with the approval of the court, make at his cost those improvements and alterations that a prudent administrator would make." La. C.C. art. 558.

 iii. "The right of usufruct extends to the accessories of the thing at the commencement of the usufruct." La. C.C. art. 559.

 iv. "The usufructuary is entitled to the fruits of the thing subject to usufruct." La. C.C. art. 550.

 v. **Fruits** "are produced by or derived from another thing without diminution of its substance. There are two kinds of fruits; natural fruits and civil fruits." La. C.C. art. 551.

  A. "The usufructuary's right to fruits commences on the effective date of the usufruct." La. C.C. art. 554.

  B. "**Natural fruits** are products of the earth or of animals." La. C.C. art. 551. "The usufructuary acquires the ownership of natural fruits severed during the existence of the usufruct. Natural fruits not severed at the end of the usufruct belong to the naked owner." La. C.C. art. 555.

C. "**Civil fruits** are revenues derived from a thing by operation of law or by reason of a juridical act, such as rentals, interest, and certain corporate distributions." La. C.C. art. 551. "The usufructuary acquires the ownership of civil fruits accruing during the existence of the usufruct. Civil fruits accrue day by day and the usufructuary is entitled to them regardless of when they are received." La. C.C. art. 556.

vi. "The usufructuary may cut trees growing on the land of which he has the usufruct and take stones, sand, and other materials from it, but only for his use or for the improvement or cultivation of the land." La. C.C. art. 560.

vii. "When the usufruct includes timberlands, the usufructuary is bound to manage them as a prudent administrator. The proceeds of timber operations that are derived from proper management of timberlands belong to the usufructuary." La. C.C. art. 562.

    A. Land that grows merchantable timber is timberland, even if it is not regularly managed and exploited for timber as if it were a tree farm. What constitutes management as a prudent administrator of timberland is a factual question and may include clearcutting, where appropriate under the circumstances. *Kennedy v. Kennedy*.

viii. **Stocks**.

    A. "A cash dividend declared during the existence of the usufruct belongs to the usufructuary. A liquidation dividend or a stock redemption payment belongs to the naked owner subject to the usufruct. Stock dividends and stock splits declared during the existence of the usufruct belong to the naked owner subject to the usufruct. A stock warrant and a subscription right declared during the existence of the usufruct belong to the naked owner free of the usufruct." La. C.C. art. 552.

    B. "The usufructuary has the right to vote shares of stock in corporations and to vote or exercise similar rights with respect to interests in other juridical persons, unless otherwise provided." La. C.C. art. 553.

ix. "The usufruct extends to the increase to the land caused by alluvion or dereliction." La. C.C. art. 563.

x. "The usufructuary has no right to the enjoyment of a treasure found in the property of which he has the usufruct. If the usufructuary has found the treasure, he is entitled to keep one-half of it as finder." La. C.C. art. 564.

xi. "The usufructuary has a right to the enjoyment of predial servitudes due to the estate of which he has the usufruct. When the estate is enclosed within other lands belonging to the grantor of the usufruct, the usufructuary is entitled to a gratuitous right of passage." La. C.C. art. 565.

xii. "If the usufructuary has not disposed of corporeal movables that are by their nature impaired by use, wear, or decay, he is bound to deliver them to the owner in the state in which they may be at the end of the usufruct. The usufructuary is relieved of this obligation if the things are entirely worn out by normal use, wear, or decay." La. C.C. art. 569.

b) **Under the Mineral Code**.

i. "The rights of the usufructuary and of the naked owner in mines and quarries are governed by the [Louisiana] Mineral Code" found at La. R.S. Title 31. La. C.C. Art. 561.

    A. Before the effective date of the Mineral Code, cases concerning oil and gas exploration were resolved by reference and analogy to the general provisions of usufruct law and the provisions that dealt with mines and quarries. *See*, e.g., *Gueno v. Medlenka*, which concluded that a usufructuary has no right to extract oil, gas, and other minerals from the land burdened by the usufruct but does enjoy the usufruct over proceeds from mineral production already in progress at the commencement of the usufruct. The naked owner, on the other hand, has the right to explore the land for minerals and reduce them to possession, so long as he does not impair or impede the usufructuary's enjoyment of the property.

ii. "Except as specially provided in Articles 189 through 191, the usufruct of land does not include the landowner's rights in minerals." La. M.C. art. 188.

iii. "A conventional usufruct, including one created by a donation *inter vivos* or *mortis causa*, may by express provision include the use and enjoyment of all or a specified portion of the landowner's rights in minerals." La. M.C. art. 189.

iv. "A. If a usufruct of land is that of parents during marriage, or any other legal usufruct, or if there is no provision including the use and enjoyment of mineral rights in a conventional usufruct, the usufructuary is entitled to the use and enjoyment of the landowner's rights in minerals as to mines or quarries actually worked at the time the usufruct was created.

B. If a usufruct of land is that of a surviving spouse, whether legal or conventional, and there is no contrary provision in the instrument creating the usufruct, the usufructuary is entitled to the use and enjoyment of the landowner's rights in minerals, whether or not mines or quarries were actually worked at the time the usufruct was created. However, the rights to which the usufructuary is thus entitled shall not include the right to execute a mineral lease without the consent of the naked owner." La. M.C. art. 190. *See* La. M.C. art. 191 for more information regarding what constitutes "actually worked" and how to determine when such a condition commences, based on the type of minerals being produced.

v. "If the land subject to the usufruct, or any part thereof, is subject to a lease granted by the landowner prior to the creation of the usufruct, the usufructuary is entitled only to royalties on actual or constructive production allocable to him under Article 191. If such a lease terminates, or if the land or any part thereof is not under lease at the time the usufruct is created, the usufructuary's right of use and enjoyment includes the right to execute leases as to any rights to which the usufructuary is entitled under Article 190 and, accordingly, to retain bonuses, rentals, or other payments, or the proportionate part thereof, allocable to his interest under Article 191. Such a lease executed by the usufructuary shall not extend beyond the period of his usufruct. " La. M.C. art. 192.

    A. It is clear this article applies to rights under La. M.C. art. 190(A), but it is unclear whether the adoption of La. M.C. 190(B) impliedly repealed this article's grant to a surviving spouse of the right to enter into a mineral lease without the consent of the naked owner.

vi. "One who has the usufruct of a mineral right, as distinguished from the usufruct of land, is entitled to all of the benefits of use and enjoyment that would accrue to him if he were the owner of the right. He may, therefore, use the right according to its nature for the duration of his usufruct." La. M.C. art. 193.

vii. "A usufructuary of land benefitting under Article 190 or 191 or a usufructuary of a mineral right is not obligated to account to the naked owner of the land or of the mineral right for production or the value thereof or any other income to which he is entitled." La. M.C. art. 194.

viii. "If a usufruct of land does not include mineral rights, the naked owner of the land has all of the rights in minerals that he would have if the land were not subject to the usufruct. The rights may not be exercised in coal or lignite which is to be produced through surface mining techniques without first obtaining the consent of the usufructuary. If the usufructuary is entitled to the benefits provided in Article 190 and 191, the rights of the landowner are subject thereto." La. M.C. art. 195.

ix. "In enjoying the right recognized by Article 195, the naked owner is entitled to use only so much of the surface of the land as is reasonably necessary for his operations, but he is responsible to the usufructuary or those holding rights under him for the value of such use and for all damages caused by the naked owner's mining activities or operations. If the activities or operations are conducted by one to whom the naked owner has granted a mineral right, the naked owner and his grantee are liable *in solido* for damages suffered by the usufructuary or those holding rights under him." La. M.C. art. 196.

3. **Legal powers of the usufructuary**.

a) "The usufructuary may institute against the naked owner or third persons all actions that are necessary to insure the possession, enjoyment, and preservation of his right." La. C.C. art. 566.

b) **Lease, disposition, and encumbrance**.

i. "The usufructuary may lease, alienate, or encumber his right. All such contracts cease of right at the end of the usufruct. If the usufructuary leases, alienates, or encumbers his right, he is responsible to the naked owner for the abuse that the person with whom he has contracted makes of the property." La. C.C. art. 567.

ii. "A lease granted by a usufructuary terminates upon the termination of the usufruct. The lessor is liable to the lessee for any loss caused by such termination, if the lessor failed to disclose his status as a usufructuary." La. C.C. art. 2716.

A. Note that the lease terminates at the end of the usufruct, whether or not the lessor disclosed that he or she was only a usufructuary. *Sparks v. Dan Cohen Co.*

iii. "The usufructuary may not dispose of nonconsumable things unless the right to do so has been expressly granted to him. Nevertheless, he may dispose of corporeal movables that are gradually and substantially impaired by use, wear, or decay, such as equipment, appliances, and vehicles, provided that he acts as a prudent administrator. The right to dispose of a nonconsumable thing includes the rights to lease, alienate, and encumber the thing. It does not include the right to alienate by donation *inter vivos*, unless that right is expressly granted." La. C.C. art. 568.

    iv. "If a thing subject to the usufruct is donated *inter vivos* by the usufructuary, he is obligated to pay to the naked owner at the termination of the usufruct the value of the thing as of the time of the donation. If a thing subject to the usufruct is otherwise alienated by the usufructuary, the usufruct attaches to any money or other property received by the usufructuary.... If, at the time of the alienation, the value of the property received by the usufructuary is less than the value of the thing alienated, the usufructuary is bound to pay the difference to the naked owner at the termination of the usufruct." La. C.C. art. 568.1.

    v. "The right to dispose of a nonconsumable thing includes the right to lease the thing for a term that extends beyond the termination of the usufruct. If, at the termination of the usufruct, the thing remains subject to the lease, the usufructuary is accountable to the naked owner for any diminution in the value of the thing at that time attributable to the lease." La. C.C. art. 568.2.

    vi. "If, at the termination of the usufruct, the thing subject to the usufruct is burdened by an encumbrance established by the usufructuary to secure an obligation, the usufructuary is bound to remove the encumbrance." La. C.C. art. 568.3.

4. **Obligations of the usufructuary**.

  a) **Inventory and security**.

    i. "The usufructuary shall cause an inventory to be made of the property subject to the usufruct [in accordance with La. C.C.P. arts. 3131–3137]. In the absence of an inventory the naked owner may prevent the usufructuary's entry into possession of the property." La. C.C. art. 570.

    ii. "The usufructuary shall give security that he will use the property subject to the usufruct as a prudent administrator and that he will faithfully fulfill all the obligations imposed on him by law or by the act that established the usufruct unless security is dispensed with. If security is required, the court may order that it be provided in accordance with law." La. C.C. art. 571.

      A. "The security shall be in the amount of the total value of the property subject to the usufruct.
      The court may increase or reduce the amount of the security, on proper showing, but the amount shall not be less than the value of the movables subject to the usufruct." La. C.C. art. 572.

      B. "Security is dispensed with when any of the following occur:
      (1) A person has a legal usufruct under [La. C.C. arts.] 223 or 3252.
      (2) A surviving spouse has a legal usufruct under [La. C.C. art.] 890 unless the naked owner is not a child of the usufructuary or if the naked owner is a child of the usufructuary and is also a forced heir of the decedent, the naked owner may obtain security but only to the extent of his legitime.
      (3) A parent has a legal usufruct under [La. C.C. art.] 891 unless the naked owner is not a child of the usufructuary.
      (4) A surviving spouse has a legal usufruct under [La. C.C. art.] 2434 unless the naked owner is a child of the decedent but not a child of the usufructuary.
      B. A seller or donor of property under reservation of usufruct is not required to give security." La. C.C. art. 573.

    C. Forced heirs may compel an executor to furnish security in connection with that role even if he is also a usufructuary of the succession property who would typically not be required to furnish security as usufructuary. *Succession of Watson.*

  iii. "A delay in giving security does not deprive the usufructuary of the fruits derived from the property since the commencement of the usufruct." La. C.C. art. 574.

  iv. "If the usufructuary does not give security, the court may order that the property be delivered to an administrator appointed in accordance with [La. C.C.P. arts. 3111–3113] for administration on behalf of the usufructuary. The administration terminates if the usufructuary gives security." La. C.C. art. 575.

b) **Repairs, preservation efforts, and charges**.

  i. **Repairs**.

    A. "**Extraordinary repairs** are those for the reconstruction of the whole or of a substantial part of the property subject to the usufruct. All others are **ordinary repairs**." La. C.C. art. 578.

    B. "The usufructuary is responsible for ordinary maintenance and repairs for keeping the property subject to the usufruct in good order, whether the need for these repairs arises from accident or *force majeure*, the normal use of things, or his fault or neglect.
The naked owner is responsible for extraordinary repairs, unless they have become necessary as a result of the usufructuary's fault or neglect in which case the usufructuary is bound to make them at his cost." La. C.C. art. 577.

    C. Delictual liability to a third party caused by a defect in the property subject to usufruct may depend on who had the responsibility to correct the defect. For example, in *Walker v. Holt*, 888 So. 2d 255 (La. App. 3d. Cir. 2004), a person sustained injuries after stepping in a hole in the yard. The court held that filling such a hole was an ordinary repair and therefore the responsibility of the usufructuary. Thus, the usufructuary was responsible for the liability related to failing to fill the hole, and the naked owner was not liable for any part of the damages.

    D. "During the existence of the usufruct, the naked owner may compel the usufructuary to make the repairs for which the usufructuary is responsible.
The usufructuary may not compel the naked owner to make the extraordinary repairs for which the owner is responsible. If the naked owner refuses to make them, the usufructuary may do so, and he shall be reimbursed without interest by the naked owner at the end of the usufruct. " La. C.C. art. 579.

    E. "If, after the usufruct commences and before the usufructuary is put in possession, the naked owner incurs necessary expenses or makes repairs for which the usufructuary is responsible, the naked owner has the right to claim the cost from the usufructuary and may retain the possession of the things subject to the usufruct until he is paid." La. C.C. art. 580.

    F. "The usufructuary is answerable for all expenses that become necessary for the preservation and use of the property after the commencement of the usufruct." La. C.C. art. 581.

    G. When a person is both a usufructuary of succession property and the succession representative with seizin of that property he or she is in possession of the usufruct and therefore personally responsible for the maintenance and repair of the property as specified by usufruct law. *Succession of Crain*.

ii. **Abandonment**. "The usufructuary may release himself from the obligation to make repairs by abandoning the usufruct or, with the approval of the court, a portion thereof, even if the owner has instituted suit to compel him to make repairs or bear the expenses of them, and even if the usufructuary has been cast in judgment. He may not release himself from the charges of the enjoyment during the period of his possession, nor from accountability for the damages that he, or persons for whom he is responsible, may have caused." La C.C. art. 582.

iii. "Neither the usufructuary nor the naked owner is bound to restore property that has been totally destroyed through accident, *force majeure*, or age.
If the naked owner elects to restore the property or to make extraordinary repairs, he shall do so within a reasonable time and in the manner least inconvenient and onerous for the usufructuary." La. C.C. art. 583.

c) **Payments of debts**.

   i. **Charges**. "The usufructuary is bound to pay the periodic charges, such as property taxes, that may be imposed, during his enjoyment of the usufruct." La. C.C. art. 584.

   ii. **Usufruct *inter vivos***.

      A. "When the usufruct is established *inter vivos*, the usufructuary is not liable for debts of the grantor, but if the debt is secured by an encumbrance of the thing subject to the usufruct, the thing may be sold for the payment of the debt." La. C.C. art. 586.

      B. "When property subject to a usufruct established *inter vivos* is encumbered to secure a debt before the commencement of the usufruct, the usufructuary may advance the funds needed to discharge the indebtedness. If he does so, the naked owner shall reimburse the usufructuary, without interest, at the termination of the usufruct, for the principal of the debt the usufructuary has discharged, and for any interest the usufructuary has paid that had accrued on the debt before the commencement of the usufruct." La. C.C. art. 588.

   iii. **Usufruct *mortis causa***.

      A. "When the usufruct is established *mortis causa*, the usufructuary is not liable for estate debts, but the property subject to the usufruct may be sold for the payment of estate debts, in accordance with" law. La. C.C. art. 587.

      B. "If the usufructuary of a usufruct established *mortis causa* advances funds to discharge an estate debt charged to the property subject to the usufruct, the naked owner shall reimburse the usufructuary, without interest, at the termination of the usufruct, but only to the extent of the principal of the debt he has discharged and for any interest he has paid that had accrued on the debt before the commencement of the usufruct." La. C.C. art. 589. *See Succession of Davis* for an application of the prior articles this one is based on.

   iv. "If the usufructuary fails or refuses to advance the funds needed to discharge a debt secured by property subject to the usufruct, or an estate debt that is charged to the property subject to the usufruct, the naked owner may advance the funds needed. If he does so, the naked owner may demand that the usufructuary pay him interest during the period of the usufruct. If the naked owner does not advance the funds, he may demand that all or part of the property be sold as needed to discharge the debt." La. C.C. art. 590.

v. "If property subject to the usufruct is sold to pay an estate debt, or a debt of the grantor, the usufruct attaches to any proceeds of the sale of the property that remain after payment of the debt." La. C.C. art. 591.

vi. "If there is more than one usufructuary of the same property, each contributes to the payment of estate debts that are charged to the property in proportion to his enjoyment of the property. If one or more of the usufructuaries fails to advance his share, those of them who advance the funds shall have the right to recover the funds they advance from those who do not advance their shares." La. C.C. art. 592.

vii. "Unless there is a governing testamentary disposition, the legacy of an annuity that is chargeable to property subject to a usufruct is payable first from the fruits and products of the property subject to the usufruct and then from the property itself." La. C.C. art. 593.

5. **Termination of usufruct**.

   a) **Causes of termination**. The Civil Code enumerates many occurrences that will terminate a usufruct:

     i. The death of the usufructuary. La. C.C. art. 607.

     ii. The dissolution or liquidation of a usufructuary who is a juridical person. The conversion, merger, or succession of juridical persons does not terminate the usufruct. La. C.C. art. 608.

     iii. For usufructs in favor of a juridical person, the passage of 30 years. La. C.C. art. 608.

     iv. For a "legacy of revenues from specified property[,]... [the] death of the legatee unless a shorter period has been expressly stipulated." La. C.C. art. 609.

     v. Where the usufruct is established for a term or subject to a condition[,]... the expiration of the term or the happening of the condition." La. C.C. art. 610.

     vi. "A usufruct granted until a third person reaches a certain age is a usufruct for a term. If the third person dies, the usufruct terminates [when] the deceased would have reached the designated age." La. C.C. art. 612.

     vii. Where "the usufructuary is charged to restore or transfer the usufruct to another person,... when the time for restitution or delivery arrives." La. C.C. art. 611.

     viii. For "[t]he usufruct of nonconsumables, by the permanent and total loss, extinction, or destruction through accident, force majeure or decay of the property subject to the usufruct." La. C.C. art. 613. But when the loss "is attributable to the fault of a third person, the usufruct does not terminate but attaches to any claim for damages and the proceeds therefrom." La. C.C. art. 614.

       A. A usufructuary may serve as administrator for tort claims related to injuries to both the use and ownership of the thing subject to usufruct, so the naked owners are not indispensable parties to the action. *Barry v. United States Fidelity & Guaranty Company*.

       B. Where a usufruct includes both structures and land, the demolition of the structures constitutes only a partial loss of the part of the usufruct pertaining to the buildings. The usufruct of the land persists. *Bond v. Green*.

ix. "[B]y the enforcement of an encumbrance established upon the property prior to the creation of the usufruct to secure a debt." But "[t]he judicial sale of the usufruct by creditors of the usufructuary deprives the usufructuary of his enjoyment of the property but does not terminate the usufruct." La. C.C. art. 620.

    A. The usufruct attaches to any proceeds remaining after the mortgage debt is satisfied because the enforcement of a preexisting mortgage only terminates the usufruct as to that portion of the proceeds required to satisfy the debt. *Watson v. Federal Land Bank of Jackson*.

x. "[B]y the prescription of nonuse if neither the usufructuary nor any other person acting in his name exercises the right during a period of ten years." La. C.C. art. 621.

xi. "[B]y confusion when the usufruct and the naked ownership are united in the same person[,]" provided the act uniting the two is not later annulled. La. C.C. art. 622.

xii. "[B]y an express written renunciation[,]" which can be annulled by a creditor of the usufructuary who is prejudiced by this renunciation. La. C.C. art. 626.

xiii. **Termination for cause**. The naked owner may terminate the usufruct "if the usufructuary commits waste, alienates things without authority, neglects to make ordinary repairs, or abuses his enjoyment in any other manner." La. C.C. art. 623.

    A. *Remedies*. The court may terminate the usufruct or return the property to the naked owner "on the condition that he shall pay to the usufructuary a reasonable annuity until the end of the usufruct." La. C.C. art. 624.

    B. *Defenses*. "The usufructuary may prevent termination of the usufruct or delivery of the property to the naked owner by giving security to insure that he will take appropriate corrective measures within a period fixed by the court." La. C.C. art. 624.

    C. *Creditors' rights*. "A creditor of the usufructuary may intervene and may prevent termination of the usufruct and delivery of the property to the naked owner by offering to repair the damages caused by the usufructuary and by giving security for the future." La. C.C. art. 625.

xiv. "A usufruct by donation *mortis causa* is not considered revoked merely because the testator has made changes in the property after the date of his testament. The effect of the legacy is determined by application of the rules contained in the Title: Of donations *inter vivos* and *mortis causa*." La. C.C. art. 619.

b) **Consequences of termination; accounting**.

i. "Upon termination of the usufruct, the usufructuary or his heirs have the right to retain possession of the property until reimbursed for all expenses and advances for which they have recourse against the owner or his heirs." La. C.C. art. 627.

ii. "Upon termination of a usufruct of nonconsumables for a cause other than total and permanent destruction of the property, full ownership is restored. The usufructuary or his heirs are bound to deliver the property to the owner with its accessories and fruits produced since the termination of the usufruct.

If property has been lost or deteriorated through the fault of the usufructuary, the owner is entitled to the value the property otherwise would have had at the termination of the usufruct." La. C.C. art. 628.

iii. "At the termination of a usufruct of consumables, the usufructuary is bound to deliver to the owner things of the same quantity and quality or the value they had at the commencement of the usufruct." La. C.C. art. 629. *See Succession of Hayes* for an example application.

    iv. The action asserting ownership of a nonconsumable thing formerly subject to usufruct is not subject to liberative prescription. *Succession of Heckert.*

  c) **Real subrogation**.

    i. "When property subject to usufruct changes form without an act of the usufructuary [— e.g., through appropriation —] the usufruct does not terminate even though the property may no longer serve the use for which it was originally destined." Instead, the usufruct attaches to the money or other property received in the conversion. La. C.C. art. 615.

    ii. "When property subject to usufruct is sold or exchanged [through partition or by agreement], the usufruct terminates [but] the usufruct attaches to the money or other property received by the usufructuary, unless the parties agree otherwise. Any tax or expense incurred... shall be deducted from the amount due by the usufructuary to the naked owner at the termination of the usufruct." La. C.C. art. 616.

    iii. The usufruct attaches to any insurance proceeds "due on account of loss, extinction, or destruction of property subject to usufruct," unless "the usufructuary or the naked owner has separately insured his interest only[.]" La. C.C. art. 617.

      A. An insurance policy that is acquired and paid for solely by a usufructuary and that lists only the usufructuary as named insured separately insures the usufructuary's interest in the property, and all proceeds from that policy belong to the usufructuary. *Kimball v. Standard Fire Ins. Co..*

    iv. "In cases governed by Articles 614, 615, 616, and the first sentence of Article 617, the naked owner may demand" security for the proceeds. La. C.C. art. 618.

6. **Legal usufruct**.

  a) A **legal usufruct** is one "created by operation of law." La. C.C. art. 544. *Contrast* with a conventional usufruct.

  b) The following legal usufructs are enumerated in the Civil Code:

    i. Usufruct of the surviving spouse under La. C.C. art. 890.

    ii. Usufruct in favor of decedent's parents over separate property inherited by the decedent's siblings under La. C.C. art. 891.

    iii. Usufruct over the marital portion under La. C.C. art. 2434.

    iv. Usufruct over property that prevents a surviving spouse or surviving minor child from being left in necessitous circumstances under La. C.C. art. 3252.

  c) Before the 2015 revision, parents enjoyed a legal usufruct over the property of their minor children. *See* La. C.C. arts. 223–226 (1870). Provisions relating to that usufruct were repealed. La. C.C. art. 230 allows "parent [to] expend, without court approval, the fruits of the child's property for the shared benefit of the family... or for the expenses of the child's household or property." This right is not a usufruct but was intended to fill a similar function, *see* La. C.C. art. 230, Revision Comment (d) (2015).

  d) **Legal usufruct of the surviving spouse**.

    i. **The law that was**.

A. The judicial doctrine of **confirmation of the legal usufruct by testament** allowed a surviving spouse to enjoy the rights afforded by the legal usufruct of the surviving spouse with additional rights granted in the decedent's testament, including the expansion of the usufruct to burden both community and separate property under certain circumstances.

B. This doctrine was codified in La. C.C. art. 916 (1975). The Supreme Court of Louisiana noted that "[t]he testator may confirm in his will the usufruct that the surviving spouse inherits by operation of law under article 916.... In practical effect, the surviving spouse is permitted to cumulate the legal usufruct in her favor with donations mortis causa that do not exceed the disposable portion.... Hence, the legal usufruct, even when confirmed in the testament, terminates by operation of law upon the surviving spouse's remarriage." *Succession of Waldron*, 323 So. 2d 434, 436–7 (La. 1975) (citations omitted but relying principally on and reaffirming *Succession of Chauvin*, 257 So. 2d 422 (La. 1972)).

C. The test for whether a usufruct contained in a testament created a testamentary usufruct or confirmed the legal usufruct of the surviving spoused changed between *Succession of Chauvin* and *Succession of Waldron*. In the former, the provisions of the testament could not contradict the terms of the legal usufruct. By *Waldron*, a testamentary provision that gave the usufruct the same or greater rights as the legal usufruct could be considered legal.

D. Since the surviving spouse is entitled to a legal usufruct under La. C.C. art. 890, a testamentary disposition to that effect simply confirms the legal usufruct unless its terms are adverse to the legal usufruct, even if the property subject to the usufruct is separate property not typically covered by the codal usufruct. *Darby v. Rozas.*

ii. **The law that is**. "If the deceased spouse is survived by descendants, the surviving spouse shall have a usufruct over the decedent's share of the community property to the extent that the decedent has not disposed of it by testament. This usufruct terminates when the surviving spouse dies or remarries, whichever occurs first." La. C.C. art. 890 (1996).

For a legal usufruct to exist, the following requirements must be met:

A. A community property regime,

B. Intestate transfer of at least some community property, and

C. Inheritance of the decedent's property by his descendants.

e) **Testamentary usufruct of the surviving spouse**.

i. "The decedent may grant a usufruct to the surviving spouse over all or part of his property, including the forced portion, and may grant the usufructuary the power to dispose of nonconsumables as provided in the law of usufruct. The usufruct shall be for life unless expressly designated for a shorter period, and shall not require security except as expressly declared by the decedent or as permitted when the legitime is affected.

A usufruct over the legitime in favor of the surviving spouse is a permissible burden that does not impinge upon the legitime, whether it affects community property or separate property, whether it is for life or a shorter period, whether or not the forced heir is a descendant of the surviving spouse, and whether or not the usufructuary has the power to dispose of nonconsumables." La. C.C art. 1499.

A. Comment (d) to the 1996 revision of La. C.C. art. 1499 purports to "legislatively overrule[] the case of Succession of B.J. Chauvin,... which held that when the will 'merely confirmed' the legal usufruct to a surviving spouse... [it] was not a lifetime usufruct" and similarly refers to *Darby v. Rozas*. The article does not state anything of the sort, and it is unclear whether a comment to a Civil Code article could or should overrule a line of *jurisprudence constante* stretching back to 1888.

B. The power to dispose of nonconsumables must be granted explicitly.

f) **Why classification matters**. The classification of a surviving spouse's usufruct as legal or testamentary is not simply an academic matter. In the absence of contrary provisions, different default rules apply to each kind of usufruct, so the distinction remains important.

   i. *Termination*. By default, the legal usufruct under article 890 terminates upon the death or remarriage of the surviving spouse. A testamentary usufruct, on the other hand, is for life by default.

   ii. *Inheritance tax*. The usufructuary under a legal usufruct did not pay Louisiana Estate taxes, while the usufructuary under a conventional or testamentary usufruct did. This distinction is no longer important because Act 822 of the 2008 Regular Legislative Session eliminated Louisiana inheritance taxes.

   iii. *Security*. As explored below, a legal usufructuary is generally not required to give security, but a conventional usufructuary may be. *See* La. C.C. arts. 571 (usufructuaries required to give security by default) and 573 (article 890 usufructuaries not required to give security except where the naked owner is a forced heir who is not the surviving spouse's child).

   iv. *Impingement on legitime*. While the revised article 890 does not explicitly address whether the usufruct of the surviving spouse is allowed to impinge on the legitime, there is little reason to suspect that the revision intended to make a change. Conventional usufructs historically were not permitted to burden the legitime, but La. C.C. art. 1499 allows it in the case of a testamentary usufruct to the surviving spouse. *But see* La. C.C. art. 1514, which allows non-child forced heirs to demand security.

g) **Obligation to give security**. Recall that usufructuaries in general are required to give security under La. C.C. art. 571 (reproduced above), unless the grantor dispenses with it. Under La. C.C. art. 573 (reproduced above) security is not required in several cases, including that of surviving spouse's usufruct.

   i. **Before August 15, 2004**.

      A. 1990 revision of La. C.C. art. 890: the surviving spouse could be compelled to give security if the property burdened was the decedent's separate property or if the naked owners were not the usufructuary's children.

      B. 1996 revision of La. C.C. art. 890: security was dispensed with for the legal usufruct but a usufruct over separate property was necessarily testamentary and therefore required security unless dispensed with by testament or La. C.c. art. 1499.

  ii. **After August 15, 2014**.

    A. The 2004 revision of La. C.C. art. 573 dispensed with security for a surviving spouse under article 890 except where the naked owner was not a child of the usufructuary or where a child of the usufructuary was a forced heir. In the latter case, the security would be limited to the legitime.

    B. Security is dispensed with where the parent's usufruct under La. C.C. art. 891 burdens property owned by the usufructuary's children. Otherwise, security must be given in accordance with law.

    C. The article dispenses with security for the martial portion usufruct under La. C.C. art. 2434 where the naked owners are children of the usufructuary.

h) **Reduction of excessive donations**.

  i. "No charges, conditions, or burdens may be imposed on the legitime except those expressly authorized by law, such as a usufruct in favor of a surviving spouse or the placing of the legitime in trust." La. C.C. art. 1496.

  ii. "A donation, *inter vivos* or *mortis causa*, that impinges upon the legitime of a forced heir is not null but is merely reducible to the extent necessary to eliminate the impingement." La. C.C. art. 1503. But A usufruct in favor of the surviving spouse never impinges on the legitime. La. C.C. art. 1499.

  iii. "Nevertheless, the legitime may not be satisfied in whole or in part by a usufruct or an income interest in trust. When a forced heir is both income and principal beneficiary of the same interest in trust, however, that interest shall be deemed a full ownership interest for purposes of satisfying the legitime..." La. C.C. art. 1502.

  iv. The Civil Code article does not address *how* an excessive donation should be reduced either procedurally or mechanically, but Comment (b) to the 1996 revision of La. C.C. art. 1503 states that where a husband leaves his entire estate to his wife but a forced heir is due one-fourth as his legitime, the wife will receive the entire disposable portion in full ownership with a usufruct for life with the power to dispose of nonconsumables over the legitime because this is the largest legacy that could have legally been left to her. A similar result would obtain under *Winsberg v. Winsberg*, 96 So. 2d 44 (La. 1857), but that opinion relies on the doctrine of confirmation of the legal usufruct. If that doctrine has been overruled by the 1996 revision, the outcome is unclear. Nevertheless, there is no judicial or statutory justification for giving the usufruct the power to dispose of nonconsumables.

  v. The usufruct in favor of a non-spouse burdening the legitime is an impermissible burden under La. C.C. art. 1496, but it is statutorily unclear how it is to be reduced.

  vi. La. C.C. art. 1499 (1870) laid out a scheme for reducing a donation where the value of the usufruct exceeded the value of the disposable portion. Forced heirs could elect to accept the donation as intended by the testator or take the legitime in full ownership while the other party took the disposable portion in full ownership. Valuing the usufruct was very difficult, and this provision was not carried forward in later revisions.

i) **Intertemporal conflicts of law**.

  i. The date a testament was executed can determine what law applies. The redactors of the 1996 revisions intended the changes to apply prospectively to testaments executed after the effective date of the changes rather than upset existing testaments and testators' intentions.

    A. "When a testament executed prior to June 18, 1996, leaves a usufruct to the surviving spouse without specifying its duration, the law in effect at the time the testament was executed shall govern the duration of the usufruct." La. R.S. 9:2441.

  ii. But the laws applicable to succession rights are determined by the date the decedent died.

    A. "Testate and intestate succession rights, including the right to claim as a forced heir, are governed by the law in effect on the date of the decedent's death." La. C.C. art 870 (B).

  iii. And, in general, courts may consider the law in effect at the time the testament was written when interpreting a legal term in a testament. La. C.C. art. 1611.1

  iv. "An action for annulment of a testament" is "subject to a liberative prescription of five years[.]" La. C.C. art. 3497.

j) **The marital portion in usufruct**.

  i. "When a spouse dies rich in comparison with the surviving spouse, the surviving spouse is entitled to claim the marital portion from the succession of the deceased spouse." La. C.C. art. 2432.

  ii. "The marital portion is an incident of any matrimonial regime and a charge on the succession of the deceased spouse. It may be claimed by the surviving spouse, even if separated from the deceased, on proof that the separation occurred without his fault." La. C.C. art. 2433.

  iii. "The marital portion is one-fourth of the succession in ownership if the deceased died without children, the same fraction in usufruct for life if he is survived by three or fewer children, and a child's share in such usufruct if he is survived by more than three children. In no event, however, shall the amount of the marital portion exceed one million dollars." La. C.C. art. 2434.

  iv. "A legacy left by the deceased to the surviving spouse and payments due to him as a result of the death are deducted from the marital portion." La. C.C. art. 2435.

    A. "Payments due to [the usufructuary] as a result of the death" include life insurance proceeds that pass outside the succession, social security death benefits, and the social security benefits flowing from the decedent's social security contributions. *See Norsworthy v. Succession of Norstworthy.*

  v. "The right of the surviving spouse to claim the marital portion is personal and nonheritable. This right prescribes three years from the date of death." La. C.C. art. 2436.

  vi. "When, during the administration of the succession, it appears that the surviving spouse will be entitled to the marital portion, he has the right to demand and receive a periodic allowance from the succession representative.
The amount of the allowance is fixed by the court in which the succession proceeding is pending. If the marital portion, as finally fixed, is less than the allowance, the surviving spouse is charged with the deficiency." La. C.C. art. 2437.

    A. This is an advance on the marital portion.

B. The Civil Code does not prescribe a certain method for calculating the amount of the allowance, *but see Norsworthy v. Succession of Norstworthy* for an applied example. The appeal court disagreed with the trial court's computation of the widow's expected marital portion but affirmed the monthly advance amount anyway because the advance would not exhaust the marital portion under either computation.

C. La. C.C. art. 2437 anticipates a court setting the allowance before the final computation of the net estate value and the marital portion. The allowance is likely not set abusively high if the marital portion is much higher than the allowance and the estate is solvent and relatively liquid. In any case, the surviving spouse is responsible for repaying any overpayments after the final fixing of the marital portion. *Norsworthy v. Succession of Norstworthy.*

LEURY V. MAYER

Son (P) v. Buyer (D)
122 La. 486, 47 So. 839 (La. 1908)

Facts & Procedure

The Son (P) of deceased parents sued to be recognized as owner of an undivided one-half interest in 20 shares of bank stock and to partition the stock and its accrued dividends by licitation. The Son's (P) father acquired the stock as community property during his marriage to the Son's (P) mother. His mother died a few years later, leaving her half of the community stock to her Son (P). A few months after that the father purported to transfer the entire stock certificate to a Buyer (D) and died years later.

In this lawsuit, the Buyer (D) pleaded prescription and argued that the father, as usufructuary, had the legal right to sell the stock because it was subject to an imperfect or quasi-usufruct. The trial court recognized the Son (P) as the owner of his mother's undivided half interest in the stock and ordered a partition sale of the stock and accrued dividends.

The Buyer (D) appealed.

Issue

Is company stock a consumable thing subject to an imperfect usufruct?

Holding & Decision

No, company stock is not a consumable thing because it represents an investment intended to generate revenue. Accordingly, the usufructuary is entitled only to the fruits of the stock, namely dividends, and may not sell the naked owner's portion of the asset. The Court reasoned that an imperfect usufruct applied to things that would be useless to the usufructuary if not consumed or changed, e.g., money or food and drink. The stock here was not useless because it generated revenue through dividends similar to real estate rents.

The Buyer (D) argued that the father could sell the stock because it was not producing revenue, but the Court dismissed that argument out of hand after reviewing the stock's performance. The Court held that the father had the right to collect all dividends declared before his death and that he could have transferred that right to the Buyer (D). But the father only had the right to transfer ownership of his undivided half of the stock; he had no right to sell the Son's (P) undivided half.

Thus the Court affirmed the trial court's judgment and amended it to clarify that only the stock and future dividends should be sold at auction and that the Buyer (D) must account to the Son (D) for all dividends received since the father's death. The Buyer (D) was entitled to keep all dividends declared before the father's death.

Rule of Law

Company stock is a nonconsumable thing because it represents an investment intended to generate revenue. Accordingly, the usufructuary is entitled only to the fruits of the stock, namely dividends, and may not sell the naked owner's portion of the asset.

SUCCESSION OF GOODE
425 So. 2d 673 (La. 1982)

Facts & Procedure

Ronald Bruce Goode died testate, leaving an olographic testament containing specific dispositions but no residuary legacy. The fifth provision of the testament provided that "[all his] oil & gas royalty interest payments ... shall be paid to Pauline Egbert Parker for as long as she might live. After her death the amount of any payments shall be equally divided between my nieces and nephews and Linda Cosby Paine." After the testament's execution, the royalty interest and payments unexpectedly increased in value.

Opponents of the testament sought to annul the testament, arguing it constituted a prohibited substitution. The trial court agreed and invalidated the testament. The appeal court affirmed, and the Louisiana Supreme Court granted certiorari.

Issue

Does a testamentary disposition bequeathing "oil & gas royalty interest payments" to one person for life and then the "amount of any payments" to others create successive usufructs over the mineral royalty interest itself or give rise to a prohibited substitution?

Holding & Decision

Such language demonstrates the testator's intent to create successive usufructs rather than a prohibited substitution because it identifies the payments separately from the underlying royalty interest and describes the intent for the fruits of the interest to be enjoyed by successive groups. Because the language is silent as to the naked ownership, it passes via intestacy.

Initially, a divided Court held that the disposition was a valid bequest of a life usufruct of the royalty interest to Mrs. Parker and of the naked ownership to the other named legatees. The majority reasoned that the testator's deliberate use of the word "payments" distinguished the income or fruits of the royalty interest from the underlying royalty interest. To validate the testament and effectuate the testator's intent for Mrs. Parker to receive lifetime payments and the others to receive them thereafter, the Court construed the disposition as creating a usufruct. The court reversed the lower courts' judgments and dismissed the petition to annul the testament.

Justice Calogero concurred with the majority opinion that there was no prohibited substitution in the testament. He opined that the testator effectively gave Mrs. Parker a "legacy of revenues" under La. C.C. art. 609, a "kind of usufruct."

Dissent

Justice Dixon dissented from the majority and agreed with Justice Calogero that the bequest was a legacy of revenues under La. C.C. art. 609.

Justice Blanche dissented, arguing that the bequest was a prohibited substitution because it constituted a "double disposition in full ownership, as well as [an implied] charge to preserve and transmit" the property to the second owners. The charge was implied, in the justice's opinion, because future payments to the second set of owners depend entirely on the preservation of the royalty interests. This impaired her right to alienate that interest and kept the interests out of commerce.

Justice Watson agreed with Justice Blanche's analysis.

Rehearing

On rehearing, the Court again reversed the lower courts but refined its interpretation. It held that the provision created successive usufructs: first, a usufruct of the mineral royalty in favor of Mrs. Parker for her lifetime, and then, upon her death, a second usufruct of the same mineral royalty in favor of the nieces, nephews, and Mrs. Paine. The Court again reasoned that the testator's consistent use of "payments" for both sets of legatees demonstrated his intent to grant them the benefits flowing from the royalty interest (i.e., a usufruct) rather than the full ownership of the royalty interest itself. Since the will made no disposition of the naked ownership of the mineral royalty and named no residuary legatee, the naked ownership devolved to the testator's intestate heirs.

The Court found this interpretation comported with testator's likely understanding and intent, especially given the relatively modest income from the royalty at the time the will was made and the testator's profession as an independent oil operator. The Court held that the second usufruct would terminate upon the death of the last surviving legatee in that group.

Rule of Law

A testamentary provision like "all oil & gas royalty interest payments owned by me shall be paid to A for life and then divided between B, C, and D" demonstrates the testator's intent to create successive usufructs rather than a prohibited substitution because it identifies the payments separately from the underlying royalty interest and describes the intent for the fruits of the interest to be enjoyed by successive groups. Because the language is silent as to the naked ownership, it passes via intestacy.

SMITH V. NELSON
Heirs (P) v. Stepfather (D)
121 La. 170, 46 So. 200 (La. 1908)

Facts & Procedure

After their mother's death, Mrs. Smith's Heirs (P) sued her second husband, Mr. Nelson (D), to partition property they inherited in indivision with him from their mother's succession. Mrs. Smith was widowed from Michael Smith, the plaintiffs' father, and then married the defendant, Mr. Nelson (D).

She bequeathed to the Heirs (P) all her community property from the first marriage and an undivided one-half interest in the property held in community with Mr. Nelson (D). She also bequeathed Mr. Nelson (D) the usufruct over all the property she acquired during her marriage to him.

After Mrs. Smith's death, the Heirs (P) were recognized as full owners of the former community property from their parents' marriage and as owners of an undivided one-half interest in the community property of her marriage to Mr. Nelson (D), subject to his usufruct. Mr. Nelson (D) was recognized as owner of the other undivided half of the community property and as usufructuary of the rest.

Mr. Nelson (D) eventually remarried, and the two surviving Heirs (P) sued to partition the property they held in indivision, arguing that his remarriage terminated the usufruct by operation of law. They also sought an accounting of revenues flowing from the property. The plaintiffs impleaded the minor children of their deceased brother.

Mr. Nelson (D) pleaded various exceptions and argued that if a sale were ordered, he was entitled to the usufruct of the proceeds or one-third of the property in full ownership. The trial court initially ordered a sale and granted Mr. Nelson (D) the usufruct of the proceeds but dismissed the lawsuit after a retrial.

The Heirs (P) appealed.

Issue

Can the naked owners without any share of full ownership in an undivided interest in immovable property compel partition by licitation of the entire property, including the usufruct?

Holding & Decision

No, naked owners cannot compel a usufructuary or an owner with perfect title to partition his interest by licitation.

The Court first held that Mr. Nelson's (D) remarriage did not terminate his usufruct because it had been established by testament and recognized by the court in the succession proceedings. Because the plaintiffs' case assumed the usufruct terminated, they requested a simple partition of the property rather than the partition of the naked ownership or a partition subject to usufruct. The Court noted that there was no basis for an action between a naked owner on the one side and a perfect owner and usufructuary on the other because the parties held distinct fragments of a dismembered title to the same immovable and, thus, there was no thing held in common to partition. Instead, they owned distinct rights.

The Court further reasoned that if the action were viewed as an action between owners in common only of the naked title, such a sale would deprive Mr. Nelson (D) of his right to transmit his full ownership to his heirs by either permanently dismembering his title by vesting naked ownership in a purchaser while he retained only a usufruct or by extinguishing his usufruct over his own half if the entire property were sold free of the usufruct.

The Court approved the principle that naked co-owners can partition the naked ownership among themselves (even if the property is burdened by a usufruct), but they cannot compel the usufructuary to participate in a partition that involves the sale of the entire immovable.

Because the plaintiffs relied on the assumption that Mr. Nelson's (D) usufruct had terminated and it had not, their lawsuit failed. The Court affirmed the lower court's ruling.

Rule of Law

Naked owners cannot compel a usufructuary or an owner with perfect title to partition his interest by licitation.

GUENO V. MEDLENKA
Owners (P) v. Usufructuary (D)
238 La. 1081, 117 So. 2d 817 (La. 1960)

Facts & Procedure

The naked Owners (P) and their mineral lessees sued for a declaration that the Usufructuary (D) had no right to exploit the oil, gas, and minerals of the land burdened by the usufruct and that she could not grant a mineral lease to another defendant. The trial court ruled that the Owners (P) had the right to explore the land for minerals and grant mineral leases but that this right was subordinate to the Usufructuary's (D) rights to enjoy and use the property. Thus, the court ruled, the Owners (P) could not actually explore and exploit the land for minerals without the Usufructuary's (D) consent.

The Usufructuary (D) appealed.

Issue

Between the naked owner of land and the usufructuary, who has the right to explore the land for minerals and reduce them to possession?

Holding & Decision

The usufructuary has no right to extract oil, gas, and other minerals from the land burdened by the usufruct but does enjoy the usufruct over proceeds from mineral production already in progress at the commencement of the usufruct. The naked owner, on the other hand, has the right to explore the land for minerals and reduce them to possession, so long as he does not impair or impede the usufructuary's enjoyment of the property.

First, the Court considered and rejected the position that usufruct includes the right to search for and extract oil, gas, and minerals from the land, reasoning that usufructuary of a nonconsumable cannot consume and alter the substance of the thing by extracting and selling the land's products. Nevertheless, a usufructuary is entitled to the proceeds arising from mines and quarries opened before the commencement of the usufruct, and the same principle applies to oil and gas exploration. Thus, the Usufructuary (D) had no right to grant a mineral lease.

But the Court also held that a naked owner has the right to explore and exploit the land to produce oil, gas, and other minerals, despite its being burdened by a usufruct. The Court agreed with the lower court's conclusion to this effect, including the limitation that this right may not be exercised in a way that impairs the use and enjoyment of the usufruct. But the Court rejected the trial court's conclusion that the naked owner's rights are subordinate to the usufructuary's rights. Instead, the Court reasoned that the naked owner's rights are "coextensive and concurrent with, not subordinate to, the usufructuary's right of enjoyment and use."

Thus, the Court held that the Owners (P) herein did not need the Usufructuary's (D) consent to explore and exploit the land for minerals so long as these operations did not interfere with the Usufructuary's (D) enjoyment. Holding otherwise would give the usufructuary a veto and keep the property out of commerce, contrary to public policy, without any basis in law. A usufructuary would still be entitled to damages if the naked owners injured them and their rights.

The Court affirmed the trial court's declaration that the Usufructuary (D) had no mineral rights and that the Owners' (P) mineral lease was valid. It amended the judgment by deleting the trial court's declaration that the Owners' (P) rights were subordinate to the Usufructuary's (D) rights and that the Owners (P) must have the Usufructuary's (D) consent before entering the property.

Rule of Law

A usufructuary has no right to extract oil, gas, and other minerals from the land burdened by the usufruct but does enjoy the usufruct over proceeds from mineral production already in progress at the commencement of the usufruct. The naked owner, on the other hand, has the right to explore the land for minerals and reduce them to possession, so long as he does not impair or impede the usufructuary's enjoyment of the property.

KENNEDY V. KENNEDY
Usufructuary (P) v. Owner (D)
699 So. 2d 351 (La. 1997)

Facts & Procedure

The Usufructuary (P) holding a usufruct over a 143-acre tract of mature loblolly pine trees sued for declaratory judgment authorizing her to clearcut the trees and replant the stand. The Owner (D) objected.

The tract had never been managed or exploited for timber. The property mostly consisted mature and over-mature pines aged 60–75 years old and included about 30 acres of younger trees. The Usufructuary's (P) forestry expert endorsed the plan to clearcut nearly all of merchantable trees and replant seedlings, leave some hardwoods near watersheds and streams to reduce erosion, and selectively cut the larger trees in the young section of the property. The Owner (D) opposed the clear-cut, advocating for a selective cut or no cut at all, arguing a clear-cut would deplete the substance of the land.

The trial court adopted the opinion of Usufructuary's (P) forester and approved his plan. The appeal court reversed, limiting the Usufructuary (P) to a selective cut from only the 30-acre stand of younger trees. The Louisiana Supreme Court granted writs and, on original hearing, affirmed appeal court's decision. After rehearing, the Court reversed.

Issue

1. Does land containing valuable, mature timber that has never been previously managed or exploited for timber operations constitute "timberlands" for the purposes of La. C.C. art. 562?

2. If so, can a clear-cut of such previously unmanaged timberland, followed by replanting, constitute "proper management" by a "prudent administrator" under La. C.C. art. 562?

Holding & Decision

1. Yes, land that grows merchantable timber is timberland, even if it is not regularly managed and exploited for timber as if it were a tree farm. The Court reviewed the legislative history of La. C.C. art. 562, noting that the drafters specifically removed language from an earlier draft that would have required prior regular exploitation of timberland for a usufructuary to continue such operations (*Cf.* the "open mines" doctrine for minerals). The Court specifically rejected the notion that "timberland" in Art. 562 is synonymous with a "tree farm," which implies prior, regular management for generating sustained timber yields. Adopting the generally prevailing and technical forestry definitions, the Court found the 143-acre tract, being covered with marketable timber, clearly qualified as "timberland."

2. Yes, what constitutes management as a prudent administrator is a factual question and may include clearcutting, where appropriate under the circumstances. The Court found the trial court was not manifestly erroneous in accepting the Usufructuary's (P) expert's opinion that it was prudent to largely clearcut and replant the previously unmanaged tract of mature and over-mature pines at issue. The expert testimony indicated that selective cutting of the old, suppressed trees would be ineffective for rehabilitation and that leaving them standing posed risks of insect infestation, disease, and ecological succession by less desirable hardwoods. The "prudent administrator" standard is flexible. While a clear-cut might not be prudent for a well-managed tree farm, it might be warranted for previously unmanaged timberland under specific circumstances like those present here.

Thus the Court reversed the appeal court's judgment and reinstated the trial court's judgment, noting that the Usufructuary (P) was entitled to the proceeds from the timber operations as approved by the trial court.

Dissent

Justice Johnson adopted the opinion of the Owner's (P) experts that a selective cutting was more prudent. He argued that a clearcut would deplete the substance of the property and deprive the naked owner his due under La. C.C. art. 562.

Rule of Law

1. Land that grows merchantable timber is timberland, even if it is not regularly managed and exploited for timber as if it were a tree farm.

2. What constitutes management as a prudent administrator of timberland is a factual question and may include clearcutting, where appropriate under the circumstances.

SPARKS V. DAN COHEN CO.
Owners (P) v. Lessee (D)
187 La. 830, 175 So. 590 (La. 1937)

Facts & Procedure

The Owners (P) of a commercial retail building inherited it from their uncle, James L. Nelson. Mr. Nelson also bequeathed a life usufruct of his estate, including the building, to his widow, Mrs. Martha Nelson. On February 1, 1934, Mrs. Nelson leased the store building to the Lessee (D) herein for a five-year term with an option to renew for another five years.

The lease referred to Mrs. Nelson simply as "lessor" and did not disclose her status as usufructuary. Several of Mrs. Nelson's relatives who later became plaintiffs in this suit negotiated the lease on her behalf. They uniformly testified that the Lessee (D) had been informed during the negotiations that Mrs. Nelson was the usufructuary and not the owner of the building. The Lessee (D) denied that knowledge throughout the trial.

Four days after Mrs. Nelson's death, the Owners (P) notified the Lessee (D) the lease terminated along with the usufruct upon Mrs. Nelson's demise. The Lessee (D) disagreed. After accepting Mrs. Nelson's succession along with other heirs, the Owners (P) formally demanded the Lessee (D) vacate and filed this suit to declare the lease terminated.

The Lessee (D) pleaded estoppel, arguing that by unconditionally accepting Mrs. Nelson's succession, the plaintiffs assumed her warranty obligations under the lease and were thus barred from challenging it. The trial court ruled for the Owners (P), finding that the Lessee (D) knew that Mrs. Nelson was merely a usufructuary, declared the lease terminated, awarded the Owners (P) rent incurred during the proceedings, and evicted the Lessee (D).

The Lessee (D) appealed.

Issue

Does a lease granted by a usufructuary terminate at the end of the usufruct, regardless of whether the lessee knew that the usufructuary was not the owner of the property?

Holding & Decision

Yes, under La. C.C. art. 2716 a "lease granted by a usufructuary terminates upon the termination of the usufruct[,]" whether or not the lessee knew that the lessor was merely a usufruct. The Court noted that, while a lease terminates with the end of the usufruct, under the same law a lessee would be entitled to indemnification from the usufructuary's heirs if he or she were not informed that the lessor was not the owner. The Owners (P) here were among Mrs. Nelson's heirs, and the Lessee (D) sought such indemnity. But the Court noted that, even if a lessee were entitled to indemnity, that remedy did not extend the lease.

The Court rejected the Lessee's (D) estoppel and indemnity arguments after reviewing the trial court's factual finding that the Lessee (D) had been informed that Mrs. Nelson was merely a usufructuary. To support that conclusion, the trial court and the Court noted that the lease negotiations were conducted on Mrs. Nelson's behalf by several of the plaintiffs in this case or their spouses, all of whom were experienced businessmen who would have been incentivized to make that disclosure and who all testified that they did so. Further, Mrs. Nelson's status was apparent from the public records.

The Court affirmed the trial court's judgment. The Court denied the Lessee's (D) petition for rehearing after issuing a short *per curiam* opinion clarifying some language in the original opinion.

Rule of Law

Under La. C.C. art. 2716 a "lease granted by a usufructuary terminates upon the termination of the usufruct[,]" whether or not the lessee knew that the lessor was merely a usufruct

SUCCESSION OF WATSON
Heirs (P) v. Widower (D)
517 So. 2d 276 (La. App. 1st Cir. 1987)

Facts & Procedure

This case concerns a dispute over whether a joint usufructuary-executor can be compelled to furnish security. Frances Doyle Watson died, leaving the forced portion to her son, daughter, and granddaughter from a predeceased son. She left the disposable portion to her Widower (D), the father of the living heirs and grandfather of the child representing her deceased father. Mrs. Watson also named the Widower (D) testamentary executor of her estate and "dispense[d] him from furnishing security" by testament.

The daughter and granddaughter filed a petition to compel the Widower (D) to furnish security for his role as executor. The trial court held La. C.C.P. art. 3154 allowed forced heirs to compel an executor to furnish security, regardless of the decedent's testamentary dispensation. Since the petitioners were forced heirs, the provision applied.

The Trial court ordered the Widower (D) to furnish $30,000 of security. The Widower (D) appealed.

Issue

May a usufructuary be compelled to furnish security in connection with his role as executor of a succession containing property burdened by his usufruct?

Holding & Decision

Yes, forced heirs may compel an executor to furnish security in connection with that role even if he is also a usufructuary of the succession property who would typically not be required to furnish security as usufructuary. Both the trial court and the appeal court cited La. C.C.P. art. 3154 as the controlling law. The appeal court distinguished between the Widower's (D) two roles — usufructuary and executor — and concluded that, even though the petitioners could not force the surviving spouse to furnish security for his performance as usufructuary, article 3154 specifically allowed them to do so in connection with his performance as executor. The Widower's (D) status as both usufructuary and executor did not affect the petitioner's rights to have an executor furnish security.

The appeal court affirmed the trial court's judgment.

Rule of Law

Forced heirs may compel an executor to furnish security in connection with that role even if he is also a usufructuary of the succession property who would typically not be required to furnish security as usufructuary.

SUCCESSION OF CRAIN
Stepdaughter v. Widow
450 So. 2d 1374 (La. App. 1st Cir. 1984)

Facts & Procedure

Eros Crosby Crain died, leaving a Widow and two daughters from a prior marriage. The decedent's testament confirmed the legal usufruct in favor of the Widow over his share of the community property, including the family home, and named her testamentary executrix. The daughters were his residuary legatees and accordingly naked owners of the family home.

Disputes arose during the succession administration regarding who bore responsibility for paying expenses related to the family home and penalties for late payment of estate taxes. The Widow sought payment from the succession for repairs to the home and other maintenance expenses, like security system fees, termite treatment, and plumbing repairs. Some other repairs were substantial, including roof repairs and repairs to a boat dock and slip. The Widow's Stepdaughter sought to charge all home-related expenses and tax penalties to the Widow individually because she enjoyed the sole use of the house or, in the alternative, to charge her rent.

The trial court ordered the succession to bear one-half of the approved repair costs, one-half of the mortgage payments, and one-half of various maintenance expenses (yard upkeep, security, etc.). It also held the succession, not the Widow personally, liable for the estate tax penalties and interest.

The Stepdaughter appealed.

Issue

May a person in possession of a home who is both usufructuary and executrix of the estate that owns the home charge the estate for ordinary repairs made to the home?

Holding & Decision

No, when a person is both a usufructuary of succession property and the succession representative with seizin of that property he or she is in possession of the usufruct and therefore personally responsible for the maintenance and repair of the property as specified by usufruct law. The appeal court reasoned that La. C.C.P. art. 3221, the provision that requires a succession representative like the Widow to repair and maintain succession property, did not apply because a succession representative who is also a legatee and who has seizin is deemed to be in possession of his or her legacy. Therefore, the Widow was in possession as a usufructuary of her usufruct over the family home and was required to fulfill the obligations of that role.

The appeal court quickly noted that a usufructuary is responsible for ordinary maintenance and repairs and that a usufructuary cannot compel the naked owners to make or pay for extraordinary repairs during the pendency of the usufruct. Instead, the usufructuary may demand reimbursement from the naked owner at the termination of the usufruct.

The court noted that many of the repairs and maintenance activities at issue were "ordinary repairs," including painting, repairing leaks, replacing glass, and repairing home HVAC and plumbing systems. The court held that the Widow was responsible for paying for these repairs. The court categorized several other items as "extraordinary repairs," including repairs to the dock, boat slip, and roof. But the court held that the usufructuary was not entitled to reimbursement until the usufruct's termination. Therefore, the Widow was responsible for all the repair and maintenance charges and was unable to shift them to the succession.

The appeal court also agreed with the trial court that the Widow was not personally liable for the estate tax penalties and interest. The trial curt carefully reviewed the record and found no fault in the Widow's handling of the federal taxes. Accordingly, the penalties and interest were properly charged to the succession.

Thus, the appeal court reversed the portion of the trial court's judgment holding the succession liable for half of the maintenance and repair charges, declared the Widow responsible for them, and affirmed the portion of the judgment holding the estate responsible for the tax penalties and interest.

Rule of Law

When a person is both a usufructuary of succession property and the succession representative with seizin of that property he or she is in possession of the usufruct and therefore personally responsible for the maintenance and repair of the property as specified by usufruct law.

Succession of Davis
Forced Heirs v. Widow
536 So. 2d 498 (La. App. 1st Cir. 1988)

Facts & Procedure

Charles Edward Davis died intestate, leaving a Widow and three children from a prior marriage. The decedent and his wife had two outstanding debts when he died: one automobile loan and a mortgage secured by an immovable. The Widow acquired a legal usufruct as surviving spouse over the deceased's undivided one-half of the community property, including both the car and the immovables, while the Forced Heirs inherited the naked ownership. Mrs. Davis also served as the administratrix of the succession.

During the administration, Mrs. Davis paid off the car note and made installment payments on the mortgage totaling $6,899.10. She filed a tableau of distribution seeking reimbursement from the Forced Heirs for their share of these debts. The Forced Heirs, on the other hand, argued that the Widow, as usufructuary, was solely responsible for the mortgage debts.

The trial court, relying on *Succession of Crain*, ruled in favor of the Forced Heirs, and the Widow appealed.

Issue

Is a usufructuary of property encumbered by a mortgage personally liable for the payment of the secured debt?

Holding & Decision

No, a usufructuary is not personally liable for the succession debts secured by a mortgage on the property subject to the usufruct, but the property could be seized and sold to pay the debts. A usufructuary who pays the debt to avoid liquidation is entitled to reimbursement for those payments without interest at the end of the usufruct. A naked owner who pays the debt is entitled to be paid interest by the usufructuary.

The appeal court reviewed the applicable Civil Code articles and found that the Widow had no legal obligation to pay the mortgage on the property subject to usufruct. Nevertheless, such payments would prevent the seizure and sale of the property and allow her to enjoy the usufruct. The court found that the then-current La. C.C. art. 592 regulated the rights of whichever party — usufructuary or naked owner — pays the debt. (*Cf.* revised La. C.C. arts. 589–90 which restate and clarify the substance of former art. 592.)

But the court noted that the parties confused the interest owed to a naked owner who paid the debt. The interest is not the interest on the note that is paid to the holder of the note. Rather the interest owed by the usufructuary to the naked owner who pays the debt is calculated at the legal rate of interest on the entire debt paid by the naked owner.

With that modification, the appeal court affirmed the trial court's judgment.

Rule of Law

A usufructuary is not personally liable for the succession debts secured by a mortgage on the property subject to the usufruct, but the property could be seized and sold to pay the debts. A usufructuary who pays the debt to avoid liquidation is entitled to reimbursement for those payments without interest at the end of the usufruct. A naked owner who pays the debt is entitled to be paid interest by the usufructuary.

Barry v. United States Fidelity & Guaranty Company

Usufructuary (P) v. Driver (D)
236 So. 2d 229 (La. App. 3d Cir. 1970)

Facts & Procedure

In this tort suit over an automobile accident, a Usufructuary (P) and another Driver (D) collided, totaling the Usufructuary's (P) car. At trial the parties stipulated that the car was worth $1,125 and retained a salvage value of $200. The car had been part of the community between the Usufructuary (P) and her deceased husband, so she owned an undivided one-half interest in the car and held the usufruct over the other undivided half. The Usufructuary's (P) children were the naked owners of the their father's undivided one-half interest in the car.

The trial court found the other Driver (D) 100% at fault for the accident but rejected the Usufructuary's (P) claim for damages for the loss of the car.

The Usufructuary (P) appealed.

Issue

Are the naked owners indispensable parties to an action by the usufructuary to recover damages for the destruction of an automobile totaled due to a third party's fault?

Holding & Decision

No, a usufructuary may serve as administrator for tort claims related to injuries to both the use and ownership of the thing subject to usufruct, so the naked owners are not indispensable parties to the action.

On appeal, the other Driver (D) argued that the usufruct terminated upon the destruction of the automobile and that, as a result, the naked owners were indispensable parties to this litigation. The appeal court rejected this argument, finding that the usufruct did not terminate but instead attached to the tort claim and resulting damages. The appeal court noted that while former La. C.C. arts. 613–615 apply to a purely accidental loss (viz., not one caused by another's fault), French and other continental jurisprudence and doctrine suggest that the usufruct attaches to the damage claim for a loss caused by another's fault. Further, former La. C.C. art. 613 was inapplicable to usufructs under universal title like the usufruct of the surviving spouse at issue. Finally, Louisiana law specifically provides that the usufruct of the surviving spouse does not terminate when the property subject to the usufruct changes form, as here. Instead, the principle of real subrogation allows the usufructuary to sue in his or her own name and to recover payments that are then subject to usufruct for the remainder of its term.

The court then held that, since the usufruct did not terminate, the naked owners were not indispensable parties. The Usufructuary (P) could administer the claim and recover the loss in her own name. She could, of course, implead the naked owners if she chose but she was not required to.

Therefore, the court amended the trial court's judgment to award the Usufructuary (P) $925 ($1,125 value less $200 salvage value) in damages for the destroyed automobile and otherwise affirmed the judgment.

Rule of Law

A usufructuary may serve as administrator for tort claims related to injuries to both the use and ownership of the thing subject to usufruct, so the naked owners are not indispensable parties to the action.

BOND V. GREEN

Owners (P) v. Usufructuaries (D)
401 So. 2d 639 (La. App. 3d Cir. 1981)

Facts & Procedure

The Owners (P) of a parcel of land sued to evict the Usufructuaries (D) because their usufruct had terminated. Alternatively, they sought a judicial determination of the boundaries of the property subject to usufruct.

In 1966, the soon-to-be Usufructuaries (D) owned the property at issue and sold it to Lloyd Love. They reserved the usufruct over the house they lived in, another house nearby, and "the yards surrounding" their residence. At the commencement of the usufruct, the two houses were very dilapidated. Mr. Love testified that he considered them worthless because of their condition, and the trial court heard testimony that they became progressively worse and more hazardous after the sale.

Nevertheless, the Usufructuaries occupied the larger house for years and attempted to make repairs as they could. Despite these efforts, the houses were falling down by 1976, and the Usufructuaries (D) had them demolished with Mr. Love's permission. They replaced the structures with two mobile homes in approximately the same locations.

The chain of title between Mr. Love and the Owners (P) herein is unclear, but they filed this action to evict the Usufructuaries (D), arguing that their usufruct terminated with the complete destruction of the houses through neglect and because they failed to pay the property taxes. The trial court rejected the Owners' (P) claims, recognized the usufruct, and ordered the Usufructuaries (D) to reimburse the Owners (P) for property taxes they paid.

The Owners (P) appealed.

Issue

Does a usufruct of structures and the yards surrounding them terminate when the structures are demolished?

Holding & Decision

No, where a usufruct includes both structures and land, the demolition of the structures constitutes only a partial loss of the part of the usufruct pertaining to the buildings. The usufruct of the land survives the demolition of the buildings.

The appeal court noted that the comments to La. C.C. art. 613 specifically contemplate the the usufruct over an estate continuing after its buildings are destroyed. The court also rejected the claim that the usufruct terminated because the Usufructuaries (D) abused the usufruct and failed to make ordinary repairs to the buildings. The facts demonstrated that the buildings were old and in disrepair at the commencement of the usufruct. Further, usufructuaries are not bound to restore property "destroyed because of age."

Finally, the court rejected the claim that the usufruct terminated because the Usufructuaries (D) failed to pay property taxes, noting that the Owner's (P) only remedy was an action for reimbursement. Failing to meet the obligation to pay taxes did not terminate the usufruct.

After finding that the usufruct had not terminated, the appeal court reviewed the trial court's determination of the usufruct's boundary. The court approved of the trial court's reception of parol evidence from Mr. Love to clarify the ambiguous language "yards surrounding said residence" contained in the reservation.

The court affirmed the trial court's judgment.

Rule of Law

Where a usufruct includes both structures and land, the demolition of the structures constitutes only a partial loss of the part of the usufruct pertaining to the buildings. The usufruct of the land persists.

KIMBALL V. STANDARD FIRE INS. CO.
Usufructuary (P) v. Insurer (D)
578 So. 2d 546 (La. App. 3d Cir. 1991)

Facts & Procedure

The Usufructuary (P) secured and paid for an insurance policy insuring against fire on the former community home over which she enjoyed the surviving spouse's usufruct. While the Usufructuary (P) was in jail for conspiracy to murder her husband, the house burned down under mysterious circumstances after being emptied of furnishings.

The Usufructuary (P) sued the insurance company to collect on the policy, and the administrator of her husband's succession notified the insurer that he intended to intervene to collect the succession's portion of the insurance proceeds. Before the intervention was filed, the insurance company inexplicably sent the Usufructuary (P) a check for $110,000, which she cashed. She then disappeared with the money. The succession eventually intervened in the lawsuit seeking additional money from the insurance company.

The trial court dismissed the intervention after finding that the Usufructuary (P) intended to and and did insure only her interest in the property.

The intervenors appealed.

Issue

Are the naked owners covered by an insurance policy acquired and paid for by the usufructuary that only lists her as the named insured?

Holding & Decision

No, an insurance policy that is acquired and paid for solely by a usufructuary and that lists only the usufructuary as named insured separately insures the usufructuary's interest in the property, and all proceeds from that policy belong to the usufructuary.

The appeal court adopted the trial court's reasons for judgment. The trial court noted the murder, arson, likely insurance fraud, and other scandalous facts surrounding this case but concluded that the Usufructuary (D) intended only to insure her interest in the property. She made a sworn statement to that effect, renewed the policy in her name alone, paid the premium herself, and was listed as the sole named insured. The trial court did not note any contrary evidence presented by the intervenors despite their having an insurable interest.

Under La. C.C. art. 617, if a usufructuary separately insures her interest, the policy proceeds belong to the usufructuary. The trial court concluded that the Usufructuary (P) did so and that the intervenors had no claim to any insurance proceeds under the policy. Further, the court noted that the usufruct of the community home would have converted to a usufruct over the insurance proceeds in any case, so the intervention was premature at best.

The appeal court affirmed the trial court's judgment dismissing the intervention.

Rule of Law

An insurance policy that is acquired and paid for solely by a usufructuary and that lists only the usufructuary as named insured separately insures the usufructuary's interest in the property, and all proceeds from that policy belong to the usufructuary.

WATSON V. FEDERAL LAND BANK OF JACKSON
Owner & Usufructuary (P) v. Co-owners' Creditor (D)
606 So. 2d 920 (La. App. 3d Cir 1992)

Facts & Procedure

This is a factually and procedurally complicated case concerning the rights of a usufructuary and the naked owners' creditors to excess funds left over after the property burdened by the usufruct was seized and sold to satisfy a mortgage debt. C. Winston Estes owned a separate-property home that he encumbered with a mortgage in favor of The Prudential Insurance Company of America. He died, leaving a testament naming his wife Margie (P) the usufructuary over all his property, including the mortgaged home and leaving the naked ownership split evenly between his four children.

Three of the children incurred significant debts, and money judgments were entered against them in favor of the defendant Federal Land Bank of Jackson (D) after their father's death. Two judgments were in the amount of $620,408.30, and the third was in the amount of $742,166.79. The fourth child and plaintiff herein, Irmaleta Estes Watson Pousson, was not named in any of the judgments.

No one paid the mortgage on the home, and it was seized and sold to satisfy the mortgage debt. After satisfying the debt, $360,408.30 of excess funds remained, which Prudential paid to Land Bank (D) to partially satisfy the three naked owners' judgments.

Margie and Irma (P) filed this suit to recover the excess funds paid to the Land Bank (D). The plaintiffs filed a motion for summary judgment to recognize Margie's (P) usufruct over the entire balance and the wrongful conversion of Irma's (P) one-quarter interest in the proceeds. The Land Bank (D) also filed a motion for summary judgment to deny Margie's (P) claims. In all, the trial court denied the portion of the plaintiff's motion seeking to recognize Margie's (P) usufruct, granted the portion recognizing Irma's (P) right to one-quarter of the proceeds, and granted the Land Bank's (D) cross-motion denying Margie's (P) claims.

Margie (P) appealed the summary judgment in favor of the Land Bank (D). No one appealed the judgment recognizing Irma's (P) interest in the proceeds.

Issue

Does a usufruct on property subject to a prior mortgage attach to any excess proceeds left after the property is sold at judicial sale to satisfy the debt?

Holding & Decision

Yes, the usufruct attaches to any proceeds remaining after the mortgage debt is satisfied because the enforcement of a preexisting mortgage only terminates the usufruct as to the portion of the proceeds required to satisfy the debt. The appeal court noted that La. C.C. art. 620 explicitly terminates a usufruct when a preexisting mortgage is enforced against the property but read that provision *in pari materia* with La. C.C. art. 615, which provides that the usufruct attaches to the proceeds when property subject to usufruct is converted to money without the usufructuary's action. Thus, the court concluded, the usufruct is terminated only with respect to the portion of the proceeds required to satisfy the debt; the remainder remains subject to the usufruct.

The court noted that the opposite result was untenable because it would enrich the naked owners at the expense of the usufructuary. Further, the interests of the naked owners and their creditors were adequately protected by La. C.C. art. 618, under which the interested party could demand security from the usufructuary.

The appeal court reversed the trial court's judgment and remanded the matter for further proceedings.

Rule of Law

The usufruct attaches to any proceeds remaining after the mortgage debt is satisfied because the enforcement of a preexisting mortgage only terminates the usufruct as to that portion of the proceeds required to satisfy the debt.

SUCCESSION OF HAYES
Heirs v. Usufructuary-Administrator
33 La. Ann. 1143 (La. 1881)

Facts & Procedure

Sarah E. Hayes died in 1862 during the Civil War without issue and left her husband, Jesse B. Clark, the usufruct over her share of the community property. Mrs. Hayes's legal Heirs inherited the naked ownership of the community and rest of her estate. Mr. Clark served as administrator of the succession and filed an accounting.

The Heirs opposed several items in the accounting, but this appeal concerned itself with two: 1. a credit of $1,055.55 Mr. Clark claimed for cotton sold for worthless Confederate money and bonds and 2. a credit of $2,000 Mr. Clark claimed for bringing separate property, including animals, and funds into the community. The Heirs opposed the cotton claim entirely and sought to reduce the larger claim by $254.

The trial court dismissed the Heirs' opposition, and the Heirs appealed.

Issue

Does a usufructuary who also acts as succession administrator have to reimburse the succession at the end of the usufruct for the value of consumables harvested and sold in the usufructuary's name?

Holding & Decision

Yes, where the usufructuary harvests a consumable and sells it in his own name, he is bound to return to the naked owner at the end of the usufruct the value the thing had at the commencement of the usufruct or like things.

The Court summarized the opposing arguments. If Mr. Clark harvested and sold the cotton as executor it could have been construed as a prudent action meant to protect the succession's asset from the ravages of war. Therefore, he would not be required to reimburse the Heirs. On the other hand, if he acted as usufructuary, reimbursement would be required at the end of the usufruct. The Court noted specifically that Mr. Clark invested the funds from the sale of the cotton in his own name and commingled the funds with his own separate funds. Based on the facts and Mr. Clark's pleadings, the Court found that Mr. Clark sold the cotton as usufructuary and was required to return the value or like things to the naked owners at the termination of the usufruct. Thus, he was not entitled to the $1,055.55 credit.

The Court also found that Mr. Clark himself valued the animals he brought into the community at $254. Thus, he was not entitled to reimbursement for these animals as part of his separate property.

The Court amended the trial court's judgment by striking the $1,055.55 credit and reducing the $2,000 credit by $254 to $1,746. In addition, the Court increased the bond required of Mr. Clark as usufructuary to $2,500. Otherwise, the Court affirmed the judgment.

Rule of Law

Where the usufructuary harvests a consumable and sells it in his own name, he is bound to return to the naked owner at the end of the usufruct the value the thing had at the commencement of the usufruct or like things.

SUCCESSION OF HECKERT
Children v. Second Wife
160 So. 2d 375 (La. App. 4th Cir. 1964)

Facts & Procedure

John Earl Heckert and Anna I. Buch were married and had two children. Mrs. Buch died intestate, and Mr. Heckert was recognized as the owner of a one-half undivided interest in the community property and usufructuary over the rest as surviving spouse. The children inherited the naked ownership of their mother's estate, including one-half of the community property.

The succession's inventory listed the community's 710 shares of stock in S.H. Kress and Company. The community owned an addition 300 shares of stock that were not included in the inventory. Mr. Heckert had possession of all 1,010 shares and collected the dividends.

Some time later, Mr. Heckert married Eunice Knobloch, and the usufruct terminated by law. Mr. Heckert did not return the children's half of the shares to them, and they did not object to his keeping them and collecting the dividends. Over 20 years later, Mr. Heckert died and left the disposable portion of his estate to Mrs. Kobloch and the legitime to his children.

At the time of his death, Mr. Heckert only retained 3 stock certificates for 100 shares each. The parties demonstrated during the succession proceedings that Mr. Heckert donated a total of 400 shares of the stock to his second wife.

The children sued Mrs. Knobloch Heckert to invalidate the donations, claiming that they owned an undivided interest in the donated shares and because the donations lessened their legitime. Alternatively, they demanded the stocks be returned to their father's succession to recalculate the legitime. Mrs. Knobloch Heckert asserted that the lawsuit amounted to a demand for an accounting and that such an action was prescribed by ten-year liberative prescription.

The trial court found in favor of the children and held that they were entitled to 505 shares from their mother's succession. The court awarded them 450 shares of stock, including the three 100 share certificates still in Mr. Heckert's possession and part of those certificates donated to Mrs. Knobloch Heckert, and the cash value of the remaining 55 shares from Mr. Heckert's estate. Mrs. Knobloch Heckert appealed.

Issue

Is the action for the return of nonconsumable property improperly divested by a usufructuary subject to ten-year liberative prescription?

Holding & Decision

No, the action asserting ownership of a nonconsumable thing formerly subject to usufruct is not subject to liberative prescription. At the outset, the appeal court rejected Mrs. Knobloch Heckert's argument that the children sought an accounting. Instead, the court found that the children were asserting ownership of property they inherited from their mother and for the preservation of their legitime.

The appeal court adopted the trial court's reasons for judgment as its opinion. The court reviewed the law regarding the transfer of stock and found that the law protected the company and transferee from harm caused by inappropriate transfers; it did not enlarge the transferor's powers to transfer stock. Stocks are nonconsumables, so a usufructuary cannot sell or otherwise dispose of the naked owners' rights in the stocks. If he did so, the court reasoned, this would be a breach of duty for which the usufructuary would be answerable.

The court further reasoned that the action for an accounting for an imperfect usufruct (of consumables) was subject to liberative prescription but that prescription does not run against the rights of naked owners under a perfect usufruct (of nonconsumables) as here. Finally, the court held that a usufructuary, as a precarious possessor, cannot acquisitively prescribe against the naked owners.

Since Mr. Heckert lacked authority to sell his children's stock, the court returned to the children all the stock remaining in Mr. Heckert's succession and directed the return of one-half of the stock he donated to Mrs. Knobloch Heckert. There was not enough stock left to make the children whole, so the court ordered Mr. Heckert's succession to make up the difference in cash.

The appeal court affirmed the trial court's judgment.

Rule of Law

The action asserting ownership of a nonconsumable thing formerly subject to usufruct is not subject to liberative prescription.

DARBY V. ROZAS
Stepchildren (P) v. Usufructuary (D)
580 So. 2d 984 (La. App. 3d Cir. 1991)

Facts & Procedure

Dr. Sidney J. Rozas died in 1986 and left a testament that, among other things, bequeathed to his wife the family home, a car, and the usufruct of all property he owned, "including the usufruct of all royalties and minerals." The testament did not address the duration of the usufruct or any resolutory conditions. He also left additional cash and other liquid assets to the Usufructuary (D) so that she inherited half of the net value of his estate and left the other half to his children from a previous marriage, the Usufructuary's (D) Stepchildren (P).

The Usufructuary (D) remarried a few years later, and her Stepchildren (P) sued to terminate the usufruct and recover any fruits paid to the Usufructuary (D) after her remarriage. The trial court held that the usufruct did not terminate upon remarriage, and the Stepchildren (P) appealed.

Issue

Can a usufruct contained in a testament in favor of a spouse sometimes qualify as a legal usufruct in favor of the surviving spouse under the Civil Code and terminate upon remarriage?

Holding & Decision

Yes, since the surviving spouse is entitled to a legal usufruct under La. C.C. art. 890, a testamentary disposition to that effect is a legal usufruct unless its terms are adverse to the legal usufruct, even if the property subject to the usufruct is separate property not typically covered by the codal usufruct.

The appeal court reviewed the history of La. C.C. art. 890, the cases interpreting it (most importantly *Succession of Waldron*, 323 So. 2d 434 (La. 1975), and *Succession of Chauvin*, 260 La. 828, 257 So. 2d 422 (La. 1972)) and the doctrine supporting "confirmation of the legal usufruct by will." Under *Waldron* and *Chauvin*, the surviving spouse enjoys the legal usufruct until death or remarriage unless a the testator makes a testamentary disposition "adverse to the legal usufruct[]," such as giving a larger portion to another legatee or simply disclaiming the usufruct. The courts have held that, although the La. C.C. art. 890 usufruct only burdens the decedent's community property, a testamentary provision expanding it to also include his separate property is not a disposition "adverse to the legal usufruct" sufficient to make that bequest a testamentary usufruct instead of a legal one.

The classification of the usufruct is important because, unless otherwise provided in the testament, the legal usufruct terminates upon remarriage, does not incur estate taxes, often does not require security, and is not an imposition on the legitime. The testamentary usufruct, on the other hand, is by default for the life of the usufructuary, does trigger estate taxes, often requires security, and can constitute an impermissible burden on the legitime.

The appeal court noted that the testator's intent to confirm a legal usufruct or create a testamentary one may be ascertained from the testament. Viz., a bequest that is "adverse to the legal usufruct" demonstrates the testator's intent to create a testamentary usufruct instead.

The court reviewed the record and the testament and concluded that it could find no support for the Usufructuary's (D) contention that Dr. Rozas intended to create a testamentary usufruct for life. Thus, it held that Dr. Rozas intended to confirm the legal usufruct over both his community and separate property. Since he did not specify that it was for life, the legal usufruct terminated upon the Usufructuary's (D) remarriage.

The appeal court reversed the trial court's judgment and remanded the matter for an accounting of what had been paid to the Usufructuary (D) after her remarriage.

Dissent

Judge Foret dissented and would have affirmed the result of the trial court's judgment for other reasons. He noted that the volume of doctrinal sources cited by the majority underscores the uncertainty surrounding this area of the law. Further, he asserted that the doctrine of confirming the legal usufruct was a judicial fiction that arose in order to avoid estate taxes. In his view, a usufruct contained in a testament is a testamentary or conventional usufruct, not a legal one.

The judge also noted that a bill to amend La. C.C. art. 890 codifying the concept of confirming the usufruct of the surviving spouse had been indefinitely tabled by the legislature. This legislative inaction indicated that the majority opinion's reliance on the concept is opposite the legislature's intent and the law.

Instead, Judge Foret would have found from the testament that it was Dr. Rozas's intent to grant the usufruct for life, reasoning that Dr. Rozas was learned and resourced enough to have written that the usufruct was only until remarriage if that had been his intention.

Rule of Law

Since the surviving spouse is entitled to a legal usufruct under La. C.C. art. 890, a testamentary disposition to that effect simply confirms the legal usufruct unless its terms are adverse to the legal usufruct, even if the property subject to the usufruct is separate property not typically covered by the codal usufruct.

Norsworthy v. Succession of Norsworthy

Surviving Spouse (P) v. Succession (D)
704 So. 2d 953 (La. App. 2d Cir. 1997)

Facts & Procedure

A Surviving Spouse (P) claimed the marital portion from her husband's estate, which consisted entirely of separate property. The trial court awarded the Surviving Spouse (P) a periodic allowance of $2,500 per month and as part of its reasons computed the net estate value and the likely marital portion. The Succession (D) appealed the judgment, arguing that the calculation overstated the marital portion and thus the allowance against the marital portion.

Issue

Is it an abuse of discretion for a trial court to set a periodic allowance under La. C.C. art. 2437 before the net value of the estate and its marital portion are finally calculated?

Holding & Decision

No, La. C.C. art. 2437 anticipates a court setting the allowance before the final computation of the net estate value and the marital portion. The allowance is likely not set abusively high if the marital portion is much higher than the allowance and the estate is solvent and relatively liquid. In any case, the surviving spouse is responsible for repaying any overpayments after the final determination of the marital portion.

The appeal court noted that the Surviving Spouse (P) received bequests and life insurance proceeds that should have been counted against the marital portion. The trial court simply used the net estate value from the Succession's (D) federal tax return to calculate the marital portion, but that sum ignored life insurance and potentially other assets that should have been deducted from the calculation of the marital portion. The appeal court produced a non-binding, illustrative estimate of the martial portion in connection with its opinion that suggested the martial portion would likely be around $185,000.

Nevertheless, the appeal court held that neither it nor the trial court had determined the value of the estate or the marital portion thereof. Instead, the trial court's calculations were made only to determine the allowance, which is not required to be any particular fraction of the marital portion.

The appeal court elected to avoid the question of correctness of the trial court's calculation because the $2,500 allowance was a small fraction of either court's estimate of the likely marital portion and a reasonable administration of the succession would be completed long before exhausting the marital portion, whatever it would be.

The appeal court also rejected the Succession's (D) argument that the value of the martial portion should be discounted to its present value, taking into account the likely lifespan of the Surviving Spouse (P). Under La. C.C. art. 2434, the marital portion is one-fourth of the value of the succession subject to lifetime usufruct; no present-value discounting is called for by law.

The appeal court affirmed the trial court's judgment awarding a $2,500 per month allowance.

Rule of Law

La. C.C. art. 2437 anticipates a court setting the allowance before the final computation of the net estate value and the marital portion. The allowance is likely not set abusively high if the marital portion is much higher than the allowance and the estate is solvent and relatively liquid. In any case, the surviving spouse is responsible for repaying any overpayments after the final fixing of the marital portion.

Chapter 18

Dedication to Public Use

1. **Dedication to public use**.

   a) The public has the right to use things subject to public use, and the state and its political subdivisions may regulate such use. This right is sometimes conceptualized as or analogized to a servitude in favor of the public.

   b) Recall the definition of public things:
   "Public things are owned by the state or its political subdivisions in their capacity as public persons.
   Public things that belong to the state are such as running waters, the waters and bottoms of natural navigable water bodies, the territorial sea, and the seashore.
   Public things that may belong to political subdivisions of the state are such as streets and public squares." La. C.C. art. 450.

   c) But "[p]rivate things may [also] be subject to public use in accordance with law or by dedication." La. C.C. art. 455.

      i. The owner may still exercise control and derive benefits from his ownership so long as it does not interfere with the public use.

   d) "A road may be either public or private.
   A **public road** is one that is subject to public use. The public may own the land on which the road is built or merely have the right to use it.
   A **private road** is one that is not subject to public use." La. C.C. art. 457.

   e) **Obstructions and encroachments**.

      i. "Works built without lawful permit on public things, including the sea, the seashore, and the bottom of natural navigable waters, or on the banks of navigable rivers, that obstruct the public use may be removed at the expense of the persons who built or own them at the instance of the public authorities, or of any person residing in the state.
      The owner of the works may not prevent their removal by alleging prescription or possession." La. C.C. art. 458.

      ii. "A building that merely encroaches on a public way without preventing its use, and which cannot be removed without causing substantial damage to its owner, shall be permitted to remain. If it is demolished from any cause, the owner shall be bound to restore to the public the part of the way upon which the building stood." La. C.C. art. 459.

      iii. Obstructions and encroachments on a thing subject to public use do not give rise to a right to possess or support acquisitive prescription because the thing is "inalienable, imprescriptible, and exempt from seizure as long as [it is] subject to, or needed for, public use." C.L.P. at 894.

f) **Private rights of enjoyment**. A **concession** is a private right granted concerning a thing subject to public use, e.g., an oil and gas lease covering the bed of a navigable water bottom.

      i. Concessions should not obstruct or exclude public use.

      ii. A concession may be revoked on its own terms, if provided, or taken by expropriation for public utility.

      iii. A concession on a private thing subject to public use can be made only with the owner's consent.

g) The state and its subdivisions may use property for uses other than that to which it was dedicated, so long as the use is not contrary to the public interest.

h) There is no full, formal body of legislation concerning the methods and manners of dedicating things to public use, but the courts have crafted the jurisprudence explored below.

      i. E.g., under the law in force before the passage of the 1974 cemetery laws "a graveyard becomes dedicated for cemetery purposes by virtue of a long and exclusive usage of this property for [such] purposes." *Haines v. St. Joseph Baptist Church*

2. **Types of dedication**.

a) **Formal dedication**. Dedication via written act.

      i. A dedication need not comply with the formalities governing donations or other transfers.

      ii. A formal dedication may be made by a written juridical act without authentic form or any formal acceptance.

      iii. A formal dedication transfers ownership unless it is explicitly retained.

          A. *But see Webb v. Franks Investment Co.*, which held that a formal dedication may transfer ownership of the roadbed but the intent must be determined from the instrument and, if ambiguous, from the extrinsic proof of the parties' intent.

      iv. The grantor may not revoke a formal dedication, but a dedication may contain a clause reverting the dedication on some condition. The state or political subdivision may revoke a dedication if it is no longer needed for public purposes.

b) **Implied dedication**. Dedication via informal offer to subject things to public use followed by acceptance through actual use, e.g., a sale referring to a plot plan showing future public roads or public spaces that are then built and used.

      i. Indispensable elements of an implied dedication:

          A. Proof of the intent to dedicate (the "offer") and

          B. Proof of acceptance, generally by public use.

      ii. Longtime public use alone is not sufficient to create an implied dedication.

A. Longstanding use of a boat launch and canal by the public with the permission or tacit consent of the owner is insufficient to demonstrate the requisite intent to dedicate the property to public use. The owners' continued maintenance, posting of the property, enforcement of rules, and removal of trespassers all demonstrate their intent to maintain control and full ownership of the property. *Cenac v. Public Access Water Rights Ass'n.*

iii. The doctrine of implied dedication is borrowed from the common law, and is sometimes called "common law dedication."

iv. Implied dedications are generally created by the sale of lots with references to a city plan or subdivision plan that identifies public places like streets or squares.

A. Land that is designated as a public plaza on a published development plan and advertised by the developer as a public plaza is formally dedicated to public use when actually used by the public for many years and is out of commerce. *City of Baton Rouge v. Bird.*

B. A landowner who consents to having a public sidewalk constructed entirely on his property impliedly dedicates the land used for the sidewalk to public use when it is actually used by the public. *City of Houma v. Cunningham.*

C. A tract of land is impliedly dedicated to public use when a plat of subdivision is recorded that designates the tract something like "park" and lots are subsequently sold in the subdivision. The subdivider should not be able to profit at the purchasers' expense by altering the use of the designated park. *White v. Kinberger.*

v. A donation that makes reference to a similar city or subdivision plan does not create a dedication.

vi. *Changing analytical approach.* Historically, courts did not reach the question of whether a dedication transfers the ownership of the ground under the public space because the nature of the cases was addressable simply by determining the right to use or obstruct use. By the 20th century courts generally began asserting that dedication only creates a servitude of public use.

c) **Statutory dedication**. Dedication via the formalities in La. R.S. 33:5051, e.g. through a recorded subdivision plan with explicit dedications.

i. The statutory requirements were originally enacted in 1896 and remain in force with amendments and re-enactments.

ii. Under modern jurisprudence, **substantial compliance** with the statute is considered to be the same as a dedication by deed, resulting in the transfer of ownership of the dedicated land to the public. *Cf.* the creation of a servitude under an implied dedication.

A. There is no established test for what constitutes "substantial compliance."

B. If a plat or plan has not been recorded or has been recorded by someone other than the subdivider, there is no substantial compliance.

C. The statute requires a "formal dedication" but does not define that concept.

D. A recorded plat that substantially but imperfectly complies with the statutory dedication requirements dedicates the streets, alleys, public squares, and other public areas to public use and transfers their ownership to the public, even without a formal dedication. *Garrett v. Pioneer Production Corp.*

    iii. Noncompliance with the statute may still create other forms of dedication.

    iv. The dedication is completed upon recording the plat.

d) **Tacit dedication**. Dedication via La. R.S. 48:491 and the public maintenance of a road for public use for three years.

    i. "(a) All roads and streets in this state which have been or hereafter are **kept up, maintained, or worked for a period of three years** by [a government body] shall be public roads or streets, as the case may be, if there is actual or constructive knowledge of such work by adjoining landowners exercising reasonable concern over their property....
(c) Actual or constructive knowledge is conclusively presumed within all parishes and municipalities... if the total period of such maintenance is **four years or more**, unless prior thereto and within sixty days of such actual or constructive knowledge, the prescription is interrupted or suspended in any manner provided by law." La. R.S. 48:491(B) (emphasis added).

      A. Token maintenance of private property like occasionally cutting the grass or dumping dirt does not establish the tacit dedication of that land as a street. *Jackson v. Town of Logansport.*

      B. A government resolution alone cannot convert a private road to a public one, but it can demonstrate that the government intended to begin maintaining the road and authorized such maintenance, thereby beginning the period required for tacit dedication. *Meyers v. Denton.*

      C. Once a road is tacitly dedicated by three years of public maintenance it remains a public road even if maintenance ceases unless the servitude of use is extinguished by ten-year prescription of nonuse. *Martin v. Cheramie.*

      D. The retroactive application of La. R.S. 48:491(B) would constitute an unconstitutional taking, so it is only applicable where the three-year period began on or after the effective date in 1954. *See Town of Eunice v. Childs*, 205 So. 2d 897 (La. App. 3d Cir. 1967).

    ii. "All roads or streets made on the front of their respective tracts of lands by individuals when the lands have their front on any of the rivers or bayous within this state shall be public roads when located outside of municipalities and shall be public streets when located inside of municipalities." La. R.S. 48:491(C).

3. **Termination of public use**. Upon the termination of public use, the owner regains full rights in the property.

a) **Abandoning highways**. Under La. R.S. 48:224(A), "[w]hen the secretary determines that certain sections of the state highway system cease to be used by the public to the extent that the original public purpose is no longer being served, he may... declare that the highway is to be abandoned." The parishes through with the highway runs may agree to take over the highway and its maintenance. La. R.S. 48:224(B). If they do not, the former owners may purchase it for the higher of it original cost or the appraised market value. La. R.S. 48:224(C). Failing that, the property may be sold at public or private sale. *Id.*

b) A public road may only be abandoned by a formal act of revocation under La. R.S. 48:701, relocation of the road by the government, or clear proof of intent of abandonment by the government. Failure to maintain the road does not constitute proof of intent to abandon the road. *Fore v. Volentine*.

c) Parishes and municipalities may revoke dedications of property to public use if the property has been abandoned or is no longer needed for public use under La. R.S. 48:701 (roads, streets, and alleyways) and La. R.S. 33:4718 (parks, squares, or plots).

   i. When a dedication of a road, street, or alleyway is revoked, the land up to the centerline reverts to the owners of the adjacent land. La. R.S. 48:701, 714.

   ii. When the dedication of a park, square, or other plot is revoked, the ownership reverts to the former owners at the time of the dedication or their successors. La. R.S. 33:4718.

   iii. A parish with a population less than 325,000 may not sell roads, streets, or alleyways, even if they have been determined to be unneeded for public purposes; it may only revoke the dedication, which transfers the ownership to the contiguous landowners under La. R.S. 48:701. *Walker v. Coleman*.

d) Certain parishes may dispose of roads, streets, and alleys that are "no longer needed for the public use" by revocation of the dedication, sale at public auction or private sale, or exchange for property of approximately equal value. La. R.S. 48:711–712.

   i. A municipality has broad discretion to close streets to the public and dispose of them when they are no longer needed for public purposes so long as that finding is neither arbitrary nor capricious. *Coliseum Square Association v. City of New Orleans*.

e) Unilaterally rescinding the abandonment of a road would unconstitutionally divest the landowner of his rights in the now-private road. *St. Martin Parish Police Jury v. Michel*.

HAINES V. ST. JOSEPH BAPTIST CHURCH
Neighbor (P) v. Church (D)
96 So. 3d 1256 (La. App. 5th Cir. 2012)

Facts & Procedure

A Neighbor (P) owned a residential property with a structure that encroached a few feet onto the adjacent Lot 210-A owned by a Church (D). The Neighbor (P) sued the Church (D) for recognition of his ownership of the part of Lot 210-A on which he and his ancestors in title had built the encroaching structure through 30-year acquisitive prescription. The Church (D) opposed this action, arguing that the cemetery was and is in the public domain and therefore not subject to acquisitive prescription.

The parties filed cross-motions for summary judgment. The Neighbor (P) presented documents and testimony proving his chain of title back to the 1920s and showing that the encroaching structure had been built in the 1940s. A survey from the 1990s showed the structure encroaching on Lot 210-A by 11 feet. The Neighbor (P) also presented a quitclaim deed from 1996 in which an entity purported to transfer Lot 210-A to the Church (D).

The Church (D), on the other hand, offered a 1996 survey labeling Lot 210-A as a cemetery containing at least one grave and an 1983 Affidavit of Ownership by a former pastor who averred that the lot was known as the St. Joseph Cemetery and that the Church (D) conducted burials there. That affidavit also referenced a 1921 subdivision plan that allegedly dedicated the plot as a cemetery owned and controlled by the Church (D).

The trial court found that jurisprudential rules governed the identification and management of cemeteries rather than the statutes passed on that topic in 1974 and determined that the encroaching building did not violate any of those rules. The court granted the Neighbor's (P) motion for summary judgment and denied the Church's (D).

The Church (D) appealed, and the appeal court reviewed the matter *de novo*.

Issue

When is a parcel used as a cemetery dedicated to public use such that it is no longer susceptible of acquisitive prescription?

Holding & Decision

The appeal court briefly reviewed the jurisprudence of cemeteries and concluded that under the law in force before the passage of the 1974 cemetery laws "a graveyard becomes dedicated for cemetery purposes by virtue of a long and exclusive usage of this property for [such] purposes."

It reviewed a 1955 case, *Locke v. Lester*, 78 So. 2d 14 (La.App. 2d Cir. 1955), which held that a plot used as a cemetery without any restriction as to who could be buried there for over fifty years had been informally dedicated to public use. This dedication occurred without acceptance or other formality when the owner demonstrated its intention to give it over to public use and the public actually used it.

Here, the appeal court found that the record contained at least one issue of material fact, namely, how long Lot 210-A had been a cemetery. The affidavit indicated it had been used as a cemetery for some time before 1983, and the 1921 subdivision plan indicated the use could have started in 1921 or before. The starting date was a material issue for determining if and when Lot 210-A had been dedicated to public use. Therefore, summary judgment was inappropriate.

The court reversed the judgment granting the Neighbor's (P) summary judgment, affirmed the denial of the Church's (D) motion for summary judgment, and remanded the case for further proceedings.

Rule of Law

Under the law in force before the passage of the 1974 cemetery laws "a graveyard becomes dedicated for cemetery purposes by virtue of a long and exclusive usage of this property for [such] purposes."

CITY OF BATON ROUGE V. BIRD
City (P) v. Heirs (D)
21 La. Ann. 244 (La. 1869)

Facts & Procedure

The Heirs (D) of Elie Beauregard claimed ownership of two squares of land in Baton Rouge known as "Mexico Square" and "Government Landing" and sought to have them partitioned and sold. The City of Baton Rouge (P) sued to enjoin the sale and to be declared owner of the squares, arguing that they had been dedicated to public use by Elie Beauregard and that the public had actually used them for many years.

The trial court found for the Heirs (D), and the City (P) appealed.

Issue

Is land designated as a public plaza in a published development plan advertised by the developer-owner dedicated to public use if it is actually used by the public?

Holding & Decision

Yes, land that is designated as a public plaza on a published development plan and advertised by the developer as a public plaza is formally dedicated to public use when actually used by the public for many years and is therefore out of commerce.

On appeal, the Court reviewed the history of the squares at issue and found that Elie Beauregard subdivided part of his plantation into what would become a large part of Baton Rouge. He prepared a plan for the proposed city and published notice of the plan and the plan itself around 1803.

The map of the proposed development shows both squares at issue, one of which was designated "Plaza de Mexico." The other was originally described as "Plaza de Colomb" but was eventually renamed "Government Landing" as it sits at the foot of government street. The advertisement highlighted the development's "seven public plazas," described the dimensions of Mexico Plaza, and suggested that it could be ornamented with a fountain. Several people testified at the trial that they were familiar with the squares and that, in their memory, both squares had been used as public places and no one claimed them as private property.

The Court noted that two factors were required to dedicate a thing to public use: the assent of the owner and the use for public purposes. Once so dedicated, the owner of his heirs could not revoke the dedication. The Court found that the published plan represented the squares in question as public places and that they had always been so regarded. The squares were never taxed as private property and were left open as common space until 1865 when the City (P) planted trees in Mexico Square. Thus, the Court held that the squares had been dedicated to public use and were out of commerce.

The Court reversed the trial court's judgment and found in favor of the City (P), quieted its title to the two squares, and made the injunction against its sale permanent.

Rule of Law

Land that is designated as a public plaza on a published development plan and advertised by the developer as a public plaza is formally dedicated to public use when actually used by the public for many years and is out of commerce.

CENAC V. PUBLIC ACCESS WATER RIGHTS ASS'N
Owner (P) v. Nonprofit (D)
851 So. 2d 1006 (La. 2003)

Facts & Procedure

The Owner (P) of a large tract known as the Golden Ranch Plantation in Lafourche Parish sued a local Nonprofit (D) to enjoin it and and associated people from interfering with the Owner's (P) right to fence off a boat launch on the property. The boat launch had been used for many years to access a man-made canal that connected several nearby public canals and bodies of water. The Nonprofit (D) asserted that the public had gained a servitude of use over the boat launch and the canal and that they both had been dedicated to public use.

The facts are not overly complicated, but there are a lot of them. At trial the parties demonstrated that the Gheens family and subsequently their family foundation, the current Owner's (D) ancestors in title, allowed the public to use the boat launch and the canal for decades. Several locals testified that they believed the boat launch and canal were public and that they had used it for years without asking permission. Members of the public conducted minor maintenance on the boat launch (e.g., filling potholes in the parking lot with shells and installing tie-downs), and the Army Corps of Engineers sprayed the canal to control invasive vegetation and maintain its navigability.

The Gheenses and their foundation posted and maintained private property signs around the property and canal. Employees testified that the public could generally use the boat launch and canal so long as users did not violate the few rules the family set. Employees were directed to patrol the property and eject trespassers who did not follow those rules (e.g., hunters, commercial fishermen, and air boats). Further, the employees testified that they were under strict order not to allow the use of public funds for property maintenance.

The former owners signed hunting leases with various parties and allowed the lessees to use the boat launch and canal. The former owners also built a private boat launch for the lessees across the canal from the boat launch at issue, allowing them to avoid the crowded boat launch used by the public.

Finally, an attorney who represented the Gheenses and who was later a Vice President of the Gheens Foundation testified that the Gheenses intentionally avoided giving up or compromising any rights to the property, including the boat launch and canal. The public was permitted to use the launch and canal, but the family had no intent to give the public any rights in the property. This, he testified, was evidenced by the Foundation's transfer of the launch and canal to the Owner (P) herein without any disclosure of a servitude in favor of the public, despite noting other encumbrances on parts of the land.

The trial court concluded that there was insufficient evidence supporting the Nonprofit's (D) contention that the boat launch had been dedicated to public use and granted the Owner (P) a permanent injunction barring the defendants from using the boat launch. But the court also found that the canal had been built for navigation and that the canal had been impliedly dedicated to public use. The court decreed that the Owner (P) owned the canal but that it was burdened by a servitude of public use.

Everyone appealed parts of the judgment. The appeal court affirmed the portion of the judgment granting the injunction but reversed the portion of the judgment recognizing the servitude over the canal, finding that the Nonprofit (D) failed to establish the owners' intent to dedicate the canal and launch to public use.

The Nonprofit (D) appealed again.

Issue

Does an owner demonstrate its intent to dedicate a canal and boat launch to the public use when he or she allows the public to use the property for decades so long as the public follows certain rules, the public and government do some maintenance, and the owners' agents police the property and enforce the owners' rules?

Holding & Decision

No, longstanding use by the public of a boat launch and canal with the permission or tacit consent of the owner is insufficient to demonstrate the requisite intent to dedicate the property to public use. The owners' continued maintenance, posting of the property, enforcement of rules, and removal of trespassers all demonstrate their intent to maintain control and full ownership of the property.

The Court began its analysis with a quick overview of the importation of implied dedication from the common law through *jurisprudence constante*. The Court noted that "implied dedication requires an unequivocally manifested intent to dedicate on the part of the owner" but does not require maintenance by a municipality. Some cases added this latter requirement, but the Court repudiated those cases explicitly. Where the owner makes an implied dedication, ownership of the land remains with the owner but the public at large receives a servitude of use. But in any case, longstanding use by the public without the requisite intent to dedicate is insufficient to create a dedication.

Although implied dedication is a jurisprudential construct, the legislature enacted La. R.S. 9:1251, which prevents a servitude of use from coming into existence over a boat launch or other property that a private owner allows the public to use for access to waterways. The courts all agreed this statute applied to the boat launch but not the canal. Nevertheless, the owner could have manifested the intent to dedicate the launch to the public.

The Court agreed with the trial court that the Nonprofit (D) failed to demonstrate the owners' intent to dedicate the boat launch and its parking lot to public use. But the Court held that the trial court erred by applying the wrong test to the canal. The trial court based its finding on the establishment and use of the canal for navigation rather than finding that the owners intended to dedicate the canal to public use.

The Court reviewed the record *de novo* and found that the Nonprofit (D) "failed to prove a plain and positive intent to dedicate [the canal to public use] by language or acts so clear as to exclude every other hypothesis." The Court discounted the facts showing that the local government and Army Corps of Engineers provided minor maintenance and emphasized the owners' continued maintenance responsibilities and well as the testimony of employees and the family attorney that the Gheenses maintained control and intended to maintain ownership of the entire property, including the canal and boat launch. In sum, the Court concluded that the Gheens permitted the public to use the facilities but retained the right to revoke permission, which they did when users violated the rules.

Thus, the Court affirmed the judgment of the appeal court.

Dissent

Justice Weimer concurred with the majority that the boat launch was not dedicated to public use, citing La. R.S. 9:1251, but he dissented and would have reinstated the trial court's judgment that the canal had been dedicated to public use. The justice argued that there was no evidence the Gheenses ever intended to close the canal to navigation. Instead, the promoted the use of the canal for navigation. He distinguished navigation from other uses, which the family did regulate (e.g., trespassing and hunting). The justice also found it more relevant than the majority that the Army Corps of Engineers sprayed herbicide to keep vegetation in the canal down and maintain navigability.

Under this reading and weighting of the facts, Justice Weimer opined that the trial court was not manifestly erroneous and that the courts should not have upset its findings on appeal.

Rule of Law

Longstanding use of a boat launch and canal by the public with the permission or tacit consent of the owner is insufficient to demonstrate the requisite intent to dedicate the property to public use. The owners' continued maintenance, posting of the property, enforcement of rules, and removal of trespassers all demonstrate their intent to maintain control and full ownership of the property.

CITY OF HOUMA V. CUNNINGHAM
City (P) v. Resident (D)
225 So. 2d 613 (La. App. 1st Cir. 1969)

Facts & Procedure

The City of Houma (P) sued a Resident (D) to collect an assessment for the construction of curbs, sidewalks, drains and other improvements in front of his property. The City (P) sued about three years after initially assessing the charge. The Resident (D) answered that the city constructed the sidewalk entirely on his property, which differed from his neighbors, and that this constituted an illegal taking that entitled him to damages.

At trial, evidence showed that the Resident's (D) property sat at the corner of two narrow streets and that the Resident (D) allowed the City (P) to construct a new sidewalk entirely on his property in order to widen the street. He maintained that this consent was conditioned on his neighbors likewise allowing the sidewalks to be moved onto their property so that the street could be widened.

The street was only widened in front of the Resident's (D) property, and his sidewalk had to be poured with sharp curves to connect to the neighbor's sidewalk that remained in the customary place next to the narrower part of the street. The Resident (D) refused to sign a right-of-way agreement regarding the sidewalk at least twice, but other evidence suggests that he refused not because he did not want the sidewalk placed on his property but because he was unhappy with the workmanship, which was repaired.

The City (P) argued that the sidewalk was placed on the Resident's (D) property and the street was widened solely for his personal benefit. Thus, he impliedly dedicated the sidewalk strip to public use. No evidence showed that the Resident (D) objected to the construction at any time.

The trial court found for the City (P), ordered the Resident (D) to pay the assessment, and dismissed the Resident's (D) reconventional demand for damages.

The Resident (D) appealed.

Issue

Does a landowner who consents to having a public sidewalk constructed entirely on his property impliedly dedicate the land used for the sidewalk to public use?

Holding & Decision

Yes, a landowner who consents to having a public sidewalk constructed entirely on his property impliedly dedicates the land used for the sidewalk to public use when it is actually used by the public.

The appeal court found that the Resident (D) consented to the placement of the sidewalk on his property and that he intended to dedicate the strip of land where the sidewalk was constructed to public use. The court noted that the doctrine of implied dedication is well established in Louisiana jurisprudence and operates by estoppel when an owner tacitly consents and the public uses the dedicated thing. The court held that the Resident (D) impliedly dedicated a right-of-way over the sidewalk strip to the public through his acts detailed above.

Thus, the court affirmed the trial court's judgment.

Rule of Law

A landowner who consents to having a public sidewalk constructed entirely on his property impliedly dedicates the land used for the sidewalk to public use when it is actually used by the public.

WHITE V. KINBERGER
Developer (P) v. Neighbors (D)
611 So. 2d 810 (La. App. 3d Cir. 1992)

Facts & Procedure

A Developer (P) acquired and sought to subdivide a 4,000 acre tract of land that had been designated as a park on a plat of the Charles Park Addition Subdivision. The Developers (P) acquired the tract from Paul D. White, Sr. in 1985. Paul White, in turn, had purchased the property from Charles N. White, the person who recorded the original plat of subdivision. The plat contained formal language dedicating the streets and utility easements to public use, as required by La. R.S. 33:5051 for a statutory dedication. The plat labeled the tract at issue "PARK" but did not contain any language explicitly dedicating it to public use.

The Neighbors (D) and the City of Alexandria claimed that the tract had been dedicated to public use as a park, and city denied the Developers (P) permission to develop the tract. The Developers (P) filed a possessory action against the Neighbors (D), the city, and others claiming that they had disturbed the Developer's (P) peaceful possession of the tract by recording certain documents. The parties filed cross-motions for summary judgment to determine whether the tract was a public thing. The Developer (P) also sought a declaration that the Neighbors (D) had converted the lawsuit to a petitory action in which they would be required to prove title.

On summary judgment, the trial court reviewed the plat and received an affidavit from Charles N. White, the original developer, that he intended for the tract to remain undeveloped "for the use and benefit of the owners of lots located in" the subdivision. The trial court concluded that the tract had been dedicated to public use via implied dedication and granted the Neighbors' (D) motion for summary judgment.

The Developer (P) appealed.

Issue

Is a tract of land impliedly dedicated to public use when a plat of subdivision is recorded that designates the tract something like "park" if lots are subsequently sold in the subdivision?

Holding & Decision

Yes, a tract of land is impliedly dedicated to public use when a plat of subdivision is recorded that designates the tract something like "park" and lots are subsequently sold in the subdivision. The subdivider should not be able to profit at the purchasers' expense by altering the use of the designated park.

The appeal court noted that the intent to dedicate a thing to the public use must be proved but that the recording of a subdivision plan creates a presumption of the intent to dedicate. No particular language is required to created an implied dedication.

The court reviewed two cases. In *O'Quinn v. Burks*, 231 So.2d 660 (La. App. 2nd Cir. 1970), the developer recorded a plat designating some land as a "proposed park." The court did not find an implied dedication. On the other hand, the court in *Town of Vinton v. Lyons*, 131 La. 673, 60 So. 54 (La. 1912), found that the word "Park" inscribed on a plat demonstrated the intent to dedicate that land to public use. The appeal court analogized this case to *Vinton* because of identical wording of the inscription and distinguished it from *O'Quinn* because that park was simply proposed, not promised. The court also relied on the original developer's statement that he intended the tract to remain a park in determining his intent at the time he recorded the plat.

The court found that the plat complied with the statutory requirements to dedicate the streets and utility easements as well as supporting an implied dedication of the park. After a learned discussion of doctrinal arguments, the court concluded that there was no reason a single plat could not create both statutory and implied dedications.

Finally, the court held that the tract at issue was the subject of an implied dedication and rejected the Developer's (P) claim that the defendants converted the action to a petitory action. Proving that land is a public thing is a defense against the possessory action. Thus, the court affirmed the trial court's judgment.

Dissent

Chief Judge Domengeaux dissented, arguing that the explicit dedication of the streets and utility easements excluded an implicit dedication of the park. Further, the chief judge was unconvinced that the developer intended the parcel to be a *public* park. Instead, it appears from the record that he intended it to be, at most, a private park for the subdivision residents. This is further evidenced by the developer later selling the would-be park to another private owner. Finally, the chief judge questioned the likelihood that the residents wanted a public park open to all in their neighborhood and noted that the park had never been used as a park and that the City of Alexandria required the record owners to maintain it.

Rule of Law

A tract of land is impliedly dedicated to public use when a plat of subdivision is recorded that designates the tract something like "park" and lots are subsequently sold in the subdivision. The subdivider should not be able to profit at the purchasers' expense by altering the use of the designated park.

GARRETT V. PIONEER PRODUCTION CORP.
Claimants (P) v. City (D)
390 So. 2d 851 (La. 1980)

Facts & Procedure

The Claimants (P) claimed ownership of the land underlying the streets of the City of Jennings (D) and filed a petitory action against the City (D) for recognition of their ownership. Both the Claimants' (P) mineral lessees and the City's (D) mineral lessees were included as parties to the lawsuit.

At trial the Claimants (P) proved that their ancestors in title had acquired two large tracts around the turn of the 20th Century and began selling parcels to others in 1901. No plat of subdivision was recorded at that time, but the acts of sale designated each parcel's lot and block numbers. In 1905, someone recorded plats for both large tracts. It is unclear who recorded them, but some subsequent acts of sale referred to the plats. Many of the streets at issue appeared on the plats, and the lot numbering scheme on the plats matched all the acts of sale.

The trial court held that the Claimants' (P) ancestors in title substantially complied with the statute requiring plat recordation and, therefore, the streets had been statutorily dedicated to public use. This transferred ownership in the land under them to the City (D). On appeal, the appeal court reversed, concluding that there was no proof the subdividers themselves recorded the plat.

Everyone appealed.

Issue

Does a recorded plat that complies with some but not all of the statutory dedication requirements dedicate designated streets and other public areas to the public use?

Holding & Decision

Yes, a recorded plat that substantially but imperfectly complies with the statutory dedication requirements dedicates the streets, alleys, public squares, and other public areas to the public use and transfers their ownership to the public, even without a formal dedication.

The Court delivered a lengthy excursus on the history of statutory dedication in Louisiana. In short, Act 134 of 1896 required subdividers to record plats that contained the particulars of the subdivision, including the numbers and dimensions of all lots, the names of all streets, a certificate from the Parish Surveyor, and a formal dedication of streets to public use. While the ownership of the soil under public streets was of little practical import before the advent of the mineral industry, early jurisprudence held that the public owned the soil under public roads. Later jurisprudence distinguished between major and minor roads and between rural roads and municipal streets, typically finding that the public owned the soil under municipal streets.

Only "substantial compliance" with the elements of the law was required to effect a statutory dedication. Perfect compliance was not required, and the only penalty for failing to comply was a fine for the owner. Streets were dedicated once a lot was sold under the plat. The Court noted that the recordation in this case was deficient in several ways, i.e., it was recorded after the first sale, some of the streets were not named, it contained no surveyor's certificate, and there was no formal dedication. Nevertheless, the Court found the recordation substantially compliant based on cases addressing each of the kinds of deficiency.

The Court rejected the appeal court's opinion that there was no proof that the subdividers themselves recorded the plat, noting that they made several sales with reference to an unrecorded plat before the recordation, made sales that conformed to the lot and block numbers in the plat that was later recorded, and made sales after the recordation "according to plat." Taken together with the fact that the genuineness of an ancient document is presumed, the Court found that the subdividers did record the plats and that they intended to dedicate the streets to public use.

But not all the roads were present on the plats.The Court noted that Carter Street and the former road running south from South Street were not on the plats. Therefore, they were not dedicated to public use.

Thus the Court reversed the appeal court's judgment, recognized the City (D) as the owner of all the streets other than the two missing from the plats, maintained the City's (D) mineral lessees in their leases over the streets shown on the plats, and recognized that the lessees were entitled to cancel the portions of the leases over the two streets missing from the plats. The Court remanded the case for an accounting of sums due the Claimants (P) in light of the judgment.

Rule of Law

A recorded plat that substantially but imperfectly complies with the statutory dedication requirements dedicates the streets, alleys, public squares, and other public areas to public use and transfers their ownership to the public, even without a formal dedication.

WEBB V. FRANKS INVESTMENT CO.
Landowners (P) v. Mineral Companies (D)
105 So. 3d 764 (La. App. 2d Cir. 2012), *cert denied 2013*

Facts & Procedure

This appeal involves two consolidated cases with unrelated parties but the same issue. In both cases, large tracts of land in different parts of Caddo Parish were split by a formally dedicated road. The Landowners (P) executed the same standard form dedication provided by the parish in the years 1913, 1914, 1924, and 1928. The forms all provided that the owner "dedicate[d land] to the public use for a public road," described the strip to be used as a road, and included the preprinted statement "The said property to be used for public road purposes only." The dedications were made without compensation.

In both cases, the Landowners (P) and their heirs eventually conveyed the land to others but retained the mineral rights. In time, they leased or sold the rights to be exploited. The determination of the road bed's owner determined who owned the mineral rights and whether working one side of the road was sufficient to interrupt the prescription of nonuse with respect to the other side of the road. If the two sides were separate tracts because a third party owned the road in the middle, activity on one side would not interrupt prescription on the other side.

The form dedications had been the subject of a great deal of attention in Caddo Parish as the mineral production industry grew. As part of the motion practice, the parties showed that in 1930, the Parish Engineer wrote to an out-of-state landowner that a dedication using the same form would not allow the Parish to exploit minerals. In 1957, the Caddo Parish Police Jury passed a resolution disclaiming the ownership of the mineral rights under another dedication made on the same form. And in 1983, the Caddo Parish Police Jury passed and recorded another resolution expressly waiving "all present and future claims to fee title and to mineral rights relating to the property described in" the form agreements.

The trial court heard motions for summary judgment in both cases and found that, as a matter of law, Caddo Parish owned the roads and the land under them.

The Landowners (P) appealed.

Issue

Does a formal dedication of property to use as a public road necessarily transfer the ownership of that property?

Holding & Decision

No, a formal dedication may transfer ownership of the roadbed but the intent must be determined from the instrument and, if ambiguous, from the extrinsic proof of the parties' intent.

The appeal court referred to an 1848 case in which the Louisiana Supreme Court held that the public has a servitude over soil dedicated to use as a public road. *Hatch v. Arnault*, 3 La. Ann. 482. That Court based its reasoning on La. C.C. art. 654 (1825), carried into the Code of 1870 as article 658(2), which provided that "the soil of public roads belongs to the owner of the land." That article was adapted in part into La. C.C. 457 in 1978, and the revision comments noted that the provision was not intended to change the law. La. C.C. art. 457 does not contain the exact language quoted above from La. C.C art 654 (1825).

The appeal court also recognized the case of *St. Charles Parish School Board v. P & L Inv. Corp.*, 675 So. 2d 218 (La. 1996), which cited Yiannopoulos's opinion that a formal dedication transfers ownership unless ownership is expressly or impliedly retained. The court distinguished the cases at bar from *St. Charles Parish School Board* because that case concerned a tacit dedication instead of a formal one as in this case. Nonetheless, the court insisted that Yiannopoulos's quotation be read *in pari materia* with other sections of his Property treatise to mean that the object of a right of way agreement is a question of fact but is generally meant to create a servitude rather than a transfer.

After reviewing the record, the court concluded that the dedications themselves indicate that only a servitude was given because they lacked consideration, did not include language conveying title, limited the use of the strip, and because public policy did not require ownership to use it as a road. But even if the intent were ambiguous on the face of the dedications themselves, extrinsic evidence of the acts of the Parish Engineer and Police Juries described above made the intent and understanding of the parties clear.

Finally, the court noted that even if the dedication had been statutory (instead of formal) and conveyed ownership, the resolutions passed by the Caddo Police Jury sufficed to revoke the transfers and relinquish the Parish's ownership interest and mineral rights.

The Court reversed the trial court's judgment and remanded the matter.

Rule of Law

Judge Moore dissented, decrying as "revisionism" the majority's reading of *St. Charles School Board* and distinguishing it from the case at bar. He would have held that the dedication contained no retention or reservations of any kind and, therefore, constituted formal donations that transferred ownership of the land. He would have considered the dedications donations made onerous by the condition that the property be used only for road purposes. Finally, he called on the Louisiana Supreme Court to revisit *St. Charles School Board* in light of the changing economic realities brought on by the rise of the mineral industry.

Rule of Law

A formal dedication may transfer ownership of the roadbed but the intent must be determined from the instrument and, if ambiguous, from the extrinsic proof of the parties' intent.

JACKSON V. TOWN OF LOGANSPORT
Landowner (P) v. Town (D)
322 So. 2d 281 (La. App. 2d Cir. 1975)

Facts & Procedure

A Landowner (P) sought to enjoin the Town (D) from constructing a street across his property. The Town (D) maintained that it acquired a public servitude because the Landowner's (P) property was part of a "grass street" connecting two established streets about a block apart.

Town (D) employees cut the grass of the grass street near the Landowner's (P) property about once a year, but there was no evidence that they cut the grass on his property. Similarly, another employee testified that in the previous thirteen years, two or three loads of dirt had been dumped on the grass street to maintain it, but again there was no evidence the dirt was placed on the Landowner's (P) property.

The trial court issued a preliminary injunction against the Town (D), and the Town (D) appealed.

Issue

Does minor, occasional maintenance suffice to establish the tacit dedication of a street?

Holding & Decision

No, token maintenance of private property like occasionally cutting the grass or dumping dirt does not establish the tacit dedication of that land as a street.

The appeal court reviewed the methods of dedication and rejected most out of hand. It noted that informal dedication — either through implied dedication or tacit dedication under La. R.S. 48:491 — was the only possible dedication potentially applicable to these facts. But the court rejected implied dedication because it requires the owner to intend to dedicate the land to public use, and the Landowner (P) had clearly attempted to prevent the public use of his property by erecting fence posts and barricades, complaining about the roadwork, and ultimately filing suit to stop it. That leaves tacit dedication as the only possible source of the public's right to use the property.

Under La. R.S. 48:491, a street that is maintained by a parish government is tacitly dedicated to public use. "'Brushing up' or token maintenance" are insufficient. The court found that the town's activities described by their employees, even assuming they were done directly to the Landowner's (P) property, were not sufficient to establish a tacit dedication.

The court affirmed the trial court's judgment.

Rule of Law

Token maintenance of private property like occasionally cutting the grass or dumping dirt does not establish the tacit dedication of that land as a street.

MEYERS V. DENTON
848 So. 2d 759 (La. App. 3d Cir. 2003)

Facts & Procedure

This dispute concerns the tacit dedication of a road running across the Dentons' (D) property and, as a result, whether they may prevent neighbors like the Meyers (P) from using the road to access their land. The Dentons (D) purchased a 552 acre tract in multiple transactions in April 1996 and February 1997. A road known as the Upper Little River Road ran across the property. The Dentons (P) gated the road, maintaining that it was private.

The Meyers (P) owned land west of the Dentons (D) and had regularly used the Upper Little River Road to access their property. They filed suit to remove the gates because the road was a public road. The Pooles also owned land reached by the road and intervened in the suit. Along the way, the Dentons (D) filed a reconventional demand alleging that others were unjustly enriched by the improvements the Dentons (D) made to the road.

Early on, the trial court entered a temporary restraining order that saw the plaintiffs receiving keys to the gates. The trial court later granted the Meyers' (P) motion for summary judgment and found that the road at issue was a public road. The Dentons (D) appealed, and the appeal court reversed the summary judgment because issues of material fact remained.

After remand, the parties tried the case and presented evidence that the road was initially built in the early 1970s by the U.S. Army Corps of Engineers to support a construction project on the Little River. Catahoula Parish Police Jury passed a resolution declaring the road "open to public traffic" in 1973, and the Parish began to maintain it. A cast of witnesses who worked for the Parish testified that the Parish frequently graded the road, maintained its ditches, filled holes, and fixed problems. This maintenance continued until 1995 or 1996.

The evidence also showed that the Parish cataloged the Upper Little River Road as being 4.3 miles long, which is the distance from its junction with another road to where the Dentons (D) erected the gates. The Dentons (D) contended that they were told that the public road and public maintenance of the road ended at the 4.3 mile marker. Some Parish-related witnesses corroborated this position, but some of the testimony suggested the Parish conducted work beyond the 4.3 mile limit. The Dentons (D) claimed that they had made $9,592 of improvements to the road on their property under the understanding that the Parish maintenance stopped where the gates were placed.

The trial court again found that the Upper Little River Road was a public road, finding that the Catahoula Parish Police Jury identified it as a road and began maintaining it in 1973 and continued to do so for more than three years. The trial court also rejected the Dentons' (D) unjust enrichment claim, and declined to determine whether the road was a public river road subject to the riparian servitude under La. C.C. art. 665.

The Meyers (P) and the Dentons (D) both appealed.

Issue

Does a government resolution that a private road is "open to public traffic" dedicate it to public use?

Holding & Decision

No, a government resolution alone cannot convert a private road to a public one, but it can demonstrate that the government intended to begin maintaining the road and authorized such maintenance, thereby beginning the period required for tacit dedication.

The appeal court noted that the public or private nature of a road is a factual determination and, under La. R.S. 48:491(B), a private road becomes a public road when maintained by a government body for three years. This tacit dedication does not require the landowner's consent or his intent to dedicate the road. But the maintenance must be substantial; infrequent minor maintenance does not suffice to tacitly dedicate a road to the public use.

After reviewing the evidence adduced at trial, the appeal court found that the trial court was not clearly wrong in interpreting the facts to find that the Parish maintained the road for more than three years and that such maintenance served to tacitly dedicate the road to public use under La. R.S. 48:491(B). The appeal court noted that the Policy Jury's resolution opening the road to public traffic did not dedicate the road to public use because the Police Jury lacked that power. Instead, it evidenced the Police Jury's intent to begin maintaining the road. This led to its tacit dedication three years later.

The court also agreed that it was unnecessary to address whether the road was a public river road under La. C.C. art. 665. Finally, the appeal court agreed that the plaintiffs were not unjustly enriched. The court noted that the Dentons (D) knew the character of the road was disputed and continued to make improvements regardless. Further the gates barred the Parish from conducting necessary maintenance, and the improvements the Dentons (D) made were not necessary. As a result, others were not unjustly enriched.

The appeal court affirmed the lower court's judgment.

Rule of Law

A government resolution alone cannot convert a private road to a public one, but it can demonstrate that the government intended to begin maintaining the road and authorized such maintenance, thereby beginning the period required for tacit dedication.

MARTIN V. CHERAMIE
264 So. 2d 285 (La. App. 4th Cir. 1972)

Facts & Procedure

The Martins (P) and their family company operated a marina in Grand Isle which had been accessed for many years via a blacktop road running across the adjacent property owned by the Cheramies (D). In 1970, the Cheramies (D) barricaded the blacktop road by placing metal drums across it. The Martins (P) removed the drums, and the Cheramies (D) replaced the drums with the assistance of the Mayor of Grand Isle, who threatened to jail the Martins (P) if they disturbed the barrels again.

The Martins (P) sued to enjoin the Cheramies (D) to remove the barrels and to stop blocking the blacktop road. The parties agreed that the disputed strip had been owned by the Cheramies (D), but the Martins (P) alleged that the strip had been tacitly dedicated as a public road because it had been maintained for more than three years by the Louisiana Department of Highways ("LDH").

The evidence at trial showed that in 1953, the Jefferson Parish Police Jury contracted with the LDH to maintain the road. At the time it was a shell road, and the LDH added shells and graded it approximately quarterly between 1953 and 1958 or 1959, when the LDH blacktopped the road. After blacktopping, the road required little regular maintenance, Hurricane Betsy partially washed the road away in 1965. The LDH repaired the broken section.

Around that time, the Cheramies (D) began claiming the road as private property and refused to permit the LDH entrance. Public maintenance of the blacktop road ceased. Instead, the LDH built or rebuilt another road that also runs to the Martins' (P) marina, albeit not as conveniently from the main highway. Many witnesses testified that the road at issue had been used as public road to the marina until the Cheramies (D) blocked it.

The trial court denied the Martins' (P) request for injunctive relief, and they appealed.

Issue

Does a tacitly dedicated road revert to a private thing if the government stops maintaining it?

Holding & Decision

No, once a road is tacitly dedicated by three years of public maintenance it remains a public road even if maintenance ceases unless the servitude of use is extinguished by ten-year prescription of nonuse. The appeal court noted that the trial court ruled as it did because the LDH stopped maintaining the blacktop road. The court discarded this reasoning, finding that the discontinuance of maintenance did not change the character of the blacktop road. The facts would be different if the public had ceased using it for ten years, but the length of time it went unmaintained was irrelevant. Even if no one had used the road since the Cheramies (D) ran the LDH off in 1965, ten years had not passed by the time the Martins (P) filed suit in 1970. Thus the servitude of use had not prescribed.

The court also rejected the Cheramies' (D) argument that their consent was required for a tacit dedication and that the maintenance performed was insufficient to trigger La. R.S. 48:491. While consent is not required to tacitly dedicate a road, the appeal court found that the Cheramies (D) consented to and invited the public maintenance of the road on their property for thirteen years before changing their minds. Additionally, the court found that the LDH's periodic shelling, grading, and blacktopping in the 1950s were sufficient maintenance to support a dedication under the law.

Finally, the appeal court rejected the Cheramie's (D) contention that the road was used to provide access to the water and, therefore, was excluded from dedication by La. R.S. 9:1251. To the contrary, the court found, the road provided access to the Martins' (P) property, not the water. The Martins' (P) marina, on the other hand, provided access to the water.

Thus, the appeal court reversed the trial court's judgment in part, ordered the Cheramies (D) to remove the barricades, and enjoined them from blocking access to the blacktop road.

Rule of Law

Once a road is tacitly dedicated by three years of public maintenance it remains a public road even if maintenance ceases unless the servitude of use is extinguished by ten-year prescription of nonuse.

COLISEUM SQUARE ASSOCIATION V. CITY OF NEW ORLEANS

Neighborhood Association (P) v. City (D)
544 So. 2d 351 (La. 1989)

Facts & Procedure

The City (D) and Trinity Episcopal Church reached an agreement whereby the City (D) would close the 2100 block of Chestnut Street and lease it to the Church. The Church owned all the property on both sides of that block and operated a school there. The Neighborhood Association (P) sued to enjoin the City (D) from closing the street and leasing it, arguing that the City (D) lacked the authority to do so and, if it had the authority, the action was arbitrary and capricious.

The City (D) and the Church conducted an extensive analysis of the effects of closing the street, including a traffic study, suggestions for alternate traffic routes in the neighborhood, proposals to improve the appearance and function of the neighborhood and bike lanes, and other items. Both the City (D) Planning Commission and Council reviewed the analysis and studies before approving the plan. Opponents argued that the plan would damage the historical character of the neighborhood. Proponents argued it would increase security and safety for the campus and those using the facilities, increase the aesthetic quality and value of the neighborhood, and create a positive impact on New Orleans by furthering the Church's educational mission.

The trial and appeal courts sided with the City (D), finding that it had the authority to enter into the transaction and that the decision to do so was neither arbitrary nor capricious.

The Neighborhood Association (P) appealed.

Issue

Does a municipality have the authority to close streets to the public and lease them to a private entity?

Holding & Decision

Yes, a municipality has broad discretion to close streets to the public and dispose of them when they are no longer needed for public purposes so long as that finding is neither arbitrary nor capricious.

The Court first analyzed whether the City (D) had the legal authority to close and lease the street to the Church. Reviewing the law, the Court found that there was no constitutional prohibition against such a transaction and held that the City (D) was explicitly given the authority to lease property under both its home rule charter and the Louisiana law.

Next, the Court examined whether the City (D) acted arbitrarily or capriciously in deciding to close the street and lease it to the Church. The Court initially noted that the mere use of street did not necessarily mean that the street was needed. The determination of need was to be made by the Council after reviewing the evidence. The Court reviewed the extensive study the City (D) conducted and identified the pro and con positions the Council had weighed in coming to its decision. Given the extensive analysis and consideration reflected in the record, the Court held that the City (D) did not act arbitrarily or capriciously.

Thus the Court affirmed the lower courts' judgments.

Rule of Law

A municipality has broad discretion to close streets to the public and dispose of them when they are no longer needed for public purposes so long as that finding is neither arbitrary nor capricious.

FORE V. VOLENTINE
385 So. 2d 860 (La. App. 2d Cir. 1980)

Facts & Procedure

The Fores (P) sued to have a road running across the Volentines' (D) property declared a public road and to enjoin them to repair the road and desist from further interference with its use. In the 1940s, the Parish built the road at issue across the Volentines' (D) and others' land and terminating on the Fores' (P) land. The Parish regularly maintained the road for decades but stopped about eight years before the Fores (P) filed this lawsuit. In the years before the lawsuit, the Volentines (D) fenced across the road and allowed their lessees to plow and plant the road.

The trial court held that the road was tacitly dedicated to public use under La. R.S. 48:491 and that the servitude of use had not been terminated by ten years' nonuse. It ordered the Volentines (D) to restore the road and cease interfering with its use.

The Volentines (D) appealed.

Issue

Short of 10-year nonuse, can a public road be abandoned by the failure to conduct maintenance?

Holding & Decision

No, a public road may only be abandoned by a formal act of revocation under La. R.S. 48:701, relocation of the road by the government, or clear proof of intent of abandonment by the government. Failure to maintain the road does not constitute proof of intent to abandon the road.

The appeal court rejected the Volentines' (D) contention that the Parish's failure to maintain the road, to object to the fencing and planting across the road, and to include the road in their road numbering system demonstrated its clear intent to abandon the road. To support this contention, they cited two cases, both of which the appeal court distinguished and about which the court expressed suspicion. Instead, the court enumerated the three ways for a government entity to abandon a road, none of which applied to these facts. Further, the right to use the road had not been abandoned since it had been used in the last ten years. Thus, the road remained a public road.

The appeal court amended the lower court's judgment to correct a typographical error and affirmed it as amended.

Rule of Law

A public road may only be abandoned by a formal act of revocation under La. R.S. 48:701, relocation of the road by the government, or clear proof of intent of abandonment by the government. Failure to maintain the road does not constitute proof of intent to abandon the road.

St. Martin Parish Police Jury v. Michel

Police Jury (P) v. Landowner (D)
229 So. 2d 463 (La. App. 3d Cir. 1969)

Facts & Procedure

The Police Jury (P) sued to prevent a Landowner (D) from blocking Richard Avenue, arguing that it was a public road. At trial, the evidence showed that Richard Avenue had been tacitly dedicated under La. R.S. 48:491. In July 1967, at the Landowner's (D) request, the Police Jury (P) passed a resolution formally abandoning Richard Avenue. After an outcry from its constituents, the Police Jury (P) then passed another resolution rescinding the previous one in August 1967. The public used the road until the Landowner fenced across it in 1969.

The Police Jury (P) sued, and the trial court granted it an injunction. The Landowner (D) appealed.

Issue

Can a government body unilaterally rescind the abandonment of a road?

Holding & Decision

No, unilaterally rescinding the abandonment of a road would unconstitutionally divest the landowner of his rights in the now-private road.

The appeal court noted that police juries have broad power to rescind their official acts but that power does not allow them to impair contracts or divest vested rights from others. When the road was abandoned, it reverted to the Landowner (D). Rescinding the abandonment, then, would divest him of his vested ownership right in violation of the constitution.

Thus, the appeal court set aside and recalled the injunction and dismissed the Police Jury's (P) lawsuit.

Rule of Law

Unilaterally rescinding the abandonment of a road would unconstitutionally divest the landowner of his rights in the now-private road.

WALKER V. COLEMAN
540 So. 2d 93 (La. App. 2d Cir. 1989)

Facts & Procedure

At its core, this is a dispute over a small parish's ability to sell property not needed for public purposes rather than simply revoke the dedication and allow it to revert under La. R.S. 48:701. The facts are not particularly complicated, but the procedural posture is somewhat unusual.

In 1929, a developer dedicated the streets and alleyways of a subdivision by recording a plan. The street and alleyway at issue here were never improved for actual use. Decades later in 1985, the Ouachita Parish Police Jury (D) adopted an ordinance formally declaring that the street and alleyway were not needed for public purposes and authorizing a sale to the highest bidder. Charles D. Walker (P) won the bid for $6,100. His property abuts the north side of the alley he purportedly purchased.

Some time later, Mr. Walker (P) sued his neighbor on the other side of the alley, James A. Coleman (D), to have him remove a building that encroached on the alley. Mr. Coleman (D) filed an exception of no right of action arguing that the Mr. Walker (P) could not have title because the Police Jury (D) lacked the authority to sell the alleyway. Instead, he argued, the Police Jury (D) could only revoke the dedication, which would cause the south half of the alleyway to revert to him, obviating any encroachment. Mr. Walker (P) amended his lawsuit to implead the Police Jury (D) as a defendant and demand the return of his purchase price if Mr. Coleman's (D) argument succeeded.

The trial court sustained the exception and dismissed the suit against Mr. Coleman (D). The Police Jury (D) appealed. Mr. Walker did not appeal and instead joined Mr. Coleman (D) in opposing the Police Jury's (D) appeal.

Issue

May a parish with a population less than 325,000 sell roads, streets, or alleyways that have been determined to be unneeded for public purposes?

Holding & Decision

No, a parish with a population less than 325,000 may not sell roads, streets, or alleyways, even if they have been determined to be unneeded for public purposes; it may only revoke the dedication, which transfers the ownership to the contiguous landowners under La. R.S. 48:701.

The court found that when a property is statutorily or formally dedicated, ownership is transferred to the political subdivisions as a public thing. Public things cannot be alienated, and a dedicated street or alleyway remains a public thing until the political subdivision formally determines they are not needed for public purposes. At that time, the street or alleyway is alienable in accordance with law.

La. R.S. 33:4711 governs the alienation of parish property generally, and La. R.S. 48:701 governs streets and alleyways specifically. That law provides that in parishes with fewer than 325,000 residents, a police jury that determines a street or alleyway is no longer needed for public purpose may only revoke the dedication, not sell the property. Upon revocation, the property is split down the middle and reverts to the ownership of each adjoining owner up to the centerline.

The court rejected the Police Jury's (D) argument that La. R.S. 48:701 constitutes an unconstitutional donation of public property because the transfer is not a donation. Rather, it is a revocation, and the legislature has both the authority to require dedications and to determine the effect of their revocation.

Because Ouachita Parish had fewer than 325,000 resident, the Police Jury (D) could only revoke the dedication; it could not sell the property to Mr. Walker. Thus, the appeal court affirmed the trial court's judgment.

Rule of Law

A parish with a population less than 325,000 may not sell roads, streets, or alleyways, even if they have been determined to be unneeded for public purposes; it may only revoke the dedication, which transfers the ownership to the contiguous landowners under La. R.S. 48:701.

About the Author

Gregory W. Rome is an attorney, author, former software engineer, and father of three amazing girls. He holds a bachelor's degree in computer science, a Master of Business Administration degree with a concentration in finance, and a Juris Doctor degree with a certificate in civil law. He served as longtime law clerk to the Honorable Kirk A. Vaughn, Louisiana 34th Judicial District Court, and practiced law for a decade. Today Rome holds an IT business leadership role at a Fortune 500 company where he focuses on complex technology transactions, including software licensing agreements and global outsourcing contracts.

Rome is deeply passionate about Louisiana's civil law tradition and is dedicated to making complex legal concepts and the state's unique legal heritage accessible to students and practitioners alike. He is the co-author of The Louisiana Civil Law Dictionary, helped found the Civil Law Commentaries journal while attending Tulane Law School, and served on the journal's inaugural editorial board.

About the Cover

The cover image is adapted from *Bayou Plaquemines*, an 1881 painting by Joseph Rusling Meeker. Meeker was an American painter whose service on a Union gunboat in Louisiana during the Civil War kindled a lifelong fascination with southern swamps and bayous. The original painting belongs to the Ogden Museum of Southern Art in New Orleans, Louisiana.

www.ingramcontent.com/pod-product-compliance
Lightning Source LLC
Chambersburg PA
CBHW081801200326
41597CB00023B/4104